Designing and Managing Your Career

Advice from the Harvard Business Review

Designing and Managing Your Career

Designing
and Managing Your Career

edited by Harry Levinson

Harvard Business School Press

Boston, Massachusetts

101345

Most of the articles included in this collection are available as individual reprints. For information and ordering call 617-495-6192 or contact Operations Department, Harvard Business School Publishing Division, Boston, MA 02163 (Fax: 617-495-6985).

Printed in the United States of America
93 92 91 90 89 5 4 3 2 1

Library of Congress Cataloging-in-Publication Data
Designing and managing your career.

   (Advice from the Harvard business review)
   Includes bibliographies and index.
   1. Executives. 2. Career development. I. Levinson, Harry. II. Series.
HD38.2.D475   1988   658.4'09   88-30099
ISBN 0-87584-180-5 (alk.)

The paper used in this publication meets the requirements of the American National Standard for Permanence of Paper for Printed Library Materials Z39.49-1984.

Contents

Introduction

HARRY LEVINSON

There is an often repeated, half-humorous statement among mature adults that in one form or another, goes, "I haven't decided what I'm going to be when I grow up." For most people in our culture there's more reality than humor to the comment. Fortunately, in an open society we learn many skills and develop many interests. Sooner or later we focus on one or integrate several into an occupation. For the majority of people the choices are not easy. Some are dictated by the local availability of jobs. All too many follow from the urgings of parents and grandparents. Some evolve out of drifting from one method of earning a livelihood to another until a person stumbles into a role that provides significant gratification; others emerge when a person has become too old to start anew in entry-level jobs.

Despite the proliferation of guidance counselors in high schools and of career counselors in community service agencies, the struggle to find the right niche is difficult because on the one hand there are so many choices and on the other, so few opportunities to fit oneself into a given role. Unlike clothing, one can't take an occupational role from a rack, choosing color and style, and then try it on for size. A person could spend unrecoverable days in a trial-and-error effort to find the right role. Establishing yourself in a career is something like fitting together a psychological jigsaw puzzle: we are unaware of many of the pieces within ourselves, and the pieces are not shaped in such a way that we can fit them together neatly.

As hard as it is to choose and begin a career, it is even more difficult to become successful in one. In some cases people can chart their careers by following others who have taken the same path. It's easy, for example, to undertake a career as a management information specialist. The steps in training and those in the first several levels above entry are quite plain. However, with increasing proficiency you soon have to make a major choice. Some people will want to remain within the narrow confines of management information services. Others will have the opportunity to move into managing information services programs. Still others will move into the higher levels of organizations to plot the management services on which the corporate operations will be based.

There are multiple choice points along the way, and each person must weigh what path he or she wants to follow. In many instances you will be shooting in the dark because it's hard to know how your preferred behavior will fit a given

1

role and indeed to know the behavior required by the role. All advancement therefore necessarily involves the risk of failure. Fortunately, however, advancement also offers the opportunity for increased personal achievement and gratification if you choose carefully and well; in short, if you manage your own career.

Before looking at how you go about managing your career successfully, it will be helpful to examine why the choices have become so difficult. Then you can clear away some of the emotional underbrush that interferes with making appropriate choices. Retrospection is the foundation for introspection.

World War II was a socioeconomic watershed for the United States. Mobilization of the nation for the war effort and the fact that 11 million men and women were, or had been, in uniform meant that when the war was over there would be a drastic reintegration: of individuals, of ways of doing business, of organizing community life, of technical innovation, of geographical mobility, and of educational aspiration. Many, many people had to rethink their roles as human beings.

Well into the twentieth century children learned their occupational skills at the knees of their parents. As the industrial age matured they moved on to the factory or other large-scale enterprises. And after World War II more people came to depend on larger organizations and indeed often found in those organizations the kind of support that previously had characterized the small community. It was not without good reason that employees spoke of AT&T as "Ma Bell" and used the same appellation for Eastman Kodak. During the 50s people could count on getting a good job, in many kinds of companies, which meant a permanent job with a pension at retirement. Such secure employment became particularly desirable for those who had experienced or had been affected by the Great Depression. The name of the occupational game had been to land such a job. Indeed, had you asked most people why they went to college or a university, they would have responded, "To prepare myself to find a good job."

When millions of World War II veterans went back to universities, under the GI Bill of Rights, most, even those who got advanced degrees, were seeking good jobs in large organizations. There were several developments that accompanied this trend. The word *career* came into vogue. It was fine for people at lower levels to seek a *job* in an organization that would have some permanence, but those at higher levels, particularly managerial ranks, spoke of *career*, because for them advancement was the name of the occupational game. Professional schools, including schools of management, expanded, and people in managerial and professional ranks began to move from one organization to another more quickly as they saw opportunities to advance. The subject of reaching certain stages in one's career at certain ages became popular.

Research into careers and into stages of adult development was also begun. Much of this research and conceptualization arose out of concurrent psychoanalytic theorizing and the so-called human potential movement. People began to ask themselves more openly and more directly what it was they wanted to get out of their lives and, indeed, where they were going with their lives. There were more separations and divorces as people expressed their dissatisfactions in very concrete ways. We began to hear more about self-centeredness and ultimately, "the culture of narcissism."

The 1950s carried much of the prewar momentum of the wish for stability and continuity, but the 1960s brought forth a vast social rebellion that encompassed not only dress but also attitude. The then younger generation objected to the lifestyle of its predecessor with its pressures toward conformity and control. Young people asserted their independence and their wish to follow their own bent. The discontent was fanned by the Vietnam War and by the sense that institutions were controlling people's destinies. The young rebelled against institutions, whether universities or schools, churches, or corporations. They demanded their right to be free, to "do their own thing."

The pursuit of career in the traditional sense was no longer viable. Economic downturns and recessions had taught employees not only that loyalty to organizations did not pay, that they could readily lose their jobs no matter how dedicated they had been, but also that organizations that failed to keep up technically would soon be out of business. Recessions and mergers forced companies to reorganize; the resulting tenuousness of organizational life gave a new dimension to the meaning of career.

Organizations also had to change more quickly as worldwide competition increased the momentum of product obsolescence. Some products became obsolete before they came off the drawing boards. Furthermore, people's interests and values changed quickly in a highly mobile society. People pressed for greater novelty in clothing, hair styles, home furnishings, automobiles, and technical devices. Those who met their needs successfully responded ever more quickly.

What had been a generalized cultural orientation began to fractionate quite rapidly. A population that had once had enough common interests to sustain a magazine like the *Saturday Evening Post* became so diverse that publications like the *Post* went out of business. At the same time, many small special-interest magazines sprang up and were quite profitable. Similarly, organizations divided themselves into many more differentiated units to deal with various markets, and they, too, rose and fell with the quickly changing interests of consumers. A vast corporation like General Motors found itself outpaced by the Japanese, and it still has not adapted to the rapid change global competition requires. The same thing happened to many other organizations. There has been a dramatic shift from a manufacturing orientation to a service orientation, resulting in a loss of a wide range of jobs and roles.

Many skills became obsolete in a few years, particularly those that had an academic base. This was an acute problem for engineers and became an equally acute one for physicians and other professionals who were pressured to upgrade their skills constantly. It became apparent that much of what had been learned in school had a half-life of about ten years because, it was said, over a ten-year period half of what had been learned became obsolete and the other half turned out to be wrong. The advent of new technologies, often characterized as "high tech," allowed people to go off in many different highly specialized directions as a vast array of occupational possibilities opened up.

We began to hear about mid-life crises and mid-life transitions. Many people who had followed the dictates of the culture and their parents in their career choice and development by middle age recognized that they really didn't like what they were doing. Others became satiated and bored, and sought new arenas. Refresher courses and new developments, however, often did not come in sufficient quantity to renew their interest. People simply needed new stimulation.

More highly educated than their parents, they demanded and expected more of themselves and of their environments. They wanted to master new problems and undertake new activities and challenges that, in turn, would gratify them and give them a sense of continued development. Simultaneously, the wider range of choices and more financial security allowed people a greater opportunity to do what they wanted. With life spans increasing, even CEOs who are retiring must choose what they are going to do in their so-called retirement. Many people who have retired from organizations find their retirement experiences hollow unless they have some form of gratifying work that stimulates them.

Larger numbers of women have come into the work place, some directly from school and others after they have had children. Particularly for the latter, the idea of a job was far removed from the concept of career. Yet, as it had been for many years for men, identity for women increasingly became intertwined with career. A woman's career was no longer limited to the roles of teacher, nurse, or housewife. It had to include elements of continued achievement, contribution, and gratification. Of course, for many women, especially for those who were divorced and had children, survival was a fundamental issue. But beyond survival were the questions: Who am I? What is life all about?

The issue of what people wanted to do with their lives became more pressing. The young people of the 1960s had asserted their need for freedom of choice. When they matured and when others who had not been part of that rebellion also matured, the questions were still the same: What do I do with my life? What makes it all worthwhile?

Given further momentum by downsizing, mergers, reorganizations, and the major transitions of socioeconomic life, these trends led to more widespread self-exploration. People understood that they had to take charge of their own lives and make their own choices. More of them wanted a greater degree of control over their own fate, partly because they could not trust organizations to do so anymore, partly because work—career, if you will—and the meaning of life itself had become so intertwined. To achieve a given role in an organization, worthy though the attainment might be, would no longer necessarily provide a sense of inner satisfaction. To fight for and gain a position in an organizational hierarchy might well turn out to be a hollow victory if you expected a psychological pot of gold at the end of the occupational rainbow.

Taken together these changes mean that preparing yourself for a job in an organization is much too limited a way of thinking about career. Even undertaking a professional role is too limited in the sense that your interest within a profession might become more refined or broadened or take off in directions that you had not thought of in the beginning. This does not mean that people should not prepare themselves for jobs or that they should not work in organizations. It means that people should prepare themselves to be their own means for achieving career and personal gratification. Essentially, they need to strengthen themselves to use themselves better in their own self-interest.

I am told that in China people cannot get a license to drive a car without first passing an examination in which they demonstrate their understanding of automobile mechanics because the country has so few mechanics and garages. In a certain sense, that's what's happening with respect to careers in America. Not that there aren't many models to follow. Not that there aren't batteries of psychological tests, guidance counselors, outplacement counselors, and other advisers. Not that you don't have to become proficient in something to earn a livelihood. No. But models, tests, and mentors are only components of what, in today's terms, we want to think of as careers.

So the issue of career has become a lifelong concern in our own country and increasingly for people in other developed countries who have to make occupational and life choices.

We are called upon to choose and then develop orientations and skills that will help us adapt to changing socioeconomic and cultural circumstances. Doing that, in turn, will allow us to sustain our freedom of enterprise and mobility. Essentially, we should strengthen ourselves to make our own choices in a less and less predictable world, where more and more we can count only on the services or products that we as individuals can offer.

Why this book? Aren't there already enough books on careers? What makes this one new or different or unique?

Three factors contribute to its uniqueness. First is its concern with the fundamentals of career choice, namely, your own assessment of yourself. Necessarily, all decisions that you make are based on an assumption about who you are and what you want to be. Both issues are usually quite vague and sometimes contradictory. Yet they need to be clarified for the steps that follow.

Second is that this is a book of wisdom. By that I mean that it is made up of contributions by many people. Each is an expert in a given area that relates to career success. The articles here provided many insights for readers of the *Harvard Business Review* when they were first published. Integrated around a career focus, they are not a pastiche of odds and ends but a psychological mosaic. Like a multifaceted diamond, each facet of which reflects brilliant light, each article contributes to the whole a certain psychological sparkle or vitality that enlivens career issues. Winnowed from hundreds of HBR pieces, they become something bigger than they had been in their original form—a template for examining your particular career issues.

Third, the articles were written originally for managers and executives. They are intended for practical people who must make practical decisions about their everyday career activities. They deal with issues in organizations as people fulfill managerial and executive roles, but, in addition, they deal with the broader issues of career that relate to identity and personal direction. They take up not only your career issues, but also those of others for whom you have responsibility. They take up, too, some of the struggles of aging, ethics, overload, and achievement; they express especial concern for the final phase of career that begins at retirement.

Designing and Managing Your Career is a book that any person can dip into, regardless of the stage of his or her own career. Its articles have endured because readers have found them useful, but it is not a book of recipes. Reading it is like preparing for a trip to a distant land. It brings together the maps and guidebooks, and constructs an itinerary. Like all itineraries, it may be subject to change but at least it is sufficiently consistent to give you a sense of direction and outcome. These pieces allow for many changes of course and for much reflection, introspection, and retrospection. They should help the reader think not only about where he or she is going and about how ideally to get there, but also about some of the difficulties along the way.

This book has continuity because it extends psychologically from basic choices about career through the postretirement period. It is the kind of book that you can pick up, review, put down, and pick up again. In a certain sense, it is a companion for your career. As such, it provides the opportunity for you to raise and discuss questions with colleagues and friends before you make major choices or when you are in the middle of a career dilemma.

The book is divided into five sections. Section I is devoted to "Finding What You're Good At." The intention of this section is to provide handles for the reader to get a sense of his or her own strengths and how they can be applied in a given career direction. In the second section, "Succeeding in Your Career," the articles take up the issues of mobility and how people go about maximizing what they bring to their career opportunities in organizations. In the third section, "Managing Others' Careers," the book takes up those issues that frequently impair your own career; namely, the failures and difficulties of your subordinates, and how to deal with them. Inevitably, your own progress in any organization hinges significantly on how well your subordinates do and how well you can deal with their problems. Section IV, "Handling Career Stress," looks at the inevitable struggles and pressures that anyone who pursues a career in an organization must cope with. These necessarily drain energy, become a psychological burden, and interfere with the pleasure and gratification of career pursuit. Section V, "Retiring with Grace," deals with the last phase of a career, the crowning activity that ideally integrates all the rest and enables you to look back with satisfaction on your lifetime occupational achievement.

Finally, a less obvious feature of this book should be acknowledged and placed in context. Some articles included in this book were written before researchers, writers, and editors began to take into consideration the role of women in management. These articles have been included because their insights far outweigh their anachronistic qualities. Nevertheless, the archaic use of the masculine gender and the assumption that a manager is necessarily male are regrettable. The editor and the publisher hope outdated assumptions about gender will not undermine otherwise cogent and relevant essays.

PART ONE

Finding What You're Good At

n "The Power to See Ourselves," Paul J. Brouwer tells us that management development is not the same thing as manager development. Management development is an organizational activity that helps the manager grow. Manager development is a change in the manager's self-image, the way a person thinks of himself or herself. It has to do with choices that people make based on how they see themselves and who they think they are. Changing your self-image is rarely easy, yet all of us necessarily do so as we mature. We can do so more realistically if we can examine ourselves carefully to develop the kind of insight that enables us to change our expectations of ourselves and to evolve more clearly in the directions in which we would like to go. The more realistic your view of yourself, the more guaranteed is your personal effectiveness.

The self-image exists in the context of an aspiration, an ego ideal. In "A Second Career: The Possible Dream," I elaborate on those aspects of the ego ideal that enable us to tap into our internal momentum to get a sense of both the direction and intensity of that momentum. It's extremely important to understand the relationship between the self-image and the ego ideal because taken together they address the question, "Who are you?" When you have developed an understanding of your ego ideal, together with your characteristic style of behavior, then you are in a position to fit yourself to those various options from among which you may choose.

The third article in this group, "Skills of an Effective Administrator" by Robert L. Katz, is a *Harvard Business Review* classic. This means that 15 years after its initial publication it is still in heavy demand as a reprint. Here, Katz speaks of the three kinds of skills you need to be an effective administrator: technical, human, and conceptual. They are skills because they are abilities that can be developed. The criterion for attainment of these skills is effective action under varying conditions. Technical skills refer to the specifics of doing a given task. Human skills lead to an awareness of your own perceptions, attitudes, assumptions, and beliefs, which in turn are manifested in understanding the meaning of the behavior of others. Conceptual skills involve seeing the organization as a whole in its context: Conceptual and human skills become increasingly important at higher levels in the organization, and the need for higher level conceptual skills is increasing rapidly in the contemporary business world. The capacity for conceptual skills is a given, but you can train yourself in human relations skills, the methods for doing so Katz specifies. It's important in the course of development not only to understand what skills are required for advancement and achievement, but also to become aware of those whose neglect can undermine career achievement.

Following Katz, Henry Mintzberg, writing on "The Manager's Job: Folklore and Fact," observes that the description of the manager's work as one activity after another has been much oversimplified; such continuity does not lend itself to reflective planning. He points out that there are certain regular duties: ceremonial, negotiating, and processing information, odds and ends that when pieced together illuminate the underside of issues. The strategic databank of an organization lies not in its computers, but in the minds of its managers. This private, internalized, and even unconscious knowledge works against the delegation of responsibility from manager to subordinate. Mintzberg also points out that the increasing fragmentation of managerial work and its demands for more and more verbal communication and overwork mean that the manager is caught up in roles that are informational, interpersonal, and decisional—in other words, action-oriented. This makes it imperative to understand the pressures and dilemmas of the managerial role, to find systematic ways to share privileged information, and to discharge tensions before they become stresses. Those require forcing free time into a hectic schedule and developing the skills that Katz discusses.

Abraham Zaleznik, in "Managers and Leaders: Are They Different?," differentiates these two important aspects of administrative function. Leadership requires the power to influence the thoughts and actions of people, and that entails risk. Managers are problem solvers, neither geniuses nor heroes. There is an antagonism between these two roles, and the cultures of the roles differ. The leadership role is entrepreneurial, the managerial role, conformist. Leaders and managers differ in their motivation and experience as well as in their behavior. Zaleznik's delineation of differences makes it possible for you to juxtapose your understanding of yourself and your preferred ways of behaving against the criteria that Zaleznik establishes. While Katz talked about necessary skills and Mintzberg about what managers actually do, Zaleznik makes it clear that there are significant personality and behavioral differences that require evaluation against self-images and ego ideals.

Once having measured yourself against these criteria, it's reasonable to consider next the article by Alfred W. Swinyard and Floyd A. Bond, "Who Gets Promoted?" The authors argue that more and more people who come into managerial roles have higher levels of education and tend to be more mobile. Those who go to the top will more likely come through operational activities, and chances are that younger people will move more rapidly to top management positions because of the advanced average age of top management and the fact that people need at least five years in vice presidential roles to be eligible for top management positions. They point out that careful attention must be given to the ages of senior people and therefore the degree to which they block advancement of younger people. Also important is the experience in operations or division management as contrasted with staff roles. Those with MBAs have a distinct advantage, and there is a growing demand for advanced degrees. They contend from the research data that there is a new mobility among the executives that is already making its mark.

Howard H. Stevenson and David E. Gumpert observe in "The Heart of Entrepreneurship" that there is considerable pressure from the outside environment for innovation and an equal pressure from the inside as people try to move toward their ego ideals. The critical task becomes one of identifying opportunity and making innovation, flexibility, and creativity operational. The authors call for evaluating your own needs and juxtaposing them against probable opportunity. They suggest questions that will help the reader examine the degree to which he or she is likely to be entrepreneurial, and if so, in what ways and under what conditions. Entrepreneurship does not necessarily mean going into business for yourself. It can be carried on in established organizations if people are willing to size up carefully who they are and what the organization and the environment need.

1

The Power to See Ourselves

PAUL J. BROUWER

A psychological fact is that manager development means change in the manager's self-concept. Each of us, whether we realize it or not, has a self-image. We see ourselves in some way—smart, slow, kindly, well-intentioned, lazy, misunderstood, meticulous, or shrewd; we all can pick adjectives that describe ourselves. This is the "I" behind the face in the mirror, the "I" that thinks, dreams, talks, feels, and believes, the "I" that no one knows fully. In this article we will explore the meaning of the self-image, particularly in relation to changing behavior in growing managers, and how changes in self-concept come about.

One reason this self-concept is crucial is that it has a great deal to do with manager development—with being a growing person and eventually realizing one's self-potential. Note the term *manager* development rather than *management* development; the purpose of such development is to help individual managers to grow. After all, they have to do most of the job themselves. As a member of a firm of consulting psychologists to management, I can report that fact from experience—and add the further observation that no one can tell managers exactly how to grow. Rather, the most one can do is to help managers understand themselves in their own situations, and then trust them to find the best directions themselves.

Filters for Reality

In the first place, the self-concept is important because everything we do or say, everything we hear, feel, or otherwise perceive, is influenced by how we see ourselves. For example:

A businessman, who had traveled in many parts of the world, was incorrigibly curious about the customs, speech, local places of interest, history, and traditions of any place he visited. However, on a one-week visit to London—his first—on a delicate mission for his company, he might just as well have been in Indianapolis for all he learned of English ways of life. Being on a business trip, he saw himself as a businessman, and actually perceived little of what was around him. But as a vacationer in London he would have seen England in depth, because he would have seen himself coming to London for that purpose.

Photographers often slip a reddish filter over the lens when snapping pictures from reaching the film, so that the final picture shows much darker skies and more sharply whitened clouds. The self-concept is like a filter that screens out what we do not want to hear and see, passes through what we do want to see and hear. In the reverse direction, it gives an idiosyncratic flavor to our behavior. Don't we all usually pick our name out of a jumble of words on a page? Or hear our name announced at an airport amidst all of the other announcements that we fail to hear? This is called selective listening, and it is a function of our self-concept. Thus, how we see ourselves determines generally what we react to, what we perceive, and, in broad terms, how we behave in general.

And this shows up in business situations too. Imagine two executives, A and B, in identical situations. Each calls in a subordinate and delegates an assignment. The italicized words below give partial indications of their self-concepts. Executive A says:

"Tom, I'm *concerned* about our relations with the XYZ Company. Its *purchases* from us have fallen off lately and *rather abruptly*. You know our history with it. *Will* you *investigate* and find out the cause of the reduced volume? *Let me know* if you run into anything you don't understand."

Executive A is confident of her ability to handle the situation. She sees herself as unthreatened, able to cope with whatever Tom's investigation discloses, and willing to delay action until the facts are gathered and studied.

Executive B, on the other hand, says:

"Jane, the XYZ Company has cut back its purchases from us for the third month in a row. *We've got to get on this and quick.* Now, you go visit it. *I wish I could but I'm tied down here.* Talk to the purchasing agent—uh, what's her name again? Uh . . . (shuffling papers) . . . here it is . . . Bailey, *See* Bailey. Oh . . . and you'd better see the chief engineer, a nice guy . . . named . . . uh . . . his name slips me *for the moment* . . . you can get it from Bailey. But don't go near Sam Awful—he'll cover up whatever's happening anyway, and might use your visit as a sign we're scared of old XYZ. *I've got to have some answers on this one, Jane.* The boss is on my neck but good. So. . . ."

Executive B is obviously less confident. He feels threatened by the situation. He doesn't trust Jane to use her own common sense—as indicated by his explicit "do"s and "don't"s—probably because he himself lacks confidence.

Continuing Changes

Although the self-concept is important in understanding human behavior *generally*, it becomes critically so in understanding *manager development*, where changes in behavior are the objective. As a matter of cold, hard, psychological fact, a change in behavior on the job, for better or worse, means a change in self-concept. Thus, we are dealing with an immensely and immediately practical consideration.

Human beings constantly change their behavior, as we see if we examine ourselves (and others) critically enough. It is a superficial observation to say that so-and-so is the same person she was five years ago. Technically, she isn't exactly the same today as she was even yesterday. For one thing, she is one day older. She has learned something new, however negligible, that becomes incorporated in her apperceptive mass. As a result, her perception of today's events is different, however slightly and undetectably, from what it was yesterday. She may have had nothing "significant" happen to her—no promotion, no accident, no soul-searching upset—but she will be different, even though only a person with Solomon's wisdom would know it. Change in behavior is constant.

The difficulties managers have in thinking about changes in behavior come from their inability to detect change, and from fuzzy thinking behind such comforting, though fallacious, notions as, "You can't teach an old dog new tricks," "He was born that way," or "She's been like that ever since I've known her."

On the other hand, sometimes superficial behavior changes are erroneously thought to be basic. For example, consider the simplest level of change in behavior, which is brought about by increased knowledge or skill:

The newly appointed foreman learns his new duties, dons a white shirt, delegates jobs he used to do himself, and learns to participate in his superintendent's meetings. His company provides him with instruction through manuals, books, conferences, sessions with his boss, and management training courses. He joins the National Foremen's Association, attends lectures, and may even be sent to a two-week seminar at the local university. He learns much and becomes suitably skillful in discharging his new functions. This new way of life changes the foreman's behavior, of course; but only peripherally, just as living in a new house does not basically alter the marriage relation. He knows more, sees more, has more and better skills.

If companies do want such "simple-level" changes, and only these, then management training is called for. The new zone manager learns the policy manual, and the new vice president of manufacturing learns how the company's controller figures costs. These specific learnings are the objectives of training, and can become changes in behavior produced by training.

Keystone for Growth

If, however, a company wants growth in the *deeper* sense, then something more subtle and basic in its impact is called for in the manager development effort. Such deeper growth is, of course, a change in self-concept. Managers who once were unreliable in their judgment or who lacked drive *grow* toward reliability in judgment or toward stronger drive. Growth in this sense brings observable changes in outward behavior, because each person is now inwardly different—different, for example, in self-perception, in attitude toward job and company as both relate to his or her own life, or in a feeling of responsibility for others.

But experience shows that such growth is as difficult to achieve as it is desirable. It demands the full-fledged participation of the manager. Actually the trite expression, "Management development is self-development," is psychologically sound. Growing managers change because they want to and because they have to in response to new insights and understandings gained on the job. They do not change because they are told to, exhorted to, or because it is the thing to do.

Such growth implies changes within people—in how they use their knowledge, in the ends to which they apply their skills, and, in short, in their view of themselves. The point is clear that growing people examine themselves; and as they do so, they emerge with new depths of motivation, a sharper sense of direction, and a more vital awareness of how they want to live on the job. Growth in this sense is personalized and vital. And such growth in self-concept is at the heart of a real manager development effort.

But growth in self-concept is not always simple and clear.

Conflicts in Self-Concept

Each human being is several selves, living comfortably in the role of father or mother, husband or wife, business person, president, golfer, bridge player, the life of the party, and so on. But if there are conflicts among any of these roles, then discomfort arises. And such conflict brings with it such dynamics as tension, guilt feelings, and compensation. Let us illustrate with a familiar example:

A person sees him- or herself both as a good parent and a good business person. As a parent, he or she spends time with the children; but as a business person, the time demands can be overwhelming. Now what can be done? It obviously is not possible to be home most evenings with the family and also be out of town on necessary business trips. Both self-concepts cannot be realized simultaneously. So what happens? The business gets the time Monday through Friday, and the family gets the weekends.

This seems like an easy resolution. What, then, is the problem? The person in our example has had to modify both self-concepts and may feel deeply dissatisfied with such a necessity. So the dissatisfaction, the psychological discomfort, the basic conflict in self-concepts, may show in his or her behavior — being unduly critical of business associates (or subordinates) who will not follow this example and give up their family life during the week; resenting the children, who blithely go about their own activities on the weekend, ignoring their parents. And if by chance the teen-age child develops any emotional problems which are ascribed to "parental neglect," our person really hits the ceiling! "Neglect? How can that be? Haven't I given my children every weekend?"

In the deeper sense, conflicts lie behind many self-concepts, but it is beyond our scope to explore them. In an individual case, this is a matter for professional study and expert handling. By definition, effective, consistent behavior is integrated behavior, while unintegrated behavior is the behavior of conflict.

Unrealism in Self-Concept

In addition to conflicts between self-concepts as a cause of ineffective behavior, there is the crucial matter of disparity between "how I see myself" and "how others see me." Unrealistic self-appraisal has cost many a manager his or her job. Think of people you know who have been fired, eased out, or moved laterally because they no longer "seemed up to the job." Has there not been in many such cases the subtle flavor of unadaptability, of a rigid inability in a manager to adjust his or her sights to a new role as times have changed?

Most familiar are the unnecessarily tragic cases of those who cannot grow old gracefully. Next are those uncounted misfits who fail through lack of realistic insight into their true worth. For example, take the good vice president who flunks as president because he never realized his inability to endure the rigors of being top person. There are endless instances of failures owing to a disparity between "who I am" and "who I think I am."

Unfortunately, not only outright failure may come from disparities in self-concept; more insidious is the effect of partial or fuzzy self-appraisal. In fact, if the proposition is right that realism in the individual's self-view has a one-to-one relationship with effectiveness on the job, then it surely follows that all of us can improve our effectiveness by the simple expedient of developing a more realistic, more accurate self-concept!

In short, the more realistic one's view of oneself, the more guaranteed is personal effectiveness. Here is an example that underscores this point:

George H., the vice president of sales for a $50-million company with a staff of 250 sales and service people, was in serious organizational trouble. The group had increased in size so rapidly that it had long since outgrown its organizational pattern. There were constant complaints such as: "Whom do I work for?" "Nobody knows whether I'm doing well or poorly." "We haven't any system to follow in service to customers." The executives under George tried valiantly to do twice and three times as much as they had always done. The situation was, frankly, a mess.

George as a person was well liked and respected. He was democratic, attentive to others, soft-spoken, unlikely to "order," always likely to "suggest," and unsure of himself as an administrator. In general he was a person who saw himself as a stimulator and coordinator of his people, an excellent personal salesperson, but not a supervisor. Somehow he had completely missed sensing that his people waited for directions from him. He felt that a sensible district sales manager should know what to do. His own perception of himself and his people's perception of him as vice president of sales were poles apart.

The impasse was breached when an outsider on whom George relied heavily (and who also had the confidence of the top people in the department) finally told him bluntly, "George, your people are waiting for you to clear the air. They'll follow any organizational plan you want them to. This step only you can take. They respect you and want your leadership. They value you. Don't ask them; tell them, for goodness' sake, how you're going to organize their activities."

George tried to integrate this new dimension into his self-concept. At first, he swung to one extreme and "got tough:" He made explicit, directive demands; he swore; he told everybody, in effect, "I want what I want when I want it— and that's right now!" But soon he abandoned his pretense and absorbed into his self-concept the new "take-charge" aspect of his functioning. He defined an organizational plan, set up policies and procedures which sorted out sales and service duties, discussed them fully with all involved, and said, in effect, "This is it. Let's go."

This example is, of course, an over-simplification; it highlights the fact that disparity in perception can reduce managerial effectiveness. What George saw himself to be in the office of vice president of sales precluded his seeing the needs of his people. And this blind spot nearly cost him prolonged chaos, if not the loss of his job.

Finally, it is manifestly clear that change in self-concept as a function of executive growth has a payoff. Recall situations where a critical appointment has to be made. Who gets the nod? Usually it is the one who *as a person* is thought to have potential and who is able to make a contribution to the "mix" of key executives. Consequently, many companies, in selecting their handpicked future executives, feed in "trainees" with liberal arts degrees. They are looking for the *people*, not their knowledge or special skills. By the same token, as the young people grow, it is their self-concept that will change and come more into line with what they are becoming in relation to their potential. It is on the basis of their self-concept that young people emerge as top executives. To twist an old adage, it isn't what you know that finally counts; it's who you *are*.

Natural Resistance

But there is still one big question to answer. If changes in the self-concept of the executive are desirable, just what brings them about? In fact, are changes in self-concept possible? Of course changes are possible, but there is one obvious block to growth.

Even when executives want to change, the lurking suspicion that such effort is futile tends to vitiate the process of change. Faint mutterings of self-discontent tend to get quashed by the notion that "an old dog can't learn new tricks." And the basic comfort of the status quo seems to outweigh the value of the new mode of behavior.

One reason for such feelings of resistance is that, psychologically, the mature person resists change. By definition, the self-concept is an organization or patterning of attitudes, habits, knowledge, drives, and the like. And also, by definition, the fact of organization means a cementing together of all these complex components.

For example, people who for many years have been highly and aggressively competitive cannot, except with difficulty, either suddenly or gradually become insightfully cooperative; they will still tend to see themselves as needing to surpass others. They retain a pattern, a consistency, and basic characteristics; and in this sense resist change. Indeed, this is a good thing, or we still would all be going through the throes of "finding ourselves" as we did as adolescents.

When mature people change, therefore, they do so against a natural resistance; but whether this resistance is a deeply stabilizing influence that helps them to retain their basic direction and character, or whether it is a cocoon that makes them unreachable, is a moot question. Resistance, though built in, may thus be either a roadblock or a gyroscope.

We have noted that changes in the self-concept of executives are "gut-level," not peripheral. They are changes in perception and attitude and understanding, not changes in knowledge or experience or skills. So our exploration of how change occurs must include those factors which seem to operate more deeply within the individual and which polarize new directions and behaviors. We are looking for those basic vital factors which, as they operate, really change people beyond their power of dissimulation or pretense. This is change in the fundamental makeup of people, not change in their apparel. When such changes occur, the person is different.

Steps to Maturity

Let us be clear about one point. Growth does not proceed in clear-cut, discrete, logical steps. Sometimes it occurs in inexplicable spurts; at other times, with agonizing slowness. There are cases where real learning is so deeply unconscious that no overt behavior change shows up for a long time. Even regressions will occur, as when an adolescent, perhaps troubled by a day's activities, will sleep with a special blanket as he or she did at age six. The process of growth is a nebulous, multifactored, fluid, dynamic process, often astounding, and usually only partially controllable.

But for the sake of discussion, and understanding, we can postulate a sequence of steps.

Self-Examination

If we were to attempt a systematic analysis of what happens when growth in managers occurs, we would need to begin with self-examination. For here individuals first know that they *don't know* or first get an inkling that they wish their behavior were different in some respect. They are forced, either by circumstance or their own conscious introspection, to look at themselves critically. This is what happens when golfers see movies of their swing, or when a parent scolds a child by saying, "Just look at yourself—all dirty." Or when the supervisor's thinly veiled anger over a subordinate's sloppy work finally becomes known. People see themselves every time they look in the mirror, but do they really examine what they see? Do they appraise and evaluate and study what manner of people they are?

The function of self-examination is to lay the groundwork for insight, without which no growth can occur. Insight is the "oh, I see now" feeling which must, consciously or unconsciously, precede change in behavior. Insights—real, genuine glimpses of ourselves as we really are—are reached only with difficulty and sometimes with real psychic pain. But they are the building blocks of growth. Thus self-examination is a preparation for insight, a groundbreaking for the seeds of self-understanding which gradually bloom into changed behavior.

Self-Expectation

As individuals raise their sights for themselves, as they get insights into the direction in which they want to grow, as they "see" themselves in a particular respect they do not like, then they are changing their self-expectations. (This is the next step.) New demands on themselves are set up, not by anyone else, just by themselves. This is another way of saying what the theologians insist on, namely, that a conviction of sin precedes salvation. Or, as the psychologists put it, first accept the fact that *you* have the problem—not anyone else—and then you are ready to find a solution. Here are two cases that illustrate the importance of self-expectation through insight:

Mary D. was a chronic complainer. Nothing was ever her fault. She frequently and self-pityingly inveighed against her boss, her subordinates, her peers, and the competition. She was capable, knowledgeable, a hard worker, critical. And never once, when she sang the old refrain, "Why does this always happen to me? did an inner voice whisper back, "It's no different for you, old girl, than for anyone else. It's just the way you take it."

Efforts by her boss and her friends to develop some insight in Mary seemed wasted. Logical explanations, patiently made, were of course futile. Anger toward her only proved to her she was picked on. Gentle tolerance only gave her a bigger pool to wallow in.

One day in a meeting of executives to find answers to a particular crisis that had hit everyone (an unexpected price slash by a major competitor), she held forth at length on the uselessness of market research, on the futility of keeping a "pipeline" on the competitor's situation, on how her department (sales) couldn't be blamed for not anticipating the vagaries of the competition's pricing policy, and so on. She finally stopped. And, as though by prearrangement, the whole group, perhaps in complete disgust at her immaturity and irrelevance, sat in stony silence.

At length the silence became so oppressive that it suddenly dawned on the complainer that she was just that—an immature complainer. She recalled the words of her colleagues and her own dim awareness that she did complain a lot. Insight finally occurred.

At long last she was ready to begin to grow out of her immaturity. She saw (and disliked) herself at this point. Now her growth could become self-directed; she could easily find many opportunities to quash feelings of self-pity and to face reality in a more stateswomanlike fashion, because now she expected more stateswomanlike attitudes of herself.

Pete B., age 58, was vice president of engineering of a company that made fine-quality capital goods equipment. He had been with his company 35 years. He was a good engineer, who knew the product inside out; and through the years he had learned to know the customers, too. He felt proud of and personally involved in each installation of the product. It was not unusual to see him on an evening, coatless and with his tie loose, perched on a stool before a drafting board, surrounded by young engineers, digging at a tough installation problem. While some thought Pete did too much himself, others felt that with him on the job the customer would be satisfied.

About four years ago, however, the president, whose family owned the company, sold it to a large corporation, and the company became a wholly owned subsidiary. One allied product line was acquired, then another. Finally Pete's department was asked to do the engineering work for several subsidiaries that were not set up to do their own.

Now Pete's job had changed, subtly but surely, and trouble began to brew for Pete because he couldn't seem to change with the situation.

Psychologically, Pete saw himself as a one-person department (with assistants as trainees) who personally engineered the product for the customer, his friend. He resisted the impersonality of working on engineering problems of "sister companies" whose customers and products he barely knew and cared less about. The new fangled system of a "home office" engineering vice president who was "staff" seemed to him just another unnecessary complication. Nothing worked the way it used to. He saw himself bypassed by progress and change.

So, unconsciously, he began to resist and to fight. His yearning for the "good old days" subconsciously forced him to run faster and faster in order to know more customers and more product lines; to work more evenings; to press new systems into the form of old procedures. And, of course, he began to slip, and badly. Gradually, Pete was viewed by his superiors as "good old Pete, but let's not get him in on this matter or he'll have to take it over himself and we'll get bogged down," and by his subordinates as a fine fellow, but stodgy and old-fashioned.

Fortunately, before the situation compelled a major organizational shift, Pete took stock of his situation, and really saw himself as he was. He got the insight that his self-image of a kind of personal engineer was no longer applicable to the corporation's greatly expanded needs. And right then, with this new glimpse of himself (and the courage and self-honesty to face it), he began to change. He started by focusing on how his years of experience could be applied to the coaching of his subordinates. He put himself in the shoes of the staff vice president and could then see how to mesh gears better. Then he stopped resisting the new fangled data processing and automation procedures. His growth began with a new self-expectation.

Change in Self-Expectation

How do people get a new self-demand, a new self-expectation? How do they find out that their self-concept is inadequate? How do people know not only that they can be different but should be as well? Unfortunately for those who like recipes or formulas, such questions are perenially bothersome because there is no one best way.

What can be done to stimulate change in self-expectation besides honest, realistic, self-appraising introspection? In the business context, the constructive pointing up of executives' needs for growth by their superiors is a tremendous source of insight. The emphasis, of course, is on the word *constructive*, which means helpful, insightful ideas from the superior and not, as so often happens, a ceremonial, judgmental, "I'll tell you what I think about you" appraisal.

Of further source of insight is husbands and wives—the perceptive ones, that is. Perceptive ones have unique ways of jerking spouses up short when their self-images become distorted.

In fact, anything which enables people to get a new perception—reading, observing, studying, going to conferences, attending meetings, and participating in clubs—can provide insight into themselves. *Out of insight comes change in self-expectation.*

And, of course, life situations which are kaleidoscopic always enable perceptive people to see themselves in a new light. Here is another example:

Katherine W. was acutely self-critical, often to the point where her fear of failure immobilized her. She delayed decisions, fussed endlessly with details, and generally strained to be perfect. In time her relation with the psychologist, who genuinely accepted her without criticism, praise, blame, or hostility, enabled her to "see" how her self-critical attitudes really stemmed from her self-pride. She felt she had to be perfect because it was "safer" to be free from criticism and failure. But she finally "rejoined the human race" and demanded of herself only that she do her best. The insight that she was human after all freed her to change her self-expectations.

Self-Direction

People are masters of their own destiny in the sense that they take charge of their own development if they want to grow. Nothing can be done to them to make them grow; they grow only as they want to and as their own insights enable them to.

The changes in self-concept that executives undergo must continue primarily through their own self-direction. It is clear that many development programs miss their mark badly at this point. They make the naive assumption that exposure to experiences or people or books or courses is enough to produce growth. Not so. They effect change in the participants only as they reach out and appropriate something—a bit of wisdom, a new idea, or a new concept—that stretches them, and gives them answers to their own self-generated problem.

Put another way, we might say that, just as learning is impossible without motivation, so real executive development is impossible unless executives seek it. Furthermore, the strength of their desire is infinitely stronger if they seek development because they want to develop than if they are merely trying to please their bosses or do what is expected of them. As any teacher knows, the pupils who listen and learn merely in order to pass the course are far poorer learners than those who want to learn.

Fundamentally, this is the age-old problem of motivation, of keeping steam up in the boiler. The maintenance of a growing edge, as executives emerge from insight to insight to realize their potential, is a consequence of intrinsic motivation. They are driven toward unrealized objectives, perhaps toward unrealizable goals.

After developing insight into themselves *in relation to what they want to be*, the power that keeps executives growing is the veritable necessity of doing things that to them are intrinsically, basically, and lastingly worthwhile. Growing executives are so because they derive their strength and desire and drive from inner, unachieved goals; and their satisfactions from self-realization. This is intrinsic motivation as it relates to self-concept.

Broadened Perceptions

The dynamics of this factor of growth are very clear: people must see themselves in relation to their environment, both personal and impersonal, and must develop their image of themselves partly in response to what they see around them. So if they see a very small world (as a child does), their concept of themselves must necessarily be narrow; if they see themselves as citizens of the world (as a world traveler might), their self-concept embraces the world. This is the difference between the real provincial, such as a hillbilly, and the true sophisticate.

A most common complaint of superiors is that subordinates are too narrow in their outlooks. For example, the sales manager promoted to vice president of sales irritates her peers in manufacturing or research by having "only a salesperson's point of view." The former production supervisor, now a vice president, is derided by the people in sales for his attitude of "We'll make it at low cost; it's up to you to sell it, and don't bother me with special runs for special customers or model changes—sell 'em." Both people suffer from constraint of the self-concept: they perceive their jobs (and themselves) too narrowly. For instance:

A vice president of sales was brought in from outside the company to gear up the effort of merchandising a new line of products. He did a magnificent job, old pro that he was, of shaping up and vitalizing a sales force. Volume of sales picked up excellently, and he was the hero of the hour.

But after a year, when he felt on top of his job, some of his attitudes and habits reasserted themselves, annoying others and stalling progress. For instance, he persisted in making frequent references to his former (and larger) company. He climbed on manufacturing for delivery delays, and on research and engineering for perfectionism before releasing the specifications for what he felt were needed product changes. The time it took to explain to him, pacify him, and argue with him was ill-spent and futile. He was rapidly becoming a block in the path of progress.

One day the president approached him directly. "George," said the president, "what's your title?"

"Why," said George, puzzled, "vice president of sales."

"Right. And what does *vice president* mean to you?"

George paused. What was the president getting at? "Well," he said, "it means a lot of things, I guess. Responsibility for sales, building a. . . ."

"Stop right there," interrupted the president. "Responsibility for sales, you say. True in a way. But sales managers also have this responsibility, don't they?"

"Well, yes."

"Then what do the words *vice president* mean in your title?"

"Oh, I see. . . . Well, I guess they mean seeing or having responsibility for the sales function of the company from the point of view of the company . . . that part of your office."

"You got my point before I mentioned it, George," said the president. "Vice presidents speak from the company point of view, not just of their departments. They try to keep the overall good of the company in mind."

George thought this conversation over. He got the point. He realized the narrowness of his own view. He has been thinking of himself as "on loan" from his former employer to straighten things out here. As he pondered the president's comments, he broadened his perception of job—and of himself. And sometime later he began to act as an officer of the total company.

Self-Realization Power

It is not enough, however, just to see ourselves as we are now. Such understanding is a necessary starting point, or basis on which to build. But we must also see what our real selves *could* be, and grow into that.

The strong people of history have had one psychological characteristic in common: they seem always to have been themselves as persons—

. . . Beethoven, continuing to compose after he became deaf;

. . . Milton, who didn't allow blindness to interfere with his writing;

. . . Keller, becoming a lecturer on opportunities for the handicapped despite being both deaf and blind.

Such people have given meaning to the phrase, "fulfilling one's destiny."

In less dramatic form, strong executives fulfill themselves as they live lives that are an unfolding of their potential. They must be themselves. In this sense, the self-concept of the strong executive is a constantly evolving, changing thing as they continuously realize themselves. This is, indeed, genuine growth and the kind that continues until senescence sets in.

Can all people aspire to be this strong—to accomplish such a self-realization? Of course not. But growing people (by definition) have unrealized power if their self-concept, their self-expectation, their self-direction, and their constantly broadening perceptions (wisdom) allow them to find it. The difference between a strong person and a weak person may not be a difference in ability, for many clerks have keen intelligence; or in drive, for many ambitious people get nowhere; or in opportunity, for somehow, strong people *make* opportunity. No, the difference lies in self-concept. How much do I value my life? What do I want to do with it? What must I do to be myself? Strong people have emerged with clear-cut answers to such questions; weak ones equivocate and temporize and never dare.

Thus growth, finally, is the evolvement of personal goals and the sense of venture in pursuing them. This is the meaning of dedicated people. Their personal goals, their company goals, and their job goals have coincidence to a great extent; and their personal power is directed single-mindedly toward seeing themselves in relation to the fulfillment of their executive potential.

2

A Second Career: The Possible Dream

HARRY LEVINSON

Just two years after his appointment as director of marketing services, 35-year-old Tom Conant started thinking about leaving his job and enrolling in law school. He had fantasies of addressing the bench in an attempt to persuade the judge to side with his position. Tom imagined how it would feel to demolish the opposing lawyer by asking the witness penetrating questions that led inexorably to the conclusion he sought. He couldn't wait to get started.

Tom had joined the company right after business school and in 12 years there had topped one success with another. His marketing acumen, his ability to innovate, do research, and carry through new programs brought the company important new business. In other respects, too, Tom had been a model manager to his superiors and his subordinates. He was marked as a comer. Tom's initial impatience to sink his teeth into new challenges had posed some problems, but as he received new responsibilities, Tom began to relax and seemed to enjoy his work and his colleagues.

When he found himself thinking of a career in law, Tom surprised himself. He had thought that he might be wooed by competitors, but he had never expected to think of abandoning his career. Leo Burns, Tom's predecessor as manager of marketing services and his mentor, hoped to see his protégé follow him to the vice presidency. Tom knew that his resignation would shatter Leo, and that knowledge annoyed him. He didn't want to fight or disappoint Leo.

Anger at Leo slowly mounted. In his fantasy Tom tried to explain to Leo his reasons for leaving, to describe the soul-searching he had done in the last year, but Leo wouldn't listen. He pictured Leo's disappointment turning to irritation. The imaginary drama came to a climax with Leo insisting that Tom leave the company immediately. "Marketing doesn't need you!" Tom imagined Leo shouting. "Just get on with your plans and get out!"

When Tom had these fantasies, he always had second thoughts about making such a move. He had a good career ahead of him. He was a loyal company person, and the company had been good to him. His recent promotion had given him new responsibilities and a reputation in the industry. And he hadn't really been that bored for the last two years.

Yet in calmer moments Tom remembered other managers who had switched careers. An engineer he knew had left a responsible job in product development at the age of 40 to go to law school and was now a patent attorney. He boasted that it was a change he was glad he had made: "I was going to spend the rest of my life putting new faces on old products. Now I can use what I know about engineering to help people who are going to make real changes happen."

Tom reflected also about the many people in the news who were on their second, or even third, careers. California ex-governor Jerry Brown had been a Jesuit seminarian before entering politics; Henry Kissinger had been a professor before becoming a diplomat. Several business school deans had been CEOs, and university presidents have become business executives.

As always, Tom concluded his reverie with a farewell handshake; he was leaving his old friends behind. He imagined them thinking that they, too, should have undertaken second careers.

Almost everyone at some point thinks of a second career. Many people have good reasons. Tom's law school fantasy was based in part on a cool assessment of his own life and the contemporary business situation. He believed that growing consumer movements would force the marketing field to change radically in the next decade. Despite their temporary relaxation, he thought that federal, state, and local regulations controlling advertising and promotion would increase. By combining his marketing experience with a law school education, Tom reasoned he could steal a march on this trend and build a solid future for himself either as an in-house counsel or as a consultant.

As the years pass, most people — regardless of their professions or skills — find their jobs or careers less interesting, stimulating, or rewarding. By midlife, many feel the need for new and greener occupational fields. They yearn for opportunities to reassert their independence and maturity and to express the needs and use the talents of a different stage of life.

Some people feel they are no longer in the running for advancement, some that their talents and skills are not being fully used, and some that they have outgrown their jobs, companies, or disciplines. Others, feeling blocked by being in the wrong company, industry, or position, are bored. Some are in over their heads, while others had merely drifted into their jobs or chosen directions prematurely. One or a combination of these feelings can make a person hate to go to work in the morning and can trigger thoughts of a way out.

The realities of contemporary organizational life also stimulate a manager to think about a second career: the competition is stiffer every year. Even to the young manager, the accelerating pace of change makes obsolescence a threat. Rapid technological changes (which demand higher levels of education and training), more differentiated markets, and unpredictable economic circumstances all make it improbable that a manager will have a life-long career in one field or one organization.

By their middle or late 30s, managers usually know how far their careers will take them. By comparing his promotion rate to those of peers, a manager can tell if he has leveled off. If a manager's latest assignment takes him out of the organization's prescribed route to the top, the upward movement probably has ended.

Other factors behind the wish for second careers are the effects aging and growth have on people. Although an intense period of skills training, job rotation, long hours of overtime, and much traveling may have satisfied them when they were younger and just beginning their careers, managers as they get older probably find the pace exhausting and the rewards insufficiently attractive to compensate for the loss of other gratifications.

But the reasons for thinking about a second career are not always positive. Some people want to change because they are always dissatisfied with themselves; some are depressed and angry; some have anxiety about death that induces restlessness; and some have overvalued themselves and believe they are more talented or capable than they really are. Some managers can't tolerate bosses. Others think they should have been CEO a long time ago. Some are unwilling to acquire experience, while others are competing with old classmates. Some are just competing— and not as well as they'd like.

Seeking a new career for these reasons is an exercise in futility. If a manager blames the job, the boss, or the company when the source of his discontent is really himself, his second career is likely to be as disappointing as his first. Therefore a manager, before embarking on choosing a second career, must have an honest picture of himself and understand the changes he probably will go through.

Stages in Adult Development

As middle age approaches, thoughts about a second career intensify.[1] Building on the work of Sigmund Freud, psychoanalyst Erik H. Erikson has outlined three stages of adulthood: intimacy, generativity, and integrity.[2] Each stage has a psychosocial crisis and each has its task.

The first adult stage, intimacy, which lasts from about age 21 to age 35, is the most spontaneously creative period. It is an innovative and productive time. The young adult channels great energies into choosing and launching a career and, usually, into contracting a marriage and establishing a family. The third and final stage, integrity, begins at approximately age 55. Ideally, at this age a person ties together his life experience and comes to terms with his life. At work, he prepares for retirement and reflects on his career.

In between, during the stage of generativity, from about age 35 to age 55, the adult lays the foundations for the next generation. Commonly called the mid-life transition, this is the time of reevaluation. At home, the children are leaving the nest and husbands and wives have to rethink their relationship to each other. At work, the drive to compete and excel is peaking, and executives pay more attention to bringing other, younger managers along.

The transition between intimacy and generativity is, according to Daniel Levinson, the time during which the adult makes his last assertion for independence.[3] Levinson calls this "the BOOM [becoming one's own man] effect." His studies of executives indicate that at about age 37, the adult throws off the guidance or protection of older mentors or managers and takes full charge of himself. Those that are able to make this last stand for independence go on to new heights. They demand more responsibility or start their own companies. Others either don't assert themselves or are rejected when they make demands. The BOOM effect is an impetus for seeking a new career.

In our culture people have opportunities to do many things. In youth they choose one and leave the others behind, but they promise themselves they'll come back to them. Fifteen years out of school, people tend to feel satiated with what they're doing—even if it is something with high status and high pay— and itch to fulfill old promises to themselves. They tend to become restless when circumstances keep them from doing so and become dismayed when they realize that they can't go back and start all over again.

When people are in this stage of life, they need to seek counsel, to talk at length about their reasons, and to listen to others' experiences and perceptions. They also need the support of others who are important to them through this difficult decision-making and transition period. Such assistance can ensure that the manager will make a sound second-career choice rather than flee impulsively from frustration or boredom. It might even result in a wise decision on the part of a promising executive to remain, with renewed enthusiasm, in his organization. A manager who thinks through the issues of a second career also readies himself to help others with the same concerns.

Who Are You?

The most critical factor for people to consider in choosing a gratifying second career is their ego ideal. It can serve as a road map. Central to a person's aspirations, the ego ideal is an idealized image of oneself in the future. It includes the goals people would like to achieve and how they would like to see themselves. At an early age, children identify with parents and other power figures, find out how to please or resist them, and learn to adapt to feeling small and helpless in comparison with them. How they do these things, as well as other unconscious factors, determines how their ego ideals develop. During childhood and adolescence, the young person incorporates rising aspirations built on academic or career achievements into the ego ideal and, as time goes on, also includes successive models, each of which has a more specialized competence.

Throughout life people strive toward their ego ideals, but no one ever achieves it. With successive accomplishments, aspirations rise. But as people feel they are progressing toward their ego ideals, their self-pictures are more rather than less positive. The closer a person gets to the ego ideal, therefore, the better he feels about himself. The greater the gap between one's ego ideal and one's current self-image, the angrier one is at oneself and the more inadequate, guilty, and depressed one feels.

When a career helps satisfy the ego ideal, life and work are rewarding and enjoyable. When a career does not help meet these self-demands, work is a curse. In short, the wish to attain the ego ideal, to like oneself, is the most powerful of motivating forces. Delivery on the promises one makes to oneself is an important aspect of choosing a new direction.

Tapping into the Ego Ideal

Because people begin to form their ego ideals in earliest childhood, developing an accurate understanding of them is difficult. A careful review of family history and school and work experiences can go a long way in outlining the needs that are important to the ego ideal. A manager can help the process along by discussing with a listener or a friend answers to the following questions (although this exercise may strike you as off the point, there are very good reasons for carrying it out):

1. What were your father's or father substitute's values? Not what did your father say or do, but what did he stand for? What things were important to him? What was the code he lived by? And then, what were your mother's values?

2. What was the first thing you did that pleased your mother? Small children try hard to please their mothers, who are the most important figures

in their lives. Every child's earliest efforts to please mother become ingrained behavior. They are, therefore, a significant part of each person's characteristic way of behaving and have an important influence on subconscious goals. Later, children try to please the father, too.

(Sometimes, especially for women, it may be the mother's values that are more important and the activities that pleased father that weigh more heavily.)

3. Who were your childhood heroes or heroines? Did you idolize athletes, movie stars, or political figures? What kind of people do you now enjoy reading about or watching on TV? What kind of achievements do you admire?

4. Who are and were your models — relatives, teachers, scoutmasters, preachers, bosses, characters in stories? What did they say or do that made you admire them?

5. When you were able to make choices, what were they? What elective subjects did you take in high school? What major did you pursue in college? What jobs have you accepted? At first glance, these choices may seem to have been random, but they were not. And when you take a retrospective look at them, a pattern emerges.

6. What few experiences in your lifetime have been the most gratifying? Which gave you the greatest pleasure and sense of elation? The pleasure you took in the experience was really the pleasure you took in yourself. What were you doing?

7. Of all the things you've done, at which were you the most successful? What were you doing and how were you doing it?

8. What would you like your epitaph or obituary to say? What would you like to be remembered for? What would you like to leave as a memorial?

The answers to these questions will help managers sketch the outlines of their ego ideals and give them a sense of the main thrust of their lives.

If you still have some doubts about direction after you've talked these questions through, you might take a battery of psychological tests to complement the definition of your ego ideal. Many counseling psychologists provide interest, aptitude, and values inventories as well as tests of intelligence, reasoning, and other capacities. They can interpret the test results and advise you about their significance for your career choice.

How Do You Like to Act?

The next step is to determine the kinds of occupational activities that fit the way you like to behave, how you like to do your job or deal with co-workers. The point here is to determine whether you are temperamentally fit for the job you're thinking of moving to. For instance, Tom in the opening vignette had always wanted to take on new responsibilities and challenges and to act alone taking risks rather than in a group, where interdependence is important. If Tom decided to go to law school to become a consultant working on his own, he would be making a choice consistent with how he worked best. He would be choosing an environment in which he would be psychologically comfortable.

In determining how your personality will fit with a job, a listener's or friend's questions and insights will be valuable. Explore the following areas:

How do you handle aggressive energy? Do you channel it into the organization and administration of projects? Are you reluctant to express it? For instance, do you have difficulty taking people to task or confronting colleagues or subordinates? How do you react when someone challenges your opinion?

Channeling aggressive energy into the organization and administration of projects means that the person can comfortably take charge and can focus his achievement effort into organizational achievement rather than personal aggrandizement. A person who is reluctant to express his aggression may have difficulty speaking up at the right time or representing himself adequately or analyzing problems and discussions with other people. Difficulty in taking people to task or confronting colleagues is also a product of reluctance to express aggression and usually reflects a good deal of underlying unconscious guilt.

A person who is unable to take people to task cannot take charge as a manager; and one who is unable to confront others cannot give colleagues or subordinates honest performance appraisals.

How do you handle affection? Some people prefer to be independent, while others enjoy working closely with people. Do you need constant approval and encouragement or does the quality of your work satisfy you? Can you praise others or do you find it difficult to express positive feelings?

While some people enjoy the affectionate interchange and camaraderie of working closely with others, some people prefer to be independent. The latter may either deny their need for other people's praise, approval, and affection or simply feel more comfortable keeping a distance.

Many managers have great difficulty telling others when they do good work. It is as if any expression of emotion is difficult for them. For some, this is a matter of conscience: they feel like hypocrites for praising work that isn't outstanding. For others, praise may seem to invite a closer relationship with the person being praised or may violate the picture of stoic self-control they want to present.

How do you handle dependency? Do you have trouble making decisions without your manager's OK? Do you work better when you're in charge or in a number 2 position? Do you work as well independently as on a team? Do you have difficulty asking for and using the help of others?

Although most of us fear becoming helplessly dependent on others, in organizations we are necessarily dependent on a lot of other people to get our work done. But some people can't tolerate this aspect of themselves. They need to do everything on their own. It is all right for other people to lean on them, and indeed sometimes they encourage it, but it is not all right for them to lean on other people. Such people disdain others' advice or guidance, even when seeking professional help is appropriate.

On the other hand, some people do well only when they can lean on somebody else's guidance or direction and panic when they don't have that. And while some people may work well by themselves, they may not accept other people's needs to depend on them. Such people will not be good bosses.

Listeners' or friends' special knowledge of a manager's working habits will enable them to be perceptive in questioning the manager in these areas. In addition, the manager should ask others—friends, co-workers, colleagues—to share with him their perceptions of his characteristic behavior. Sometimes they can tell the manager about working habits that he himself is not aware of. For instance, over a period of time friends might have noticed that Tom, from the opening vignette, enjoyed bearing full responsibility and risk for a project and making it work through his own expertise. This information could help Tom choose whether to join a company as in-house counsel or to become an independent consultant. A friend could point out that given his characteristic working style, Tom would probably enjoy the latter better.

In some cases, of course, friends may not be very perceptive or may have their own interests at heart and not be very helpful. At times like these, managers should definitely seek professional help.

Which Way to Go?

Armed with an understanding of his ego ideal and working style, the manager is now ready to weigh options more wisely. He may choose to launch a second career or he may decide to stick with his course in the organization. Whatever his decision, his friends' support and his deeper understanding of himself and his motivation will equip him to attack his chosen career with new dedication and enthusiasm.

Second careers are evolutionary. They stem from some interest that has lain dormant or has been abandoned in favor of another occupation. Asked if he had any idea of what he wanted to do when he left the chairmanship of Dain, Kalman & Quail, an investment banking firm in Minneapolis, for a new vocation, Wheelock Whitney answered, "Yes, really. I thought I'd like to pursue some other things that I cared about." Among these interests was the Johnson Institute, a center studying and treating the chemically dependent. Whitney had become deeply involved in the institute eight years earlier when his wife was undergoing treatment for alcoholism.[4]

Many turn to second careers that extend a previous occupational thrust; they may go into business for themselves in fields they already know. By searching the past for those budding interests that had no chance to flower, a manager can draw a long list of career options. At the same time, a manager can eliminate those that are no longer interesting or pleasurable. In choosing his second career, William Damroth said he switched from the chairmanship of Lexington Corporation because "to me the main thing was that I couldn't continue doing what I enjoy the most, which is the creative role, the intense bringing together of all factors, saying, 'It ought to look like this.' For instance, what I'm doing today is much more satisfying than the long-range planning you have to do for a company. Today's satisfaction is immediate."[5]

After eliminating undesirable options, a manager should investigate what additional training is required for each of the remaining possibilities and how much he can afford to invest. To pick up some careers, managers need to spend years in full-time professional or academic training; others they can approach through a course of reading, night school, or correspondence study. By seeing how the remaining options fit with how he prefers to behave and by understanding his ego ideal, a manager can usually narrow the field to one or two general directions. At this point, a manager considering a career change should again ask a friend or counselor to act as a sounding board, letting the manager talk through options and refine his ideas.

Finally, before a manager makes a choice, he should consider a number of other critical issues:

1. **Family.** Whom do you have responsibility for—a mother-in-law, an uncle, a grandfather, a handicapped sister or brother? Do these responsibil-

ities limit your options? Do your responsibilities to your spouse and children impose geographic or financial constraints?

2. **Present job.** If a manager comes to a premature judgment or acts impulsively, he risks leaving his present job thinking that the company left much to be desired. Will your peers and boss see the move as a rejection of the company and of your work together? Feeling abandoned, they might attack you. The possibility of anger and disappointment is especially high when you and your superior have worked closely together and when you respect and admire each other. Furthermore, some people, disappointed that they failed to act when the time was right, will be jealous. They may unload on you their anger with them-selves. Are you prepared for these conflicts?

It will help you to think about what it means to lose these peers and mentors. Rather than thinking that you are being disloyal, recognize that people who prepare themselves for a second career are doing the organization as well as themselves a favor by making space for younger, talented managers looking forward to promotion.

3. **Status.** One's status in the community is directly related to one's status at work. Choosing another career may well result in changing one's status. How important is that to you? How important is it that you associate with the same people you have associated with before, that you play golf at the same clubs or take part in the same social activities? Because your spouse and children will also be affected, the family must discuss this issue together. The sacrifices may well be severe.

4. **Rebuilding.** If you're thinking of starting a new business or launch-ing a new career, chances are that you will have to build a clientele. Rarely does a person move from one organization to another and take with him all of his accounts. For example, a lawyer told me that when he and his colleagues left a large firm to start their own, they expected their clients to follow them. Only a small fraction did, and the new firm had to build its clientele from scratch. Anyone starting his own business should expect it to take from two to five years to build a stable of customers.

5. **Freedom v. constraints.** For a mature manager in the BOOM pe-riod, the pressure to be autonomous, to do what he wants to do, to be free of commitments to somebody else, is very high. Therefore, in choosing an activity or direction, it is important to choose, insofar as you can, something that allows you maximum freedom to come and go, to do as you wish, while meeting the formal obligations of the role. As William Damroth comments: "My time is my own. I can lie on my back for two hours if I want. Instead of saying, 'This is what I want' and moving toward it, I've said 'This is what I don't like,' and I've eliminated it. I've cut away all the things that make life unhappy for me. I don't have any tension headaches in the mornings."[6]

But one doesn't always achieve freedom so easily. As we go through life we aspire to many things—promotions, new roles, different experiences. And we often ask ourselves, "Who am I to want to do that? What right do I have to seek that goal?" Self-critical feelings often prevent us from moving toward aspirations that we have every right to work toward and achieve.

The issue becomes particularly important with respect to a second career. Because a mature manager recognizes, if he hasn't before, that he has every right to pursue anything he wants to, now is the time to act. Anyone is eligible for any aspiration. One may not achieve it, but one has as much right as anybody else to want it and try for it.

6. **Year-long depression.** I have never seen a person make a significant career shift without experiencing a year-long depression. I don't mean that people are down in the dumps for a year but that they feel loss, ambivalence, and fear that things may not work out. Caught in an ambiguous situation in which they are not yet rooted, they feel detached from their stable routines.

The longer the manager has been with an organization, the more likely he has come to depend on it; the closer his relationships have been with his colleagues, the greater will be the sense of loss. The more his family has been tied to the organization, the more profound these feelings are likely to be.

7. **Talk.** All change is loss and all loss requires mourning.[7] Even when promoted, one loses the support of colleagues, friends, and known ways of doing things. To dissipate the inevitable sorrow, you have to turn it into words. To detach yourself from old ties and give up old habits, you have to talk about the experience. Feeling that they have to be heroic, some managers, men particularly, either deny that they are having such experiences or grit their teeth and try to plow through them. That way of acting doesn't deal with the depression; it only buries it and makes one vulnerable to physiological symptoms and overreactions when traumas occur.

It is important to have somebody to talk to and to be able to talk to that person freely. But even with the most careful and sensitive support from spouse and friends, you may get sidetracked, spin your wheels and get stuck in the mire. If after such talk you are no clearer about your choice, it may be time to consult a professional. The issues and feelings any careful self-appraisal touches on are often too complex to examine or discuss without professional help.

8. **Joint experiences.** Husbands' and wives' careers often separate them. When one member of the marriage makes a career change, new problems having to do with adult development emerge. Early in a marriage the spouses go in different directions, the husband usually to earn a livelihood and the wife usually to bear children. After her childrearing is done, the wife may return to work, but chances are nevertheless that the two spouses will still go in different occupational directions. Their only common interest tends to be the children or family problems.

Usually by the time a person has reached midcareer, the children are out on their own or close to it. The spouses now have to talk to each other. But if they have gone in different directions, they may have trouble communicating. A second career can help spouses reunite. One couple, for example, became interested in antiques. Together they went to antique shows and searched for old glass. When they gave up their old careers, they decided to run an antique store together. What was originally a shared hobby gave the couple financial security while they worked together.

Sometimes a new career threatens an old relationship. One manager was successful and widely respected in his organization. Although unequal to him in status or earning power, his wife also had professional training. When they decided to have children, she left her job to rear them. During those years, he was a supportive helpmate. When she was able, she went to law school and subsequently entered a prestigious law firm. Her status and income now exceed her husband's. He has taken a backseat to her and, with some feelings of embarrassment, carries on some of the household and family maintenance activities that she formerly handled. He speaks of his new situation with mingled pride and shame and is now considering a second career himself.

9. **Open options.** Even if you have exercised great care in choosing a second career, the change won't necessarily work out. Economic vagaries as well as factors that you couldn't foresee may cut your second career short. If you left your old job on a positive note, however, it may be possible to get it back. Many organizations recognize that a manager who has tested himself elsewhere and wants to return is likely to be an even better and more highly motivated employee.

REFERENCES

1. See my article, "On Being a Middle-Aged Manager," HBR July-August 1969, p. 57.
2. Erik H. Erikson, *Childhood and Society*, 2d ed. (New York: Norton, 1963).
3. Daniel Levinson, Charlotte N. Darrow, Edward B. Klein, Maria H. Levinson, and Braxton McKee, *The Seasons of a Man's Life* (New York: Alfred A. Knopf, 1978).
4. See "Don't Call It 'Early Retirement,'" HBR interview with Wheelock Whitney and William G. Damroth, HBR September-October 1975, p. 103.
5. Ibid., p. 113.
6. Ibid., p. 118.
7. See my article, "Easing the Pain of Personal Loss," HBR September-October 1972, p. 80.

3

Skills of an Effective Administrator

ROBERT L. KATZ

Although the selection and training of good administrators is widely recognized as one of American industry's most pressing problems, there is surprisingly little agreement among executives or educators on what makes a good administrator. The executive development programs of some of the nation's leading corporations and colleges reflect a tremendous variation in objectives.

At the root of this difference is industry's search for the traits or attributes which will objectively identify the "ideal executive" who is equipped to cope effectively with any problem in any organization. As one observer of U.S. industry recently noted:

"The assumption that there is an executive type is widely accepted, either openly or implicitly. Yet any executive presumably knows that a company needs all kinds of managers for different levels of jobs. The qualities most needed by a shop superintendent are likely to be quite opposed to those needed by a coordinating vice president of manufacturing. The literature of executive development is loaded with efforts to define the qualities needed by executives, and by themselves these sound quite rational. Few, for instance, would dispute the fact that a top manager needs good judgment, the ability to make decisions, the ability to win respect of others, and all the other well-worn phrases any management man could mention. But one has only to look at the successful managers in any company to see how enormously their particular qualities vary from any ideal list of executive virtues."[1]

Yet this quest for the executive stereotype has become so intense that many companies, in concentrating on certain specific traits or qualities, stand in danger of losing sight of their real concern: *what a man can accomplish.*

It is the purpose of this article to suggest what may be a more useful approach to the selection and development of administrators. This approach is based not on what good executives *are* (their innate traits and characteristics), but rather on what they *do* (the kinds of skills which they exhibit in carrying out their jobs effectively). As used here, a *skill* implies an ability which can be developed, not necessarily inborn, and which is manifested in performance, not merely in potential. So the principal criterion of skillfulness must be effective action under varying conditions.

This approach suggests that effective administration rests on *three basic developable skills* which obviate the need for identifying specific traits and which may provide a useful way of looking at and understanding the administrative process. This approach is the outgrowth of firsthand observation of executives at work coupled with study of current field research in administration.

In the sections which follow, an attempt will be made to define and demonstrate what these three skills are; to suggest that the relative importance of the three skills varies with the level of administrative responsibility; to present some of the implications of this variation for selection, training, and promotion of executives; and to propose ways of developing these skills.

Three-Skill Approach

It is assumed here that an administrator is one who (a) directs the activities of other persons and (b) undertakes the responsibility for achieving certain objectives through these efforts. Within this definition, successful administration appears to rest on three basic skills, which we will call *technical, human,* and *conceptual.* It would be unrealistic to assert that these skills are not interrelated, yet there may be real merit in examining each one separately, and in developing them independently.

Technical Skill

As used here, technical skill implies an understanding of, and proficiency in, a specific kind of activity, particularly one involving methods, processes, procedures, or techniques. It is relatively easy for us to visualize the technical skill of the surgeon, the musician, the accountant, or the engineer when each is performing his own special function. Technical skill involves specialized knowledge, analytical ability within that specialty, and facility in the use of the tools and techniques of the specific discipline.

Of the three skills described in this article, technical skill is perhaps the most familiar because it is the most concrete, and because, in our age of specialization, it is the skill required of the greatest number of people. Most of our vocational and on-the-job training programs are largely concerned with developing this specialized technical skill.

Human Skill

As used here, human skill is the executive's ability to work effectively as a group member and to build cooperative effort within the team he leads. As *technical* skill is primarily concerned with working with "things" (processes or physical objects), so *human* skill is primarily concerned with working with people. This skill is demonstrated in the way the individual perceives (and recognizes the perceptions of) his superiors, equals, and subordinates, and in the way he behaves subsequently.

The person with highly developed human skill is aware of his own attitudes, assumptions, and beliefs about other individuals and groups; he is able to see the usefulness and limitations of these feelings. By accepting the existence of viewpoints, perceptions, and beliefs which are different from his own, he is skilled in understanding what others really mean by their words and behavior. He is equally skillful in communicating to others, in their own contexts, what he means by *his* behavior.

Such a person works to create an atmosphere of approval and security in which subordinates feel free to express themselves without fear of censure or ridicule, by encouraging them to participate in the planning and carrying out of those things which directly affect them. He is sufficiently sensitive to the needs and motivations of others in his organization so that he can judge the possible reactions to, and outcomes of, various courses of action he may undertake. Having this sensitivity, he is able and willing to *act* in a way which takes these perceptions by others into account.

Real skill in working with others must become a natural, continuous activity, since it involves sensitivity not only at times of decision making but also in the day-by-day behavior of the individual. Human skill cannot be a "sometime thing." Techniques cannot be randomly applied, nor can personality traits be put on or removed like an overcoat. Because everything which an executive says and does (or leaves unsaid or undone) has an effect on his associates, his true self will, in time, show through. Thus, to be effective, this skill must be naturally developed and unconsciously, as well as consistently, demonstrated in the individual's every action. It must become an integral part of his whole being.

Because human skill is so vital a part of everything the administrator does, examples of inadequate human skill are easier to describe than are highly skillful performances. Perhaps consideration of an actual situation would serve to clarify what is involved:

When a new conveyor unit was installed in a shoe factory where workers had previously been free to determine their own work rate, the production manager asked the industrial engineer who had designed the conveyor to serve as foreman, even though a qualified foreman was available. The engineer, who reported directly to the production manager, objected, but under pressure he agreed to take the job "until a suitable foreman could be found," even though this was a job of lower status than his present one. Then this conversation took place:

Production Manager: "I've had a lot of experience with conveyors. I want you to keep this conveyor going at all times except for rest periods, and I want it going at top speed. Get these people thinking in terms of 2 pairs of shoes a minute, 70 dozen pairs a day, 350 dozen pairs a week. They are all experienced operators on their individual jobs, and it's just a matter of getting them to do their jobs in a little different way. I want you to make that base rate of 250 dozen pair a week work!" [Base rate was established at slightly under 75% of the maximum capacity. This base rate was 50% higher than under the old system.]

Engineer: "If I'm going to be foreman of the conveyor unit, I want to do things my way. I've worked on conveyors, and I don't agree with you on first getting people used to a conveyor going at top speed. These people have never seen a conveyor. You'll scare them. I'd like to run the conveyor at one-third speed for a couple of weeks and then gradually increase the speed.

"I think we should discuss setting the base rate [production quota before incentive bonus] on a daily basis instead of a weekly basis. [Workers had previously been paid on a daily straight piecework basis.]

"I'd also suggest setting a daily base rate at 45 or even 40 dozen pair. You have to set a base rate low enough for them to make. Once they know they can make the base rate, they will go after the bonus."

Production Manager: "You do it your way on the speed; but remember it's the results that count. On the base rate, I'm not discussing it with you; I'm telling you to make the 250 dozen pair a week work. I don't want a daily base rate."[2]

Here is a situation in which the production manager was so preoccupied with getting the physical output that he did not pay attention to the people through whom that output had to be achieved. Notice, first, that he made the engineer who designed the unit serve as foreman, apparently hoping to force the engineer to justify his design by producing the maximum output. However, the production manager was oblivious to (a) the way the engineer perceived this appointment, as a demotion, and (b) the need for the engineer to be able to control the variables if he was to be held responsible for maximum output. Instead the production manager imposed a production standard and refused to make any changes in the work situation.

Moreover, although this was a radically new situation for the operators, the production manager expected them to produce immediately at well above their previous output—even though the operators had an unfamiliar production system to cope with, the operators had never worked together as a team before, the operators and their new foreman had never worked together before, and the foreman was not in agreement with the production goals or standards. By ignoring all these human factors, the production manager not only placed the engineer in an extremely difficult operating situation but also, by refusing to allow the engineer to "run his own show," discouraged the very assumption of responsibility he had hoped for in making the appointment.

Under these circumstances, it is easy to understand how the relationship between these two men rapidly deteriorated, and how production, after two months' operation, was at only 125 dozen pairs per week (just 75% of what the output had been under the old system).

Conceptual Skill

As used here, conceptual skill involves the ability to see the enterprise as a whole; it includes recognizing how the various functions of the organization depend on one another, and how changes in any one part affect all the others; and it extends to visualizing the relationship of the individual business to the industry, the community, and the political, social, and economic forces of the nation as a whole. Recognizing these relationships and perceiving the significant elements in any situation, the administrator should then be able to act in a way which advances the over-all welfare of the total organization.

Hence, the success of any decision depends on the conceptual skill of the people who make the decision and those who put it into action. When, for example, an important change in marketing policy is made, it is critical that the effects on production, control, finance, research, and the people involved be considered. And it remains critical right down to the last executive who must implement the new policy. If each executive recognizes the over-all relationships and significance of the change, he is almost certain to be more effective in administering it. Consequently the chances for succeeding are greatly increased.

Not only does the effective coordination of the various parts of the business depend on the conceptual skill of the administrators involved, but so also does the whole future direction and tone of the organization. The attitudes of a top executive color the whole character of the organization's response and determine the "corporate personality" which distinguishes one company's ways of doing business from another's. These attitudes are a reflection of the administrator's conceptual skill (referred to by some as his "creative ability"—the way he perceives and responds to the direction in which the business should grow, company objectives and policies, and stockholders' and employees' interests.

Conceptual skill, as defined above, is what Chester I. Barnard, former president of the New Jersey Bell Telephone Company, is implying when he says: ". . . the essential aspect of the [executive] process is the sensing of the organization as a whole and of the total situation relevant to it."[3] Examples of inadequate conceptual skill are all around us. Here is one instance:

In a large manufacturing company which had a long tradition of job-shop type operations, primary responsibility for production control had been left to the foremen and other lower-level supervisors. "Village" type operations with small working groups and informal organizations were the rule. A heavy influx of orders following World War II tripled the normal production requirements and severely taxed the whole manufacturing organization. At this point, a new production manager was brought in from outside the company, and he established a wide range of controls and formalized the entire operating structure.

As long as the boom demand lasted, the employees made every effort to conform with the new procedures and environment. But when demand subsided to prewar levels, serious labor relations problems developed, friction was high among department heads, and the company found itself saddled with a heavy indirect labor cost. Management sought to reinstate its old procedures; it fired the production manager and attempted to give greater authority to the foremen once again. However, during the four years of formalized control, the foremen had grown away from their old practices, many had left the company, and adequate replacements had not been developed. Without strong foreman leadership, the traditional job-shop operations proved costly and inefficient.

In this instance, when the new production controls and formalized organizations were introduced, management did not foresee the consequences of this action in the event of a future contraction of business. Later, when conditions changed and it was necessary to pare down operations, management was again unable to recognize the implications of its action and reverted to the old procedures, which, under the circumstances, were no longer appropriate. This compounded *conceptual* inadequacy left the company at a serious competitive disadvantage.

Because a company's over-all success is dependent on its executives' conceptual skill in establishing and carrying out policy decisions, this skill is the unifying, coordinating ingredient of the administrative process, and of undeniable over-all importance.

Relative Importance

We may notice that, in a very real sense, conceptual skill embodies consideration of both the technical and human aspects of the organization. Yet the concept of *skill*, as an ability to translate knowledge into action, should enable one to distinguish between the three skills of performing the technical activities (technical skill), understanding and motivating individuals and groups (human skill), and coordinating and integrating all the activities and interests of the organization toward a common objective (conceptual skill).

This separation of effective administration into three basic skills is useful primarily for purposes of analysis. In practice, these skills are so closely interrelated that it is difficult to determine where one ends and another begins. However, just because the skills are interrelated does not imply that we cannot get some value from looking at them separately, or by varying their emphasis. In playing golf the action of the hands, wrists, hips, shoulders, arms, and head are all interrelated; yet in improving one's swing it is often valuable to work on one of these elements separately. Also, under different playing conditions the relative importance of these elements varies. Similarly, although all three are of importance at every level of administration, the technical, human, and conceptual skills of the administrator vary in relative importance at different levels of responsibility.

At Lower Levels

Technical skill is responsible for many of the great advances of modern industry. It is indispensable to efficient operation. Yet it has greatest importance at the lower levels of administration. As the administrator moves further and further from the actual physical operation, this need for technical skill becomes less important, provided he has skilled subordinates and can help them solve their own problems. At the top, technical skill may be almost nonexistent, and the executive may still be able to perform effectively if his human and conceptual skills are highly developed. For example:

In one large capital-goods producing company, the controller was called on to replace the manufacturing vice president, who had been stricken suddenly with a severe illness. The controller had no previous production experience, but he had been with the company for more than 20 years and knew many of the key production personnel intimately. By setting up an advisory staff, and by delegating an unusual amount of authority to his department heads, he was able to devote himself to coordination of the various functions. By so doing, he produced a highly efficient team. The results were lower costs, greater productivity, and higher morale than the production division had ever before experienced. Management had gambled that this man's ability to work with people was more important than his lack of a technical production background, and the gamble paid off.

Other examples are evident all around us. We are all familiar with those "professional managers" who are becoming the prototypes of our modern executive world. These men shift with great ease, and with no apparent loss in effectiveness, from one industry to another. Their human and conceptual skills seem to make up for their unfamiliarity with the new job's technical aspects.

At Every Level

Human skill, the ability to work with others, is essential to effective administration at every level. One recent research study has shown that human skill is of paramount importance at the foreman level, pointing out that the chief function of the foreman as an administrator is to attain collaboration of people in the work group.[4] Another study reinforces this finding and extends it to the middle-management group, adding that the administrator should be primarily concerned with facilitating communication in the organization.[5] And still another study, concerned primarily with top management, underscores the need for self-awareness and sensitivity to human relationships by executives at that level.[6] These findings would tend to indicate that human skill is of great importance at every level, but notice the difference in emphasis.

Human skill seems to be most important at lower levels, where the number of direct contacts between administrators and subordinates is greatest. As we go higher and higher in the administrative echelons, the number and frequency of these personal contacts decrease, and the need for human skill becomes proportionately, although probably not absolutely, less. At the same time, conceptual skill becomes increasingly more important with the need for policy decisions and broad-scale action. The human skill of dealing with individuals then becomes subordinate to the conceptual skill of integrating group interests and activities into a whole.

In fact, a recent research study by Professor Chris Argyris of Yale University has given us the example of an extremely effective plant manager who, although possessing little human skill as defined here, was nonetheless very successful:

This manager, the head of a largely autonomous division, made his supervisors, through the effects of his strong personality and the "pressure" he applied, highly dependent on him for most of their "rewards, penalties, authority, perpetuation, communication, and identification."

As a result, the supervisors spent much of their time competing with one another for the manager's favor. They told him only the things they thought he wanted to hear, and spent much time trying to find out his desires. They depended on him to set their objectives and to show them how to reach them. Because the manager was inconsistent and unpredictable in his behavior, the supervisors were insecure and continually engaged in interdepartmental squabbles which they tried to keep hidden from the manager.

Clearly, human skill as defined here was lacking. Yet, by the evaluation of his superiors and by his results in increasing efficiency and raising profits and morale, this manager was exceedingly effective. Professor Argyris suggests that employees in modern industrial organizations tend to have a "built-in" sense of dependence on superiors which capable and alert men can turn to advantage.[7]

In the context of the three-skill approach, it seems that this manager was able to capitalize on this dependence because he recognized the interrelationships of all the activities under his control, identified himself with the organization, and sublimated the individual interests of his subordinates to *his* (the organization's) interest, set his goals realistically, and showed his subordinates how to reach these goals. This would seem to be an excellent example of a situation in which strong conceptual skill more than compensated for a lack of human skill.

At the Top Level

Conceptual skill, as indicated in the preceding sections, becomes increasingly critical in more responsible executive positions where its effects are maximized and most easily observed. In fact, recent research findings lead to the conclusion that at the top level of administration this conceptual skill becomes the most important ability of all. As Herman W. Steinkraus, president of Bridgeport Brass Company, said:

"One of the most important lessons which I learned on this job [the presidency] is the importance of coordinating the various departments into an effective team, and, secondly, to recognize the shifting emphasis from time to time of the relative importance of various departments to the business."[8]

It would appear, then, that at lower levels of administrative responsibility, the principal need is for technical and human skills. At higher levels, technical skill becomes relatively less important while the need for conceptual skill increases rapidly. At the top level of an organization, conceptual skill becomes the most important skill of all for successful administration. A chief executive may lack technical or human skills and still be effective if he has subordinates who have strong abilities in these directions. But if his conceptual skill is weak, the success of the whole organization may be jeopardized.

Implications for Action

This three-skill approach implies that significant benefits may result from redefining the objectives of executive development programs, from re-considering the placement of executives in organizations, and from revising procedures for testing and selecting prospective executives.

Executive Development

Many executive development programs may be failing to achieve sat-isfactory results because of their inability to foster the growth of these admin-istrative skills. Programs which concentrate on the mere imparting of information or the cultivation of a specific trait would seem to be largely unproductive in enhancing the administrative skills of candidates.

A strictly informative program was described to me recently by an officer and director of a large corporation who had been responsible for the executive-development activities of his company, as follows:

"What we try to do is to get our promising young men together with some of our senior executives in regular meetings each month. Then we give the young fellows a chance to ask questions to let them find out about the company's history and how and why we've done things in the past."

It was not surprising that neither the senior executives nor the young men felt this program was improving their administrative abilities.

The futility of pursuing specific traits becomes apparent when we consider the responses of an administrator in a number of different situations. In coping with these varied conditions, he may appear to demonstrate one trait in one instance—e.g., dominance when dealing with subordinates—and the directly opposite trait under another set of circumstances—e.g., submissiveness when dealing with superiors. Yet in each instance he may be acting appropriately to achieve the best results. Which, then, can we identify as a desirable characteristic? Here is a further example of this dilemma:

A Pacific Coast sales manager had a reputation for decisiveness and positive action. Yet when he was required to name an assistant to understudy his job from among several well-qualified subordinates, he deliberately avoided making a decision. His associates were quick to observe what appeared to be obvious indecisiveness.

But after several months had passed, it became clear that the sales manager had very unobtrusively been giving the various salesmen opportunities to dem-onstrate their attitudes and feelings. As a result, he was able to identify strong sentiments for one man whose subsequent promotion was enthusiastically ac-cepted by the entire group.

In this instance, the sales manager's skillful performance was improperly in-terpreted as "indecisiveness." Their concern with irrelevant traits led his asso-ciates to overlook the adequacy of his performance. Would it not have been more appropriate to conclude that his human skill in working with others enabled him to adapt effectively to the requirements of a new situation?

Cases such as these would indicate that it is more useful to judge an administrator on the results of his performance than on his apparent traits. Skills are easier to identify than are traits and are less likely to be misinterpreted. Furthermore, skills offer a more directly applicable frame of reference for executive development, since any improvement in an administrator's skills must necessarily result in more effective performance.

Still another danger in many existing executive development programs lies in the unqualified enthusiasm with which some companies and colleges have embraced courses in "human relations." There would seem to be two inherent pitfalls here: (1) Human relations courses might only be imparting information or specific techniques, rather than developing the individual's human skill. (2) Even if individual development does take place, some companies, by placing all of their emphasis on human skill, may be completely overlooking the training requirements for top positions. They may run the risk of producing men with highly developed human skill who lack the conceptual ability to be effective top-level administrators.

It would appear important, then, that the training of a candidate for an administrative position be directed at the development of those skills which are most needed at the level of responsibility for which he is being considered.

Executive Placement

This three-skill concept suggests immediate possibilities for the creating of management teams of individuals with complementary skills. For example, one medium-size midwestern distributing organization has as president a man of unusual conceptual ability but extremely limited human skill. However, he has two vice presidents with exceptional human skill. These three men make up an executive committee which has been outstandingly successful, the skills of each member making up for deficiencies of the others. Perhaps the plan of two-man complementary conference leadership proposed by Robert F. Bales, in which the one leader maintains "task leadership" while the other provides "social leadership," might also be an example in point.[9]

Executive Selection

In trying to predetermine a prospective candidate's abilities on a job, much use is being made these days of various kinds of testing devices. Executives are being tested for everything from "decisiveness" to "conformity." These tests, as a recent article in *Fortune* points out, have achieved some highly questionable results when applied to performance on the job.[10] Would it not be much more productive to be concerned with skills of doing rather than with a number of traits which do not guarantee performance?

This three-skill approach makes trait testing unnecessary and substitutes for it procedures which examine a man's ability to cope with the actual problems and situations he will find on his job. These procedures, which indicate what a man can *do* in specific situations, are the same for selection and for measuring development. They will be described in the section on developing executive skills which follows.

This approach suggests that executives should *not* be chosen on the basis of their apparent possession of a number of behavior characteristics or traits, but on the basis of their possession of the requisite skills for the specific level of responsibility involved.

Developing the Skills

For years many people have contended that leadership ability is inherent in certain chosen individuals. We talk of "born leaders," "born executives," "born salesmen." It is undoubtedly true that certain people, naturally or innately, possess greater aptitude or ability in certain skills. But research in psychology and physiology would also indicate, first, that those having strong aptitudes and abilities can improve their skill through practice and training, and, secondly, that even those lacking the natural ability can improve their performance and over-all effectiveness.

The *skill* conception of administration suggests that we may hope to improve our administrative effectiveness and to develop better administrators for the future. This skill conception implies *learning by doing*. Different people learn in different ways, but skills are developed through practice and through relating learning to one's own personal experience and background. If well done, training in these basic administrative skills should develop executive abilities more surely and more rapidly than through unorganized experience. What, then, are some of the ways in which this training can be conducted?

Technical Skill

Development of technical skill has received great attention for many years by industry and educational institutions alike, and much progress has been made. Sound grounding in the principles, structures, and processes of the individual specialty, coupled with actual practice and experience during which the individual is watched and helped by a superior, appear to be most effective. In view of the vast amount of work which has been done in training people in the technical skills, it would seem unnecessary in this article to suggest more.

Human Skill

Human skill, however, has been much less understood, and only recently has systematic progress been made in developing it. Many different approaches to the development of human skill are being pursued by various universities and professional men today. These are rooted in such disciplines as psychology, sociology, and anthropology.

Some of these approaches find their application in "applied psychology," "human engineering," and a host of other manifestations requiring technical specialists to help the businessman with his human problems. As a practical matter, however, the executive must develop his own human skill, rather than lean on the advice of others. To be effective, he must develop his own personal point of view toward human activity, so that he will (a) recognize the feelings and sentiments which he brings to a situation; (b) have an attitude about his own experiences which will enable him to re-evaluate and learn from them; (c) develop ability in understanding what others by their actions and words (explicit or implicit) are trying to communicate to him; and (d) develop ability in successfully communicating his ideas and attitudes to others.[11]

This human skill can be developed by some individuals without formalized training. Others can be individually aided by their immediate superiors as an integral part of the "coaching" process to be described later. This aid depends for effectiveness, obviously, on the extent to which the superior possesses the human skill.

For larger groups, the use of case problems coupled with impromptu role playing can be very effective. This training can be established on a formal or informal basis, but it requires a skilled instructor and organized sequence of activities.[12] It affords as good an approximation to reality as can be provided on a continuing classroom basis and offers an opportunity for critical reflection not often found in actual practice. An important part of the procedure is the self-examination of the trainee's own concepts and values, which may enable him to develop more useful attitudes about himself and about others. With the change in attitude, hopefully, there may also come some active skill in dealing with human problems.

Human skill has also been tested in the classroom, within reasonable limits, by a series of analyses of detailed accounts of actual situations involving administrative action, together with a number of role-playing opportunities in which the individual is required to carry out the details of the action he has proposed. In this way an individual's understanding of the total situation and his own personal ability to do something about it can be evaluated.

On the job, there should be frequent opportunities for a superior to observe an individual's ability to work effectively with others. These may appear to be highly subjective evaluations and to depend for validity on the human skill of the rater. But does not every promotion, in the last analysis, depend on someone's subjective judgment? And should this subjectivity be berated, or should we make a greater effort to develop people within our organizations with the human skill to make such judgments effectively?

Conceptual Skill

Conceptual skill, like human skill, has not been very widely understood. A number of methods have been tried to aid in developing this ability, with varying success. Some of the best results have always been achieved through the "coaching" of subordinates by superiors.[13] This is no new idea. It implies that one of the key responsibilities of the executive is to help his subordinates to develop their administrative potentials. One way a superior can help "coach" his subordinate is by assigning a particular responsibility, and then responding with searching questions or opinions, rather than giving answers, whenever the subordinate seeks help. When Benjamin F. Fairless, now chairman of the board of the United States Steel Corporation, was president of the corporation, he described his coaching activities:

"When one of my vice presidents or the head of one of our operating companies comes to me for instructions, I generally counter by asking him questions. First thing I know, he has told me how to solve the problem himself."[14]

Obviously, this is an ideal and wholly natural procedure for administrative training, and applies to the development of technical and human skill, as well as to that of conceptual skill. However, its success must necessarily rest on the abilities and willingness of the superior to help the subordinate.

Another excellent way to develop conceptual skill is through trading jobs, that is, by moving promising young men through different functions of the business but at the same level of responsibility. This gives the man the chance literally to "be in the other fellow's shoes."

Other possibilities include: special assignments, particularly the kind which involve inter-departmental problems; and management boards, such as the

McCormick Multiple Management plan, in which junior executives serve as advisers to top management on policy matters.

For larger groups, the kind of case-problems course described above, only using cases involving broad management policy and interdepartmental coordination, may be useful. Courses of this kind, often called "General Management" or "Business Policy," are becoming increasingly prevalent.

In the classroom, conceptual skill has also been evaluated with reasonable effectiveness by presenting a series of detailed descriptions of specific complex situations. In these the individual being tested is asked to set forth a course of action which responds to the underlying forces operating in each situation and which considers the implications of this action on the various functions and parts of the organization and its total environment.

On the job, the alert supervisor should find frequent opportunities to observe the extent to which the individual is able to relate himself and his job to the other functions and operations of the company.

Like human skill, conceptual skill, too, must become a natural part of the executive's makeup. Different methods may be indicated for developing different people, by virtue of their backgrounds, attitudes, and experience. But in every case that method should be chosen which will enable the executive to develop his own personal skill in visualizing the enterprise as a whole and in coordinating and integrating its various parts.

Conclusion

The purpose of this article has been to show that effective administration depends on three basic personal skills, which have been called *technical*, *human*, and *conceptual*. The administrator needs: (a) sufficient technical skill to accomplish the mechanics of the particular job for which he is responsible; (b) sufficient human skill in working with others to be an effective group member and to be able to build cooperative effort within the team he leads; (c) sufficient conceptual skill to recognize the interrelationships of the various factors involved in his situation, which will lead him to take that action which is likely to achieve the maximum good for the total organization.

The relative importance of these three skills seems to vary with the level of administrative responsibility. At lower levels, the major need is for technical and human skills. At higher levels, the administrator's effectiveness depends largely on human and conceptual skills. At the top, conceptual skill becomes the most important of all for successful administration.

This three-skill approach emphasizes that good administrators are not necessarily born; they may be developed. It transcends the need to identify specific traits in an effort to provide a more useful way of looking at the administrative process. By helping to identify the skills most needed at various levels of responsibility, it may prove useful in the selection, training, and promotion of executives.

Retrospective Commentary

When this article was first published nearly 20 years ago, there was a great deal of interest in trying to identify a set of ideal personality traits that would readily distinguish potential executive talent. The search for these traits was vigorously pursued in the hope that the selection and training of managers could be conducted with greater reliability.

This article was an attempt to focus attention on demonstrable skills of performance rather than on innate personality characteristics. And, while describing the three kinds of administrative skill (technical, human, and conceptual), it also attempted to highlight the importance of conceptual skill as a uniquely valuable managerial capability, long before the concept of corporate strategy was well defined or popularly understood.

It still appears useful to think of managerial ability in terms of these three basic, observable skills. It also still appears that the relative importance of these skills varies with the administrative level of the manager in the organization. However, my experience over the past 20 years, in working with senior executives in a wide variety of industries, suggests that several specific points require either sharp modification or substantial further refinement.

Human Skill

I now believe that this kind of skill could be usefully subdivided into (a) leadership ability within the manager's own unit and (b) skill in intergroup relationships. In my experience, outstanding capability in one of these roles is frequently accompanied by mediocre performance in the other.

Often, the most internally efficient department managers are those who have committed themselves fully to the unique values and criteria of their specialized functions, without acknowledging that other departments' differing values have any validity at all. For example, a production manager may be most efficient if he puts all his emphasis on obtaining a high degree of reliability in his production schedule. He would then resist any external pressures that place a higher priority on criteria other than delivering the required output on time. Or a sales manager may be most efficient if he puts all his emphasis on maintaining positive relationships with customers. He would then resist all pressures that would emphasize other values, such as ease of production or selling the highest gross margin items. In each case, the manager will probably receive strong support from his subordinates, who share the same values. But he will encounter severe antagonism from other departments with conflicting values.

To the extent that two departments' values conflict with each other, skillful intergroup relationships require some equivocation. But compromise is often perceived by departmental subordinates as a "sellout." Thus the manager is obliged to choose between gaining full support from subordinates or enjoying full collaboration with peers and/or superiors. Having both is rarely possible. Consequently, I would revise my original evaluation of human skill to say now that internal *intragroup* skills are essential in lower and middle management roles and that *intergroup* skills become increasingly important in successively higher levels of management.

Conceptual Skill

In retrospect, I now see that what I called conceptual skill depends entirely on a specific way of thinking about an enterprise. This "general management point of view," as it has come to be known, involves always thinking in terms of the following: relative emphases and priorities among conflicting objectives and criteria; relative tendencies and probabilities (rather than certainties); rough correlations and patterns among elements (rather than clear-cut cause-and-effect relationships).

I am now far less sanguine about the degree to which this way of thinking can be developed on the job. Unless a person has learned to think this way early in life, it is unrealistic to expect a major change on reaching executive status. Job rotation, special interdepartmental assignments, and working with case problems certainly provide opportunities for a person to enhance previously developed conceptual abilities. But I question how easily this way of thinking can be inculcated after a person passes adolescence. In this sense, then, conceptual skill should perhaps be viewed as an *innate* ability.

Technical Skill

In the original article, I suggested that specific technical skills are unimportant at top management levels. I cited as evidence the many professional managers who move easily from one industry to another without apparent loss of effectiveness.

I now believe this mobility is possible only in very large companies, where the chief executive has extensive staff assistance and highly competent, experienced technical operators throughout the organization. An old, established, large company has great operational momentum that enables the new chief executive to concentrate on strategic issues.

In smaller companies, where technical expertise is not as pervasive and seasoned staff assistance is not as available, I believe the chief executive has a much greater need for personal experience in the industry. He not only needs to know the right questions to ask his subordinates; he also needs enough industry background to know how to evaluate the answers.

Role of the Chief Executive

In the original article, I took too simplistic and naïve a view of the chief executive's role. My extensive work with company presidents and my own personal experience as a chief executive have given me much more respect for the difficulties and complexities of that role. I now know that every important executive action must strike a balance among so many conflicting values, objectives, and criteria that it will *always* be suboptimal from any single viewpoint. *Every* decision or choice affecting the whole enterprise has negative consequences for some of the parts.

The chief executive must try to perceive the conflicts and trace accurately their likely impact throughout the organization. Reluctantly, but wittingly, he may have to sacrifice the interests of a single unit or part for the good of the whole. He needs to be willing to accept solutions that are adequate and feasible in the total situation rather than what, from a single point of view, may be elegant or optimum.

Not only must the chief executive be an efficient operator, but he must also be an effective strategist. It is his responsibility to provide the framework and direction for overall company operations. He must continually specify where the company will place its emphasis in terms of products, services, and customers. He must define performance criteria and determine what special competences the company will emphasize. He also needs to set priorities and timetables. He must establish the standards and controls necessary to monitor progress and to place limits on individual actions. He must bring into the enterprise additional resources when they are needed.

Moreover, he must change his management style and strike different balances among his personal skills as conditions change or as his organization grows in size and complexity. The *remedial* role (saving the organization when it is in great difficulty) calls for drastic human action and emphasizes conceptual and technical skills. The *maintaining* role (sustaining the organization in its present posture) emphasizes human skills and requires only modest technical or strategic changes. But the *innovative* role (developing and expanding the organization) demands high competence in both conceptual and intergroup skills, with the technical contribution provided primarily by subordinates.

In my view, it is impossible for anyone to perform well in these continually changing roles without help. Yet because effective management of the total enterprise involves constant suboptimizing, it is impossible for the chief executive to get unanimous or continuous support from his subordinates. If he is overly friendly or supportive, he may compromise his effectiveness or his objectivity. Yet somewhere in the organization, he needs to have a well-informed, objective, understanding, and supportive sounding board with whom he can freely discuss his doubts, fears, and aspirations. Sometimes this function can be supplied by an outside director, the outside corporate counsel, or the company auditor. But such a confidant requires just as high a degree of conceptual and human skills as the chief executive himself; and to be truly helpful, he must know all about the company's operations, key personnel, and industry. This role has been largely overlooked in discussions of organizational requirements, but in my view, its proper fulfillment is essential to the success of the chief executive and the enterprise.

Conclusion

I now realize more fully that managers at all levels require some competence in each of the three skills. Even managers at the lowest levels must continually use all of them. Dealing with the external demands on a manager's unit requires conceptual skill; the limited physical and financial resources available to him tax his technical skill; and the capabilities and demands of the persons with whom he deals make it essential that he possess human skill. A clear idea of these skills and of ways to measure a manager's competence in each category still appears to me to be a most effective tool for top management, not only in understanding executive behavior, but also in the selection, training, and promotion of managers at all levels.

REFERENCES

1. Perrin Stryker, "The Growing Pains of Executive Development," *Advanced Management*, August 1954, p. 15.

2. From a mimeographed case in the files of the Harvard Business School, copyrighted by the President and Fellows of Harvard College.

3. *Functions of the Executive* (Cambridge: Harvard University Press, 1948), p. 235.

4. A. Zaleznik, *Foreman Training in a Growing Enterprise* (Boston: Division of Research, Harvard Business School, 1951).

5. Harriet O. Ronken and Paul R. Lawrence, *Administering Changes* (Boston: Division of Research, Harvard Business School, 1952).

6. Edmund P. Learned, David H. Ulrich, and Donald R. Booz, *Executive Action* (Boston: Division of Research, Harvard Business School, 1950).

7. *Executive Leadership* (New York: Harper & Brothers, 1953), see also "Leadership Pattern in the Plant," HBR January–February 1954, p. 63.

8. "What Should a President Do?" *Dun's Review*, August 1951, p. 21.

9. "In Conference," HBR March–April 1954, p. 44.

10. William H. Whyte, Jr., "The Fallacies of 'Personality' Testing," *Fortune*, September 1954, p. 117.

11. For a further discussion of this point, see F.J. Roethlisberger, "Training Supervisors in Human Relations," HBR September 1951, p. 47.

12. See, for example, A. Winn, "Training in Administration and Human Relations," *Personnel*, September 1953, p. 139; see also, Kenneth R. Andrews, "Executive Training by the Case Method," HBR September–October 1951, p. 58.

13. For a more complete development of the concept of "coaching," see Myles L. Mace, *The Growth and Development of Executives* (Boston: Division of Research, Harvard Business School, 1950).

14. "What Should a President Do?" *Dun's Review*, July 1951, p. 14.

4

The Manager's Job: Folklore and Fact

HENRY MINTZBERG

If you ask a manager what he does, he will most likely tell you that he plans, organizes, coordinates, and controls. Then watch what he does. Don't be surprised if you can't relate what you see to these four words.

When he is called and told that one of his factories has just burned down, and he advises the caller to see whether temporary arrangements can be made to supply customers through a foreign subsidiary, is he planning, organizing, co-ordinating, or controlling? How about when he presents a gold watch to a retiring employee? Or when he attends a conference to meet people in the trade? Or on returning from that conference, when he tells one of his employees about an interesting product idea he picked up there?

The fact is that these four words, which have dominated management vocabulary since the French industrialist Henri Fayol first introduced them in 1916, tell us little about what managers actually do. At best, they indicate some vague objectives managers have when they work.

The field of management, so devoted to progress and change, has for more than half a century not seriously addressed *the* basic question: What do managers do? Without a proper answer, how can we teach management? How can we design planning or information systems for managers? How can we improve the practice of management at all?

Our ignorance of the nature of managerial work shows up in various ways in the modern organization—in the boast by the successful manager that he never spent a single day in a management training program; in the turnover of cor-porate planners who never quite understood what it was the manager wanted; in the computer consoles gathering dust in the back room because the managers never used the fancy on-line MIS some analyst thought they needed. Perhaps most important, our ignorance shows up in the inability of our large public organizations to come to grips with some of their most serious policy problems.

Somehow, in the rush to automate production, to use management science in the functional areas of marketing and finance, and to apply the skills of the behavioral scientist to the problem of worker motivation, the manager—that person in charge of the organization or one of its subunits—has been forgotten.

My intention in this article is simple: to break the reader away from Fayol's words and introduce him to a more supportable, and what I believe to be a more useful, description of managerial work. This description derives from my review and synthesis of the available research on how various managers have spent their time.

In some studies, managers were observed intensively ("shadowed" is the term some of them used); in a number of others, they kept detailed diaries of their activities; in a few studies, their records were analyzed. All kinds of managers were studied—foremen, factory supervisors, staff managers, field sales managers, hospital administrators, presidents of companies and nations, and even street gang leaders. These "managers" worked in the United States, Canada, Sweden, and Great Britain.

A synthesis of these findings paints an interesting picture, one as different from Fayol's classical view as a cubist abstract is from a Renaissance painting. In a sense, this picture will be obvious to anyone who has ever spent a day in a manager's office, either in front of the desk or behind it. Yet, at the same time, this picture may turn out to be revolutionary, in that it throws into doubt so much of the folklore that we have accepted about the manager's work.

I first discuss some of this folklore and contrast it with some of the discoveries of systematic research—the hard facts about how managers spend their time. Then I synthesize these research findings in a description of ten roles that seem to describe the essential content of all managers' jobs. In a concluding section, I discuss a number of implications of this synthesis for those trying to achieve more effective management, both in classrooms and in the business world.

Some Folklore and Facts about Managerial Work

There are four myths about the manager's job that do not bear up under careful scrutiny of the facts.

1. *Folklore: The manager is a reflective, systematic planner.* The evidence on this issue is overwhelming, but not a shred of it supports this statement.

Fact: Study after study has shown that managers work at an unrelenting pace, that their activities are characterized by brevity, variety, and discontinuity, and that they are strongly oriented to action and dislike reflective activities. Consider this evidence:

Half the activities engaged in by the five chief executives of my study lasted less than nine minutes, and only 10% exceeded one hour.[1] A study of 56 U.S. foremen found that they averaged 583 activities per eight-hour shift, an average of 1 every 48 seconds.[2] The work pace for both chief executives and foremen was unrelenting. The chief executives met a steady stream of callers and mail from the moment they arrived in the morning until they left in the evening. Coffee breaks and lunches were inevitably work related, and ever-present subordinates seemed to usurp any free moment.

A diary study of 160 British middle and top managers found that they worked for a half hour or more without interruption only about once every two days.[3]

Of the verbal contacts of the chief executives in my study, 93% were arranged on an ad hoc basis. Only 1% of the executives' time was spent in open-ended observational tours. Only 1 out of 368 verbal contacts was unrelated to a specific issue and could be called general planning. Another researcher finds that "in *not one single case* did a manager report the obtaining of important external information from a general conversation or other undirected personal communication."[4]

No study has found important patterns in the way managers schedule their time. They seem to jump from issue to issue, continually responding to the needs of the moment.

Is this the planner that the classical view describes? Hardly. How, then, can we explain this behavior? The manager is simply responding to the pressures of his job. I found that my chief executives terminated many of their own activities, often leaving meetings before the end, and interrupted their desk work to call in subordinates. One president not only placed his desk so that he could look down a long hallway but also left his door open when he was alone—an invitation for subordinates to come in and interrupt him.

Clearly, these managers wanted to encourage the flow of current information. But more significantly, they seemed to be conditioned by their own work loads. They appreciated the opportunity cost of their own time, and they were continually aware of their ever-present obligations—mail to be answered, callers to attend to, and so on. It seems that no matter what he is doing, the manager is plagued by the possibilities of what he might do and what he must do.

When the manager must plan, he seems to do so implicitly in the context of daily actions, not in some abstract process reserved for two weeks in the organization's mountain retreat. The plans of the chief executives I studied seemed to exist only in their heads—as flexible, but often specific, intentions. The traditional literature notwithstanding, the job of managing does not breed reflective planners; the manager is a real-time responder to stimuli, an individual who is conditioned by his job to prefer live to delayed action.

2. *Folklore: The effective manager has no regular duties to perform.* Managers are constantly being told to spend more time planning and delegating, and less time seeing customers and engaging in negotiations. These are not, after all, the true tasks of the manager. To use the popular analogy, the good manager, like the good conductor, carefully orchestrates everything in advance, then sits back to enjoy the fruits of his labor, responding occasionally to an unforeseeable exception.

But here again the pleasant abstraction just does not seem to hold up. We had better take a closer look at those activities managers feel compelled to engage in before we arbitrarily define them away.

Fact: In addition to handling exceptions, managerial work involves performing a number of regular duties, including ritual and ceremony, negotiations, and processing of soft information that links the organization with its environment. Consider some evidence from the research studies:

A study of the work of the presidents of small companies found that they engaged in routine activities because their companies could not afford staff specialists and were so thin on operating personnel that a single absence often required the president to substitute.[5]

One study of field sales managers and another of chief executives suggest that it is a natural part of both jobs to see important customers, assuming the managers wish to keep those customers.[6]

Someone, only half in jest, once described the manager as that person who sees visitors so that everyone else can get his work done. In my study, I found that certain ceremonial duties—meeting visiting dignitaries, giving out gold watches, presiding at Christmas dinners—were an intrinsic part of the chief executive's job.

Studies of managers' information flow suggest that managers play a key role in securing "soft" external information (much of it available only to them because of their status) and in passing it along to their subordinates.

3. *Folklore: The senior manager needs aggregated information, which a formal management information system best provides.* Not too long ago, the words *total information system* were everywhere in the management literature. In keeping with the classical view of the manager as that individual perched on the apex of a regulated, hierarchical system, the literature's manager was to receive all his important information from a giant, comprehensive MIS.

But lately, as it has become increasingly evident that these giant MIS systems are not working — that managers are simply not using them — the enthusiasm has waned. A look at how managers actually process information makes the reason quite clear. Managers have five media at their command — documents, telephone calls, scheduled and unscheduled meetings, and observational tours.

Fact: Managers strongly favor the verbal media — namely, telephone calls and meetings. The evidence comes from every single study of managerial work. Consider the following:

In two British studies, managers spent an average of 66% and 80% of their time in verbal (oral) communication.[7] In my study of five American chief executives, the figure was 78%.

These five chief executives treated mail processing as a burden to be dispensed with. One came in Saturday morning to process 142 pieces of mail in just over three hours, to "get rid of all the stuff." This same manager looked at the first piece of "hard" mail he had received all week, a standard cost report, and put it aside with the comment, "I never look at this."

These same five chief executives responded immediately to 2 of the 40 routine reports they received during the five weeks of my study and to four items in the 104 periodicals. They skimmed most of these periodicals in seconds, almost ritualistically. In all, these chief executives of good-sized organizations initiated on their own — that is, not in response to something else — a grand total of 25 pieces of mail during the 25 days I observed them.

An analysis of the mail the executives received reveals an interesting picture — only 13% was of specific and immediate use. So now we have another piece in the puzzle: not much of the mail provides live, current information — the action of a competitor, the mood of a government legislator, or the rating of last night's television show. Yet this is the information that drove the managers, interrupting their meetings and rescheduling their workdays.

Consider another interesting finding. Managers seem to cherish "soft" information, especially gossip, hearsay, and speculation. Why? The reason is its timeliness; today's gossip may be tomorrow's fact. The manager who is not accessible for the telephone call informing him that his biggest customer was seen golfing with his main competitor may read about a dramatic drop in sales in the next quarterly report. But then it's too late.

To assess the value of historical, aggregated, "hard" MIS information, consider two of the manager's prime uses for his information — to identify problems and opportunities[8] and to build his own mental models of the things around him (e.g., how his organization's budget system works, how his customers buy his product, how changes in the economy affect his organization, and so on). Every bit of evidence suggests that the manager identifies decision situations and builds models not with the aggregated abstractions an MIS provides, but with specific tidbits of data.

Consider the words of Richard Neustadt, who studied the information-collecting habits of Presidents Roosevelt, Truman, and Eisenhower:

"It is not information of a general sort that helps a President see personal stakes; not summaries, not surveys, not the *bland amalgams*. Rather . . . it is the odds and ends of *tangible detail* that pieced together in his mind illuminate the underside of issues put before him. To help himself he must reach out as widely as he can for every scrap of fact, opinion, gossip, bearing on his interests and relationships as President. He must become his own director of his own central intelligence."[9]

The manager's emphasis on the verbal media raises two important points:

First, verbal information is stored in the brains of people. Only when people write this information down can it be stored in the files of the organization—whether in metal cabinets or on magnetic tape—and managers apparently do not write down much of what they hear. Thus the strategic data bank of the organization is not in the memory of its computers but in the minds of its managers.

Second, the manager's extensive use of verbal media helps to explain why he is reluctant to delegate tasks. When we note that most of the manager's important information comes in verbal form and is stored in his head, we can well appreciate his reluctance. It is not as if he can hand a dossier over to someone; he must take the time to "dump memory"—to tell that someone all he knows about the subject. But this could take so long that the manager may find it easier to do the task himself. Thus the manager is damned by his own information system to a "dilemma of delegation"—to do too much himself or to delegate to his subordinates with inadequate briefing.

4. *Folklore: Management is, or at least is quickly becoming, a science and a profession.* By almost any definitions of *science* and *profession*, this statement is false. Brief observation of any manager will quickly lay to rest the notion that managers practice a science. A science involves the enaction of systematic, analytically determined procedures or programs. If we do not even know what procedures managers use, how can we prescribe them by scientific analysis? And how can we call management a profession if we cannot specify what managers are to learn? For after all, a profession involves "knowledge of some department of learning or science" (*Random House Dictionary*).[10]

Fact: The managers' programs—to schedule time, process information, make decisions, and so on—remain locked deep inside their brains. Thus, to describe these programs, we rely on words like *judgment* and *intuition*, seldom stopping to realize that they are merely labels for our ignorance.

I was struck during my study by the fact that the executives I was observing —all very competent by any standard—are fundamentally indistinguishable from their counterparts of a hundred years ago (or a thousand years ago, for that matter). The information they need differs, but they seek it in the same way—by word of mouth. Their decisions concern modern technology, but the procedures they use to make them are the same as the procedures of the nineteenth-century manager. Even the computer, so important for the specialized work of the organization, has apparently had no influence on the work procedures of general managers. In fact, the manager is in a kind of loop, with increasingly heavy work pressures but no aid forthcoming from management science.

Considering the facts about managerial work, we can see that the manager's job is enormously complicated and difficult. The manager is overburdened with obligations; yet he cannot easily delegate his tasks. As a result, he is driven to overwork and is forced to do many tasks superficially. Brevity, fragmentation, and verbal communication characterize his work. Yet these are the very characteristics of managerial work that have impeded scientific attempts to improve it. As a result, the management scientist has concentrated his efforts on the specialized functions of the organization, where he could more easily analyze the procedures and quantify the relevant information.[11]

But the pressures of the manager's job are becoming worse. Where before he needed only to respond to owners and directors, now he finds that subordinates with democratic norms continually reduce his freedom to issue unexplained orders, and a growing number of outside influences (consumer groups, government agencies, and so on) expect his attention. And the manager has had nowhere to turn for help. The first step in providing the manager with some help is to find out what his job really is.

Back to a Basic Description of Managerial Work

Now let us try to put some of the pieces of this puzzle together. Earlier, I defined the manager as that person in charge of an organization or one of its subunits. Besides chief executive officers, this definition would include vice presidents, bishops, foremen, hockey coaches, and prime ministers. Can all of these people have anything in common? Indeed they can. For an important starting point, all are vested with formal authority over an organizational unit. From formal authority comes status, which leads to various interpersonal relations, and from these comes access to information. Information, in turn, enables the manager to make decisions and strategies for his unit.

The manager's job can be described in terms of various "roles," or organized sets of behaviors identified with a position. My description, shown in *Exhibit I*, comprises ten roles. As we shall see, formal authority gives rise to the three interpersonal roles, which in turn give rise to the three informational roles; these two sets of roles enable the manager to play the four decisional roles.

Interpersonal Roles

Three of the manager's roles arise directly from his formal authority and involve basic interpersonal relationships.

1. First is the *figurehead* role. By virtue of his position as head of an organizational unit, every manager must perform some duties of a ceremonial nature. The president greets the touring dignitaries, the foreman attends the wedding of a lathe operator, and the sales manager takes an important customer to lunch.

The chief executives of my study spent 12% of their contact time on ceremonial duties; 17% of their incoming mail dealt with acknowledgments and requests related to their status. For example, a letter to a company president requested free merchandise for a crippled schoolchild; diplomas were put on the desk of the school superintendent for his signature.

Duties that involve interpersonal roles may sometimes be routine, involving little serious communication and no important decision making. Nevertheless, they are important to the smooth functioning of an organization and cannot be ignored by the manager.

2. Because he is in charge of an organizational unit, the manager is responsible for the work of the people of that unit. His actions in this regard constitute the *leader* role. Some of these actions involve leadership directly — for example, in most organizations the manager is normally responsible for hiring and training his own staff.

In addition, there is the indirect exercise of the leader role. Every manager must motivate and encourage his employees, somehow reconciling their individual needs with the goals of the organization. In virtually every contact the manager has with his employees, subordinates seeking leadership clues probe his actions: "Does he approve?" "How would he like the report to turn out?" "Is he more interested in market share than high profits?"

The influence of the manager is most clearly seen in the leader role. Formal authority vests him with great potential power; leadership determines in large part how much of it he will realize.

3. The literature of management has always recognized the leader role, particularly those aspects of it related to motivation. In comparison, until recently it has hardly mentioned the *liaison* role, in which the manager makes

Exhibit I   The Manager's Roles

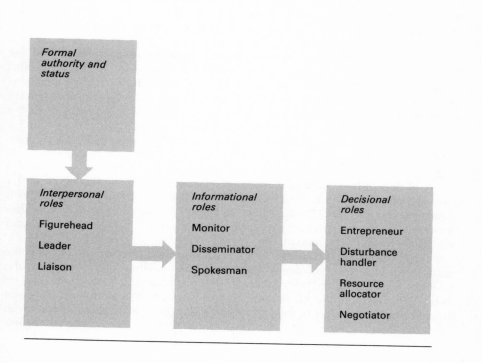

Formal authority and status

Interpersonal roles	Informational roles	Decisional roles
Figurehead	Monitor	Entrepreneur
Leader	Disseminator	Disturbance handler
Liaison	Spokesman	Resource allocator
		Negotiator

contacts outside his vertical chain of command. This is remarkable in light of the finding of virtually every study of managerial work that managers spend as much time with peers and other people outside their units as they do with their own subordinates—and, surprisingly, very little time with their own superiors.

In Rosemary Stewart's diary study, the 160 British middle and top managers spent 47% of their time with peers, 41% of their time with people outside their unit, and only 12% of their time with their superiors. For Robert H. Guest's study of U.S. foremen, the figures were 44%, 46%, and 10%. The chief executives of my study averaged 44% of their contact time with people outside their organizations, 48% with subordinates, and 7% with directors and trustees.

The contacts the five CEOs made were with an incredibly wide range of people: subordinates; clients, business associates, and suppliers; and peers—managers of similar organizations, government and trade organization officials, fellow directors on outside boards, and independents with no relevant organizational affiliations. The chief executives' time with and mail from these groups is shown in *Exhibit II* on page 56. Guest's study of foremen shows, like-wise, that their contacts were numerous and wide ranging, seldom involving fewer than 25 individuals, and often more than 50.

As we shall see shortly, the manager cultivates such contacts largely to find information. In effect, the liaison role is devoted to building up the manager's own external information system—informal, private, verbal, but, nevertheless, effective.

Informational Roles

By virtue of his interpersonal contacts, both with his subordinates and with his network of contacts, the manager emerges as the nerve center of his organizational unit. He may not know everything, but he typically knows more than any member of his staff.

Studies have shown this relationship to hold for all managers, from street gang leaders to U.S. presidents. In *The Human Group*, George C. Homans explains how, because they were at the center of the information flow in their own gangs and were also in close touch with other gang leaders, street gang leaders were better informed than any of their followers.[12] And Richard Neustadt describes the following account from his study of Franklin D. Roosevelt:

"The essence of Roosevelt's technique for information-gathering was competition. 'He would call you in,' one of his aides once told me, 'and he'd ask you to get the story on some complicated business, and you'd come back after a couple of days of hard labor and present the juicy morsel you'd uncovered under a stone somewhere, and *then* you'd find out he knew all about it, along with something else you *didn't* know. Where he got this information from he wouldn't mention, usually, but after he had done this to you once or twice you got damn careful about *your* information.' "[13]

We can see where Roosevelt "got this information" when we consider the relationship between the interpersonal and informational roles. As leader, the manager has formal and easy access to every member of his staff. Hence, as noted earlier, he tends to know more about his own unit than anyone else does. In addition, his liaison contacts expose the manager to external information to which his subordinates often lack access. Many of these contacts are with other managers of equal status, who are themselves nerve centers in their own organization. In this way, the manager develops a powerful data base of information.

The processing of information is a key part of the manager's job. In my study, the chief executives spent 40% of their contact time on activities devoted exclusively to the transmission of information; 70% of their incoming mail was purely informational (as opposed to requests for action). The manager does not leave meetings or hang up the telephone in order to get back to work. In large part, communication *is* his work. Three roles describe these informational aspects of managerial work.

1. As *monitor*, the manager perpetually scans his environment for information, interrogates his liaison contacts and his subordinates, and receives unsolicited information, much of it as a result of the network of personal contacts he has developed. Remember that a good part of the information the manager collects in his monitor role arrives in verbal form, often as gossip, hearsay, and speculation. By virtue of his contacts, the manager has a natural advantage in collecting this soft information for his organization.

2. He must share and distribute much of this information. Information he gleans from outside personal contacts may be needed within his organization. In his *disseminator* role, the manager passes some of his privileged information directly to his subordinates, who would otherwise have no access to it. When his subordinates lack easy contact with one another, the manager will sometimes pass information from one to another.

3. In his *spokesman* role, the manager sends some of his information to people outside his unit—a president makes a speech to lobby for an organization cause, or a foreman suggests a product modification to a supplier. In addition, as part of his role as spokesman, every manager must inform and satisfy the influential people who control his organizational unit. For the foreman, this may simply involve keeping the plant manager informed about the flow of work through the shop.

The president of a large corporation, however, may spend a great amount of his time dealing with a host of influences. Directors and shareholders must be advised about financial performance; consumer groups must be assured that the organization is fulfilling its social responsibilities; and government officials must be satisfied that the organization is abiding by the law.

Decisional Roles

Information is not, of course, an end in itself; it is the basic input to decision making. One thing is clear in the study of managerial work: the manager plays the major role in his unit's decision-making system. As its formal authority, only he can commit the unit to important new courses of action; and as its nerve center, only he has full and current information to make the set of decisions that determines the unit's strategy. Four roles describe the manager as decisionmaker.

1. As *entrepreneur*, the manager seeks to improve his unit, to adapt it to changing conditions in the environment. In his monitor role, the president is constantly on the lookout for new ideas. When a good one appears, he initiates a development project that he may supervise himself or delegate to an employee (perhaps with the stipulation that he must approve the final proposal).

There are two interesting features about these development projects

Exhibit II The Chief Executives' Contacts

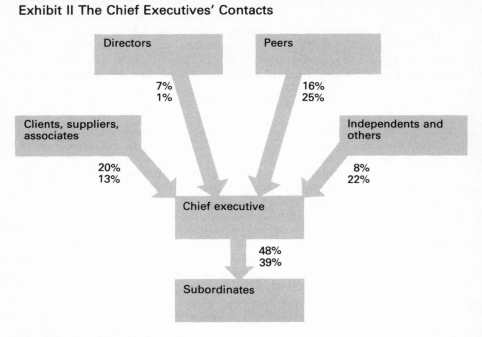

Note: The top figure indicates the proportion of total contact time spent with each group and the bottom figure, the proportion of mail from each group.

at the chief executive level. First, these projects do not involve single decisions or even unified clusters of decisions. Rather, they emerge as a series of small decisions and actions sequenced over time. Apparently, the chief executive prolongs each project so that he can fit it bit by bit into his busy, disjointed schedule and so that he can gradually come to comprehend the issue, if it is a complex one.

Second, the chief executives I studied supervised as many as 50 of these projects at the same time. Some projects entailed new products or processes; others involved public relations campaigns, improvement of the cash position, reorganization of a weak department, resolution of a morale problem in a foreign division, integration of computer operations, various acquisitions at different stages of development, and so on.

The chief executive appears to maintain a kind of inventory of the development projects that he himself supervises — projects that are at various stages of development, some active and some in limbo. Like a juggler, he keeps a number of projects in the air; periodically, one comes down, is given a new burst of energy, and is sent back into orbit. At various intervals, he puts new projects on-stream and discards old ones.

2. While the entrepreneur role describes the manager as the voluntary initiator of change, the *disturbance handler* role depicts the manager involuntarily

responding to pressures. Here change is beyond the manager's control. He must act because the pressures of the situation are too severe to be ignored: a strike looms, a major customer has gone bankrupt, or a supplier reneges on his contract.

It has been fashionable, I noted earlier, to compare the manager to an orchestra conductor, just as Peter F. Drucker wrote in *The Practice of Management*:

"The manager has the task of creating a true whole that is larger than the sum of its parts, a productive entity ʟ‚at turns out more than the sum of the resources put into it. One analogy is the conductor of a symphony orchestra, through whose effort, vision and leadership individual instrumental parts that are so much noise by themselves become the living whole of music. But the conductor has the composer's score; he is only interpreter. The manager is both composer and conductor."[14]

Now consider the words of Leonard R. Sayles, who has carried out systematic research on the manager's job:

"[The manager] is like a symphony orchestra conductor, endeavouring to maintain a melodious performance in which the contributions of the various instruments are coordinated and sequenced, patterned and paced, while the orchestra members are having various personal difficulties, stage hands are moving music stands, alternating excessive heat and cold are creating audience and instrument problems, and the sponsor of the concert is insisting on irrational changes in the program."[15]

In effect, every manager must spend a good part of his time responding to high-pressure disturbances. No organization can be so well run, so standardized, that it has considered every contingency in the uncertain environment in advance. Disturbances arise not only because poor managers ignore situations until they reach crisis proportions, but also because good managers cannot possibly anticipate all the consequences of the actions they take.

3. The third decisional role is that of *resource allocator*. To the manager falls the responsibility of deciding who will get what in his organizational unit. Perhaps the most important resource the manager allocates is his own time. Access to the manager constitutes exposure to the unit's nerve center and decision-maker. The manager is also charged with designing his unit's structure, that pattern of formal relationships that determines how work is to be divided and coordinated.

Also, in his role as resource allocator, the manager authorizes the important decisions of his unit before they are implemented. By retaining this power, the manager can ensure that decisions are interrelated; all must pass through a single brain. To fragment this power is to encourage discontinuous decision making and a disjointed strategy.

There are a number of interesting features about the manager's authorizing others' decisions. First, despite the widespread use of capital budgeting procedures—a means of authorizing various capital expenditures at one time—executives in my study made a great many authorization decisions on an ad hoc basis. Apparently, many projects cannot wait or simply do not have the quantifiable costs and benefits that capital budgeting requires.

Second, I found that the chief executives faced incredibly complex choices. They had to consider the impact of each decision on other decisions and on the organization's strategy. They had to ensure that the decision would be acceptable to those who influence the organization, as well as ensure that resources would not be overextended. They had to understand the various costs and benefits as well as the feasibility of the proposal. They also had to consider questions of timing. All this was necessary for the simple approval of someone else's proposal. At the same time, however, delay could lose time, while quick approval could be ill considered and quick rejection might discourage the subordinate who had spent months developing a pet project.

One common solution to approving projects is to pick the man instead of the proposal. That is, the manager authorizes those projects presented to him by people whose judgment he trusts. But he cannot always use this simple dodge.

4. The final decisional role is that of *negotiator*. Studies of managerial work at all levels indicate that managers spend considerable time in negotiations: the president of the football team is called in to work out a contract with the holdout superstar; the corporation president leads his company's contingent to negotiate a new strike issue; the foreman argues a grievance problem to its conclusion with the shop steward. As Leonard Sayles puts it, negotiations are a "way of life" for the sophisticated manager.

These negotiations are duties of the manager's job; perhaps routine, they are not to be shirked. They are an integral part of his job, for only he has the authority to commit organizational resources in "real time," and only he has the nerve center information that important negotiations require.

The Integrated Job

It should be clear by now that the ten roles I have been describing are not easily separable. In the terminology of the psychologist, they form a gestalt, an integrated whole. No role can be pulled out of the framework and the job be left intact. For example, a manager without liaison contacts lacks external information. As a result, he can neither disseminate the information his employees need nor make decisions that adequately reflect external conditions. (In fact, this is a problem for the new person in a managerial position, since he cannot make effective decisions until he has built up his network of contacts.)

Here lies a clue to the problems of team management.[16] Two or three people cannot share a single managerial position unless they can act as one entity. This means that they cannot divide up the ten roles unless they can very carefully reintegrate them. The real difficulty lies with the informational roles. Unless there can be full sharing of managerial information—and, as I pointed out earlier, it is primarily verbal—team management breaks down. A single managerial job cannot be arbitrarily split, for example, into internal and external roles, for information from both sources must be brought to bear on the same decisions.

To say that the ten roles form a gestalt is not to say that all managers give equal attention to each role. In fact, I found in my review of the various research studies that

. . . sales managers seem to spend relatively more of their time in the interpersonal roles, presumably a reflection of the extrovert nature of the marketing activity;

. . . production managers give relatively more attention to the decisional roles, presumably a reflection of their concern with efficient work flow;

. . . staff managers spend the most time in the informational roles, since they are experts who manage departments that advise other parts of the organization.

Nevertheless, in all cases the interpersonal, informational, and decisional roles remain inseparable.

Toward More Effective Management

What are the messages for management in this description? I believe, first and foremost, that this description of managerial work should prove more important to managers than any prescription they might derive from it. That is to say, *the manager's effectiveness is significantly influenced by his insight into his own work.* His performance depends on how well he understands and responds to the pressures and dilemmas of the job. Thus managers who can be introspective about their work are likely to be effective at their jobs. The insert on page 61 offers 14 groups of self-study questions for managers. Some may sound rhetorical; none is meant to be. Even though the questions cannot be answered simply, the manager should address them.

Let us take a look at three specific areas of concern. For the most part, the managerial logjams—the dilemma of delegation, the data base centralized in one brain, the problems of working with the management scientist—revolve around the verbal nature of the manager's information. There are great dangers in centralizing the organization's data bank in the minds of its managers. When they leave, they take their memory with them. And when subordinates are out of convenient verbal reach of the manager, they are at an informational disadvantage.

1. *The manager is challenged to find systematic ways to share his privileged information.* A regular debriefing session with key subordinates, a weekly memory dump on the dictating machine, the maintaining of a diary of important information for limited circulation, or other similar methods may ease the logjam of work considerably. Time spent disseminating this information will be more than regained when decisions must be made. Of course, some will raise the question of confidentiality. But managers would do well to weigh the risks of exposing privileged information against having subordinates who can make effective decisions.

If there is a single theme that runs through this article, it is that the pressures of his job drive the manager to be superficial in his actions—to overload himself with work, encourage interruption, respond quickly to every stimulus, seek the tangible and avoid the abstract, make decisions in small increments, and do everything abruptly.

2. *Here again, the manager is challenged to deal consciously with the pressures of superficiality by giving serious attention to the issues that require it, by stepping back from his tangible bits of information in order to see a broad picture, and by making use of analytical inputs.* Although effective managers have to be adept at responding quickly to numerous and varying problems, the danger in managerial work is that they will respond to every issue equally (and that means abruptly) and that they will never work the tangible bits and pieces of informational input into a comprehensive picture of their world.

As I noted earlier, the manager uses these bits of information to build models of his world. But the manager can also avail himself of the models of the specialists. Economists describe the functioning of markets, operations researchers simulate financial flow processes, and behavioral scientists explain the needs and goals of people. The best of these models can be searched out and learned.

In dealing with complex issues, the senior manager has much to gain from a close relationship with the management scientists of his own organization.

They have something important that he lacks—time to probe complex issues. An effective working relationship hinges on the resolution of what a colleague and I have called "the planning dilemma."[17] Managers have the information and the authority; analysts have the time and the technology. A successful working relationship between the two will be effected when the manager learns to share his information and the analyst learns to adapt to his manager's needs. For the analyst, adaptation means worrying less about the elegance of the method and more about its speed and flexibility.

It seems to me that analysts can help the top manager especially to schedule his time, feed in analytical information, monitor projects under his supervision, develop models to aid in making choices, design contingency plans for disturbances that can be anticipated, and conduct "quick-and-dirty" analysis for those that cannot. But there can be no cooperation if the analysts are out of the mainstream of the manager's information flow.

3. *The manager is challenged to gain control of his own time by turning obligations to his advantage and by turning those things he wishes to do into obligations.* The chief executives of my study initiated only 32% of their own contacts (and another 5% by mutual agreement). And yet to a considerable extent they seemed to control their time. There were two key factors that enabled them to do so.

First, the manager has to spend so much time discharging obligations that if he were to view them as just that, he would leave no mark on his organization. The unsuccessful manager blames failure on the obligations; the effective manager turns his obligations to his own advantage. A speech is a chance to lobby for a cause; a meeting is a chance to reorganize a weak department; a visit to an important customer is a chance to extract trade information.

Second, the manager frees some of his time to do those things that he—perhaps no one else—thinks important by turning them into obligations. Free time is made, not found, in the manager's job; it is forced into the schedule. Hoping to leave some time open for contemplation or general planning is tantamount to hoping that the pressures of the job will go away. The manager who wants to innovate initiates a project and obligates others to report back to him; the manager who needs certain environmental information establishes channels that will automatically keep him informed; the manager who has to tour facilities commits himself publicly.

The Educator's Job

Finally, a word about the training of managers. Our management schools have done an admirable job of training the organization's specialists— management scientists, marketing researchers, accountants, and organizational development specialists. But for the most part they have not trained managers.[18]

Management schools will begin the serious training of managers when skill training takes a serious place next to cognitive learning. Cognitive learning is detached and informational, like reading a book or listening to a lecture. No doubt much important cognitive material must be assimilated by the manager-to-be. But cognitive learning no more makes a manager than it does a swimmer. The latter will drown the first time he jumps into the water if his coach never takes him out of the lecture hall, gets him wet, and gives him feedback on his performance.

In other words, we are taught a skill through practice plus feedback, whether in a real or a simulated situation. Our management schools need to identify the skills managers use, select students who show potential in these skills, put the students into situations where these skills can be practiced, and then give them systematic feedback on their performance.

My description of managerial work suggests a number of important managerial skills — developing peer relationships, carrying out negotiations, motivating subordinates, resolving conflicts, establishing information networks and subsequently disseminating information, making decisions in conditions of extreme ambiguity, and allocating resources. Above all, the manager needs to be introspective about his work so that he may continue to learn on the job.

Many of the manager's skills can, in fact, be practiced, using techniques that range from role playing to videotaping real meetings. And our management schools can enhance the entrepreneurial skills by designing programs that encourage sensible risk taking and innovation.

No job is more vital to our society than that of the manager. It is the manager who determines whether our social institutions serve us well or whether they squander our talents and resources. It is time to strip away the folklore about managerial work, and time to study it realistically so that we can begin the difficult task of making significant improvements in its performance.

Self-Study Questions for Managers

1.
Where do I get my information, and how? Can I make greater use of my contacts to get information? Can other people do some of my scanning for me? In what areas is my knowledge weakest, and how can I get others to provide me with the information I need? Do I have powerful enough mental models of those things I must understand within the organization and in its environment?

2.
What information do I disseminate in my organization? How important is it that my subordinates get my information? Do I keep too much information to myself because dissemination of it is time-consuming or inconvenient? How can I get more information to others so they can make better decisions?

3.
Do I balance information collecting with action taking? Do I tend to act before information is in? Or do I wait so long for all the information that opportunities pass me by and I become a bottleneck in my organization?

4.
What pace of change am I asking my organization to tolerate? Is this change balanced so that our operations are neither excessively static nor overly disrupted? Have we sufficiently analyzed the impact of this change on the future of our organization?

5.
Am I sufficiently well informed to pass judgment on the proposals that my subordinates make? Is it possible to leave final authorization for more of the proposals with subordinates? Do we have problems of coordination because subordinates in fact now make too many of these decisions independently?

6.
What is my vision of direction for this organization? Are these plans primarily in my own mind in loose form? Should I make them explicit in order to guide the decisions of others in the organization better? Or do I need flexibility to change them at will?

7.
How do my subordinates react to my managerial style? Am I sufficiently sensitive to the powerful influence my actions have on them? Do I fully understand their reactions to my actions? Do I find an appropriate balance between encouragement and pressure? Do I stifle their initiative?

8.
What kind of external relationships do I maintain, and how? Do I spend too much of my time maintaining these relationships? Are there certain types of people whom I should get to know better?

9.
Is there any system to my time scheduling, or am I just reacting to the pressures of the moment? Do I find the appropriate mix of activities, or do I tend to concentrate on one particular function or one type of problem just because I find it interesting? Am I more efficient with particular kinds of work at special times of the day or week? Does my schedule reflect this? Can someone else (in addition to my secretary) take responsibility for much of my scheduling and do it more systematically?

10.
Do I overwork? What effect does my work load have on my efficiency? Should I force myself to take breaks or to reduce the pace of my activity?

11.
Am I too superficial in what I do? Can I really shift moods as quickly and frequently as my work patterns require? Should I attempt to decrease the amount of fragmentation and interruption in my work?

12.
Do I orient myself too much toward current, tangible activities? Am I a slave to the action and excitement of my work, so that I am no longer able to concentrate on issues? Do key problems receive the attention they deserve? Should I spend more time reading and probing deeply into certain issues? Could I be more reflective? Should I be?

13.
Do I use the different media appropriately? Do I know how to make the most of written communication? Do I rely excessively on face-to-face communication, thereby putting all but a few of my subordinates at an informational disadvantage? Do I schedule enough of my meetings on a regular basis? Do I spend enough time touring my organization to observe activity at first hand? Am I too detached from the heart of my organization's activities, seeing things only in an abstract way?

14.
How do I blend my personal rights and duties? Do my obligations consume all my time? How can I free myself sufficiently from obligations to ensure that I am taking this organization where I want it to go? How can I turn my obligations to my advantage?

REFERENCES

1. All the data from my study can be found in Henry Mintzberg, *The Nature of Managerial Work* (New York: Harper & Row, 1973).

2. Robert H. Guest, "Of Time and the Foreman," *Personnel*, May 1956, p. 478.

3. Rosemary Stewart, *Managers and Their Jobs* (London: Macmillan, 1967); see also Sune Carlson, *Executive Behaviour* (Stockholm: Strömbergs, 1951), the first of the diary studies.

4. Francis J. Aguilar, *Scanning the Business Environment* (New York: Macmillan, 1967), p. 102.

5. Unpublished study by Irving Choran, reported in Mintzberg, *The Nature of Managerial Work*.

6. Robert T. Davis, *Performance and Development of Field Sales Managers* (Boston: Division of Research, Harvard Business School, 1957); George H. Copeman, *The Role of the Managing Director* (London: Business Publications, 1963).

7. Stewart, *Managers and Their Jobs*; Tom Burns, "The Directions of Activity and Communication in a Departmental Executive Group," *Human Relations* 7, no. 1 (1954): 73.

8. H. Edward Wrapp, "Good Managers Don't Make Policy Decisions," HBR September-October 1967, p. 91; Wrapp refers to this as spotting opportunities and relationships in the stream of operating problems and decisions; in his article Wrapp raises a number of excellent points related to this analysis.

9. Richard E. Neustadt, *Presidential Power* (New York: John Wiley, 1960), pp. 153-154; italics added.

10. For a more thorough, though rather different, discussion of this issue, see Kenneth R. Andrews, "Toward Professionalism in Business Management," HBR March-April 1969, p. 49.

11. C. Jackson Grayson, Jr., in "Management Science and Business Practice," HBR July-August 1973, p. 41, explains in similar terms why, as chairman of the Price Commission, he did not use those very techniques that he himself promoted in his earlier career as a management scientist.

12. George C. Homans, *The Human Group* (New York: Harcourt, Brace & World, 1950), based on the study by William F. Whyte entitled *Street Corner Society*, rev. ed. (Chicago: University of Chicago Press, 1955).

13. Neustadt, *Presidential Power*, p. 157.

14. Peter F. Drucker, *The Practice of Management* (New York: Harper & Row, 1954), pp. 341-342.

15. Leonard R. Sayles, *Managerial Behavior* (New York: McGraw-Hill, 1964), p. 162.

16. See Richard C. Hodgson, Daniel J. Levinson, and Abraham Zaleznik, *The Executive Role Constellation* (Boston: Division of Research, Harvard Business School, 1965), for a discussion of the sharing of roles.

17. James S. Hekimian and Henry Mintzberg, "The Planning Dilemma," *The Management Review*, May 1968, p. 4.

18. See J. Sterling Livingston, "Myth of the Well-Educated Manager," HBR January-February 1971, p. 79.

5

Managers and Leaders: Are They Different?

ABRAHAM ZALEZNIK

What is the ideal way to develop leadership? Every society provides its own answer to this question, and each, in groping for answers, defines its deepest concerns about the purposes, distributions, and uses of power. Business has contributed its answer to the leadership question by evolving a new breed called the manager. Simultaneously, business has established a new power ethic that favors collective over individual leadership, the cult of the group over that of personality. While ensuring the competence, control, and the balance of power relations among groups with the potential for rivalry, managerial leadership unfortunately does not necessarily ensure imagination, creativity, or ethical behavior in guiding the destinies of corporate enterprises.

Leadership inevitably requires using power to influence the thoughts and actions of other people. Power in the hands of an individual entails human risks: first, the risk of equating power with the ability to get immediate results; second, the risk of ignoring the many different ways people can legitimately accumulate power; and third, the risk of losing self-control in the desire for power. The need to hedge these risks accounts in part for the development of collective leadership and the managerial ethic. Consequently, an inherent conservatism dominates the culture of large organizations. In *The Second American Revolution*, John D. Rockefeller, 3rd. describes the conservatism of organizations:

"An organization is a system, with a logic of its own, and all the weight of tradition and inertia. The deck is stacked in favor of the tried and proven way of doing things and against the taking of risks and striking out in new directions."[1]

Out of this conservatism and inertia organizations provide succession to power through the development of managers rather than individual leaders. And the irony of the managerial ethic is that it fosters a bureaucratic culture in business, supposedly the last bastion protecting us from the encroachments and controls of bureaucracy in government and education. Perhaps the risks associated with power in the hands of an individual may be necessary ones for business to take if organizations are to break free of their inertia and bureaucratic conservatism.

Manager vs. Leader Personality

Theodore Levitt has described the essential features of a managerial culture with its emphasis on rationality and control:

"Management consists of the rational assessment of a situation and the systematic selection of goals and purposes (what is to be done?); the systematic development of strategies to achieve these goals; the marshalling of the required resources; the rational design, organization, direction, and control of the activities required to attain the selected purposes; and, finally, the motivating and rewarding of people to do the work."[2]

In other words, whether his or her energies are directed toward goals, resources, organization structures, or people, a manager is a problem solver. The manager asks himself, "What problems have to be solved, and what are the best ways to achieve results so that people will continue to contribute to this organization?" In this conception, leadership is a practical effort to direct affairs; and to fulfill his task, a manager requires that many people operate at different levels of status and responsibility. Our democratic society is, in fact, unique in having solved the problem of providing well-trained managers for business. The same solution stands ready to be applied to government, education, health care, and other institutions. It takes neither genius nor heroism to be a manager, but rather persistence, tough-mindedness, hard work, intelligence, analytical ability and, perhaps most important, tolerance and good will.

Another conception, however, attaches almost mystical beliefs to what leadership is and assumes that only great people are worthy of the drama of power and politics. Here, leadership is a psychodrama in which, as a precondition for control of a political structure, a lonely person must gain control of him or herself. Such an expectation of leadership contrasts sharply with the mundane, practical, and yet important conception that leadership is really managing work that other people do.

Two questions come to mind. Is this mystique of leadership merely a holdover from our collective childhood of dependency and our longing for good and heroic parents? Or, is there a basic truth lurking behind the need for leaders that no matter how competent managers are, their leadership stagnates because of their limitations in visualizing purposes and generating value in work? Without this imaginative capacity and the ability to communicate, managers, driven by their narrow purposes, perpetuate group conflicts instead of reforming them into broader desires and goals.

If indeed problems demand greatness, then, judging by past performance, the selection and development of leaders leave a great deal to chance. There are no known ways to train "great" leaders. Furthermore, beyond what we leave to chance, there is a deeper issue in the relationship between the need for competent managers and the longing for great leaders.

What it takes to ensure the supply of people who will assume practical responsibility may inhibit the development of great leaders. Conversely, the presence of great leaders may undermine the development of managers who become very anxious in the relative disorder that leaders seem to generate. The antagonism in aim (to have many competent managers as well as great leaders) often remains obscure in stable and well-developed societies. But the antagonism surfaces during periods of stress and change, as it did in the Western countries during both the Great Depression and World War II. The tension also appears in the struggle for power between theorists and professional managers in revolutionary societies.

It is easy enough to dismiss the dilemma I pose (of training managers while we may need new leaders, or leaders at the expense of managers) by saying that the need is for people who can be *both* managers and leaders. The truth of the matter as I see it, however, is that just as a managerial culture is different from the entrepreneurial culture that develops when leaders appear in organizations, managers and leaders are very different kinds of people. They differ in motivation, personal history, and in how they think and act.

A technologically oriented and economically successful society tends to depreciate the need for great leaders. Such societies hold a deep and abiding faith in rational methods of solving problems, including problems of value, economics, and justice. Once rational methods of solving problems are broken down into elements, organized, and taught as skills, then society's faith in technique over personal qualities in leadership remains the guiding conception for a democratic society contemplating its leadership requirements. But there are times when tinkering and trial and error prove inadequate to the emerging problems of selecting goals, allocating resources, and distributing wealth and opportunity. During such times, the democratic society needs to find leaders who use themselves as the instruments of learning and acting, instead of managers who use their accumulation of collective experience to get where they are going.

The most impressive spokesman, as well as exemplar of the managerial viewpoint, was Alfred P. Sloan, Jr. who, along with Pierre du Pont, designed the modern corporate structure. Reflecting on what makes one management successful while another fails, Sloan suggested that "good management rests on a reconciliation of centralization and decentralization, or 'decentralization with coordinated control.' "[3]

Sloan's conception of management, as well as his practice, developed by trial and error, and by the accumulation of experience. Sloan wrote:

"There is no hard and fast rule for sorting out the various responsibilities and the best way to assign them. The balance which is struck . . . varies according to what is being decided, the circumstances of the time, past experience, and the temperaments and skills of the executive involved."[4]

In other words, in much the same way that the inventors of the late nineteenth century tried, failed, and fitted until they hit on a product or method, managers who innovate in developing organizations are "tinkerers." They do not have a grand design or experience the intuitive flash of insight that, borrowing from modern science, we have come to call the "breakthrough."

Managers and leaders differ fundamentally in their world views. The dimensions for assessing these differences include managers' and leaders' orientations toward their goals, their work, their human relations, and their selves.

Attitudes toward Goals

Managers tend to adopt impersonal, if not passive, attitudes toward goals. Managerial goals arise out of necessities rather than desires, and therefore, are deeply embedded in the history and culture of the organization.

Frederic G. Donner, chairman and chief executive officer of General Motors from 1958 to 1967, expressed this impersonal and passive attitude toward goals in defining GM's position on product development:

". . . To meet the challenge of the marketplace, we must recognize changes in customer needs and desires far enough ahead to have the right products in the right places at the right time and in the right quantity.

"We must balance trends in preference against the many compromises that are necessary to make a final product that is both reliable and good looking, that performs well and that sells at a competitive price in the necessary volume. We must design, not just the cars we would like to build, but more importantly, the cars that our customers want to buy."[5]

Nowhere in this formulation of how a product comes into being is there a notion that consumer tastes and preferences arise in part as a result of what manufacturers do. In reality, through product design, advertising, and promotion, consumers learn to like what they then say they need. Few would argue that people who enjoy taking snapshots *need* a camera that also develops pictures. But in response to novelty, convenience, a shorter interval between acting (taking the snap) and gaining pleasure (seeing the shot), the Polaroid camera succeeded in the marketplace. But it is inconceivable that Edwin Land responded to impressions of consumer need. Instead, he translated a technology (polarization of light) into a product, which proliferated and stimulated consumers' desires.

The example of Polaroid and Land suggests how leaders think about goals. They are active instead of reactive, shaping ideas instead of responding to them. Leaders adopt a personal and active attitude toward goals. The influence a leader exerts in altering moods, evoking images and expectations, and in establishing specific desires and objectives determines the direction a business takes. The net result of this influence is to change the way people think about what is desirable, possible, and necessary.

Conceptions of Work

What do managers and leaders do? What is the nature of their respective work?

Leaders and managers differ in their conceptions. Managers tend to view work as an enabling process involving some combination of people and ideas interacting to establish strategies and make decisions. Managers help the process along by a range of skills, including calculating the interests in opposition, staging and timing the surfacing of controversial issues, and reducing tensions. In this enabling process, managers appear flexible in the use of tactics: they negotiate and bargain, on the one hand, and use rewards and punishments, and other forms of coercion, on the other. Machiavelli wrote for managers and not necessarily for leaders.

Alfred Sloan illustrated how this enabling process works in situations of conflict. The time was the early 1920s when the Ford Motor Co. still dominated the automobile industry using, as did General Motors, the conventional water-cooled engine. With the full backing of Pierre du Pont, Charles Kettering dedicated himself to the design of an air-cooled engine, which, if successful, would have been a great technical and market coup for GM. Kettering believed in his product, but the manufacturing division heads at GM remained skeptical and later opposed the new design on two grounds: first, that it was technically unreliable, and second, that the corporation was putting all its eggs in one basket by investing in a new product instead of attending to the current marketing situation.

In the summer of 1923 after a series of false starts and after its decision to recall the copper-cooled Chevrolets from dealers and customers, GM management reorganized and finally scrapped the project. When it dawned on Kettering that the company had rejected the engine, he was deeply discouraged and wrote to Sloan that without the "organized resistance" against the project it would succeed and that unless the project were saved, he would leave the company.

Alfred Sloan was all too aware of the fact that Kettering was unhappy and indeed intended to leave General Motors. Sloan was also aware of the fact that, while the manufacturing divisions strongly opposed the new engine, Pierre du Pont supported Kettering. Furthermore, Sloan had himself gone on record in a letter to Kettering less than two years earlier expressing full confidence in him. The problem Sloan now had was to make his decision stick, keep Kettering in the organization (he was much too valuable to lose), avoid alienating du Pont, and encourage the division heads to move speedily in developing product lines using conventional water-cooled engines.

The actions that Sloan took in the face of this conflict reveal much about how managers work. First, he tried to reassure Kettering by presenting the problem in a very ambiguous fashion, suggesting that he and the Executive Committee sided with Kettering, but that it would not be practical to force the divisions to do what they were opposed to. He presented the problem as being a question of the people, not the product. Second, he proposed to reorganize around the problem by consolidating all functions in a new division that would be responsible for the design, production, and marketing of the new car. This solution, however, appeared as ambiguous as his efforts to placate and keep Kettering in General Motors. Sloan wrote: "My plan was to create an independent pilot operation under the sole jurisdiction of Mr. Kettering, a kind of copper-cooled-car division. Mr. Kettering would designate his own chief engineer and his production staff to solve the technical problems of manufacture."[6]

While Sloan did not discuss the practical value of this solution, which included saddling an inventor with management responsibility, he in effect used this plan to limit his conflict with Pierre du Pont.

In effect, the managerial solution that Sloan arranged and pressed for adoption limited the options available to others. The structural solution narrowed choices, even limiting emotional reactions to the point where the key people could do nothing but go along, and even allowed Sloan to say in his memorandum to du Pont, "We have discussed the matter with Mr. Kettering at some length this morning and he agrees with us absolutely on every point we made. He appears to receive the suggestion enthusiastically and has every confidence that it can be put across along these lines."[7]

Having placated people who opposed his views by developing a structural solution that appeared to give something but in reality only limited options, Sloan could then authorize the car division's general manager, with whom he basically agreed, to move quickly in designing water-cooled cars for the immediate market demand.

Years later Sloan wrote, evidently with tongue in cheek, "The copper-cooled car never came up again in a big way. It just died out, I don't know why."[8]

In order to get people to accept solutions to problems, managers need to coordinate and balance continually. Interestingly enough, this managerial work has much in common with what diplomats and mediators do, with Henry Kissinger apparently an outstanding practitioner. The manager aims at shifting balances of power toward solutions acceptable as a compromise among conflicting values.

What about leaders, what do they do? Where managers act to limit choices, leaders work in the opposite direction, to develop fresh approaches to long-standing problems and to open issues for new options. Stanley and Inge Hoffmann, the political scientists, liken the leader's work to that of the artist. But unlike most artists, the leader himself is an integral part of the aesthetic product.

One cannot look at a leader's art without looking at the artist. On Charles de Gaulle as a political artist, they wrote: "And each of his major political acts, however tortuous the means or the details, has been whole, indivisible and un-mistakably his own, like an artistic act."[9]

The closest one can get to a product apart from the artist is the ideas that occupy, indeed at times obsess, the leader's mental life. To be effective, however, the leader needs to project his ideas into images that excite people, and only then develop choices that give the projected images substance. Consequently, leaders create excitement in work.

John F. Kennedy's brief presidency shows both the strengths and weaknesses connected with the excitement leaders generate in their work. In his inaugural address he said, "Let every nation know, whether it wishes us well or ill, that we shall pay any price, bear any burden, meet any hardship, support any friend, oppose any foe, in order to assure the survival and the success of liberty."

This much-quoted statement forced people to react beyond immediate con-cerns and to identify with Kennedy and with important shared ideals. But upon closer scrutiny the statement must be seen as absurd because it promises a position which if in fact adopted, as in the Viet Nam War, could produce disastrous results. Yet unless expectations are aroused and mobilized, with all the dangers of frustration inherent in heightened desire, new thinking and new choice can never come to light.

Leaders work from high-risk positions, indeed often are temperamentally disposed to seek out risk and danger, especially where opportunity and reward appear high. From my observations, why one individual seeks risks while another approaches problems conservatively depends more on his or her personality and less on conscious choice. For some, especially those who become managers, the instinct for survival dominates their need for risk, and their ability to tolerate mundane, practical work assists their survival. The same cannot be said for leaders who sometimes react to mundane work as to an affliction.

Relations with Others

Managers prefer to work with people; they avoid solitary activity be-cause it makes them anxious. Several years ago, I directed studies on the psy-chological aspects of career. The need to seek out others with whom to work and collaborate seemed to stand out as important characteristics of managers. When asked, for example, to write imaginative stories in response to a picture showing a single figure (a boy contemplating a violin, or a man silhouetted in a state of reflection), managers populated their stories with people. The following is an example of a manager's imaginative story about the young boy contem-plating a violin:

"Mom and Dad insisted that junior take music lessons so that someday he can become a concert musician. His instrument was ordered and had just arrived. Junior is weighing the alternatives of playing football with the other kids or playing with the squeak box. He can't understand how his parents could think a violin is better than a touchdown.

"After four months of practicing the violin, junior has had more than enough, Daddy is going out of his mind, and Mommy is willing to give in reluctantly to the men's wishes. Football season is now over, but a good third baseman will take the field next spring."[10]

This story illustrates two themes that clarify managerial attitudes toward human relations. The first, as I have suggested, is to seek out activity with other people (i.e., the football team), and the second is to maintain a low level of emotional involvement in these relationships. The low emotional involvement appears in the writer's use of conventional metaphors, even clichés, and in the depiction of the ready transformation of potential conflict into harmonious decisions. In this case, Junior, Mommy, and Daddy agree to give up the violin for manly sports.

These two themes may seem paradoxical, but their coexistence supports what a manager does, including reconciling differences, seeking compromises, and establishing a balance of power. A further idea demonstrated by how the manager wrote the story is that managers may lack empathy, or the capacity to sense intuitively the thoughts and feelings of others. To illustrate attempts to be empathic, here is another story written to the same stimulus picture by someone considered by his peers to be a leader:

"This little boy has the appearance of being a sincere artist, one who is deeply affected by the violin, and has an intense desire to master the instrument.

"He seems to have just completed his normal practice session and appears to be somewhat crestfallen at his inability to produce the sounds which he is sure lie within the violin.

"He appears to be in the process of making a vow to himself to expend the necessary time and effort to play this instrument until he satisfies himself that he is able to bring forth the qualities of music which he feels within himself.

"With this type of determination and carry through, this boy became one of the great violinists of his day."[11]

Empathy is not simply a matter of paying attention to other people. It is also the capacity to take in emotional signals and to make them mean something in a relationship with an individual. People who describe another person as "deeply affected" with "intense desire," as capable of feeling "crestfallen" and as one who can "vow to himself," would seem to have an inner perceptiveness that they can use in their relationships with others.

Managers relate to people according to the role they play in a sequence of events or in a decision-making *process*, while leaders, who are concerned with ideas, relate in more intuitive and empathic ways. The manager's orientation to people, as actors in a sequence of events, deflects his or her attention away from the substance of people's concerns and toward their roles in a process. The distinction is simply between a manager's attention to *how* things get done and a leader's to *what* the events and decisions mean to participants.

In recent years, managers have taken over from game theory the notion that decision-making events can be one of two types: the win-lose situation (or zero-sum game) or the win-win situation in which everybody in the action comes out ahead. As part of the process of reconciling differences among people and maintaining balances of power, managers strive to convert win-lose into win-win situations.

As an illustration, take the decision of how to allocate capital resources among operating divisions in a large, decentralized organization. On the face of it, the dollars available for distribution are limited at any given time. Presumably, therefore, the more one division gets, the less is available for other divisions.

Managers tend to view this situation (as it affects human relations) as a conversion issue: how to make what seems like a win-lose problem into a win-win problem. Several solutions to this situation come to mind. First, the manager focuses others' attention on procedure and not on substance. Here the actors become engrossed in the bigger problem of *how* to make decisions, not *what* decisions to make. Once committed to the bigger problem, the actors have to support the outcome since they were involved in formulating decision rules. Because the actors believe in the rules they formulated, they will accept present losses in the expectation that next time they will win.

Second, the manager communicates to his subordinates indirectly, using "signals" instead of "messages." A signal has a number of possible implicit positions in it while a message clearly states a position. Signals are inconclusive and subject to reinterpretation should people become upset and angry, while messages involve the direct consequence that some people will indeed not like what they hear. The nature of messages heightens emotional response, and, as I have indicated, emotionally makes managers anxious. With signals, the question of who wins and who loses often becomes obscured.

Third, the manager plays for time. Managers seem to recognize that with the passage of time and the delay of major decisions, compromises emerge that take the sting out of win-lose situations; and the original "game" will be superseded by additional ones. Therefore, compromises may mean that one wins and loses simultaneously, depending on which of the games one evaluates.

There are undoubtedly many other tactical moves managers use to change human situations from win-lose to win-win. But the point to be made is that such tactics focus on the decision-making process itself and interest managers rather than leaders. The interest in tactics involves costs as well as benefits, including making organizations fatter in bureaucratic and political intrigue and leaner in direct, hard activity and warm human relationships. Consequently, one often hears subordinates characterize managers as inscrutable, detached, and manipulative. These adjectives arise from the subordinates' perception that they are linked together in a process whose purpose, beyond simply making decisions, is to maintain a controlled as well as rational and equitable structure. These adjectives suggest that managers need order in the face of the potential chaos that many fear in human relationships.

In contrast, one often hears leaders referred to in adjectives rich in emotional content. Leaders attract strong feelings of identity and difference, or of love and hate. Human relations in leader-dominated structures often appear turbulent, intense, and at times even disorganized. Such an atmosphere intensifies individual motivation and often produces unanticipated outcomes. Does this intense motivation lead to innovation and high performance, or does it represent wasted energy?

Senses of Self

In *The Varieties of Religious Experience*, William James describes two basic personality types, "once-born" and "twice-born."[12] People of the former personality type are those for whom adjustments to life have been straightforward and whose lives have been more or less a peaceful flow from the moment of their births. The twice-borns, on the other hand, have not had an easy time of it. Their lives are marked by a continual struggle to attain some sense of order. Unlike the once-borns they cannot take things for granted. According to James, these personalities have equally different world views. For a once-born personality, the sense of self, as a guide to conduct and attitude, derives from a feeling of being at home and in harmony with one's environment. For a twice-born, the sense of self derives from a feeling of profound separateness.

A sense of belonging or of being separate has a practical significance for the kinds of investments managers and leaders make in their careers. Managers see themselves as conservators and regulators of an existing order of affairs with which they personally identify and from which they gain rewards. Perpetuating and strengthening existing institutions enhances a manager's sense of self-worth: he or she is performing in a role that harmonizes with the ideals of duty and responsibility. William James had this harmony in mind—this sense of self as flowing easily to and from the outer world—in defining a once-born personality. If one feels oneself as a member of institutions, contributing to their well-being, then one fulfills a mission in life and feels rewarded for having measured up to ideals. This reward transcends material gains and answers the more fundamental desire for personal integrity which is achieved by identifying with existing institutions.

Leaders tend to be twice-born personalities, people who feel separate from their environment, including other people. They may work in organizations, but they never belong to them. Their sense of who they are does not depend upon memberships, work roles, or other social indicators of identity. What seems to follow from this idea about separateness is some theoretical basis for explaining why certain individuals search out opportunities for change. The methods to bring about change may be technological, political, or ideological, but the object is the same: to profoundly alter human, economic, and political relationships.

Sociologists refer to the preparation individuals undergo to perform in roles as the socialization process. Where individuals experience themselves as an integral part of the social structure (their self-esteem gains strength through participation and conformity), social standards exert powerful effects in maintaining the individual's personal sense of continuity, even beyond the early years in the family. The line of development from the family to schools, then to career is cumulative and reinforcing. When the line of development is not reinforcing because of significant disruptions in relationships or other problems experienced in the family or other social institutions, the individual turns inward and struggles to establish self-esteem, identity, and order. Here the psychological dynamics center on the experience with loss and the efforts at recovery.

In considering the development of leadership, we have to examine two different courses of life history: (1) development through socialization, which prepares the individual to guide institutions and to maintain the existing balance of social relations; and (2) development through personal mastery, which impels an individual to struggle for psychological and social change. Society produces its managerial talent through the first line of development, while through the second leaders emerge.

Development of Leadership

The development of every person begins in the family. Each person experiences the traumas associated with separating from his or her parents, as well as the pain that follows such frustration. In the same vein, all individuals face the difficulties of achieving self-regulation and self-control. But for some, perhaps a majority, the fortunes of childhood provide adequate gratifications and sufficient opportunities to find substitutes for rewards no longer available. Such individuals, the "once-borns," make moderate identifications with parents and find a harmony between what they expect and what they are able to realize from life.

But suppose the pains of separation are amplified by a combination of parental demands and the individual's needs to the degree that a sense of isolation, of being special, and of wariness disrupts the bonds that attach children to parents and other authority figures? Under such conditions, and given a special aptitude, the origins of which remain mysterious, the person becomes deeply involved in his or her inner world at the expense of interest in the outer world. For such a person, self-esteem no longer depends solely upon positive attachments and real rewards. A form of self-reliance takes hold along with expectations of performance and achievement, and perhaps even the desire to do great works.

Such self-perceptions can come to nothing if the individual's talents are negligible. Even with strong talents, there are no guarantees that achievement will follow, let alone that the end result will be for good rather than evil. Other factors enter into development. For one thing, leaders are like artists and other gifted people who often struggle with neuroses; their ability to function varies considerably even over the short run, and some potential leaders may lose the struggle altogether. Also, beyond early childhood, the patterns of development that affect managers and leaders involve the selective influence of particular people. Just as they appear flexible and evenly distributed in the types of talents available for development, managers form moderate and widely distributed attachments. Leaders, on the other hand, establish, and also break off, intensive one-to-one relationships.

It is a common observation that people with great talents are often only indifferent students. No one, for example, could have predicted Einstein's great achievements on the basis of his mediocre record in school. The reason for mediocrity is obviously not the absence of ability. It may result, instead, from self-absorption and the inability to pay attention to the ordinary tasks at hand. The only sure way an individual can interrupt reverie-like preoccupation and self-absorption is to form a deep attachment to a great teacher or other benevolent person who understands and has the ability to communicate with the gifted individual.

Whether gifted individuals find what they need in one-to-one relationships depends on the availability of sensitive and intuitive mentors who have a vocation in cultivating talent. Fortunately, when the generations do meet and the self-selections occur, we learn more about how to develop leaders and how talented people of different generations influence each other.

While apparently destined for a mediocre career, people who form important one-to-one relationships are able to accelerate and intensify their development through an apprenticeship. The background for such apprenticeships, or the psychological readiness of an individual to benefit from an intensive relationship, depends upon some experience in life that forces the individual to turn inward. A case example will make this point clearer. This example comes from the life of Dwight David Eisenhower, and illustrates the transformation of a career from competent to outstanding.[13]

Dwight Eisenhower's early career in the Army foreshadowed very little about his future development. During World War I, while some of his West Point classmates were already experiencing the war firsthand in France, Eisenhower felt "embedded in the monotony and unsought safety of the Zone of the Interior . . . that was intolerable punishment."[14]

Shortly after World War I, Eisenhower, then a young officer somewhat pessimistic about his career chances, asked for a transfer to Panama to work under General Fox Connor, a senior officer whom Eisenhower admired. The army turned down Eisenhower's request. This setback was very much on Eisenhower's mind when Ikey, his first-born son, succumbed to influenza. By some sense of responsibility for its own, the army transferred Eisenhower to Panama, where he took up his duties under General Connor with the shadow of his lost son very much upon him.

In a relationship with the kind of father he would have wanted to be, Eisenhower reverted to being the son he lost. In this highly charged situation, Eisenhower began to learn from his mentor. General Connor offered, and Eisenhower gladly took, a magnificent tutorial on the military. The effects of this relationship on Eisenhower cannot be measured quantitatively, but, in Eisenhower's own reflections and the unfolding of his career, one cannot overestimate its significance in the reintegration of a person shattered by grief.

As Eisenhower wrote later about Connor, "Life with General Connor was a sort of graduate school in military affairs and the humanities, leavened by a man who was experienced in his knowledge of men and their conduct. I can never adequately express my gratitude to this one gentleman. . . . In a lifetime of association with great and good men, he is the one more or less invisible figure to whom I owe an incalculable debt."[15]

Some time after his tour of duty with General Connor, Eisenhower's breakthrough occurred. He received orders to attend the Command and General Staff School at Fort Leavenworth, one of the most competitive schools in the army. It was a coveted appointment, and Eisenhower took advantage of the opportunity. Unlike his performance in high school and West Point, his work at the Command School was excellent; he was graduated first in his class.

Psychological biographies of gifted people repeatedly demonstrate the important part a mentor plays in developing an individual. Andrew Carnegie owed much to his senior, Thomas A. Scott. As head of the Western Division of the Pennsylvania Railroad, Scott recognized talent and the desire to learn in the young telegrapher assigned to him. By giving Carnegie increasing responsibility and by providing him with the opportunity to learn through close personal observation, Scott added to Carnegie's self-confidence and sense of achievement. Because of his own personal strength and achievement, Scott did not fear Carnegie's aggressiveness. Rather, he gave it full play in encouraging Carnegie's initiative.

Mentors take risks with people. They bet initially on talent they perceive in younger people. Mentors also risk emotional involvement in working closely with their juniors. The risks do not always pay off, but the willingness to take them appears crucial in developing leaders.

Can Organizations Develop Leaders?

The examples I have given of how leaders develop suggest the importance of personal influence and the one-to-one relationship. For organizations to encourage consciously the development of leaders as compared with managers would mean developing one-to-one relationships between junior and senior executives and, more important, fostering a culture of individualism and possibly elitism. The elitism arises out of the desire to identify talent and other qualities suggestive of the ability to lead and not simply to manage.

The Jewel Companies Inc. enjoy a reputation for developing talented people. The chairman and chief executive officer, Donald S. Perkins, is perhaps a good example of a person brought along through the mentor approach. Franklin J. Lunding, who was Perkins's mentor, expressed the philosophy of taking risks with young people this way:

"Young people today want in on the action. They don't want to sit around for six months trimming lettuce."[16]

This statement runs counter to the culture that attaches primary importance to slow progression based on experience and proved competence. It is a high-risk philosophy, one that requires time for the attachment between senior and junior people to grow and be meaningful, and one that is bound to produce more failures than successes.

The elitism is an especially sensitive issue. At Jewel the MBA degree symbolized the elite. Lunding attracted Perkins to Jewel at a time when business school graduates had little interest in retailing in general, and food distribution in particular. Yet the elitism seemed to pay off: not only did Perkins become the president at age 37, but also under the leadership of young executives recruited into Jewel with the promise of opportunity for growth and advancement, Jewel managed to diversify into discount and drug chains and still remain strong in food retailing. By assigning each recruit to a vice president who acted as sponsor, Jewel evidently tried to build a structure around the mentor approach to developing leaders. To counteract the elitism implied in such an approach, the company also introduced an "equalizer" in what Perkins described as "the first assistant philosophy." Perkins stated:

"Being a good first assistant means that each management person thinks of himself not as the order-giving, domineering boss, but as the first assistant to those who 'report' to him in a more typical organizational sense. Thus we mentally turn our organizational charts upside-down and challenge ourselves to seek ways in which we can lead ... by helping ... by teaching ... by listening ... and by managing in the true democratic sense ... that is, with the consent of the managed. Thus the satisfactions of leadership come from helping others to get things done and changed—and not from getting credit for doing and changing things ourselves."[17]

While this statement would seem to be more egalitarian than elitist, it does reinforce a youth-oriented culture since it defines the senior officer's job as primarily helping the junior person.

A myth about how people learn and develop that seems to have taken hold in the American culture also dominates thinking in business. The myth is that people learn best from their peers. Supposedly, the threat of evaluation and even humiliation recedes in peer relations because of the tendency for mutual identification and the social restraints on authoritarian behavior among equals. Peer training in organizations occurs in various forms. The use, for example, of task forces made up of peers from several interested occupational groups (sales, production, research, and finance) supposedly removes the restraints of authority on the individual's willingness to assert and exchange ideas. As a result, so the theory goes, people interact more freely, listen more objectively to criticism and other points of view and, finally, learn from this healthy interchange.

Another application of peer training exists in some large corporations, such as Philips, N.V. in Holland, where organization structure is built on the principle of joint responsibility of two peers, one representing the commercial end of the business and the other the technical. Formally, both hold equal responsibility for geographic operations or product groups, as the case may be. As a practical matter, it may turn out that one or the other of the peers dominates the management. Nevertheless, the main interaction is between two or more equals.

The principal question I would raise about such arrangements is whether they perpetuate the managerial orientation, and preclude the formation of one-to-one relationships between senior people and potential leaders.

Aware of the possible stifling effects of peer relationships on aggressiveness and individual initiative, another company, much smaller than Philips, utilizes joint responsibility of peers for operating units, with one important difference. The chief executive of this company encourages competition and rivalry among peers, ultimately appointing the one who comes out on top for increased responsibility. These hybrid arrangements produce some unintended consequences that can be disastrous. There is no easy way to limit rivalry. Instead, it permeates all levels of the operation and opens the way for the formation of cliques in an atmosphere of intrigue.

A large, integrated oil company has accepted the importance of developing leaders through the direct influence of senior on junior executives. One chairman and chief executive officer regularly selected one talented university graduate whom he appointed his special assistant, and with whom he would work closely for a year. At the end of the year, the junior executive would become available for assignment to one of the operating divisions, where he would be assigned to a responsible post rather than a training position. The mentor relationship had acquainted the junior executive firsthand with the use of power, and with the important antidotes to the power disease called *hubris*—performance and integrity.

Working in one-to-one relationships, where there is a formal and recognized difference in the power of the actors, takes a great deal of tolerance for emotional interchange. This interchange, inevitable in close working arrangements, probably accounts for the reluctance of many executives to become involved in such relationships. *Fortune* carried an interesting story on the departure of a key executive, John W. Hanley, from the top management of Procter & Gamble, for the chief executive officer position at Monsanto.[18] According to this account, the chief executive and chairman of P&G passed over Hanley for appointment to the presidency and named another executive vice president to this post instead.

The chairman evidently felt he could not work well with Hanley who, by his own acknowledgement, was aggressive, eager to experiment and change practices, and constantly challenged his superior. A chief executive officer naturally has the right to select people with whom he feels congenial. But I wonder whether a greater capacity on the part of senior officers to tolerate the competitive impulses and behavior of their subordinates might not be healthy for corporations. At least a greater tolerance for interchange would not favor the managerial team player at the expense of the individual who might become a leader.

I am constantly surprised at the frequency with which chief executives feel threatened by open challenges to their ideas, as though the source of their authority, rather than their specific ideas, were at issue. In one case a chief executive officer, who was troubled by the aggressiveness and sometimes outright rudeness of one of his talented vice presidents, used various indirect methods such as group meetings and hints from outside directors to avoid dealing with his subordinate. I advised the executive to deal head-on with what irritated him. I suggested that by direct, face-to-face confrontation, both he and his subordinate would learn to validate the distinction between the authority to be preserved and the issues to be debated.

To confront is also to tolerate aggressive interchange, and has the net effect of stripping away the veils of ambiguity and signaling so characteristic of managerial cultures, as well as encouraging the emotional relationship leaders need if they are to survive.

REFERENCES

1. John D. Rockefeller, 3rd., *The Second American Revolution* (New York: Harper-Row, 1973), p. 72.

2. Theodore Levitt, "Management and the Post Industrial Society," *The Public Interest*, Summer 1976, p. 73.

3. Alfred P. Sloan, Jr., *My Years with General Motors* (Garden City, N.Y.: Doubleday & Co., 1964), p. 429.

4. Ibid., p. 429.

5. Ibid., p. 440.

6. Ibid., p. 91.

7. Ibid., p. 91.

8. Ibid., p. 93.

9. Stanley and Inge Hoffmann, "The Will for Grandeur: de Gaulle as Political Artist," *Daedalus*, Summer 1968, p. 849.

10. Abraham Zaleznik, Gene W. Dalton, and Louis B. Barnes, *Orientation and Conflict in Career* (Boston: Division of Research, Harvard Business School, 1970), p. 316.

11. Ibid., p. 294.

12. William James, *Varieties of Religious Experience* (New York: Mentor Books, 1958).

13. This example is included in Abraham Zaleznik and Manfred F.R. Kets de Vries, *Power and the Corporate Mind* (Boston: Houghton Mifflin, 1975).

14. Dwight D. Eisenhower, *At Ease: Stories I Tell to Friends* (Garden City, N.Y.: Doubleday, 1967), p. 136.

15. Ibid., p. 187.

16. "Jewel Lets Young Men Make Mistakes," *Business Week*, January 17, 1970, p. 90.

17. "What Makes Jewel Shine so Bright," *Progressive Grocer*, September, 1973, p. 76.

18. "Jack Hanley Got There by Selling Harder," *Fortune*, November, 1976.

6

Who Gets Promoted?

ALFRED W. SWINYARD AND FLOYD A. BOND

Here are some of the important trends we discovered in a survey of more than 11,000 executives taken at the time they were promoted to vice president or president of a major U.S. company:

New entrants into the ranks of U.S. top management are better educated than their predecessors and their nonbusiness peers.

The largest percentage of advanced degrees are held in business administration (advanced degrees in law and engineering are next most prevalent).

At the same time, the newly promoted executives are not likely to be any younger than their forebears when they "make the grade."

Those who reach the level of president in their organizations will most likely have been group vice presidents (not senior or executive vice presidents) chosen from inside the company, and they will probably not have spent more than four years in their previous positions.

Top executives now tend to be more mobile because of changes in promotional patterns and in their own opportunities. This tendency is increasing and may prove beneficial in the long run, given the superior educational backgrounds and more diversified business experiences of the candidates.

These findings come from our research on high-level executives promoted during the period 1967 through 1976. Our research effort's main purpose was to identify the character of a new, seemingly younger breed of top manager, about whom exceedingly little has been written. (Most recent books, research reports, and articles on the characteristics of the U.S. business executive concentrate on longtime members of the executive family listed in standard directories.)

In fact, we know of no longitudinal study that relies on in-depth surveys to analyze the characteristics of newly promoted executives—executives who will be leading U.S. industry in the coming decade. What we discovered is reassuring and reinforces the overall impression that, as a whole, American business people are now better informed and more sophisticated—just at the time they most need to be. (For a more detailed analysis of our methods and survey, see page 83.)

Better Educated at the Top

The newly promoted executive is indeed well educated. More than ever before, he or she is certain to have gone to college and, increasingly, to graduate school. In fact, as a group, the executives in our study have more formal education than either the general population or their college peers.

The percentage of those participating in the study without college degrees, for example, dropped from about 18% in 1967 to 11% in 1976—a decline of 39%. At the same time, the percentage of executives holding a master's degree increased from 18% to 25%—a rise of 39% (see *Exhibit I*).

In contrast, the percentage of executives completing only a bachelor's degree remained relatively constant. Law degree recipients also made up about the same portion in 1976 as in 1967, but the percentage reporting other advanced degrees (such as PhDs or MDs) increased slightly. In total, the proportion of graduate degrees increased from 33% in 1967 to 41% in 1976.

These trends are consistent with earlier studies.[1] When we compared our 1976 data to Mabel Newcomer's 1950 data, we saw that, proportionately, (1) only one-tenth as many executives reported highest educational level as high school or less, (2) only half as many reported highest level achieved as some college education but no degree, and (3) more than twice as many held graduate degrees.

Data from other sources reveal some differences between our executives and their fellow Americans of the same age. Figures available from the National Center for Educational Statistics, for example, indicate that over the period 1947–1957, when about 60% of our executives completed their educations, only 16% as many master's as bachelor's degrees were awarded in the United States. For those 60% from our study, however, the ratio was more than double.

Specific Fields of Interest

The information about our executives' undergraduate education shows that their most common field of study was business administration (27%), followed closely by engineering (26%), and social and behavioral science—including economics (22%). Fully 42% of those with undergraduate degrees went on to the graduate level.

Graduate degrees in business administration and management attracted the largest portion of our sample group. The percentage of newly promoted executives who reported their highest degree in business administration increased dramatically between 1967 and 1976 (see *Exhibit II*). Among those with bachelor's degrees in business administration who did graduate work, two-thirds achieved a master's degree in the same field, while one-third secured a law degree.

Of executives who got a bachelor's in engineering and then sought further education, about half studied business administration and about half studied law. More than half of those receiving their undergraduate degrees in the social and behavioral sciences (including economics) earned graduate or professional degrees. Most received advanced degrees in business administration, nearly a third in law, and the remainder in economics or other fields.

A summary of the educational choices of executives earning graduate degrees shows that 45% chose business administration as their major field. Law was the second choice, followed by engineering. (It is interesting to note that nearly 25%

Exhibit I Highest Degree Obtained (1967 & 1976)

Highest degree	Percentage of executives	
	1967	1976
High school graduate or less	6%	3%
Some college education	12	8
Bachelor's degree	49	48
Master's degree	18	25
Law degree	12	11
Doctorate (PhD, MD, etc.)	3	5

Exhibit II Area of Highest Degree of Newly Promoted Executives (1967 & 1976)

Area of highest degree	Percentage of executives	
	1967	1976
Business administration	22%	33%
Engineering	22	18
Law	12	11
Mathematics & science	8	6
Economics	6	6
Social & behavioral science (excluding economics)	3	5
All other	7	6
N.A. by field	2	4
No degree	18	11

of the newly promoted executives with law degrees also had undergraduate degrees in business administration.)

When separating the data by industry, we discovered some variations on the theme. Fully 33 industries (with at least 200 executives in each one) are represented by our group. But in only 14 of them did more than 40% report graduate degrees; the leaders include pharmaceuticals, real estate and land development (the field with the highest percentage of lawyers), investment banking, communications, chemicals, printing and publishing, and electronics and electronic products. Industries with less than 30% of the executives reporting graduate degrees included apparel, textiles, and construction.

The Impact of Age on Management Succession

Just as professors insist that students get younger every year, many older executives claim that the "up and coming" types are appointed at steadily younger ages. Our data, however, refute this contention. In fact, the median age of the newly promoted executives in 1967, in 1976, and for the ten-year period as a whole was 47. Slight variations occurred from year to year, but the age of the entire group remained relatively constant.

However, there are definite variations on the basis of executive position. The age of presidents who were also CEOs varied only slightly on an annual basis, hovering around 47. But presidents who were not CEOs had a median age of 49, and presidents of subsidiaries, divisions, or groups had a median age of 46.

This is similar to the case of vice presidents; executive vice presidents tended to be about three years older than group vice presidents or vice presidents, while

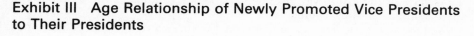

Exhibit III   Age Relationship of Newly Promoted Vice Presidents to Their Presidents

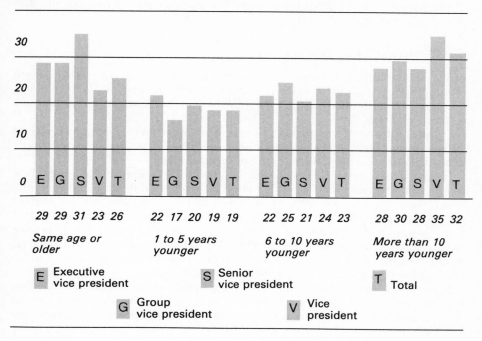

Percentage
40%

	Same age or older	1 to 5 years younger	6 to 10 years younger	More than 10 years younger
E G S V T	29 29 31 23 26	22 17 20 19 19	22 25 21 24 23	28 30 28 35 32

E Executive vice president

G Group vice president

S Senior vice president

V Vice president

T Total

the median age for senior vice presidents fell in the middle at about 47. Of the total group, 50% of the executives were between the ages of 42 and 53, with 25% younger and 25% older.

Future Career Prospects

One part of the questionnaire shed some light on future career prospects for the executives in our sample. We asked more than 6,000 vice presidents to report the age of their companies' presidents. The median age turned out to be 54, with 26% between the ages of 56 and 60, and with 13% who were 61 or older.

If we consider retirement age to be 65, we could reasonably postulate that 13% of these presidents would have to be replaced within five years, and nearly 40% within ten. But if we also assume that more than five years' service is required for any executive to be considered a candidate for president, we see that almost 42% of the newly promoted vice presidents would be too old to get the job.

Further, the future is markedly less promising for executive and senior vice presidents (who are usually the same age as or less than five years younger than their presidents) than for group vice presidents (see *Exhibit III*). That leaves about 55% of the group vice presidents as logical candidates for promotion to the presidency of their companies.

Even so, with a median age of about 46, the current new vice presidents look forward to a career that will average about another 20 years. Since many seem to be blocked from the top position in their own companies because of the age of the person they would replace, there is reason to believe that the number changing companies will increase.

What They Did Before

Two aspects of the executives' career experiences are noteworthy: length of time spent with their present companies and nature of their previous positions—including how much time they spent in that position. The first aspect is shown in *Exhibit IV*.

For the purpose of our survey, all executives were given the opportunity to indicate if they had "recently joined" their companies. A yes answer would imply that they had been hired away from another company.

In most cases, presidents reported they had a fairly long history with their companies. The presidents who were also CEOs reported that they had recently joined their companies in 24% of the cases, and they had the shortest median period of service—ten years. The percentage of other executives who had joined recently was lower, only 11% of executive and senior vice presidents. Executive vice presidents had the longest median period of service—16 years. For the total group over the decade, only 17% had recently joined their companies. Twelve years was the median length of service for all executives.

Before becoming president, an executive generally varies position often within the company. Although they may have spent a considerable amount of time in the organization, 59% of our executives had held their previous positions for less than four years—with a median of 3.4 years.

Prior Experience Varies

Our executives' previous experience ranged from general management (here considered to include operations management, division management, and administration) to functional areas (finance, marketing, manufacturing, corporate planning, and other activities). The four most common areas reported were operations (36%), finance (18%), and administration and marketing (both at 15%). Only 5% of the executives reported prior experience in corporate planning.

When we look at previous experience along position lines, we see that certain positions seem to link up with certain kinds of experience. Previous experience in operations or division management ranked first in all positions and was reported by 43% to 65% of the group vice presidents and three types of presidents (see *Exhibit IV* for a list of the varieties of presidents). Finance was a strong second among executive vice presidents and senior vice presidents, while marketing was in second position among the presidents of subsidiaries, divisions, or groups.

The data support the contention, made in a number of recent studies, that there is a decline in the percentage of top executives coming from the field of

How the Survey Was Taken

Our study includes 11,227 executives who responded to a questionnaire shortly after they became vice presidents or presidents of major U.S. corporations. Data were consistently collected on a timely basis and reported back annually to cooperating executives. The response rate of the over 20,000 executives contacted ranged from 47% to 60% on an annual basis; responses ranged from more than 800 to more than 1,300 per year.

The executives represent a good cross section of the executive community working with large companies in diversified industries throughout the United States. Following is the regional variation:

Region	Distribution (percentage)		
	1967	1976	Ten-year total
New England	7.8%	8.1%	7.0%
Mid-Atlantic	36.1	27.9	35.1
South Atlantic	2.6	5.8	5.0
East north central	28.7	24.5	25.4
East south central	1.7	2.0	1.8
West north central	5.5	7.4	6.4
West south central	4.7	8.8	6.0
Mountain	1.4	2.9	1.5
Pacific	9.5	9.5	9.6
Other & outside the U.S.	2.0	3.1	2.2
	100%	100%	100%

Our study covered highly diversified business activities. Following is the distribution of respondents by major industry groups for the ten-year period:

Industry group	Percentage of executives*
Durable manufacturing	48.1%
Nondurable manufacturing	39.2
Retail & wholesale trade	8.2
Business services	6.7
Finance, insurance & real estate	19.4
Regulated industries	16.2
Other	12.0

*Because of multiple responses in some instances, the total does not add up to 100%.

At least 500 respondents were in electronics, fabricated metals, chemicals, food, petroleum, retail trade, banking, insurance, public utilities, or transportation. Thirty-six industry groups were each mentioned by more than 200 executives.

About 31% of those comprising the study group were presidents; 29% were senior, executive, or group vice presidents; and 40% were vice presidents. Over three-quarters of the group worked in industrial companies with annual sales volumes of more than $100 million. A slightly higher percentage of vice presidents than presidents were employed in larger organizations.

Exhibit IV Time with Present Company, by Position, of Newly Promoted Executives

Position	Percentage recently joined	Median years with company
President & CEO	24%	10 yrs.
President, not CEO	16	13
President of subsidiary, division, or group	17	10
Executive vice president	11	16
Group vice president	17	11
Senior vice president	11	15
Vice president	18	12
Total	17	12

marketing. These other studies blame the decline on changing business environments and on the focus of various educational programs.

Our study suggests something else: the average marketing executive may no longer have the requisite educational background to reach the top. Patterns among more than 6,000 vice presidents in our sample show that only 17% of the marketing vice presidents had MBA degrees, compared with 30% of the finance and accounting vice presidents. The data can be looked at in another way—21% of the marketing vice presidents had no college degree, in contrast to only 8% without a bachelor's for those in finance or accounting.

Educational Background and Age

Younger executives pushing into the ranks of top management are generally better educated than their predecessors. *Exhibit V* plots the median age of the newly promoted manager by type of educational background rather than position. This exhibit also suggests that an executive with an MBA does have a clearer road to the top at an earlier age.

Newly promoted executives with MBA degrees had a median age of 44, whereas executives with other types of graduate education—such as a master's degree in another discipline or a law, doctoral, or medical degree—had a median age of 47. Executives with only a bachelor's degree had a median age of 48, while those without a college degree had a median age of 51. The median age differentials show executives with MBA degrees moving up more quickly; they are three years younger than executives with other types of advanced degrees, four years younger than those with bachelor's degrees, and seven years younger than executives without college degrees.

As we would normally expect, younger executives have been employed by their companies a shorter period of time than older ones. Newly promoted executives with advanced degrees had a median number of between seven and nine years with their companies. In contrast, executives with only bachelor's degrees had a median of 14 years, and those without college degrees, 20 years.

Exhibit V   Age, by Educational Background, of Newly Promoted Executives

Type of education	Age 35	40	45	50	55

MBA*

Other master's degrees

Law degree

Doctorate

Bachelor's degree

No college degree

Total

Mid-range (2nd & 3rd quartile)   Median

*Includes all master's degrees (MBA and others) in business administration. The MBA represents more than 90% of the group.

The executives with advanced degrees also reported more frequently that they had "recently joined" their respective companies. For example, 26% of the executives with doctoral or medical degrees and 23% with MBA degrees said they had "recently joined." The figure drops to 16% for executives with only a bachelor's degree and to 12% among those without any degree.

According to the survey, executives with advanced degrees are well represented at all levels of the top executive family. A slightly higher percentage (up to 35%) of the older executive groups are presidents, and it is these groups that have less education. More important, these older groups with less formal education have fewer vice presidents among them, and we can expect that the normal course of management succession will continue to reduce the number in top executive ranks.

Current evidence indicates that these education-linked promotion trends are, in fact, accelerating. Already in the beginning of the 1980s, about 25% of all newly promoted top executives hold MBA degrees—representing a 39% increase over the average for the decade covered by our study.

Are Old School Ties Important?

Surveys of executive characteristics sometimes concentrate on the known facts of education and experience and forget the importance of such personal attributes as determination and ambition. But the completion of graduate and professional programs is, of course, one important indication of these personal qualities, as is the type of school chosen—some traditionally require more personal determination and dedication than others. Exhibit VI lists the 15 leading schools from which our executives received their degrees.

At the bachelor's degree level, these top 15 schools awarded 30% of the total degrees. However, the leading schools do not dominate executive undergraduate education to the point that we need fear formation of a clique by future executives who have all been educated in the same tradition. Nor do these patterns of education suggest that access to the top executive community is limited to those from affluent families.

On the graduate and professional level, there is a more significant concentration of degrees in a few leading schools. Harvard heads the list. Its percentage of master's degrees awarded is nearly as large as the next five schools combined. In the case of law degrees, Harvard's 15% exceeds the combined percentages of the next two schools. Overall, it is the most frequent source of their highest degree.

The presence among the leaders of several large urban schools with well recognized evening MBA programs is significant. It points up the goal orientation and perseverance shown by some executives — who continue their educational programs despite heavy work loads.

For the most part, the schools listed by our executives include the same schools (and in about the same order) as those named in other recent studies of business executives. The current lists, however, are more diversified than those in the older studies.

A Summary of Trends

While the results of our study tend to fall in line with generally recognized historical trends, they underscore the necessity for adjustments both in our educational system and in our way of thinking about managers. Because the changes taking place were so rapid, we were able to see them clearly in a single decade. We have come to the conclusion that institutions — and commonly held opinions — are not adjusting with the same rapidity.

Exhibit VI The 15 Leading Schools from which Newly Promoted Executives Received Degrees

	Percentage receiving the degree		Percentage receiving the degree
Bachelor's degree		*Law degree*	
Yale University	3.6%	Harvard University	15.7%
Harvard University	2.7	University of Michigan	6.1
University of Michigan	2.5	Columbia University	6.1
Princeton University	2.3	Yale University	4.7
Cornell University	2.2	New York University	3.7
University of Illinois	2.1	Fordham University	3.0
University of Minnesota	1.9	University of Virginia	2.9
Dartmouth College	1.8	Cornell University	2.6
Massachusetts Institute of Technology	1.7	George Washington University	2.0

University of Wisconsin	1.6	University of Chicago	2.0
University of Pennsylvania	1.6	University of Pennsylvania	1.9
Northwestern University	1.6	Georgetown University	1.8
New York University	1.5	University of Illinois	1.5
Purdue University	1.5	University of Wisconsin	1.5
Stanford University	1.5	Stanford University	1.4
Total	30.1%	Total	56.9%
Master's degree		*Highest degree*	
Harvard University	22.5%	Harvard University	9.8%
New York University	6.1	New York University	3.2
Columbia University	4.9	University of Michigan	2.8
Massachusetts Institute of Technology	4.7	Columbia University	2.7
Stanford University	4.1	Massachusetts Institute of Technology	2.7
University of Chicago	3.9	Yale University	2.6
University of Michigan	3.6	University of Pennsylvania	2.3
University of Pennyslvania	3.2	University of Illinois	2.1
Northwestern University	1.9	Stanford University	2.0
Dartmouth College	1.5	Cornell University	1.8
Cornell University	1.3	University of Minnesota	1.8
University of Illinois	1.2	University of Chicago	1.7
Ohio State University	1.2	Northwestern University	1.6
Rutgers University	1.2	University of Wisconsin	1.5
Indiana University	1.1	Princeton University	1.4
Total	62.4%	Total	40.0%

The most obvious change is in educational background; there is a marked increase in graduate and professional education among corporate executives, a decrease in the number of those without college degrees, and a continuing rise in the importance attached to the master's degree in business administration. Our future top executives will come more and more from those holding advanced degrees. Those in our survey without college diplomas or with only a BA were several years older than better educated executives on the same level.

Despite the fact that these data indicate a demand for increasing professionalism and graduate education, administrators and counselors seem preoccupied with outmoded relationships and unwilling to admit the implications of these long-term trends. Business administration will continue to hold its position as the major career choice of entering college students, particularly women, while traditional fields, such as education and science, decline. Our educational systems must adjust to the change both by continuing to upgrade the quality of education for business administration and by making it more readily available.

Besides this educational "uplifting," the other change we note is the increasing mobility of top executives. We expect a substantial proportion of highly qualified executives to be blocked from promotion for various reasons (either they will have advanced to a certain level at too young an age, will have been shifted to a senior or executive vice presidential position from which it will be difficult to leave, or will have fallen in the competition with their equally well-educated peers).

Any of these reasons could lead directly to a desire to change companies or to transfer within the management system. (The new mobility is already making its mark — reportedly there were more than 2,000 executive search organizations at the end of 1979.) We feel, however, that the high degree of mobility will not result in chaos; the executives will not only have superior educational backgrounds but will also have extremely diversified business experiences.

REFERENCE

1. See John E. Steele and Lewis B. Ward, "MBAs: Mobile, Well Situated, Well Paid," HBR January-February 1974, p. 99; and *The Big Business Executive/1964* (New York: Scientific-American Illustrated Library, 1965), p. 34. The latter study includes data from Mabel Newcomer, *The Big Business Executive — The Factors That Made Him*: 1900-1950 (New York: Columbia University Press, 1955).

7

The Heart of Entrepreneurship

HOWARD H. STEVENSON AND
DAVID E. GUMPERT

Suddenly entrepreneurship is in vogue. If only our nation's businesses —large and small—could become more entrepreneurial, the thinking goes, we would improve our productivity and compete more effectively in the world marketplace.

But what does entrepreneurial mean? Managers describe entrepreneurship with such terms as innovative, flexible, dynamic, risk taking, creative, and growth oriented. The popular press, on the other hand, often defines the term as starting and operating new ventures. That view is reinforced by the enticing success of such upstarts as Apple Computer, Domino's Pizza, and Lotus Development.

Neither approach to a definition of entrepreneurship is precise or prescriptive enough for managers who wish to be more entrepreneurial. Everybody wants to be innovative, flexible, and creative. But for every Apple, Domino's, and Lotus, there are thousands of new restaurants, clothing stores, and consulting firms that presumably have tried to be innovative, to grow, and to show other characteristics that are entrepreneurial in the dynamic sense—but have failed.

As for the idea of equating the beginning stages of a business with entrepreneurship, note a recent study by McKinsey & Company on behalf of the American Business Conference. It concluded that many mature, medium-sized companies, having annual sales of $25 million to $1 billion, consistently develop new products and markets and also grow at rates far exceeding national averages.[1] Moreover, we're all aware of many of the largest corporations—IBM, 3M, and Hewlett-Packard are just a few of the best known—that make a practice of innovating, taking risks, and showing creativity. And they continue to expand.

So the question for the would-be entrepreneur is: How can I make innovation, flexibility, and creativity operational? To help this person discover some answers, we must first look at entrepreneurial behavior.

At the outset we should discard the notion that entrepreneurship is an all-or-none trait that some people or organizations possess and others don't. Rather, we suggest viewing entrepreneurship in the context of a range of behavior. To simplify our analysis, it is useful to view managerial behavior in terms of extremes.

At one extreme is what we might call the *promoter* type of manager, who feels confident of his or her ability to seize opportunity. This manager expects sur-

Exhibit I   Manager's Opportunity Matrix

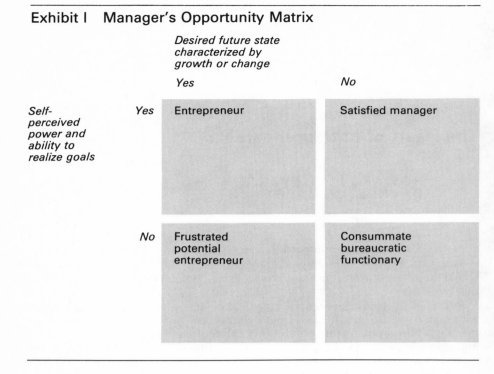

		Desired future state characterized by growth or change	
		Yes	No
Self-perceived power and ability to realize goals	Yes	Entrepreneur	Satisfied manager
	No	Frustrated potential entrepreneur	Consummate bureaucratic functionary

prises and expects not only to adjust to change but also to capitalize on it and make things happen. At the other extreme is the *trustee* type, who feels threatened by change and the unknown and whose inclination is to rely on the status quo. To the trustee type, predictability fosters effective management of existing resources while unpredictability endangers them.

Most people, of course, fall somewhere between the extremes. But it's safe to say that as managers move closer to the promoter end of the scale they become more entrepreneurial, and as they move toward the trustee end of the scale they become less so (or, perhaps, more "administrative").

When it comes to their own self-interest, the natural tendency of most people is toward the promoter end of our behavior spectrum; they know where their interests lie and pursue them aggressively. A person's most valuable assets are intelligence, energy, and experience—not money or other material things—which are well suited to the promoter role.

A close relationship exists between opportunity and individual needs. To be an entrepreneurial opportunity, a prospect must meet two tests: it must represent a desirable future state, involving growth or at least change; and the individual must believe it is possible to reach that state. This relationship often identifies four groups, which we show in *Exhibit I*.

Companies of all sizes encounter difficulty encouraging entrepreneurship when the individual's interest and the corporate interest don't coincide. Executives may enhance their position or boost their income by serving the status quo through short-term and readily measurable actions such as cost reduction or price cuts, even though such "accomplishments" may not help and may even hurt the company's long-term welfare.

To make the individual's tendency toward entrepreneurship match corporate goals and needs is no easy task for companies. First must come an understanding of the ways in which the promoter and trustee mentalities exert influence within the organization. In these pages we try to further such an understanding and we develop a framework for analyzing the essential aspects of entrepreneurship in companies of all sizes. We then use the framework to offer suggestions for encouraging entrepreneurship.

Entrepreneurial Process

Based as they often are on changes in the marketplace, pressures for extension of entrepreneurship tend to be external to the company. Limitations on entrepreneurial behavior tend to come from inside, the result of high-level decisions and the exigencies of hierarchy. In making decisions, administrators and entrepreneurs often proceed with a very different order of questions. The typical administrator asks:

What resources do I control?
What structure determines our organization's relationship to its market?
How can I minimize the impact of others on my ability to perform?
What opportunity is appropriate?

The entrepreneur, at the other end of the spectrum, tends to ask:

Where is the opportunity?
How do I capitalize on it?
What resources do I need?
How do I gain control over them?
What structure is best?

The impact of the difference in approach becomes apparent as we trace the entrepreneurial thought pattern.

Where Is the Opportunity?

Naturally, the first step is to identify the opportunity, which entails an external (or market) orientation rather than an internal (or resource) orientation. The promoter type is constantly attuned to environmental changes that may suggest a favorable chance, while the trustee type wants to preserve resources and reacts defensively to possible threats to deplete them. (See *Exhibit II*, part A.)

Entrepreneurs are not just opportunistic; they are also creative and innovative. The entrepreneur does not necessarily want to break new ground but perhaps just remix old ideas to make a seemingly new application. Many of today's fledgling microcomputer and software companies, for example, are merely altering existing technology slightly or repackaging it to accommodate newly perceived market segments.

The shakeout now going on in the publications aimed at cable TV subscribers illustrates good and bad reading of opportunity. In 1983 Time Inc. abandoned its *TV-Cable Week* after a pretax loss of $47 million. Still thriving is *The Cable Guide*, which is operated by two entrepreneurs marshaling a fraction of Time Inc.'s resources and working out of a town in Pennsylvania. By listing broadcast programs as well as those available on cable, *TV-Cable Week* aimed its content at viewers and thereby annoyed some cable operators. *The Cable Guide* focuses on cable-transmitted programs only, thereby pleasing the cable operators who distribute it.

Woolworth's recent difficulties demonstrate the challenge posed by changing opportunities. For many years the company thrived because it had the best retail locations in America's cities and towns. That approach worked fine as long as all the best locations remained in the centers of cities and in towns. As the best retail sites shifted to suburban and highway malls, however, Woolworth's was caught off guard and other mass merchandisers grabbed the new top locations. To survive, Woolworth's was forced into a defensive strategy of developing secondary suburban properties while closing old city stores.

Woolworth's is typical of many companies that, preoccupied with the strength of their resource base, are unable or unwilling to perceive momentous environmental changes. These companies turn opportunities into problems for fear of losing strength. For the entrepreneurial mentality, on the other hand, external pressures stimulate opportunity recognition. These pressures include rapid changes in:

1. Technology, which opens new doors and closes others. Advances in producing microcomputer chips helped make possible the personal computer market but at the same time shrank the minicomputer market. This development posed problems for those producers that failed to perceive the change quickly.

2. Consumer economics, which alters both the ability and willingness to pay for new products and services. The sharp rise in energy costs during the mid-1970s made popular the wood-burning stove and chain saw, and spawned the solar energy industry, among others. But these same pressures set back those huge sectors of our industrial economy that thrived on the belief in cheap energy forever.

3. Social values, which define new styles and standards of living. The burgeoning interest in physical fitness has opened up markets for special clothing, "natural" food, workout centers, and other businesses.

4. Political action and regulatory standards, which affect competition. Deregulation of airlines, financial services, and telecommunications has sparked opportunities for assorted new products and services while at the same time disrupting the economics of truckers, airlines, and many concerns in other sectors.

Unfortunately, innovation and the pursuit of opportunity impose a cost that many executives resist—the necessity of change. Like most other people, they tend to take comfort in routine and predictable situations. This is not because they are lazy; they are just more inclined to the administrative end of the organizational spectrum than to the entrepreneurial end. Among the internal pressures that move companies toward the administrative end are the following:

The "social contract." Managers feel a responsibility to employ human, manufacturing, technological, and financial resources once they have been acquired. The American steel industry, which had the best plants in the world during the 1950s but failed to update them in the face of rising foreign competition, is a prominent example of the social contract gone awry.

Performance criteria. Few executives are fired for neglecting to pursue an opportunity compared with the number punished for failing to meet ROI targets. Capacity utilization and sales growth, the typical measures of business success, are almost always based on use of existing resources.

Planning systems and cycles. Opportunities do not show up at the start of a planning cycle and last for the duration of a three- or five-year plan. Better formal planning is often the enemy of organizational adaptability.

How Do I Capitalize on It?

The ability to identify favorable circumstances is important but isn't enough to qualify a person as an entrepreneur. Many innovative thinkers never get anything done. Promoters, however, move quickly past the identification of opportunity to its pursuit. They are the hawkers with umbrellas who materialize from nowhere on Manhattan street corners at the first rumbles of thunder overhead.

For the trustee, commitment is time consuming and, once made, of long duration. Trustees move so slowly that they may appear to be stationary; once committed, they are tenacious but still very slow moving. Entrepreneurs have gamblers' reputations because of their willingness to get in and out of markets fast. But merely moving quickly does not guarantee success. First, entrepreneurs must know the territory they operate in, then they must be able to recognize patterns as they develop.

Successful risk takers have the confidence to assume that the missing elements of the pattern will take shape as they expect. Thus designers of CAD/CAM equipment feel free to engineer systems around disk drives that have yet to be built. From their knowledge of the industry, the designers feel confident the drives will be built and therefore they can get the right products on the market ahead of competitors. On the other hand, many utilities act like trustees. For example, they resist adoption of digital technology to streamline their operations and stick to electromechanical recording for readings of important data.

The pressures pushing companies toward either the entrepreneurial or administrative end of the spectrum with regard to the timing and duration of their commitment are a mixture of personal, organizational, and environmental forces. They are listed in *Exhibit II*, part B.

Administratively oriented companies approach the question whether to commit to new opportunities more cautiously. Administrators must negotiate with others on what strategy to take and must compromise to achieve necessary approvals. This process produces evolution rather than revolution. The search for perfection is the enemy of the good. Administrators often see the need to change as the result of failure of the planning process.

This disposition helps explain why managers of American electronics concerns sometimes are seen looking on in amazement as their Japanese counterparts consistently bring new electronics products—from videocassette recorders to talking calculators—to market first. These Japanese companies and other successful market-oriented businesses know that change is inevitable and, therefore, keep their organizations learning.

By endlessly studying how to reduce risk, instead of trying to deal with it, administrative companies slow the decision making. The many decision constituencies necessary to satisfy proposals for new products and services lengthen the process. If there's a project that everyone down the line agrees has a three-fourths chance of succeeding, the odds of getting that project through eight approval levels are one in ten. Many executives will justifiably say to themselves, why bother? (The Japanese have learned how to make rapid decisions by consensus without bogging down in layers of bureaucracy.)

What Resources Do I Need?

In grasping opportunities, some institutions with vast resources (such as government agencies, large nonprofit organizations, and big corporations) are tempted to commit resources heavily, to "go first class" all the way. In this way, the rationale goes, you reduce your chances of failure and increase your eventual returns.

From our observation, however, success is unrelated to the size of the resource commitment. More important is the innovativeness with which the institution commits and deploys those resources. The Apple and IBM personal computers were developed and produced by organizations that have little vertical integration. Few successful real estate developers have architects, contractors, or even space salespeople on the payroll. Yet many of these organizations rack up extraordinary ROIs and ROEs.

As necessity is proverbially the mother of invention, people who start businesses often make imaginative use of their limited resources. A computer engineer starting a peripheral equipment company will discover selling skills she never knew she possessed. The owner of a new restaurant quickly adjusts to waiting on tables. Entrepreneurs who are effective make the sparest allotment of resources.

Besides their reckless invasion of markets, people at the promoter end of our scale have reputations as gamblers because they throw everything they've got at opportunities. But in reality they throw everything they've got simply because they don't have enough. Successful entrepreneurs seek plateaus of success, where they can consolidate their gains before trying to acquire control over additional resources and further pursue the opportunity. They wish they had more to commit, but they do more with less anyway.

What level of resources is required to pursue a given opportunity? Tension prevails between the adequacy of commitment and the potential for return. Handling this tension is part of entrepreneurship's challenge and excitement. (See *Exhibit II*, part C.)

Most of the risk in entrepreneurial management lies in the effort to pursue opportunity with inappropriate resources — either too few or too many. Failures in real estate investing, for example, occur when participants attempt projects larger than their resources can handle. When the investors can't come up with more funds to tide them over unforeseen obstacles or setbacks, they fail. Large corporations tend to make the basic error of overcommitting resources.

Some large companies seem to believe that they can handle all opportunities with the resources they have behind them. But that's not always so: witness Exxon's spectacular entry into the electric motor control business and its subsequent humiliating retreat. A different error made by large corporations is rejection of openings in emerging businesses because they are "too small," thereby allowing new ventures an opportunity to gain footholds that cannot later be dislodged.

Looking beyond the size of the resource commitment, managers must consider its timing. At the administrative end of our spectrum, the tendency is to make a single decision for a total resource commitment. But during times of rapid change, such as we have experienced during the 1970s and 1980s, commitments in stages foster the most effective response to new competitors, markets, and technologies. Familiar by now is the staged entry of IBM into the full range of the microcomputer hardware and software market. Much of the genius of Procter & Gamble's marketing approach rests in trial, test, strategic experiment, and in-stage rollout of new products.

The pressures toward the gradual commitment of resources—toward the entrepreneurial end of our scale—are mostly environmental, and include:

An absence of predictable resource needs. Given the rapid pace of change in today's world, one must assume that in-course corrections will be necessary. The rapid advances have made technology forecasting hazardous, and projecting consumer economics, inflation rates, and market response has become equally difficult. A multistage commitment allows responsiveness; a one-time commitment creates unnecessary risk.

External control limits. Companies can no longer say they own the forest and will therefore do with it what they want; environmental consideration must be taken into account. Similarly, increasingly strict zoning affects companies' control of real estate. International access to resources is no longer guaranteed, as the mid-1970s oil shortages made very clear. Corporate executives must respond by matching exposure to the terms of control. They have learned the lesson in international operations but seem unwilling to apply the lesson domestically.

Social needs. The "small is beautiful" formulation of E.F. Schumacher and the argument that too large a gulf separates producers and consumers are very persuasive. Gradual commitment of resources allows managers to determine the most appropriate level of investment for a particular task.

In many of our large corporations, however, the pressure is in the opposite direction toward a single, heavy commitment of resources (at the administrative end of the scale) for the following reasons:

The need to reduce risk. Managers limit the risk they face by throwing all the resources they can muster at an opportunity from the outset, even if it means wasting assets. Such a commitment increases the likelihood of early success and reduces the likelihood of eventual failure. This stress on concentrated marshaling of assets fosters the belief that the resources themselves bring power and success.

Fragile tenure of management. At companies in which executives are either promoted every one-and-a-half to two years or exiled to corporate Siberia, they need quick, measurable results. Cash and earnings gains in each period must surpass the last. You must achieve quick, visible success or your job is in danger.

Focus on incentive compensation. Concentration of resources upfront yields quick returns and easily measurable results, which can be readily translated into a manager's bonus compensation. Small-scale strategic experiments, however, often show little in the immediate bottom line and therefore produce no effect on pay tied to ROA or ROE while consuming scarce managerial time.

Single-minded capital allocation systems. They assume that the consequences of future uncertainty can be measured now, or at least that uncertainty

Exhibit II The Entrepreneurial Culture vs. the Administrative Culture

	Entrepreneurial focus		Administrative focus	
	Characteristics	Pressures	Characteristics	Pressures
A Strategic orientation	Driven by perception of opportunity	Diminishing opportunities Rapidly changing technology, consumer economics, social values, and political rules	Driven by controlled resources	Social contracts Performance measurement criteria Planning systems and cycles
B Commitment to seize opportunities	Revolutionary, with short duration	Action orientation Narrow decision windows Acceptance of reasonable risks Few decision constituencies	Evolutionary, with long duration	Acknowledgment of multiple constituencies Negotiation about strategic course Risk reduction Coordination with existing resource base
C Commitment of resources	Many stages, with minimal exposure at each stage	Lack of predictable resource needs Lack of control over the environment	A single stage, with complete commitment out of decision	Need to reduce risk Incentive compensation Turnover in managers

Key business dimension	Entrepreneurial focus	Pressures toward this side	Administrative focus	Pressures toward this side
		Social demands for appropriate use of resources; Foreign competition; Demands for more efficient resource use		Capital budgeting systems; Formal planning systems
D Control of resources	Episodic use or rent of required resources	Increased resource specialization; Long resource life compared with need; Risk of obsolescence; Risk inherent in the identified opportunity; Inflexibility of permanent commitment to resources	Ownership or employment of required resources	Power, status, and financial rewards; Coordination of activity; Efficiency measures; Inertia and cost of change; Industry structures
E Management structure	Flat, with multiple informal networks	Coordination of key noncontrolled resources; Challenge to hierarchy; Employees' desire for independence	Hierarchy	Need for clearly defined authority and responsibility; Organizational culture; Reward systems; Management theory

a year from now will be no less than that at present. Thus a single decision point seems appropriate. Many capital budget systems make it difficult to get two bites of an apple.

In a typical case, a board of directors gets a request for $1 million next year for a start-up that, if successful, will need $3 million more in the future. The board, thinking in terms of full commitment, inquires into the return on $4 million. It fails to realize that it can buy an option and make a judgment at the $1 million stage without knowing the return on the extra $3 million. Such an approach inhibits the exercise of managerial discretion and skill, which lie in revising plans as needed and doing more with less. Hewlett-Packard and 3M are exceptions to this rule; they encourage multiple budget requests. Approval of a project means that the manager is unlikely to get all that is asked for the first time around.

Bureaucratic planning systems. A project can win the support of 99 people and then get scuttled by just one rejection. An entrepreneur, though, can be rejected 99 times but go ahead if one crucial respondent gives approval.

Once a project has begun, requests for additional resources return executives to a morass of analysis and bureaucratic delays. They try to avoid such problems by making the maximum possible upfront commitment.

An independent entrepreneur can field a salesperson when the need arises, but a corporate manager may put a salesperson in the field before necessary to avoid going through the approval process later. Easy access to small, incremental resources, allocated often on the basis of progress, has great power to motivate employees.

How Do I Control the Resources?

When one thinks of a book publishing company, one imagines large numbers of editors, typesetters, publicists, printing presses, and salespeople. And that's the way most of the nation's largest book publishers are set up. But many of today's young publishing ventures consist of just two or three people who rely heavily on outside professionals and suppliers. When one of these acquires a manuscript, it will often hire a free lance to make editorial improvements. The publisher then contracts with a typesetting company to have the manuscript set in type, a printing and binding concern to produce the volume, and a public relations firm to promote the book. People who are the equivalent of manufacturers' reps sell the book to stores.

Not coincidentally, many large, well-known New York book publishers have struggled financially in recent years, while a number of the small young book publishing ventures have thrived. Although manuscript selection and marketing decisions certainly help determine success, two key factors are the ability to reduce overhead and the acumen to take advantage of cost-lowering technological changes in the printing industry by using outside resources.

Promoter types think that all they need from a resource is the ability to use it; trustee types think that resources are inadequately controlled unless they are owned or on the payroll. Entrepreneurs learn to use other people's resources well while keeping the option open on bringing them in-house. For example: on reaching a certain volume level, the maker of an electronic product decides that it can no longer risk having a particularly valuable component made by an outside supplier who may be subject to severe market or financial pressures.

Each such decision pushes the entrepreneur toward the administrative arena. (See *Exhibit II*, part D.)

Because they try to avoid owning equipment or hiring people, entrepreneurs are often viewed as exploitive or even parasitic. But this trait has become valuable in today's fast-changing business environment, for the following reasons:

Greater resource specialization. A VLSI design engineer, a patent attorney, or state-of-the-art circuit-testing equipment may be a necessity for a company, but only occasionally. Using rather than owning enables the company to reduce its risk and its fixed costs.

Risk of obsolescence. Fast-changing technology makes ownership expensive; leasing or renting reduces the risk.

More flexibility. Using instead of owning a resource lowers the cost of pulling out of a project.

Power and status, as expressed in a hierarchy, and financial rewards push organizations toward the administrative end of the spectrum and toward ownership. In many corporations, the extent of resource ownership and control determine the degree of power, the status level, and the amount of direct and indirect compensation. Administrators argue for the ownership of resources for many sound and valid reasons, among them:

Efficiency. Execution is faster because the administrator can order a certain action without negotiation. Moreover, by avoiding having to find or share the right outside resource, companies capture (at least in the short run) all profits associated with an operation.

Stability. Effective managers are supposed to insulate the technical core of production from external shocks. To do this they need buffer inventories, control of raw materials, and control of distribution channels. Ownership also creates familiarity and an identifiable chain of command, which becomes stabilized over time.

Industry custom. If everyone else in an industry owns, it is a competitive risk to buck the tide.

What Structure Is Best?

A strangling organizational structure or a stifling bureaucracy often stirs corporate managers to think about starting or acquiring their own businesses. Rebuffed by "channels" in attempts to get their employer to consider a new product or explore a new market, they long for the freedom inherent in a small and flexible structure.

When it comes to organizing businesses, there is a distinct difference between the promoter and the trustee mentalities. Via contact with the principal actors, the promoter tries to "feel" the way events are unfolding. The trustee views relationships more formally: rights, responsibilities, and authority are conferred on different people and segments of an organization. The trustee is prepared to take action without making contact with those that are affected by the decision.

Also influencing the approach to business organization is the control of resources. To help them coordinate their activities, businesses that use and rent resources by necessity develop informal information networks both internally and externally. But organizations that own and employ resources are easily and naturally organized into hierarchies according to those resources. Because hierarchy inhibits not only the search for and commitment to opportunity but also communication and decision making, networking evolves in most companies. Usually this networking is formalized in matrix and committee structures. (See *Exhibit II*, part E.)

Commentators on organizations often criticize the entrepreneur's antipathy toward formalized structure as a liability stemming from an inability to let go. The entrepreneur is stereotyped as egocentric and unable to manage. In this view, the administrator may not be very spontaneous or innovative, but is a good manager. In reality the entrepreneur isn't necessarily a worse manager than the administrator but has simply chosen different tools to get the task done. Fashioning these tools are the following pressures:

The need to coordinate resources that are not controlled. Entrepreneurs must motivate, handle, and direct outside suppliers, professionals, and others to make sure needed goods and services are available when they're supposed to be.

The need for flexibility. In today's atmosphere of rapid change, the development of much essential operating information outside the company makes communication with external resources even more important. The notion that hierarchy provides stability does not hold true, especially if one considers that in a typical company growing 30% annually, only 40% of the employees three years down the line will have been with the company from the start. A flat and informal structure enhances communication.

Employees' desire for independence. Many of today's managers are still influenced by the antiauthoritarian values of the 1960s and the self-fulfillment values of the 1970s. Furthermore, organizations with little hierarchy breed employees accustomed to authority based on competence and persuasion; they will resist attempts to introduce structure and to rationalize authority based on hierarchy.

Of course, hierarchical organizations arise for rational reasons. According to classic management theory, a formal, well-defined structure ensures attention to all the necessary planning, organizing, and controlling activities. Among the pressures against the entrepreneurial approach and toward the administrative are the following:

The greater complexity of tasks. As planning, coordinating, communicating, and controlling functions become more involved, clearly defined authority and responsibility are needed to ensure adequate differentiation and integration.

Stratified organizational culture. If a desire for routine and order comes to dominate corporate attitudes, a more formal structure is attractive and reassuring.

Control-based reward systems. As we indicated earlier, reward systems are often based on the amount of control executives have, as measured in the organizational structure. Thus incentives reinforce formality.

It's easier, of course, to avoid adding structure than it is to reduce existing structure. Many of the high-technology companies in California's Silicon

Valley and along Route 128 in Massachusetts have been notably successful in keeping structure to a minimum by erasing distinctions between upper and lower management and encouraging such group activities as the Friday afternoon beer bust. The fewer the distinctions, the less inhibited lower-level employees will be about approaching top managers with complaints and suggestions about operations. Managers trained to expect an orderly world may feel uncomfortable in such an informal atmosphere, but the dividends in coordination and motivation can be important.

It is possible for companies with extensive structure to reduce it. Sears, Roebuck has trimmed its corporate staff way back and in the process has granted much autonomy to its operating units. Dana Corporation, like many other companies, has found that cutting out the "helping staff" has improved performance.

Stimulating Entrepreneurship

Our discussion should have made clear our belief that entrepreneurship is a trait that is confined neither to certain types of individuals nor to organizations. Obviously, it is found more in smaller and younger enterprises than in larger and older ones simply because the conditions favoring its development are more likely to be present.

For many people, the dream of being the boss and being financially self-sufficient is enough to stimulate the pursuit of opportunity. The venturesome are usually forced by capital limitations to commit resources gradually and to rent or use them rather than own them. Similarly, they recoil from the idea of bureaucracy; to them, it's vital to have an organization that can react quickly to new opportunities.

Even so, many of the nation's small businesses inhabit the administrative end of our spectrum. The owners shy from taking risks in pursuit of growth; perhaps they are preoccupied with other financial activities such as investing in real estate or the stock market, paying their children's college expenses, or providing for impending retirement. Perhaps they only want the business to provide a steady living, so they run their businesses in a way to guard what they have.

A society can do much to stimulate or inhibit the development of entrepreneurship. Government policy can do much to create opportunity. Decisions in recent years to lower the capital gains tax and deregulate certain industries have been instrumental in encouraging the establishment of many new businesses that otherwise would probably not exist today. Support of basic research in health, technology, and material science establishes a base on which opportunities are built.

Similarly, the way our colleges and universities teach business management affects approaches to entrepreneurship. Courses and departments in entrepreneurship, set up at many such institutions, will produce increasing numbers of young managers who are attuned to effective ways of pursuing opportunity and managing resources.

While government agencies and educational institutions can create conditions favorable for entrepreneurship to take hold, it's up to individual organizations to foster the conditions that allow it to flourish. That means encouraging the timely pursuit of opportunity, the most appropriate commitment and use of resources, and the breakdown of hierarchy.

Those goals of course are not easy to reach, especially if the organization must be turned around from its habitual administrative approach. We see in corporations the same type of opportunity matrix as we described for individual managers early in this article and in *Exhibit I*. As one can see in *Exhibit III*, movement to the left requires a strategic focus and the instillation of belief throughout the organization that change is acceptable and even desirable. Movement upward presupposes that corporate officers think their organization has the capacity to acquire resources as needed. To foster this belief the leadership of the organization can:

Determine its barriers to entrepreneurship. Is a manager's principal reward found in handling the company's existing resources? Are managers expected to pursue outside opportunities in its behalf only when they have extra time? Do management and director committees evaluate opportunities on an all-or-none, one-shot basis? Do superiors have to go through many levels to gain approval for capital budgets and adding personnel?

Seek to minimize risks to the individual for being entrepreneurial. When people are promoted for behaving like trustees while promoter types are shunted aside if not eased out, there's little motive to be venturesome. The leadership can work at reducing the individual's cost of failing in the pursuit of opportunity, especially if the failure is externally caused. To convince skeptical managers that the risks have indeed been reduced, the leadership must not only

---

Exhibit III   Corporate Opportunity Matrix

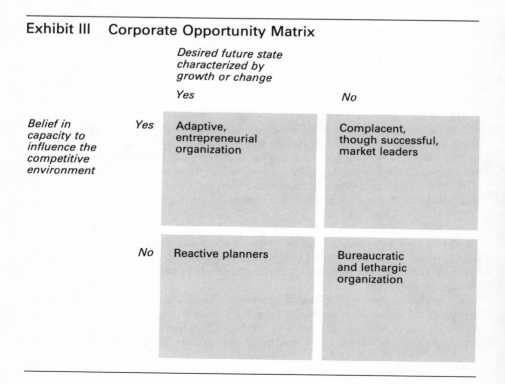

		Desired future state characterized by growth or change	
		Yes	*No*
Belief in capacity to influence the competitive environment	*Yes*	Adaptive, entrepreneurial organization	Complacent, though successful, market leaders
	No	Reactive planners	Bureaucratic and lethargic organization

recognize entrepreneurship as an organizational goal but also eliminate the bottom line as the main determinant of subordinates' success.

Exploit any resource pool. The huge resources that many companies have can be committed intelligently. Indeed, the fact that they are huge can be an important aspect of reducing the perceived risk to managers of pursuing opportunity. After all, resources per se reduce risks associated with exploiting opportunity. Excess resources can also support a thorough search process. And if enough opportunities are pursued, there can be ultimate success even if some fail.

Tailor reward systems to the situation. For some, a primary motivating force is the possibility of becoming wealthy through ownership in a growing enterprise. For a start-up or early-stage venture, then, equity in the company may be the main incentive encouraging entrepreneurial behavior on the part of the initial employees. Large organizations cannot hope to duplicate this lure without creating interest among those who are not offered such rewards. (Managers of these companies are often driven by other objectives anyway, including security and growing responsibility.) The leadership of established corporations, then, must think in terms of fostering team commitment and rewarding successful entrepreneurs with chances to do more of the same on a grander scale.

It's much easier and safer for companies to stay with the familiar than to explore the unknown. Only by encouraging change and experimentation can companies of all sizes adapt and grow in the midst of much uncertainty.

REFERENCE

1. Richard E. Cavanagh and Donald K. Clifford, Jr., "Lessons from America's Midsized Growth Companies," *McKinsey Quarterly*, Autumn 1983, p. 2.

PART
TWO

Succeeding in Your Career

Once you have sized up your self-image and ego ideal and juxtaposed these against the manager's job and differentiated the kind of role you want to perform and the kind of behavior that will be required to be innovative in whatever that role may be, you can then explore Section II. This basic understanding is the raw material of career planning and fundamental to all that follows.

Now the issue becomes: What does a career path look like? In what ways do people move along those paths? What are the trajectories and the traps? These issues are taken up in the next section. They may be regarded as career mapmaking.

John F. Veiga's discussion, "Do Managers on the Move Get Anywhere?," addresses pivotal concerns. He describes two distinct career paths followed by mobile and nonmobile managers. An important aspect of Veiga's discussion is the degree to which both organizations and the managers who work in them collude to assume that movement is the same as promotion. He offers criteria for thinking of where one is and what happens over time in typical careers.

Regardless of which path you may take, sooner or later you come to the point where you have to take charge of a unit, a company, or an activity. Sometimes this takes a long time, and at other times you have to move very quickly. In "When a New Manager Takes Charge," John J. Gabarro examines the process of taking charge and the particular activities that the manager must undertake as he or she takes charge. He looks at five predictable stages of how new managers learn and master their situations. Here Gabarro emphasizes the need to make your expectations explicit, expectations both of yourself and of others.

Rosabeth Moss Kanter contends in "Power Failure in Management Circuits" that managers fail when they do not have adequate power to do what needs to be done. In her view, power means access to resources and information, the freedom to act quickly to make it possible to accomplish more, and the ability to pass on more resources and information to subordinates; in short, "clout." She differentiates productive power from oppressive power, a differentiation that managers should be aware of.

David C. McClelland and David H. Burnham elaborate on this theme in somewhat greater detail in "Power Is the Great Motivator." They point out that good managers are motivated by a need to influence others' behavior for the good of the organization; therefore they want power for the sake of serving the organization. This the authors call power motivation. When the manager is preoccupied with obtaining power simply to advance his or her own interests, that may not be in the best interests of the organization. A concern for power is essential to good management, a step in the movement toward the ego ideal. However, it's important for the prospective or current manager to understand what kind of power he or she wants to pursue.

Joseph C. Bailey concludes from his study of top executives "that the major task of a chief executive is to resolve the conflict of codes or what others would call values." The executives' success, he reports in "Clues for Success in the President's Job," will hinge more on his or her capabilities in this limited area than on any other single segment of the executive task. Bailey also observes that the most immediate self-evident uniformity among all the CEOs he studied was their ability to cope with stress effectively. Being power-oriented in the McClelland and Burnham sense, they also view themselves as expendable. He talks about other capacities, particularly the influence of models, all of which are relevant for the person pursuing a managerial career.

1

Do Managers on the Move Get Anywhere?

JOHN F. VEIGA

One need only spend a few hours listening to middle managers talk about their career plans to discover that mobility is on their minds. Some are anxious and frustrated because they are moving too slowly—"I'm just afraid if I don't get promoted soon it's all over for me . . . the end of the ball game." Others are disillusioned by the prospects of a plateaued career—"I can't imagine anyone feeling satisfaction from doing the same thing for more than five years." No one wishes to be seen as stagnant deadwood, as a case of arrested mobility.

Many managers believe that mobility is desirable and essential for success. For some it has become synonymous with success. Unfortunately, while these managers play the mobility game, or at least pay lip service to it, few understand its rules or its dividends.

They are not alone—very little is known about how managerial careers unfold and about the forces that shape them. While executive mobility has received attention, especially through the work of Eugene E. Jennings,[1] little research has focused on the mobility patterns of middle managers, the very people who are most affected by adopting the mobility ethos.

In a large-scale study of managerial careers done over the past few years, I surveyed all the managers up to the level of vice president in three major U.S. corporations. All three companies are in manufacturing. Each employs well in excess of 100,000 people and each has more than 40 domestic plant locations. Besides having each person write a lengthy career history as well as fill out a job attitude questionnaire, I conducted follow-up interviews with more than 100 of the managers to further corroborate and amplify the survey results. The participants in the survey were 1,191 men. All of them had college educations. Their ages ranged from 29 to 64, the average being 46. Almost all of them were married (97%), and 93% of them had children. Their jobs were in all functions of their companies, the largest group working in marketing or sales (29%).

I have not included women's careers in the study because only 36 women responded to the questionnaire. This low response made separate analysis by sex impossible.

In this article, I discuss the highlights of the research by addressing four questions:

1. How mobile are managers?
2. What is a typical career?

3. Are mobile managers a breed apart?
4. What are the payoffs?

How Mobile Are Managers?

To answer this question, I looked at 6,332 job changes from the point of view of their direction (were the moves upward, lateral, or downward?), their characteristics (were they intraorganizational or interorganizational, and did they involve geographic relocation?), and their frequency (what was the average number of years between moves?).

Is up always up? Most of the managers I surveyed believe that they move almost solely in one direction—upward. At least, that's what they report: participants classified 85% of all their moves as being upward (having increased responsibility), 12% as lateral (retaining the same responsibility), but only 3% as downward (having decreased responsibility). Even for moves occurring when managers are in mid-career, when lateral transfers are common, and in late career, when downward transfers usually increase, managers continue to report that almost 70% of their moves are upward and that only 3% are downward. While there is no way to verify the actual direction of each move, average corporate estimates of directions—upward 40%, lateral 51%, and downward 9%—leave little room for doubt that serious distortions exist.

In many companies two common practices contribute heavily to this perception problem. First, seldom, if ever, does top management tell managers how it really views a particular move. All too often, a person's boss presents a move as "a real challenge," "an opportunity to grow and develop," or "a job that fills a critical need," and rarely as "a lateral move with only modest advancement potential." Second, while managers readily admit that they have no strong desire to determine the true nature of a move—they prefer to hear and say "advancement" —they are also confused and unsure about how to classify moves that are generally accompanied by "sweeteners." With lateral moves, and in some cases downward moves as well, many companies routinely offer more money, a new title, or other less tangible perquisites—e.g., "I hope you will enjoy working at our newest plant."

While it is easy to see how managers persuade themselves that lateral moves are upward ones, I was particularly curious to see how they dealt with demotions. In follow-up interviews, I had an opportunity to talk with five managers who had been recently demoted. In the eyes of top management, these moves were bona fide demotions; to those demoted, they were not. Three of these managers argued convincingly that their moves were lateral: "This move is designed to give me a chance to see how all the pieces come together." In one case, the person categorized his move as "a real step up . . . a new challenge." In all five cases, top management had so sweetened the moves and given such misleading (though well-intentioned) counseling that only one of the five was perceptive enough, or perhaps secure enough, to recognize what had really happened.

A larger study of demotions, by Fred H. Goldner, also shows such practice to be widespread and gives much evidence that "organizations tend to cloak the demotion in a good deal of ambiguity." Apparently so many moves occur in the companies studied, especially lateral ones, that it is difficult for individuals to see a demotion for what it is.[2]

Top managements in organizations are not the only culprits in clouding demotions. Evidence suggests that middle managers also play a part. Several middle managers who report downward movement on the survey offer unsolicited and sometimes lengthy explanations on the questionnaire. One manager writes, "Reorganization necessitated a decrease in my job responsibilities, but this is only temporary." Another writes, "I took this position because I was assured it could lead to bigger things." And one manager tersely notes, "My salary did not decrease . . . only the length of my title." Several of the comments reveal the writers' strong need to see their downward moves as temporary or at least as not being status reducing. Because demotions carry with them the potential for severe ego-crushing blows, which may prevent people from being able or willing to hear the truth, it is easy to understand why most top managers are reluctant to talk straight to people they demote.

Where to next? In recent years, top managers have been encountering increasing resistance when they have tried to relocate managers and their families. The problems families suffer, not to mention the difficulties dual-career couples encounter, have given relocation a bad press. But just how often do managers in large corporations have to relocate?

In the typical career profile in the three companies I studied, 35% of all career moves involved relocation before mid-career. Up to age 50, managers actually face close to a 50/50 chance of having to uproot their families every time they change jobs. While this trend could change dramatically as the number of dual-career couples increases or as managerial values change, in all likelihood for managers wishing to pursue a mobile career, relocation will continue to be a fact of life. Although this fact may be a hard pill for some managers to swallow, a significant number of them believe that the benefits far outweigh any costs. One 36-year-old engineer told me, "I've relocated four times in the last 10 years. . . . My family has enjoyed the experience, meeting new people and seeing new sights. My kids want to know, 'Where to next?'"

The career profile also reveals that managers seldom change corporate allegiances—only 10% of all moves involve such a change. Even though the average manager is not especially prone to job-hop, exceptions occur, especially before mid-career. One manager I interviewed was quite proud of the fact that he had worked for seven companies by the time he was 35 years old. Many others, while not seriously searching, make it clear that they continually assess other career opportunities and never rule out the possibility of leaving. Generally, while young managers frequently espouse this "up or out" strategy, in reality less than 10% of them sever corporate ties more than twice by the time they reach mid-career.

How fast do they run? Managers express complete confidence in being able to spot "fast-trackers," "comers," and "deadwood," yet, when faced with the question "How fast is fast?" give varying answers. While some managers think a career move every two or three years is fast, others say that that is average. Still others estimate that a move every four or five years is reasonably fast. In some cases, managers' opinions reflect their inexperience; in others, their pessimism. In any case, few managers possess accurate information about mobility.

Exhibit I reveals a wide variation in average mobility rates. While the typical manager averages a career move every 3.5 years, some average a move every

12 months, and some every 12 years. Roughly 25% can be classified as being on dormant, if not completely inactive, career paths. A like number moves very rapidly—every one to three years. Although older managers are more inclined to experience decreased mobility, age alone does not explain frequency of movement. (For the most part, the average mobility rate remains fairly constant in other industries I have looked at, including electronics, banking, insurance, and heavy and light manufacturing, although there is some variation due to organizational size and industry growth rate.)

What Is a Typical Career?

Career mobility is highest at the beginning of a managerial career and decreases gradually over its span. Significant correlations between age and geographic mobility ($r = 0.55$), intraorganizational mobility ($r = 0.43$), and interorganizational mobility ($r = 0.41$) verify this observation. As *Exhibit II* shows, when each type of mobility is plotted by age groupings, each curve reveals periods during the span of a career when the basic trend is interrupted. For example,

Exhibit I   Distribution of Career Mobility Rates

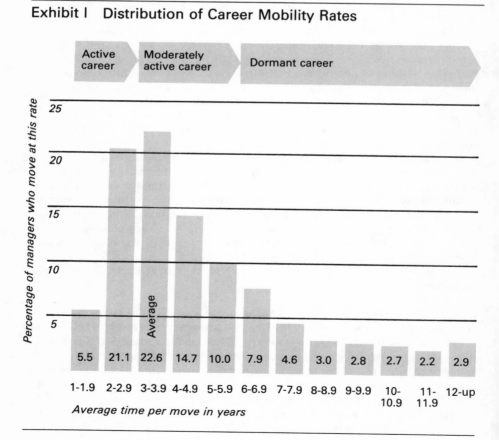

due to an increase in the numbers of managers relocating between the ages of 42 and 54, the geographic mobility curve stabilizes and remains fairly flat during that period before it continues its prior rate of descent at age 55. Now let's look at each pattern.

Geographic mobility patterns: Fairly early in their careers, managers go through a period of gradual decline in geographic moves that continues until they are about 42 years of age. Up to that time, for many managers, relocation has been a way of life; most have transferred at least twice. Many have also begun to experience some relocation fatigue — "I've transferred several times since I started working here. . . . I'd just like to stay a little longer this time. . . . You know, I'm not even sure what my address and phone number are sometimes." In making career plans, some also begin to take increasing family responsibility into more account than before and consciously avoid any potential family disruptions brought on by relocation — "Now that my kids are teenagers, I would rather avoid moving until they are on their own." These concerns constrain career options and, as can be seen from the parallel decline in both the intraorganizational and the interorganizational mobility curves, reduce the frequency of career movement.

As the curve in *Exhibit II* shows, between the ages of 42 and 54, managers begin another period of moving around. Children are now or will soon be on their own. Family matters seem less of an obstacle. A 45-year-old manager explains: "My kids are both in college and my parents are in Florida, so my wife and I are looking at the possibility of some new scenery." Seasoned managers have the perspective and skills a company can best exploit and nurture by moving managers regularly across divisional lines. If managers refuse to relocate at this stage in their careers, they are likely to do irreparable harm to their future career momentum.

Until recently, most managers reaching this stage in their careers have found their needs and their companies' well matched. With the number of wives beginning or resuming careers increasing, however, the potential for mismatches will also undoubtedly increase. Companies may be forced not only to give up job transfers to other geographic locations as a major way of revitalizing managers but also to make many more downward transfers than they used to — a trend that has already begun to gain some momentum.[3] As a consequence, it is plausible that managerial careers will begin to plateau even sooner than they do at present and that the potential for stagnation will increase markedly. Under such a scenario, keeping managers who still have a good 15 to 25 working years left motivated is going to be a real challenge for management.

The noticeably sharp decline in the geographic mobility curve after age 54 shows that for older managers career opportunities dwindle. After that age, when many careers plateau, any transfer may be a demotion in disguise. While the mid-career manager is more willing to accept relocation as the price of advancement, the older, plateaued manager is not. Unless top management can offer some unique reasons or an extremely desirable relocation, most older managers will no longer accept moves to other sites. A 61-year-old manager summed it up best by saying, "What's in it for me?"

Intraorganizational mobility: Throughout their careers, managers make intraorganizational moves more frequently and consistently than they do the other kinds. In part, this pattern is less volatile because such decisions to move are

Exhibit II   Average Career Mobility Rates over the Span of a Managerial Career

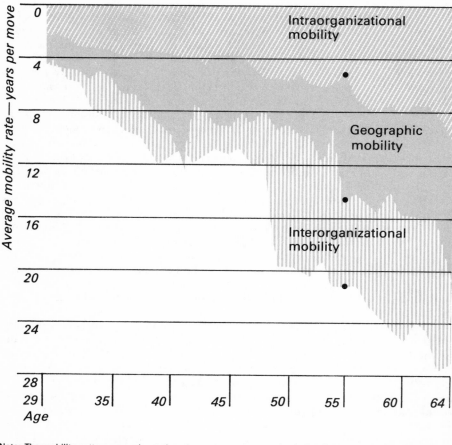

Note: The mobility patterns were located mathematically by using linear regression to fit a straight line to each curve. When the actual curve fell above or below the line for any length of the career span, the pattern is noted. Rather than attempt to look for mobility patterns by using the overall frequency of movement, I calculated separate mobility rates for each type of move and each combination of moves. When factor analyzed, the rates reduced to three, which accounted for 71% of the variance in the overall frequency of movement.

more immune from conflicts between career and family needs and because such moves are in part a function of orderly progression within a corporate hierarchy.

As they become more expert in technical functions *before* their first management assignments, many new young recruits in a company assume fairly high rates of mobility. Between the ages of 29 and 36, however, the number of moves these same people make declines. Generally, once they move into managerial positions that use their expertise, recruits become too valuable to be moved. And because they have little management experience, many are quite willing to spend time developing and improving those skills.

Once this seasoning is over, usually by the time they are 37 years old, managers enter the corporate mainstream. In an attempt to cultivate and use mature managerial talent, the company encourages younger managers to move, especially laterally. Eager to gain visibility and exposure, these managers are willing to accept a variety of assignments. Of course, managers who are anxious to move up or out and to leverage their careers create some of this movement as well as some of the directional ambiguity that accompanies it. As managers near age 46, their moves into the mainstream decline in number; by this time most executives have launched their careers. Toward the end of this stage, many of those who have not made it to the top will have to face the prospect of accepting a plateaued career or making one final attempt to migrate to yet another company.

Between the ages of 48 and 55, managers leave the mainstream. At about age 47, the number of intraorganizational moves that managers make declines significantly, showing that many careers begin to plateau at about that time (see *Exhibit II*). During this period, even though the incidence of managers classifying moves as lateral almost doubles, many still have not accepted the fact that their own careers are slowing down. Those who continue to classify their moves as upward use the term to mean "continuing responsibility and contribution" rather than "increasing responsibility and advancement" in the corporate hierarchy.

Interorganizational mobility: Over the spans of their careers, the managers I studied made more moves within companies, which may or may not have involved relocation, than moves between companies. The greatest movement occurs when the managers are under 32 years of age. This is further evidence of a job-hopping pattern among the young. The subsequent marked decline in number of moves after mid-career suggests that this pattern subsides rather quickly.

After an initial period of job-hopping and search, managers from ages 32 to 39 generally begin to concentrate on building track records. Many managers discover that job-hopping is not always fruitful and find that the ideal position is, at best, an illusion. Once they have entered the mainstream in their companies and have earned management responsibilities, their commitment to the organization reaches an all-time high. Many report feeling that they have found their niche. Besides, for many, a move to another company could necessitate another relocation, which they see as unattractive at this stage.

The curve begins to stabilize when managers are between 39 and 48 years of age and thus indicates that they are entering a second period of increasing organizational job-hopping. As we saw earlier, the number of moves within the company also increases during this time. These parallel events signal that the individual is reaching his peak career maturity, which carries with it increased anxiety as the choice of one's career path becomes narrower and seemingly irrevocable.

If managers' career expectations are not being met when they sense that they are arriving at this point, they are inclined more at this time than at any other since early career to entertain the notion of a job search. Because of their age and income, managers at mid-career find the number of job opportunities decreasing. As their peers begin to achieve executive status, and as the time for them to make it to the top begins to run out, some of these middle managers

Exhibit III Career Path Indices: Mobile versus Immobile Managers

100%					
90	Percentage of 1,191 managers above the median				
80					
70					
60					
50					
40					
30	56.8*	39.6	38.0*	69.0	65.8*	39.5
20					
10					
	M	I	M	I	M	I

Effective exposure to top management in percentages	Predecessor's length of stay in years	Number of career opportunities

Median response

7	6	3

*Significantly different at the 0.01 level (median test).

M Mobile managers

I Immobile managers

experience an increased sense of urgency about their careers. As one 46-year-old sales manager confided, "I have been really happy here. . . . I never thought I would have to seriously consider leaving . . . but as I see it now, it's a do-or-die situation. . . . I'm too young to wither on the vine."

This period of increased job-hopping occurs at a time when managers are grappling with other issues related to mid-life transition, such as the probability that they will never reach the top, which causes what Daniel J. Levinson calls "de-illusionment."[4] It is also a time when several well-documented psychological issues concerning one's career and life surface.[5] Of course no one knows to what degree this increased job-hopping is the cause or the result of a mid-career crisis. What is known is that most managers at this stage of life begin to experience the need to reexamine their career objectives and plans. For some, changing companies is the right choice; for others, it is believed to be the only choice.

After 48 years of age, managers who have not achieved executive status experience a rapid decline in career opportunities. Even though they are effective performers, their salary and career expectations are not likely to match what most prospective employers are willing to offer. In addition, by this time they have a considerable investment in what Drucker refers to as "golden fetters"— pension plans, stock options, and so forth. Making a move to another company becomes financially prohibitive. All of these factors tend to infringe on inter-organizational mobility and, as the curve shows, result in a continuous decline after 48 years of age.

Are Mobile Managers a Breed Apart?

In doing this study, I classified managers who moved every 3.9 years or less as mobile and those who moved every 4 years or more as immobile. Classifying the managers in this way created two groups of comparable size— 560 mobile managers and 631 immobile managers. The members of both groups have similar marital status, family size, and level of education, and they equally represent all functions of a company. The mobile managers average 45 years of age, while the immobile managers are on average slightly older—49.

Despite all the similarities, the career mobility patterns of the two groups are substantially different. Moving on average every 2.6 years instead of 6.9 years, mobile managers make more than double the moves of the immobile managers. On the average, the mobile managers leave their first positions in just under 2 years, while the immobile managers stay there 4 years. The fast-sprinting managers maintain relatively fast paces throughout their careers while their counterparts plod along ever more slowly.

Besides the difference in pace, mobile managers also make more moves requiring geographic relocation (39% versus 28%). Clearly, a strong connection between career mobility and willingness to relocate exists. Contrary to common belief, however, mobile managers are not prone to excessive organizational job-hopping. On the average, mobile managers change companies no more than twice; their more stay-at-home counterparts move at most once. Members of both groups believe that most of their moves are upward, a belief that is difficult to understand, given the sheer number of moves mobile managers make. However, given the sacrifices typically involved in frequently uprooting families, perhaps the job-hopping managers have good reason to view most of their moves as advancements. Without question, these two groups have significantly different career experiences, which involve different career paths and motives. Let's look at these questions next.

How do their career paths differ? Being in the right place at the right time is often stated as the formula for success. Though few managers I surveyed deny the importance of talent and experience, many believe some career paths offer greater advancement potential than others. Although many factors may influence career mobility, I looked at three especially important indices in detail—exposure to top management, predecessor's length of stay, and career opportunities (see *Exhibit III*).

1. Exposure to top management: On average, managers report both spending 14% of their time on projects that provide exposure to upper management and receiving recognition for these projects about 50% of the time. (Because effective exposure requires recognition from top management, I multiplied these two numbers together to create an exposure index—the median index was 7%, 14% times 50%.) As expected, the mobile managers, at least according to their estimates, are on career paths that give them more effective exposure to top management than the others (57% above the median versus 40%).

The reason for this higher level of exposure to upper management is inherent in the careers of those who change jobs often. Given their rate of mobility, these managers often experience broad cross-divisional exposure. With such experience, other managers are likely to seek their opinions and thus to provide even further exposure. The difference in exposure is even more evident in mid-career, when managers on the move average 35% of their time on projects involving top management, whereas others only average 15%.

Managers give several other reasons that they have, or have not, had exposure to upper management. Some describe bosses who will not share responsibility or credit. One manager states, "I worked for a plant manager who insisted upon initialing every report. I rarely got invited to important meetings. My job was to help the plant manager look good. . . . I briefed him on technical aspects and he presented the results." Others cite social and non-work-related political maneuvers such as club and church memberships as being important. Although it is difficult to determine, except through gossip, the impact that non-work-related exposure has on career advancement, almost twice as many of the managers who do not move include office politics as a primary reason for advancement (or lack of it) than those who change jobs often.

2. Predecessor's length of stay: While the length of stay of a manager's predecessor is no sure-fire measure of one's advancement potential, it does provide an important indication of how fast people on that career path move. The mobile managers I surveyed are much more likely than the other group to be following in the footsteps of managers who have themselves been mobile. As shown in *Exhibit III*, only 38% of the mobile managers are in positions in which their predecessors stayed longer than the median time of 6 years. In sharp contrast, 69% of the slow moving managers are heirs to positions from which the previous occupants took their time leaving. Overall, the mobile managers' predecessors departed after an average of 4.9 years, while the others' predecessors took half again as long, averaging 7.5 years. In addition, when the immobile managers' predecessors did depart, they moved laterally almost twice as often.

Why are mobile managers more inclined to be in management positions that have historically offered greater mobility? Is it good planning, happenstance, exposure, or merely coattailing on a mobile superior's success? For many, the corporate selection process in all likelihood plays a major role. Before filling a position, top managers ask some key questions: "Will this person be happy there?" (which can be interpreted to mean, "Can we expect this person to stay put and not get too anxious to move before we can provide another opportu-

Exhibit IV   Career Payoffs for Mobile versus Immobile Managers

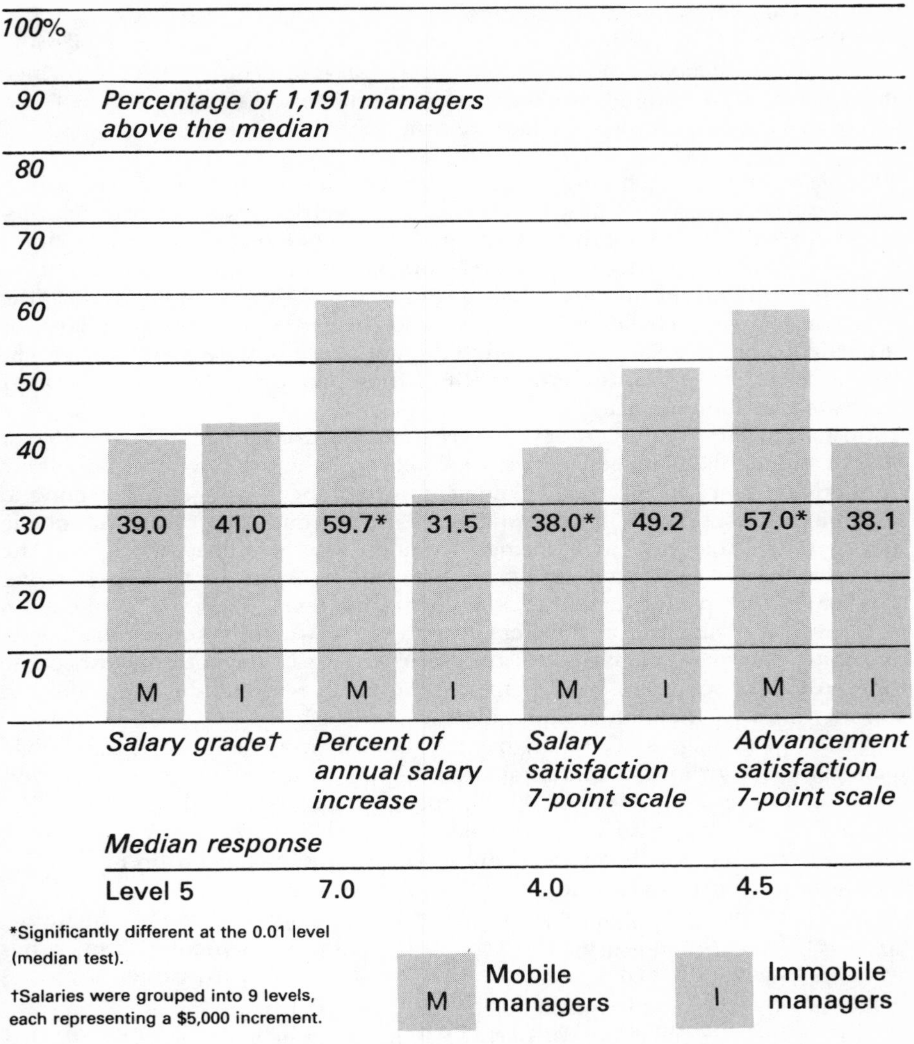

100%

90   Percentage of 1,191 managers
      above the median

80

70

60

50

40

30   39.0   41.0   59.7* 31.5   38.0* 49.2   57.0* 38.1

20

10
      M   I   M   I   M   I   M   I

Salary grade†	Percent of annual salary increase	Salary satisfaction 7-point scale	Advancement satisfaction 7-point scale

Median response

Level 5   7.0   4.0   4.5

*Significantly different at the 0.01 level
(median test).

†Salaries were grouped into 9 levels,
each representing a $5,000 increment.

M Mobile managers   I Immobile managers

nity?"). Quite often, top management is less likely to offer positions that have the potential for slowing career progress or becoming deadends to those it perceives as fast-trackers. To what degree this process is self-reinforcing or to what degree a manager can actually influence it remains open to question.

3. Career opportunities: While managers are not always the best judges of which positions they are most qualified to fill, their estimates provide an insight into how they perceive their career opportunities. Nearly 70% of the mobile managers feel they could be asked to fill at least four or more management

positions in their companies, while only 40% of the more settled managers report they have four or more opportunities available to them. Similarly, a majority of the mobile managers were certain they could duplicate their present positions in other companies, while the immobile felt their chances were at best 50/50. The latter group's pessimism seems to stem from two sources—lack of confidence in their ability to move any further and lack of effort to keep informed about career opportunities. As one manager explains, "I'm fairly satisfied with where I am, so why waste time looking around?"

What makes them run? Although mobile managers are more restless and driven than the others, it is not clear why. Managers themselves give a variety of reasons. One manager states, "I got tired of waiting for a promotion and started looking." Another states, "You just can't wait until top management spots you; cream may rise to the top, but for my career that takes too long." Others comment that "the job was no longer a challenge" or "the new job offered a much larger salary" or "I needed room to grow." Even though the stated reasons are many, the survey reveals two motives that underlie much of these managers' behavior—fear of stagnation and impatience.

Most managers are moderately concerned about career stagnation, but almost 60% of the mobile managers express a significantly higher concern than others do. Early in their careers, neither mobile nor immobile managers are willing to accept a gradual slowing in career progress. But by mid-career only the mobile managers feel this way, many facing stagnation with gloom. Realizing that the routes to the top are becoming limited and still enjoying the vitality changing jobs brings, they prefer regular reassignment to stagnation, even if, as one manager says, "It means lateral transfers every 3 years." As the immobile managers encounter slower progress, they also experience fear of stagnation, but because they no longer see themselves as marketable and are generally less willing to consider a move, they settle onto a plateau.

While few managers are totally passive about their advancement, the mobile managers as a group are quite impatient—57% scored above average on impatience, whereas only 38% of the immobile managers scored that high. The immobile managers tend to be pawnlike about their career progress, and to some, playing the mobility game is not worth it: "I work hard, I do my job. . . . I have little control over who gets promoted, so why worry if I'm next?" In contrast, the mobile managers are intensely interested in the rate at which they advance: "From the moment I started my career, I was impatient with my progress. . . . I have an internal time clock that lets me know if my career is getting bogged down."

Apparently, the mobile managers' impatience and fear of stagnation are not quelled by movement alone. In part, these needs stem from expectations that are raised early in their careers and entail a belief in what sociologists call the "unlimited success" theory, namely, that success is attainable. Given this conditioning, managers are likely to experience acute career frustration when their careers plateau. Is the race for success worth it?

What Are the Payoffs?

If you ask a mobile manager what he gets out of moving so often, you are likely to get a laundry list of payoffs—many of them intangible and unique.

The more ambivalent, slower-to-move managers, on the other hand, often answer with the question "Why would I want to be mobile?" Although the groups are not likely to agree on what the price for mobility ought to be, money and job satisfaction are central to the thinking of both of the groups.

Do mobile managers get paid more? As *Exhibit IV* shows, mobile managers do not fare better monetarily. Even though they received a larger annual increase during the previous 12 months than the other group of managers, 60% received more than a 7% increase—they do not outdistance the immobile managers on total salary earned. A study of the compensation of mobile executives reveals that, through mid-career, those who remain with the same employer actually earn higher salaries than those who move interorganizationally.[6] The executives who stay in their jobs achieve equality in compensation by being paid well for what they do and by receiving modest annual salary increases. Apparently, managers on the move have to play a catch-up game, a finding that may explain some of the differences in annual percentage increases I found. When those who become executives reach mid-career, however, jobs in various companies and a proven background of diversified corporate experience begin to pay off significantly.

Are mobile managers more satisfied with their jobs? Both groups of managers rated equally all but two major sources of job satisfaction. They were equally satisfied with their achievements, responsibilities, recognition, work, co-workers, superiors, bosses, and company policies. The two groups differ, however, about salary and advancement.

While salary is the source of greatest overall managerial dissatisfaction (the average manager rates his satisfaction with salary as 4 on a 7-point scale) mobile managers are clearly less satisfied with their salaries (see *Exhibit IV*). Although some of them pointed to specific inequities as the primary reason for their dissatisfaction ("Every time I've moved, I've been given a significant raise in pay. But I have yet to find a place where some of the older guys aren't making as much as or more than I am strictly because of longevity"), many feel their salaries have simply not kept pace to the degree that "someone with my experience and company exposure should reasonably expect."

Immobile managers do not see these "inequities" in the same way—"Fast-trackers come, and fast-trackers go. . . . a few make it, but most don't. While they are busy worrying about another move, the rest of us are keeping the place going."

After salary, advancement is the second highest source of managerial dissatisfaction, immobile managers being considerably less satisfied on this dimension than mobile managers. And yet, while unhappy about advancement, the former express no desire to leave their jobs and exhibit a patience about their progress that is hard to explain. They appear to be painting themselves into a corner by following less promising career paths and neglecting to search out career alternatives. Perhaps their ambivalence is merely a sign that they feel unable to play the mobility game.

Is moving around worth it? To managers who seem to have movement in their blood, the question is likely to be purely academic—they enjoy mobility. For those who are interested in monetary rewards, the answer is no, unless it helps them achieve a highly paying executive position eventually. And, as far as job satisfaction is concerned, the answer is also no.

But what about the challenge of playing the game and the sense of vitality a person can achieve from changing jobs? Is that not a form of payoff? For managers who enjoy playing the game and who are able to realize that upward mobility is not the only measure of a successful career, it clearly is. On the other hand, those who pursue mobility as a zero-sum game and lose will, I believe, experience a great deal of difficulty adapting to the role of an also-ran. These managers run the risk of becoming severely disillusioned when career aspirations are dashed.

A Possible Collision Course

Mobile managers give every indication that they march to the beat of a different drummer—for many, mobility is in their blood. While they are not corporate malcontents, they are considerably more restless and impatient with their careers and, I suspect, more readily frustrated and anxious about the prospects of plateauing than are immobile managers. John W. Dean epitomizes the mobile manager's perspective: "I was at the bottom of the ladder, and *instinctively* I began to climb."[7] Whether mobility is instinct or ethos, many managers following it appear to be on a collision course with the organization. Blinded by their own needs and desires to advance, they do not see some of the pitfalls of their strategy that this study reveals:

Many moves that managers think are advances are, in fact, lateral moves. Hence, managers can easily become unwitting parties to creating the illusion of advancement.

The price of rapid career movement is frequent relocation. Unless managers are willing to uproot their families frequently, especially during mid-career, they should seriously reconsider this course of action.

Mobility and compensation are not synonymous, except for the select few who achieve executive status.

Highly mobile managers all too often get caught up in a success spiral—especially during the period of peak maturity—only to emerge after mid-career disillusioned with their progress or discontent with the career choices they have made.

Being mobile does not ensure job satisfaction. Many managers who are immobile still enjoy their work.

Playing the mobility game need not be a zero-sum game—unless one equates lack of mobility with failure. Some top managements have begun to realize the collision course they are on with their managers. Top managers often face the difficult task of providing realistic appraisals while at the same time trying to avoid dampening the drives and ambitions of their talented performers. At a minimum, these realities need to be faced squarely.

To the extent that mobility is an instinct, they will have to contend with some managers who are unwilling to stay put for long. This is not an issue of poor job design or bad management but rather of realizing that some managers will want to climb the career ladder as quickly as possible—just because it's there.

It is impossible to deny that to reach the top one has to move. Most executives' careers are proof of that. What is at issue, however, is the extent to which an organization should contribute to the myth that mobility pays off or that reaching the top is an indication of worth. Those who do reach the top levels of an organization will do so myth or not; those who do not will suffer when they fail. To prevent unnecessary disappointment, top managers need to expose the illusion of advancement, to appraise managers of their realistic futures, and to create other measures of value besides the soar to the top.

Paradoxically, by encouraging managers to "take control" of their careers, top managers are also increasing the demand for career opportunities. If you encourage people to decide what it is they really want, they often presume that you are going to help them get it. Unless top managers are truly prepared to address this unspoken promise, encouraging managers to plan their careers could ultimately do them more harm than good.

Management needs to be especially vigilant concerning its motives when it encourages lateral moves. It is perfectly reasonable to use lateral moves as a way to revitalize managers; it is not all right to employ these moves to beguile talented managers who might otherwise leave. To create realistic promotion and mobility patterns, it is essential that top management see lateral moves for what they are and be candid about them.

REFERENCES

1. See Eugene E. Jennings, *The Mobile Manager* (New York: McGraw-Hill, 1971) and *Routes to the Executive Suite* (New York: McGraw-Hill, 1971).

2. See Fred H. Goldner, "Demotion in Industrial Management," *American Sociological Review*, vol. 30, 1965, p. 718.

3. See *The Career Development Bulletin*, Columbia University Center for Research in Career Development, Winter 1979, p. 1.

4. See Daniel J. Levinson, *The Seasons of a Man's Life* (New York: Alfred A. Knopf, 1978).

5. See Manfred Kets de Vries, "The Midcareer Conundrum," *Organizational Dynamics*, Autumn 1978, p. 45.

6. Gerard R. Roche, "Compensation and the Mobile Executive," HBR November-December 1975, p. 53.

7. John W. Dean, *Blind Ambition* (New York: Simon & Schuster, 1976), p. 29.

2

When a New Manager Takes Charge

JOHN J. GABARRO

The subsidiary was in serious trouble, so top management hired a young vice president of marketing with an enviable track record in another industry and gave him carte blanche. He reorganized the marketing function using a brand management concept, restructured the sales division, and devised new marketing strategies. Margins continued to erode, however, and after nine months he lost his job.

In another company top management also hired a manager from a different industry to turn around a subsidiary's heavy losses and gave him considerable latitude. He too formulated an entirely new marketing strategy along brand lines. Within a year's time margins improved, and within three years the subsidiary was very profitable and sales had doubled.

On the surface these two situations are strikingly similar. Both executives were in their middle thirties and neither had experience in his new industry. The two men implemented major changes that were remarkably alike. Furthermore, both worked for difficult bosses. Yet one succeeded and the other failed. What factors account for the different outcomes?

To answer this question, we need to look deeper and explore the contexts the two managers faced, their backgrounds, and the taking-charge process itself.

Although only dramatic examples make headlines, a recent study shows that by the time they reach their late forties, general managers have already taken charge of from three to nine management posts.[1] Despite its frequency, however, because situations are unique and managers so different, it is difficult to generalize about the taking-charge process.

Having studied 14 management successions, though, I have found issues common to all and factors that not only affect them but also influence how successful a new person is likely to be. (See the insert entitled "The Managers Taking Charge" that details the research process.)

In using the term *taking charge*, I am referring to the process of learning and taking action that a manager goes through until he (or she) has mastered a new assignment in sufficient depth to be running the organization as well as resources and constraints allow.

The taking-charge process occurs in several predictable stages, each of which has its own tasks, problems, and dilemmas. My study's findings also put to rest the myth of the all-purpose general manager who can be dropped into any situation and triumph. To the contrary, my observations indicate that managers' experiences have a profound and inescapable influence on how they take charge, what areas they focus on, and how successful they are likely to be in mastering the new situation.

The New Manager Arrives

When I looked at the taking-charge process for a period of time, two patterns stood out. First, the process can be long. In the cases studied, for senior U.S. managers, it took from two to two and a half years; some European and U.K. senior managers took even longer. Second, the taking-charge process does not involve steadily more learning or action. Rather, it is a series of alternating phases of intense learning and intense action. Also, the nature of both the managers' learning and actions changes over time.

With few exceptions, most new managers' organizational changes tended to cluster in three bursts of activity. *Exhibit I* shows these periods quite clearly. *Exhibit II* illustrates that the same bursts occur regardless of the type of succession. The data presented in *Exhibits I, II, III,* and *IV* are for completed successions only, in other words, those in which the new manager lasted in the job for two and a half years or longer. As such, the exhibits do not include data from three of the failed successions. The organizational activity measure is a composite of both structural and personnel changes managers made.

What accounts for this pervasive pattern? Why were the major changes made almost invariably in three waves of action? My observations suggest that the underlying patterns of learning and action account for these periods of intense change. They are natural consequences of how new managers learn and act as they try to master strange situations. More specifically, the data suggest that the taking-charge process occurs in five predictable stages: taking hold, immersion, reshaping, consolidation, and refinement. The length of time the executives I studied spent in each stage varied. Some spent as long as 11 months and others as little as 4 in the same stage. Thus time doesn't define a stage; rather, the nature of learning and action that characterizes it does. Let's look at each stage more carefully.

Taking Hold

The first stage, taking hold, typically lasts from three to six months and often sets the tone if not the direction for the rest of the taking-charge process. (*Exhibit III* shows the percentages of personnel and structural changes by six-month periods, which the managers made during their successions.) Taking hold is a period of intense action and learning. If the new assignment is a big promotion or change, the newcomer may at times feel overwhelmed. A new division president commented:

"You're on the edge of your seat all the time. It feels like you have no knowledge base whatsoever. You have to learn the product, the people, and the problems. You're trying like hell to learn about the organization and the people awfully fast and that's the trickiest thing. At first you're afraid to do anything for fear of upsetting the apple cart. The problem is you have to keep the business running while you're learning about it."

During this period a manager is grappling with the nature of the new situation, trying to understand the tasks and problems and assessing the organization and

The Managers Taking Charge

This article is based on a research project that consisted of two sets of field studies totalling 14 management successions. The first set was a longitudinal study of four newly assigned division presidents whom I studied over a three-year period as they went about the process of taking charge. The second set consisted of ten historical case studies of management successions, which were used to expand on and verify the longitudinal studies' results. The 14 cases were chosen to get a range of different kinds of management successions involving both functional and general managers. The successions included American and European organizations varying in sales from $1.2 million to $3 billion. The sample included turnarounds and normal situations and successions that failed as well as those that succeeded.

I studied the longitudinal cases using company documents, on-site observation, and field interviews with the new presidents and their subordinates at the end of 3, 6, 12, 15, 18, 24, 27, 30, and 36 months. For the historical studies, field interviews were conducted and company documents were used. (See "Stages in Management Succession," *Harvard Business School Course Development and Research Profile*, 1984, for a more detailed description of the site selection and methodology.)

Summary description of managers studied

Unit's business	Unit revenues*	Manager's job	Predecessor as superior	Turnaround situation	Industry-specific experience	Insider (I) or outsider (O) to organization	Location	Succession success (S) or failure (F)†
Longitudinal case studies								
Industrial and office products division	$260 million	Division president	yes	no	yes	I	U.S.	S
Machine tool division	175 million	Division president	no	yes	no	O	U.S.	S
Consumer products division	70 million	Division president	no	yes	no	O	U.S.	S
Construction products division	55 million	Division president	yes	no	no	O	U.S.	S

Historical case studies

	Revenues*	Position					Country	
Cable television subsidiary	$1.2 million	General manager	no	no	no	O	U.S.	F
Wholesale food distributor	21 million	Functional head	no	yes	no	O	U.S.	F
District sales organization (communications)	30 million	Functional head	no	no	yes	I	U.S.	S
Beverage manufacturer	90 million	General manager	no	yes	no	O	Netherlands	S
Plastic and metal products	100 million	General manager	yes	no	yes	I	U.K.	F
Beverage manufacturer	110 million	Functional head	yes	no	no	O	Italy	F
Synthetic fibers	200 million	Functional head	yes	yes	yes	I	U.K.	S
Computer and technical products	780 million	General manager	no	no	yes	I	Switzerland	S
Industrial and consumer products	3 billion	General manager	no	yes	yes	I	U.K.	S
Public education	Not available	Functional manager	no	yes	yes	I	U.S.	S

*Unit revenues expressed in 1982 U.S. dollars.

†A succession was considered a failure if the new manager was fired within the first 36 months because of his inability to meet top management's expectations of performance.

its requirements. Managers orient themselves, evaluate the situation, and develop a cognitive map. For example, one division president who was an industry outsider described his learning task as so large that even locking himself up for four days to review strategic, financial, marketing, and industry reports barely made a dent. Early in this stage, he also reported that it took him several hours to go through the morning mail, not only because the issues were new to him but also because the industry had its own technical jargon and nomenclature. Another manager in a similar situation voiced his exasperation by saying resignedly, "There aren't enough hours in the day." (All of the managers in the study happened to be men. I have every reason to believe that female managers would go through the same stages.)

Evaluation and orientation in the taking-hold stage are important even for insiders who already know of the organization and the product. A division president with more than 25 years in his organization spent the first three months in his new job testing his assumptions about key people and the division's problems. He came to several conclusions, one of which was that a senior vice president in his group was in over his head. The division president based his assessment on a number of meetings with the senior vice president, his subordinates' opinions, his plan for the previous five years, complaints about cliques in his area, problems with division functions, and the senior VP's insensitive treatment of two of the company's major overseas distributors. The last item was particularly troublesome because it made the new president doubt the man's judgment. Questioning previous perceptions and beliefs characterized most insider successions during this stage.

Actions taken during the taking-hold stage tend to be corrective. Based on their experience and what they have learned about the new situation, managers fix what problems they can. Obviously, corrective actions vary — some are short-term interventions, others take longer. For instance, in one case, although it took nearly five months before the new manager had developed a strategy for turning around the division, because of his experience, within a month he knew that the division needed both a cost system and a product-line reduction immediately.

A group CEO approached this stage quite differently, however. Having been promoted from within and having himself previously turned around the business's manufacturing operation, he did not make significant short-term corrections his first priority. Rather, focusing on product strategy and planning, he established committees and teams to address these areas. Although his actions did not have the same fix-it quality of the other turnaround, they were nonetheless corrective in that they dealt with areas the new CEO considered critical to the group's success.

The magnitude of corrective action also varies. In his third month in office, a division president with 25 years' experience in the company reorganized his new area. In contrast, the division presidents who were outsiders did not implement comparable changes until their second year in office when they were well beyond the taking-hold stage.

Immersion

Compared with the taking-hold stage, the immersion period is quiet. *Exhibit III* shows a dramatic decrease in changes after the first six months: only 6% of organizational and 9% of personnel changes occurred during the second six months, a time period that generally coincided with the beginning of the

Exhibit I   Average number of organizational changes per three-month period following succession

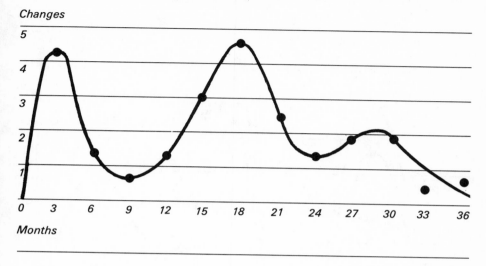

Changes

Months

immersion phase. A lull between bursts of activity, immersion is a very significant time, however, during which executives acquire greater understanding of their new situations. In the U.S. cases I studied, this stage lasted 4 to 11 months.

During immersion, new managers run the organization in a more informed fashion and steep themselves in a less hectic, finer grained learning process than was possible when they were taking hold. Consequently, by the end of this stage, they have developed a new concept or at least have greatly revised their ideas of what they need to do.

More focused learning happens during this period because managers immerse themselves in running the organization and they learn from the interactions and conflicts they deal with day to day. As their experience base grows, they can see patterns they didn't see before. In one case, for example, even though the new division manager made several momentous changes — reorganizing manufacturing by product lines and implementing better control, scheduling, and cost systems — during the taking-hold stage, manufacturing cost problems persisted. During the immersion stage, he was able to see that many of these had their roots in the product's design, and, ultimately, in how the division's engineering group was structured. It took, however, six to eight months of exploration before this underlying cause became clear.

Even when changes made in the taking-hold stage work, the immersion period still offers opportunities for further learning. New problems that had been masked or overshadowed by larger problems emerge. For example, after a division president had reorganized his division from a functional to a geographic structure, with a domestic-international split, a new set of problems surfaced during the immersion period that neither he nor his management team had foreseen. The earlier reorganization significantly increased the responsiveness,

Exhibit II Average Number of Organizational Changes per Six-Month Period Following Succession, Categorized

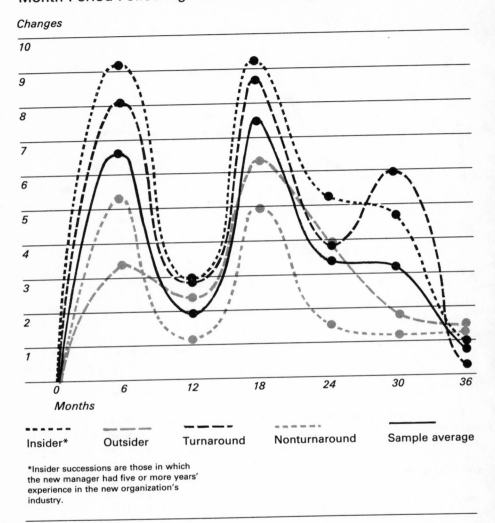

*Insider successions are those in which the new manager had five or more years' experience in the new organization's industry.

productivity, and coordination between functions in the United States and abroad, but as these areas improved, the U.S. sales force's organization and its distribution channels showed weaknesses. The old structure's cross-functional problems had hidden these weaknesses.

During immersion new managers also question whether they have the right people in place. Obvious questions about competence arose in the taking-hold stage, but now they were easier to discern. Similarly, in more than half the cases studied, the newcomers explored uncertainties they had about staff members and discussed them with others.

The analysis, probes, discussions, and, in some cases, agony of the immersion stage result in new managers' arriving at a better understanding of the more basic dynamics of the organization, people, and the industry. The concept that emerges from this stage (whether new or refined) is not necessarily radical. In 6 of the 14 cases, however, the revised concept had implications for radical changes in either strategy or organization or both. In most of the cases, it also resulted in a sharper plan of action for improving the situation further.

Reshaping

During the third stage, reshaping, the second important — and in most cases the largest — burst of activity takes place. Learning continues but in a more diminished and routine fashion. In the reshaping period, new managers direct their attention toward reconfiguring one or more aspects of the organization to implement the concept they developed or made final during the immersion stage.

The reshaping stage, like the taking-hold period, involves a great deal of organizational change. *Exhibit III* shows that more than 32% of the personnel changes and 29% of the structural changes were made during the third six-month period. Again I should caution that the stages did not neatly apportion themselves out into six-month periods. Nonetheless, after 13 to 18 months, most managers studied had reached the reshaping stage, where they were eager to act on the learning and exploration they had experienced in the immersion period. Indeed, immersion activities usually pave the way for reshaping-stage changes.

Immersion is a transition, and by the end of it new managers and often their key subordinates are impatient to get on with things. In one case, for example, a new division president had to fend off growing pressure from two of his vice presidents while he commissioned several task forces to focus on the areas of intended change. As he put it, "The task-force reports will take us to the point where there will be no surprises and a lot of added insights. The nice part of this is that everyone will know what needs to be done and they'll have ownership of the changes we decide to make. If the obvious answer is wrong, the reports will flush it out. In the meantime, I have to convince the guys down the hall that the added time this requires is worth it."

Reshaping-stage changes may involve altering processes as well as making major structural shifts. Two divisions studied went from product to functional structures.

As one would imagine, the reshaping stage is very busy, especially if it involves major changes. For example, when one manager was reorganizing both marketing and sales, he had to call two series of meetings (one with the affected managers and another with the district sales forces to explain the changes), work out details where positional changes and relocations were involved, and call on key customers and distributors. Thus, although management announced plans for the changes at the outset of this stage, their implementation took nearly eight weeks of sustained activity on the part of the new president, his new marketing VP, and his domestic sales manager. As one would expect, the learning in the reshaping stage consists mainly of feedback, for example, on the impact the sales reorganization had on key distributors and on orders.

Exhibit III Personnel and Structural Changes Made by Six-Month Periods

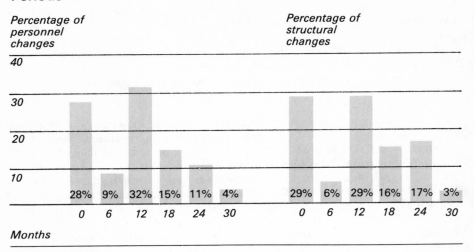

Percentage of personnel changes

Percentage of structural changes

40												
30												
20												
10	28%	9%	32%	15%	11%	4%	29%	6%	29%	16%	17%	3%

Months: 0 6 12 18 24 30   0 6 12 18 24 30

Reshaping ends when new managers have implemented as much of their concept as circumstances allow. In practice, several factors (the most common is the unavailability of people for key positions) often prevent them from completing the job.

Consolidation

The third and final wave of action in the taking-charge process occurs during the fourth stage, consolidation. Throughout this period, much of new managers' learning and action focuses on consolidating and following through on the changes they made during reshaping. The process is evaluative; for example, new managers and their key subordinates judge the consequences of the actions they took in the reshaping burst of activity and take corrective measures.

Learning at this point involves two sets of issues, the first of which is identifying what the left-over follow-through implementation problems are and how to deal with them. For instance, during his reshaping stage, a new president had reorganized his division from a product to a functional structure. But he had deferred integrating one of the former product group's manufacturing departments into the divisional manufacturing function until several other changes had been completed. When most of the reorganization had been accomplished, he and his manufacturing vice president began to study how the product group could be integrated.

A second set of issues evolves from unanticipated problems resulting from changes made during the reshaping stage. Much of the consolidation period's extraordinary activity involves diagnosing and studying these problems, then correcting them.

Finally, during consolidation, new managers deal with those aspects of their concept that they could not implement before. In several situations, for instance, managers had to wait to find a person for an important position or to transfer one of the organization's managers who could not move earlier.

Refinement

The refinement stage is a period of little organizational change. By this point executives have taken charge and their learning and actions tend to focus either on refining operations or on looking for opportunities in the marketplace, in technology, or in other areas. In one case, the manager looked at potential acquisitions; in another, the manager seriously considered divesting part of the business.

This stage marks the end of the taking-charge process. By this time managers can no longer be considered new. They no longer feel new, nor do their subordinates perceive or speak of them as new. Whatever the problems the executives now face, they do not result from newness. By now they have either established credibility and a power base or they have not. They have had enough time to shape their situations and they will be judged by the results of their actions. If they are still uncomfortable, usually it is because of pressing business problems such as a recession or mounting interest rates rather than unfamiliarity with their jobs.

Refinement is a calm period. From this stage onward, managers' learning will be more incremental and routine. Important developments in the economy, the marketplace, or technology may destroy this calmness, but whatever additional learning and action such factors lead to, they do not result from newness. For better or worse, the manager has taken charge.

What Makes a Difference?

A number of factors shape how executives progress through these stages and how successfully they take charge. Important determinants include a new manager's experience, whether the business needs turning around, the person's managerial style and personal needs, his relationships with key people by the end of the first year, and whether the manager's management style conflicts with that of his boss. Let me describe each of these in more detail.

Roots That Endure

All other things being equal, managers' functional backgrounds, managerial experiences, and special competencies appear to determine how they take charge: what actions they take and how competently they implement them.

The extent to which managers' functional experience influences their actions is quite surprising. For 13 of the 14 new managers studied, their initial actions were in areas where they had had functional experience, and the most significant changes they made during the three years also were in the areas where they had experience (see *Exhibit IV*). This pattern is not surprising for functional managers. But emergence of the same pattern among the general managers reveals the extent to which experience influences actions and points of view.

Because *Exhibit IV* is a summary, it understates both the specificity and pervasiveness of how much the new managers' experience affected their actions. *Exhibit V* looks at ten managers' experience and actions in some detail.

Exhibit IV Summary of How Managers' Functional Experience Affected Their Actions

| | Longitudinal studies | | | | Historical studies | | | | | | | | | |
| | Division presidents | | | | Other general managers | | | | | Functional managers | | | | |
Actions taken	1	2	3	4	5	6	7	8	9	10	11	12	13	14
Initial actions														
Initial activities were in area of prior functional experience.	X	X	X	X	X	X	X	X	X	X	X	NO	X	X
First structural change affected area of prior functional experience.	X	X	X	X	X	NO	NC	X	X	X	NC	NO	X	NC
Major action														
Most significant change made in first three years affected area of prior functional experience.	X	X	X	X	X	X	X	X	X	X	X	NO	X	X
Most significant structural change affected area of prior functional experience.	X	X	X	X	X	X	NC	X	X	X	NC	X	X	NC

X = yes

NO = no

NC = no change made: manager made no structural changes.

If one thinks in terms of the five taking-charge stages, this pattern is not so surprising. Indeed, one could predict that any significant additional experience base managers gain as a result of taking charge of a new assignment will not be firm until after they have experienced the deeper learning of the immersion stage, acted on this knowledge in the reshaping stage, and learned from these actions in the consolidation stage.

Insiders vs. outsiders. New managers' experience in their organization's industry also affected significantly how they took charge and what problems they encountered. First, industry insiders (managers who have five or more years' experience in the new organization's industry) take hold much more quickly than do outsiders. Insiders begin with a larger wave of action and their actions tend to be more basic. For example, fully 33% of all of the structural changes industry insiders made occurred during their first six months. Second, the number of actions insiders take is greater not only in the taking-hold stage (in the study on average insiders' actions were twice as frequent) but throughout the entire taking-charge process. Moreover, whereas three of four of the managers who did not succeed in their jobs lacked industry experience, only four of ten successful managers lacked such experience (I defined a failed appointment as one in which the new manager was fired within three years of taking charge).

One case in which a marketing manager with more than 15 years' experience in packaged goods and toiletries became marketing and sales director of a $110 million beverage division illustrates an outsider's difficulties. On the surface his background looked like a good fit, but the new industry was different from traditional packaged goods in a number of important ways. The outsider's experience had served him well in product planning and changing systems during the taking-hold period and later in restructuring the sales force. It had not, however, prepared him for dealing with the sales force or his major distributors, both of which required a hands-on approach. By the end of the taking-hold stage, he was in serious trouble with both groups. By the end of his first year, his cool, professional managerial style had alienated some key distributors so much that the division general manager had to intervene in several critical situations. These incidents undermined the new manager's ability to develop credibility with customers and subordinates.

Turning Things Around

How unfavorable a new situation was also influenced the taking-charge process in the cases I studied. In turnarounds managers feel a great deal of pressure to act on problems quickly. One might expect that in a turnaround, because of the urgency of the situation, executives would have a shorter taking-hold stage, but neither the aggregated data nor the individual case data support this. If anything, the data suggest that the taking-hold wave actually lasts longer in a turnaround.

Although the action waves are of comparable duration, the activity in the reshaping and consolidation stages peaks earlier in the turnarounds by about three to six months, a pattern which no doubt reflects the urgency experienced in turnarounds.

None of these differences between normal successions and turnarounds that the data uncovered is surprising. Others, which surfaced in manager interviews,

Exhibit V Comparison of Managers' Functional Experience and Actions Taken (Historical Studies)

Business, manager's title, and company sales	Prior assignment	Functional experience	Initial area of major involvement	Areas affected by first structural change	Areas affected by major structural change	Areas affected by most significant changes of first three years
Cable television subsidiary General manager $1.2 million	Communications engineer (in another company)	Engineering	Construction and engineering planning	Engineering installation and construction	Same	Reorganization of chief engineer's department affecting engineering, construction, and installation
Wholesale food distribution Vice president—marketing and sales $21 million	Vice president—marketing and planning (in another company)	Marketing and product management	Product planning and reduction of sales force	Creation of product manager's position and reorganization of product sales groups	Marketing (creation of product manager's responsibilities)	Introduction of product management
District sales service organization District manager $30 million	Sales service administrator (in same company)	Customer service	Sales service audit	(No structural changes made)	(No structural changes made)	Sales service training

Company	Previous position	Functional background				
Beverage manufacturer *Division general manager* *$80 million*	Division general manager (in another company)	Marketing and market planning (also experience in two prior turnarounds as general manager)	Sales force and marketing	Sales force	Creation of marketing function and reorganization of sales force	Revision of mission scope and revamping of marketing strategy affecting marketing and sales
Plastic and metal products *Group managing director* *$100 million*	Division general manager (in same company)	Manufacturing and engineering	Manufacturing rationalization	(No structural changes made)	(No structural changes made)	Manufacturing rationalization
Beverage manufacturer *Director of marketing and sales* *$110 million*	Marketing and sales director (in another company)	Marketing	Sales and sales procedures and information systems	Sales force	Sales and marketing	Sales systems and procedures
Synthetic fibers *Director of manufacturing* *$300 million*	Works manager (in same company)	Manufacturing and engineering	Restructuring of manufacturing management	Manufacturing	Same	Rationalization and restructuring of production operations

Exhibit V Continued

Business, manager's title, and company sales	Prior assignment	Functional experience	Initial area of major involvement	Areas affected by first structural change	Areas affected by major structural change	Areas affected by most significant changes of first three years
Computer and technical products Group vice president and general manager $780 million	Group general marketing manager (in same company)	Marketing, sales operations, and engineering	Marketing and sales operations	Group staff functions (finance, controller, group support functions)	Sales operations and marketing	Restructuring of sales operations
Industrial and consumer Group CEO $3 billion	Group manufacturing director (in same company)	Manufacturing management and production control (turnaround experience)	Product strategy and product planning, manufacturing operations, and production engineering	Manufacturing and production engineering	Manufacturing, product engineering, and product planning	Manufacturing operations, production engineering, quality control, and product planning
Public education Administrator	Administrator (in same system)	Educational administration (turnaround experience)	School discipline, athletics and activities, accreditation, and community involvement	(Not applicable)	(Not applicable)	Discipline, academic standards, student activities, and community involvement

are. For one thing, turnaround managers told me they knew they would have to redo later some of the changes they were making in the taking-hold stage.

In one case, the new general manager reported he knew from experience (this was his third turnaround) that it would take five to six months to design and implement a cost system that was sophisticated enough to provide all the information he needed on which products were losing money and why. He concluded that he simply did not have the time to do it perfectly and opted instead for a system that would give him as quickly as possible a better vision of the problems.

Managers don't make such suboptimal decisions gladly. When new managers and their subordinates had fewer problems to deal with (usually in the consolidation period) they would go back and improve the tourniquet systems and processes they had installed earlier.

Although the turnaround managers were under much greater pressure than their nonturnaround counterparts, they benefited from certain advantages. Generally speaking, their companies gave them much more latitude in taking action than the managers had in the normal successions. This was particularly true during the taking-hold stage. The two situations I described in the beginning of the article illustrate this well.

In the first case, after six weeks on the job, the new marketing vice president proposed a wholly new marketing strategy that top management rapidly approved. Such agreeableness is rare in nonturnaround successions. In the second case, the new manager's head office not only gave him a much greater degree of freedom than it usually gave its division general managers, but it also buffered him from corporate staff intervention for the first two years. After the manager completed the turnaround, top management told him he now had to play by the rules and conform more closely to corporate policies.

Generally, because of the urgency of the situations, the turnaround managers started with a larger power base than their counterparts and faced less rivalry from key subordinates who might have wanted their jobs. But several turnaround managers reported feeling their organizations were fearful and tense, which put additional pressure on them to settle things as quickly as possible.

The New Manager's Style

The 14 men I studied varied significantly in their styles, including how they spent their time—alone, in meetings, on tours—what kinds of meetings and interactions they preferred—one-to-one, recurrently scheduled or specially scheduled meetings, planned meetings versus ad hoc meetings—and their preferences for formality or informality.

Managerial style affects how people respond to an executive initially and influences the entire taking-charge process, including how the person makes decisions. The most dramatic example of this was one president who had a fairly hands-on approach to problems and needed control. Because he thought that the product organization prevented him from seeing problems at the functional level, he struggled throughout the immersion stage. Finally, he reorganized the division from a product to a functional structure. The implementation of this change was painful for the organization and required that several functional vice presidents split their time among three businesses, two of which were geographically separated, so that they had to travel every week. Nonetheless, the total succession went very well.

For this president, acting according to his style was a necessity. During the final debriefing in the study's fourth year, he told me that he believed he could not have turned the company around without restructuring it to fit his needs. His successor introduced a series of changes, which again made the organization more product oriented.

Relationships with Key People

Perhaps the single most salient difference between the successful and the failed transitions was the quality of the new manager's working relationships at the end of his first year. For example, at this point, three of four managers in the failed successions had poor working relationships with two or more of their key subordinates and with two or more peers, and all had poor working relationships with their superiors. In contrast, in the same time frame, only one of the new administrators in the successful transitions had a poor relationship with his boss and none had poor relationships with two or more people who reported directly to them.

Many reasons were given for these interpersonal problems, such as rivalry issues, disagreement about goals, different beliefs about what comprised effective performance, and conflicts in management style. The underlying common problem, however, was the new managers' failure to develop a set of shared expectations with their key subordinates or their bosses. Without common understanding, each side in the relationships inevitably stopped trusting the other.

The studies showed that developing effective working relationships was a critical task in the taking-hold and immersion stages. If managers didn't explore important differences in the very beginning of their successions, further problems would crop up. Managers in the successful transitions usually confronted problems by the end of the immersion stage and resolved them either by attaining agreement or by parting company.

Conflicts in Management Style

Surprisingly, many of the new managers studied (6 of 14) described a conflict in styles with their bosses as being a major problem in taking charge. Although conflicts and differences in styles also existed in relationships with subordinates, I am highlighting the problem between new managers and their bosses because this type of discord characterized all but one of the failed successions.

The conflicts always involved control and delegation. In one case, for example, a new general manager five months into the job was exasperated because his boss wouldn't stop a capital request that the manager's predecessor had submitted. The boss had asked his technical and financial staffs to review the situation and was waiting for their report before acting. This manager also reported difficulty in getting quick answers from his boss about operational questions. The manager thought his boss delegated too much and wasn't on top of details.

In contrast, another new executive felt he couldn't get his boss off his back. The situation finally exploded at the end of the first year when his boss gave him a poor performance evaluation for not being involved enough in details and for delegating too much to his subordinates.

In both these cases, the conflicts arose partly because managers hadn't clarified expectations with their bosses but mainly because of less rational factors, including profound beliefs about what is good management. Namely, a good executive sets goals clearly and delegates responsibility to subordinates without interfering versus a good manager gets involved in details and is action oriented and decisive.

How can new managers deal with differences in style? In the cases studied, the new managers had to take the initiative to work out differences and make the accommodations needed for working effectively with their bosses. In the first case, for example, the new manager stopped pressing his boss about the capital project; instead he worked with the two staff groups who were conducting the review. The second manager defined his performance targets specifically with his boss, so the boss could delegate to him more comfortably.

In the three successful transitions marked by sharp style conflicts, the managers employed similar means to deal with them.

How Stacked Is the Deck?

As we can see, many variables influence how well managers take charge. Critical factors range from managers' experience to how effectively they deal with key subordinates and their bosses. Although some are more critical than others, no one factor dominates. Evaluated together, however, they can indicate how much difficulty a new manager will face. Let me illustrate this by returning to the two vignettes that began this article. On the surface they looked so similar but they turned out so differently.

In the first case, in which the new marketing vice president lasted only nine months, his lack of industry experience hurt him considerably, especially since both his immediate boss and the division's parent management also lacked industry experience. His boss's failure to clarify his expectations about performance and a major conflict in management style between the two men further exacerbated the situation. Finally, a poor working relationship with an important peer, who sought to undermine the new manager, complicated his difficulties.

If the deck is stacked, as it was in this case, unless the new manager or his boss is insightful enough to defuse, compensate for, or in some other way minimize problems, the succession is doomed. In the other case, although the parameters were the same, the dynamics among the players were quite different, so that the second new manager prospered where the other failed.

Managing the New Manager

This study's findings offer several implications that, taken together, challenge a number of assumptions and current practices. First, we can see clearly that understanding a situation and having an impact on it do not occur overnight. Fast-track developmental assignments do not, in the end, benefit the individual, the new unit, or the organization.

Second, the all-purpose general manager who can parachute into any situation and succeed is a myth. Experience and special competencies do matter.

Finally, human variables such as managerial styles make a difference, not only to the organization's climate but also to the business decisions a new manager makes and to how he implements them.

Other soft factors such as potential conflicts in managerial styles and a newcomer's ability to develop effective working relationships also seriously affect

Taking Charge: Tasks and Dilemmas

I Taking hold: orientation and evaluation, corrective actions	Tasks	Develop an understanding of the new situation
		Take corrective actions
		Develop initial set of priorities and "map" of the situation
		Develop initial set of expectations with key subordinates
		Establish the basis for effective working relationships
	Dilemma	How quickly to act on apparent problems?
		Act too quickly—risks:
		Make a poor decision because of lack of adequate information or knowledge
		Take actions that constrain subsequent decisions that cannot be anticipated yet
		Lose advantages of the "honeymoon" period
		Act too slowly—risks:
		Lose credibility because of apparent indecisiveness
		Lose valuable time

		Tasks
II	Immersion: fine-grained, exploratory learning and managing the business	Develop a deeper, finer grained understanding of the new situation and the people
		Assess consequences of taking-hold period actions
		Reassess priorities
		Settle questions and problems concerning key personnel
		Reconfigure "map" of the situation; fill out or revise the concept
		Prepare for reshaping actions
III	Reshaping: acting on the revised concept	Reconfigure organization based on finer grained understanding
		Deal with underlying causes of residual problems
		Be open to unanticipated problems that emerge as a result of second-wave changes
IV	Consolidation: evaluative learning, follow-through, and corrective action	Follow through on reshaping actions
		Deal with unanticipated problems of reshaping stage
		Remain open to new developments
V	Refinement: refining operations, looking for new opportunities	

outcomes. These are, however, subjective factors that often fall into the non-discussable category that senior management seldom considers when it plans successions. Only the savviest planners factor them in and give them the weight they deserve.

Let me be more specific about the findings' implications for both managers who are taking charge and organizations that must be concerned with succession planning and career development.

When You Are Taking Charge

For a manager in the middle of taking charge this article may be a mixed blessing. On the one hand, it may be a relief to know that the process occurs in stages that consist of predictable learning and action tasks (see the insert entitled "Taking Charge: Tasks and Dilemmas" for a summary). On the other, to realize that there may still be considerable learning and action to accomplish after the first three to six months on the job can be a bit dismaying.

The other potentially unsettling implication is that in each of these stages the manager is on a tightrope. For example, if the taking-hold stage is a bit of a honeymoon, it is also a period in which new managers must establish their credibility. If they act too slowly, they risk losing the honeymoon period's advantages as well as valuable time, and they can appear indecisive. But if new executives act too quickly, they risk making poor decisions because of inadequate knowledge or they take actions that preclude options they may later wish they had.

Managers who are industry outsiders are on particularly slippery ground. In the absence of good advice or data, they may be better off deferring major changes until they have learned more in the immersion stage. The small first waves of action and large second waves in the outsider successions I studied probably reflect an intuitive recognition of this dilemma.

Finally, interpersonal factors emerge in one fashion or another. If, for example, newcomers find themselves in a managerial style conflict, they should not think it's bizarre; it occurred in almost half the situations I studied.

In general, a comparison of failed and effective transitions indicates that front-end work is crucial, especially in working out parameters and expectations with bosses. In the successful successions, the new managers made their mandates as specific and explicit as possible. They also made a point of keeping their superiors informed, for example, discussing with them changes they were proposing in detail—particularly during the early taking-charge stages. In contrast, the managers who failed carried vague mandates.

The successful managers were also more aware of their limitations in experience or skills and compensated for them either with selective learning or by drawing on their colleagues' abilities.

Succession Planning and Career Development

As the preceding discussion suggests, top management can take a number of steps to help minimize new administrators' problems. The most obvious of these is making the new person's charter explicit. If this is not possible (because top management doesn't understand the unit's business or the industry is in a period of turmoil), the new manager should know it. For example, in the opening vignette in which the new manager failed after nine months, headquarters hadn't told him that the most urgent priority was to reverse a decline in the newly acquired subsidiary's margins. The innocent new vice president started off buying market share, which inevitably eroded further the margins in the short term.

There are other things companies can do to facilitate the taking-charge process. General Electric, for example, runs assimilation meetings to accelerate working out expectations between new managers and their key subordinates. Conducted by the human resource staff, these meetings give new managers and those who report directly to them the opportunity to talk about expectations and other concerns early in a new manager's tenure. Top management can also anticipate the potential problems new managers who lack relevant experience face, particularly during the taking-charge stages, and lessen them by providing adequate — subordinate or corporate — backup support.

An important implication of this research for succession planning is that taking charge (defined in terms of impact and learning) takes time. Companies that make brief assignments at upper and middle levels will get quick fixes. If assignments are too short for a new manager to go beyond the taking-hold stage, the new manager will deal only with those problems that he or she knows how to fix. That may be enough if a manager's experience base is broad and deep, but when short-term assignments become company policy, both individual units and the organization as a whole suffer eventually. Taken to its extreme, such a policy feeds the obsession with short-term results that many observers have criticized.[2]

Short-term assignments also make little sense from a career development point of view. In most brief assignments, managers can't progress beyond the immersion stage. Yet the payoffs to the organization in substantive change and for the individual in important residual learning and added experience don't come until later. Significant new learning begins in the immersion stage when the outsider is familiar enough to probe underlying issues and subtle cause-and-effect relationships. Managers cannot test this new learning, though, until they act in the reshaping stage, evaluate their actions, and learn more in the consolidation and refinement stages.

The importance of experience also has several implications for succession planning and career development. All other factors being equal, an insider with industry-specific or other relevant experience is more likely to take charge with fewer difficulties than an outsider without industry-specific experience. Three of the four managers who failed were industry outsiders in well-run U.S. and European companies.

The importance of experience, which the study highlighted, also challenges the concept of the professional manager. Although turnaround specialists can succeed in a variety of situations, they are the exception, not the rule; in fact, they are themselves specialists of a kind.

I am not arguing that general management skills don't exist or that people can't transfer them into new settings. I am pointing out that lack of relevant industry or functional experience will make the taking-charge process more difficult, and companies should consider this when planning successions.

When choosing successors to managerial posts, top management has to make some difficult trade-offs in terms of what is good for the person, the unit, and the organization. If one of the organization's objectives is to develop a well-trained pool of managerial talent, then the head office should put executives in assignments that stretch them by broadening their experience. This will inevitably mean putting people with less than optimal experience in charge of units whose performance may suffer, at least in the short term. The question is whether the benefits to the person and to the larger organization are worth the costs. Also, because managers, like all human beings, learn from the feedback of bad as well as good experiences (some may argue they learn more from the ones that turn out badly), top management has to judge how long to keep executives in situations where they are having problems.

On the other hand, if management always assigns people with strong relevant experience, it forfeits giving executives broadening experiences, which become increasingly important at middle and upper levels. The guideline should be to provide developmental assignments that are not totally out of line with a manager's experience and that last long enough to produce important lessons.

REFERENCES

1. John P. Kotter, *The General Managers* (New York: Free Press, 1982).

2. Robert H. Hayes and William J. Abernathy, "Managing Our Way to Economic Decline," HBR July-August 1980, p. 67.

3

Power Failure in Management Circuits

ROSABETH MOSS KANTER

Power is America's last dirty word. It is easier to talk about money—and much easier to talk about sex—than it is to talk about power. People who have it deny it; people who want it do not want to appear to hunger for it; and people who engage in its machinations do so secretly.

Yet, because it turns out to be a critical element in effective managerial behavior, power should come out from undercover. Having searched for years for those styles or skills that would identify capable organization leaders, many analysts, like myself, are rejecting individual traits or situational appropriateness as key and finding the sources of a leader's real power.

Access to resources and information and the ability to act quickly make it possible to accomplish more and to pass on more resources and information to subordinates. For this reason, people tend to prefer bosses with "clout." When employees perceive their manager as influential upward and outward, their status is enhanced by association and they generally have high morale and feel less critical or resistant to their boss.[1] More powerful leaders are also more likely to delegate (they are too busy to do it all themselves), to reward talent, and to build a team that places subordinates in significant positions.

Powerlessness, in contrast, tends to breed bossiness rather than true leadership. In large organizations, at least, it is powerlessness that often creates ineffective, desultory management and petty, dictatorial, rules-minded managerial styles. Accountability without power—responsibility for results without the resources to get them—creates frustration and failure. People who see themselves as weak and powerless and find their subordinates resisting or discounting them tend to use more punishing forms of influence. If organizational power can "ennoble," then, recent research shows, organizational powerlessness can (with apologies to Lord Acton) "corrupt."[2]

So perhaps power, in the organization at least, does not deserve such a bad reputation. Rather than connoting only dominance, control, and oppression, *power* can mean efficacy and capacity—something managers and executives need to move the organization toward its goals. Power in organizations is analogous in simple terms to physical power: it is the ability to mobilize resources (human and material) to get things done. The true sign of power, then, is accomplishment—not fear, terror, or tyranny. Where the power is "on," the system can be productive; where the power is "off," the system bogs down.

But saying that people need power to be effective in organizations does not tell us where it comes from or why some people, in some jobs, systematically seem to have more of it than others. In this article I want to show that to discover the sources of productive power, we have to look not at the *person*—as conventional classifications of effective managers and employees do—but at the *position* the person occupies in the organization.

Where Does Power Come From?

The effectiveness that power brings evolves from two kinds of capacities: first, access to the resources, information, and support necessary to carry out a task; and, second, ability to get cooperation in doing what is necessary. (*Exhibit I* identifies some symbols of an individual manager's power.)

Both capacities derive not so much from a leader's style and skill as from his or her location in the formal and informal systems of the organization—in both job definition and connection to other important people in the company. Even the ability to get cooperation from subordinates is strongly defined by the manager's clout outward. People are more responsive to bosses who look as if they can get more for them from the organization.

We can regard the uniquely organizational sources of power as consisting of three "lines":

1. *Lines of supply.* Influence outward, over the environment, means that managers have the capacity to bring in the things that their own organizational domain needs—materials, money, resources to distribute as rewards, and perhaps even prestige.

2. *Lines of information.* To be effective, managers need to be "in the know" in both the formal and the informal sense.

3. *Lines of support.* In a formal framework, a manager's job parameters need to allow for nonordinary action, for a show of discretion or exercise of judgment. Thus managers need to know that they can assume innovative, risk-taking activities without having to go through the stifling multilayered approval process. And, informally, managers need the backing of other important figures in the organization whose tacit approval becomes another resource they bring to their own work unit as well as a sign of the manager's being "in."

Note that productive power has to do with *connections* with other parts of a system. Such systemic aspects of power derive from two sources—job activities and political alliances:

1. Power is most easily accumulated when one has a job that is designed and located to allow *discretion* (nonroutinized action permitting flexible, adaptive, and creative contributions), *recognition* (visibility and notice), and *relevance* (being central to pressing organizational problems).

2. Power also comes when one has relatively close contact with *sponsors* (higher-level people who confer approval, prestige, or backing), *peer networks* (circles of acquaintanceship that provide reputation and information, the grapevine often being faster than formal communication channels), and *subordinates* (who can be developed to relieve managers of some of their burdens and to represent the manager's point of view).

When managers are in powerful situations, it is easier for them to accomplish more. Because the tools are there, they are likely to be highly motivated and, in turn, to be able to motivate subordinates. Their activities are more likely to be on target and to net them successes. They can flexibly interpret or shape policy to meet the needs of particular areas, emergent situations, or sudden environmental shifts. They gain the respect and cooperation that attributed power brings. Subordinates' talents are resources rather than threats. And, because powerful managers have so many lines of connection and thus are oriented outward, they tend to let go of control downward, developing more independently functioning lieutenants.

The powerless live in a different world. Lacking the supplies, information, or support to make things happen easily, they may turn instead to the ultimate weapon of those who lack productive power — oppressive power: holding others back and punishing with whatever threats they can muster.

Exhibit II summarizes some of the major ways in which variables in the organization and in job design contribute to either power or powerlessness.

Positions of Powerlessness

Understanding what it takes to have power and recognizing the classic behavior of the powerless can immediately help managers make sense out of a number of familiar organizational problems that are usually attributed to inadequate people:

The ineffectiveness of first-line supervisors.

The petty interest protection and conservatism of staff professionals.

The crises of leadership at the top.

Instead of blaming the individuals involved in organizational problems, let us look at the positions people occupy. Of course, power or powerlessness in a position may not be all of the problem. Sometimes incapable people *are* at fault and need to be retrained or replaced. (See page 157 for a discussion of another special case, women.) But where patterns emerge, where the troubles associated with some units persist, organizational power failures could be the reason. Then, as Volvo President Pehr Gyllenhammar concludes, we should treat the powerless not as "villains" causing headaches for everyone else but as "victims."[3]

First-Line Supervisors

Because an employee's most important work relationship is with his or her supervisor, when many of them talk about "the company," they mean their immediate boss. Thus a supervisor's behavior is an important determinant of the average employee's relationship to work and is in itself a critical link in the production chain.

Yet I know of no U.S. corporate management entirely satisfied with the performance of its supervisors. Most see them as supervising too closely and not training their people. In one manufacturing company where direct laborers were asked on a survey how they learned their job, on a list of seven possibilities "from my supervisor" ranked next to last. (Only company training programs ranked worse.) Also, it is said that supervisors do not translate company policies into practice — for instance, that they do not carry out the right of every employee to frequent performance reviews or to career counseling.

In court cases charging race or sex discrimination, first-line supervisors are frequently cited as the "discriminating official."[4] And, in studies of innovative work redesign and quality of work life projects, they often appear as the implied

Exhibit I Some Common Symbols of a Manager's Organizational Power (influence upward and outward)

To what extent a manager can—

Intercede favorably on behalf of someone in trouble with the organization

Get a desirable placement for a talented subordinate

Get approval for expenditures beyond the budget

Get above-average salary increases for subordinates

Get items on the agenda at policy meetings

Get fast access to top decision makers

Get regular, frequent access to top decision makers

Get early information about decisions and policy shifts

villains; they are the ones who are said to undermine the program or interfere with its effectiveness. In short, they are often seen as "not sufficiently managerial."

The problem affects white-collar as well as blue-collar supervisors. In one large government agency, supervisors in field offices were seen as the source of problems concerning morale and the flow of information to and from headquarters. "Their attitudes are negative," said a senior official. "They turn people against the agency; they put down senior management. They build themselves up by always complaining about headquarters, but prevent their staff from getting any information directly. We can't afford to have such attitudes communicated to field staff."

Is the problem that supervisors need more management training programs or that incompetent people are invariably attracted to the job? Neither explanation suffices. A large part of the problem lies in the position itself—one that almost universally creates powerlessness.

First-line supervisors are "people in the middle," and that has been seen as the source of many of their problems.[5] But by recognizing that first-line supervisors are caught between higher management and workers, we only begin to skim the surface of the problem. There is practically no other organizational category as subject to powerlessness.

First, these supervisors may be at a virtual dead end in their careers. Even in companies where the job used to be a stepping stone to higher-level management jobs, it is now common practice to bring in MBAs from the outside for those positions. Thus moving from the ranks of direct labor into supervision may mean, essentially, getting "stuck" rather than moving upward. Because employees do not perceive supervisors as eventually joining the leadership circles of the organization, they may see them as lacking the high-level contacts needed to have clout. Indeed, sometimes turnover among supervisors is so high that workers feel they can outwait—and outwit—any boss.

Second, although they lack clout, with little in the way of support from above, supervisors are forced to administer programs or explain policies that they have no hand in shaping. In one company, as part of a new personnel program

Exhibit II Ways Organizational Factors Contribute to Power or Powerlessness

Factors	Generates power when factor is	Generates powerlessness when factor is
Rules inherent in the job	few	many
Predecessors in the job	few	many
Established routines	few	many
Task variety	high	low
Rewards for reliability/predictability	few	many
Rewards for unusual performance/innovation	many	few
Flexibility around use of people	high	low
Approvals needed for nonroutine decisions	few	many
Physical location	central	distant
Publicity about job activities	high	low
Relation of tasks to current problem areas	central	peripheral
Focus of tasks	outside work unit	inside work unit
Interpersonal contact in the job	high	low
Contact with senior officials	high	low
Participation in programs, conferences, meetings	high	low
Participation in problem-solving task forces	high	low
Advancement prospects of subordinates	high	low

supervisors were required to conduct counseling interviews with employees. But supervisors were not trained to do this and were given no incentives to get involved. Counseling was just another obligation. Then managers suddenly encouraged the workers to bypass their supervisors or to put pressure on them. The personnel staff brought them together and told them to demand such interviews as a basic right. If supervisors had not felt powerless before, they did after that squeeze from below, engineered from above.

The people they supervise can also make life hard for them in numerous ways. This often happens when a supervisor has himself or herself risen up from the ranks. Peers that have not made it are resentful or derisive of their former colleague, whom they now see as trying to lord it over them. Often it is easy for workers to break rules and let a lot of things slip.

Yet first-line supervisors are frequently judged according to rules and regulations while being limited by other regulations in what disciplinary actions they can take. They often lack the resources to influence or reward people; after all, workers are guaranteed their pay and benefits by someone other than their supervisors. Supervisors cannot easily control events; rather, they must react to them.

In one factory, for instance, supervisors complained that performance of their job was out of their control: they could fill production quotas only if they had the supplies, but they had no way to influence the people controlling supplies.

The lack of support for many first-line managers, particularly in large organizations, was made dramatically clear in another company. When asked if contact with executives higher in the organization who had the potential for offering support, information, and alliances diminished their own feelings of career vulnerability and the number of headaches they experienced on the job, supervisors in five out of seven work units responded positively. For them *contact* was indeed related to a greater feeling of acceptance at work and membership in the organization.

But in the two other work units where there was greater contact, people perceived more, not less, career vulnerability. Further investigation showed that supervisors in these business units got attention only when they were in trouble. Otherwise, no one bothered to talk to them. To these particular supervisors, hearing from a higher-level manager was a sign not of recognition or potential support but of danger.

It is not surprising, then, that supervisors frequently manifest symptoms of powerlessness: overly close supervision, rules-mindedness, and a tendency to do the job themselves rather than to train their people (since job skills may be one of the few remaining things they feel good about). Perhaps this is why they sometimes stand as roadblocks between their subordinates and the higher reaches of the company.

Staff Professionals

Also working under conditions that can lead to organizational powerlessness are the staff specialists. As advisers behind the scenes, staff people must sell their programs and bargain for resources, but unless they get themselves entrenched in organizational power networks, they have little in the way of favors to exchange. They are seen as useful adjuncts to the primary tasks of the organization but inessential in a day-to-day operating sense. This disenfranchisement occurs particularly when staff jobs consist of easily routinized administrative functions which are out of the mainstream of the currently relevant areas and involve little innovative decision making.

Furthermore, in some organizations, unless they have had previous line experience, staff people tend to be limited in the number of jobs into which they can move. Specialists' ladders are often very short, and professionals are just as likely to get "stuck" in such jobs as people are in less prestigious clerical or factory positions.

Staff people, unlike those who are being groomed for important line positions, may be hired because of a special expertise or particular background. But management rarely pays any attention to developing them into more general organizational resources. Lacking growth prospects themselves and working alone or in very small teams, they are not in a position to develop others or pass on power to them. They miss out on an important way that power can be accumulated.

Sometimes staff specialists, such as house counsel or organization development people, find their work being farmed out to consultants. Management considers them fine for the routine work, but the minute the activities involve risk or something problematic, they bring in outside experts. This treatment says something not only about their expertise but also about the status of their function. Since the company can always hire talent on a temporary basis, it is unclear that the management really needs to have or considers important its own staff for these functions.

And, because staff professionals are often seen as adjuncts to primary tasks, their effectiveness and therefore their contribution to the organization are often hard to measure. Thus visibility and recognition, as well as risk taking and relevance, may be denied to people in staff jobs.

Staff people tend to act out their powerlessness by becoming turf-minded. They create islands within the organization. They set themselves up as the only ones who can control professional standards and judge their own work. They create sometimes false distinctions between themselves as experts (no one else could possibly do what they do) and lay people, and this continues to keep them out of the mainstream.

One form such distinctions take is a combination of disdain when line managers attempt to act in areas the professionals think are their preserve and of subtle refusal to support the managers' efforts. Or staff groups battle with each other for control of new "problem areas," with the result that no one really handles the issue at all. To cope with their essential powerlessness, staff groups may try to elevate their own status and draw boundaries between themselves and others.

When staff jobs are treated as final resting places for people who have reached their level of competence in the organization—a good shelf on which to dump managers who are too old to go anywhere but too young to retire—then staff groups can also become pockets of conservatism, resistant to change. Their own exclusion from the risk-taking action may make them resist *anyone's* innovative proposals. In the past, personnel departments, for example, have sometimes been the last in their organization to know about innovations in human resource development or to be interested in applying them.

Top Executives

Despite the great resources and responsibilities concentrated at the top of an organization, leaders can be powerless for reasons that are not very different from those that affect staff and supervisors: lack of supplies, information, and support.

We have faith in leaders because of their ability to make things happen in the larger world, to create possibilities for everyone else, and to attract resources to the organization. These are their supplies. But influence outward—the source of much credibility downward—can diminish as environments change, setting terms and conditions out of the control of the leaders. Regardless of top management's grand plans for the organization, the environment presses. At the very least, things going on outside the organization can deflect a leader's attention and drain energy. And, more detrimental, decisions made elsewhere can have severe consequences for the organization and affect top management's sense of power and thus its operating style inside.

In the go-go years of the mid-1960s, for example, nearly every corporation officer or university president could look—and therefore feel—successful. Visible success gave leaders a great deal of credibility inside the organization, which in turn gave them the power to put new things in motion.

In the past few years, the environment has been strikingly different and the capacity of many organization leaders to do anything about it has been severely limited. New "players" have flexed their power muscles: the Arab oil bloc, government regulators, and congressional investigating committees. And managing economic decline is quite different from managing growth. It is no accident that when top leaders personally feel out of control, the control function in corporations grows.

As powerlessness in lower levels of organizations can manifest itself in overly routinized jobs where performance measures are oriented to rules and absence of change, so it can at upper levels as well. Routine work often drives out nonroutine work. Accomplishment becomes a question of nailing down details. Short-term results provide immediate gratifications and satisfy stockholders or other constituencies with limited interests.

It takes a powerful leader to be willing to risk short-term deprivations in order to bring about desired long-term outcomes. Much as first-line supervisors are tempted to focus on daily adherence to rules, leaders are tempted to focus on short-term fluctuations and lose sight of long-term objectives. The dynamics of such a situation are self-reinforcing. The more the long-term goals go unattended, the more a leader feels powerless and the greater the scramble to prove that he or she is in control of daily events at least. The more he is involved in the organization as a short-term Mr. Fix-it, the more out of control of long-term objectives he is, and the more ultimately powerless he is likely to be.

Credibility for top executives often comes from doing the extraordinary: exercising discretion, creating, inventing, planning, and acting in nonroutine ways. But since routine problems look easier and more manageable, require less change and consent on the part of anyone else, and lend themselves to instant solutions that can make any leader look good temporarily, leaders may avoid the risky by taking over what their subordinates should be doing. Ultimately, a leader may succeed in getting all the trivial problems dumped on his or her desk. This can establish expectations even for leaders attempting more challenging tasks. When Warren Bennis was president of the University of Cincinnati, a professor called him when the heat was down in a classroom. In writing about this incident, Bennis commented, "I suppose he expected me to grab a wrench and fix it."[6]

People at the top need to insulate themselves from the routine operations of the organization in order to develop and exercise power. But this very insulation can lead to another source of powerlessness—lack of information. In one multinational corporation, top executives who are sealed off in a large, distant office, flattered and virtually babied by aides, are frustrated by their distance from the real action.[7]

At the top, the concern for secrecy and privacy is mixed with real loneliness. In one bank, organization members were so accustomed to never seeing the top leaders that when a new senior vice president went to the branch offices to look around, they had suspicion, even fear, about his intentions.

Thus leaders who are cut out of an organization's information networks understand neither what is really going on at lower levels nor that their own isolation may be having negative effects. All too often top executives design "beneficial" new employee programs or declare a new humanitarian policy (e.g., "participatory management is now our style") only to find the policy ignored or mistrusted because it is perceived as coming from uncaring bosses.

The information gap has more serious consequences when executives are so insulated from the rest of the organization or from other decision makers that, as Nixon so dramatically did, they fail to see their own impending downfall. Such insulation is partly a matter of organizational position and, in some cases, of executive style.

For example, leaders may create closed inner circles consisting of "doppelgängers," people just like themselves, who are their principal sources of organizational information and tell them only what they want to know. The reasons for the distortions are varied: key aides want to relieve the leader of burdens, they think just like the leader, they want to protect their own positions of power, or the familiar "kill the messenger" syndrome makes people close to top executives reluctant to be the bearers of bad news.

Finally, just as supervisors and lower-level managers need their supporters in order to be and feel powerful, so do top executives. But for them sponsorship may not be so much a matter of individual endorsement as an issue of support by larger sources of legitimacy in the society. For top executives the problem is not to fit in among peers; rather, the question is whether the public at large and other organization members perceive a common interest which they see the executives as promoting.

If, however, public sources of support are withdrawn and leaders are open to public attack or if inside constituencies fragment and employees see their interests better aligned with pressure groups than with organizational leadership, then powerlessness begins to set in.

When common purpose is lost, the system's own politics may reduce the capacity of those at the top to act. Just as managing decline seems to create a much more passive and reactive stance than managing growth, so does mediating among conflicting interests. When what is happening outside and inside their organizations is out of their control, many people at the top turn into decline managers and dispute mediators. Neither is a particularly empowering role.

Thus when top executives lose their own lines of supply, lines of information, and lines of support, they too suffer from a kind of powerlessness. The temptation for them is to pull in every shred of power they can and to decrease the power available to other people to act. Innovation loses out in favor of control. Limits rather than targets are set. Financial goals are met by reducing "overhead" (people) rather than by giving people the tools and discretion to increase their own productive capacity. Dictatorial statements come down from the top, spreading the mentality of powerlessness farther until the whole organization becomes sluggish and people concentrate on protecting what they have rather than on producing what they can.

When everyone is playing "king of the mountain," guarding his or her turf jealously, then king of the mountain becomes the only game in town.

To Expand Power, Share It

In no case am I saying that people in the three hierarchical levels described are always powerless, but they are susceptible to common conditions that can contribute to powerlessness. *Exhibit III* summarizes the most common symptoms of powerlessness for each level and some typical sources of that behavior.

I am also distinguishing the tremendous concentration of economic and political power in large corporations themselves from the powerlessness that can beset individuals even in the highest positions in such organizations. What grows with organizational position in hierarchical levels is not necessarily the power to accomplish—productive power—but the power to punish, to prevent, to sell off, to reduce, to fire, all without appropriate concern for consequences. It is that kind of power—oppressive power—that we often say corrupts.

The absence of ways to prevent individual and social harm causes the polity to feel it must surround people in power with constraints, regulations, and laws that limit the arbitrary use of their authority. But if oppressive power corrupts, then so does the absence of productive power. In large organizations, powerlessness can be a bigger problem than power.

Exhibit III Common Symptoms and Sources of Powerlessness for Three Key Organizational Positions

Position	Symptoms	Sources
First-line supervisors	Close, rules-minded supervision Tendency to do things oneself, blocking of subordinates' development and information Resistant, underproducing subordinates	Routine, rules-minded jobs with little control over lines of supply Limited lines of information Limited advancement or involvement prospects for oneself/subordinates
Staff professionals	Turf protection, information control Retreat into professionalism Conservative resistance to change	Routine tasks seen as peripheral to "real tasks" of line organization Blocked careers Easy replacement by outside experts
Top executives	Focus on internal cutting, short-term results, "punishing" Dictatorial top-down communications Retreat to comfort of like-minded lieutenants	Uncontrollable lines of supply because of environmental changes Limited or blocked lines of information about lower levels of organization Diminished lines of support because of challenges to legitimacy (e.g., from the public or special interest groups)

David C. McClelland makes a similar distinction between oppressive and productive power:

"The negative . . . face of power is characterized by the dominance-submission mode: if I win, you lose. . . . It leads to simple and direct means of feeling powerful [such as being aggressive]. It does not often lead to effective social leadership for the reason that such a person tends to treat other people as pawns. People who feel they are pawns tend to be passive and useless to the leader who gets his satisfaction from dominating them. Slaves are the most inefficient form of labor ever devised by man. If a leader wants to have far-reaching influence, he must make his followers feel powerful and able to accomplish things on their own. . . . Even the most dictatorial leader does not succeed if he has not instilled in at least some of his followers a sense of power and the strength to pursue the goals he has set."[8]

Organizational power can grow, in part, by being shared. We do not yet know enough about new organizational forms to say whether productive power is infinitely expandable or where we reach the point of diminishing returns. But we do know that sharing power is different from giving or throwing it away. Delegation does not mean abdication.

Some basic lessons could be translated from the field of economics to the realm of organizations and management. Capital investment in plants and equipment is not the only key to productivity. The productive capacity of nations, like organizations, grows if the skill base is upgraded. People with the tools, information, and support to make more informed decisions and act more quickly can often accomplish more. By empowering others, a leader does not decrease his power; instead he may increase it — especially if the whole organization performs better.

This analysis leads to some counterintuitive conclusions. In a certain tautological sense, the principal problem of the powerless is that they lack power. Powerless people are usually the last ones to whom anyone wants to entrust more power, for fear of its dissipation or abuse. But those people are precisely the ones who might benefit most from an injection of power and whose behavior is likely to change as new options open up to them.

Also, if the powerless bosses could be encouraged to share some of the power they do have, their power would grow. Yet, of course, only those leaders who feel secure about their own power outward — their lines of supply, information, and support — can see empowering subordinates as a gain rather than a loss. The two sides of power (getting it and giving it) are closely connected.

There are important lessons here for both subordinates and those who want to change organizations, whether executives or change agents. Instead of resisting or criticizing a powerless boss, which only increases the boss's feeling of powerlessness and need to control, subordinates instead might concentrate on helping the boss become more powerful. Managers might make pockets of ineffectiveness in the organization more productive not by training or replacing individuals but by structural solutions such as opening supply and support lines.

Similarly, organizational change agents who want a new program or policy to succeed should make sure that the change itself does not render any other level of the organization powerless. In making changes, it is wise to make sure that the key people in the level or two directly above and in neighboring functions are sufficiently involved, informed, and taken into account, so that the program can be used to build their own sense of power also. If such involvement is impossible, then it is better to move these people out of the territory altogether than to leave behind a group from whom some power has been removed and who might resist and undercut the program.

In part, of course, spreading power means educating people to this new definition of it. But words alone will not make the difference; managers will need the real experience of a new way of managing.

Here is how the associate director of a large corporate professional department phrased the lessons that he learned in the transition to a team-oriented, participatory, power-sharing management process:

"Get in the habit of involving your own managers in decision making and approvals. But don't abdicate! Tell them what you want and where you're coming from. Don't go for a one-boss grass roots 'democracy.' Make the management hierarchy work for you in participation. . . .

"Hang in there, baby, and don't give up. Try not to 'revert' just because everything seems to go sour on a particular day. Open up—talk to people and tell them how you feel. They'll want to get you back on track and will do things to make that happen—because they don't really want to go back to the way it was. . . . Subordinates will push you to 'act more like a boss,' but their interest is usually more in seeing someone else brought to heel than getting bossed themselves."

Naturally, people need to have power before they can learn to share it. Exhorting managers to change their leadership styles is rarely useful by itself. In one large plant of a major electronics company, first-line production supervisors were the source of numerous complaints from managers who saw them as major roadblocks to overall plant productivity and as insufficiently skilled supervisors. So the plant personnel staff undertook two pilot programs to increase the supervisors' effectiveness. The first program was based on a traditional competency and training model aimed at teaching the specific skills of successful supervisors. The second program, in contrast, was designed to empower the supervisors by directly affecting their flexibility, access to resources, connections with higher-level officials, and control over working conditions.

After an initial gathering of data from supervisors and their subordinates, the personnel staff held meetings where all the supervisors were given tools for developing action plans for sharing the data with their people and collaborating on solutions to perceived problems. But then, in a departure from common practice in this organization, task forces of supervisors were formed to develop new systems for handling job and career issues common to them and their people. These task forces were given budgets, consultants, representation on a plantwide project steering committee alongside managers at much higher levels, and wide latitude in defining the nature and scope of the changes they wished to make. In short, lines of supply, information, and support were opened to them.

As the task forces progressed in their activities, it became clear to the plant management that the hoped-for changes in supervisory effectiveness were taking place much more rapidly through these structural changes in power than through conventional management training; so the conventional training was dropped. Not only did the pilot groups design useful new procedures for the plant, astonishing senior management in several cases with their knowledge and capabilities, but also, significantly, they learned to manage their own people better.

Several groups decided to involve shop-floor workers in their task forces; they could now see from their own experience the benefits of involving subordinates in solving job-related problems. Other supervisors began to experiment with ways to implement "participatory management" by giving subordinates more control and influence without relinquishing their own authority.

Soon the "problem supervisors" in the "most troubled plant in the company" were getting the highest possible performance ratings and were considered models for direct production management. The sharing of organizational power from the top made possible the productive use of power below.

One might wonder why more organizations do not adopt such empowering strategies. There are standard answers: that giving up control is threatening to people who have fought for every shred of it; that people do not want to share power with those they look down on; that managers fear losing their own place and special privileges in the system; that "predictability" often rates higher than "flexibility" as an organizational value; and so forth.

But I would also put skepticism about employee abilities high on the list. Many modern bureaucratic systems are designed to minimize dependence on individual intelligence by making routine as many decisions as possible. So it often comes as a genuine surprise to top executives that people doing the more routine jobs could, indeed, make sophisticated decisions or use resources entrusted to them in intelligent ways.

In the same electronics company just mentioned, at the end of a quarter the pilot supervisory task forces were asked to report results and plans to senior management in order to have their new budget requests approved. The task forces made sure they were well prepared, and the high-level executives were duly impressed. In fact, they were *so* impressed that they kept interrupting the presentations with compliments, remarking that the supervisors could easily be doing sophisticated personnel work.

At first the supervisors were flattered. Such praise from upper management could only be taken well. But when the first glow wore off, several of them became very angry. They saw the excessive praise as patronizing and insulting. "Didn't they think we could think? Didn't they imagine we were capable of doing this kind of work?" one asked. "They must have seen us as just a bunch of animals. No wonder they gave us such limited jobs."

As far as these supervisors were concerned, their abilities had always been there, in latent form perhaps, but still there. They as individuals had not changed—just their organizational power.

Women Managers Experience Special Power Failures

The traditional problems of women in management are illustrative of how formal and informal practices can combine to engender powerlessness. Historically, women in management have found their opportunities in more routine, low-profile jobs. In staff positions, where they serve in support capacities to line managers but have no line responsibilities of their own, or in supervisory jobs managing "stuck" subordinates, they are not in a position either to take the kinds of risks that build credibility or to develop their own team by pushing bright subordinates.

Such jobs, which have few favors to trade, tend to keep women out of the mainstream of the organization. This lack of clout, coupled with the greater difficulty anyone who is "different" has in getting into the information and support networks, has meant that merely by organizational situation women in management have been more likely than men to be rendered structurally powerless. This is one reason those women who have achieved power have often had family connections that put them in the mainstream of the organization's social circles.

A disproportionate number of women managers are found among first-line supervisors or staff professionals; and they, like men in those circumstances, are likely to be organizationally powerless. But the behavior of other managers can contribute to the powerlessness of women in management in a number of less obvious ways.

One way other managers can make a woman powerless is by patronizingly overprotecting her: putting her in "a safe job," not giving her enough to do to prove herself, and not suggesting her for high-risk, visible assignments. This protectiveness is sometimes born of "good" intentions to give her every chance to succeed (why stack the deck against her?). Out of managerial concerns, out of awareness that a woman may be up against situations that men simply do not have to face, some very well-meaning managers protect their female managers ("It's a jungle, so why send her into it?").

Overprotectiveness can also mask a manager's fear of association with a woman should she fail. One senior bank official at a level below vice president told me about his concerns with respect to a high-performing, financially experienced woman reporting to him. Despite *his* overwhelmingly positive work experiences with her, he was still afraid to recommend her for other assignments because he felt it was a personal risk. "What if other managers are not as accepting of women as I am?" he asked. "I know I'd be sticking my neck out; they would take her more because of my endorsement than her qualifications. And what if she doesn't make it? My judgment will be on the line."

Overprotection is relatively benign compared with rendering a person powerless by providing obvious signs of lack of managerial support. For example, allowing someone supposedly in authority to be bypassed easily means that no one else has to take him or her seriously. If a woman's immedi-

ate supervisor or other managers listen willingly to criticism of her and show they are concerned every time a negative comment comes up and that they assume she must be at fault, then they are helping to undercut her. If managers let other people know that they have concerns about this person or that they are testing her to see how she does, then they are inviting other people to look for signs of inadequacy or failure.

Furthermore, people assume they can afford to bypass women because they "must be uninformed" or "don't know the ropes." Even though women may be respected for their competence or expertise, they are not necessarily seen as being informed beyond the technical requirements of the job. There may be a grain of historical truth in this. Many women come to senior management positions as "outsiders" rather than up through the usual channels.

Also, because until very recently men have not felt comfortable seeing women as businesspeople (business clubs have traditionally excluded women), they have tended to seek each other out for informal socializing. Anyone, male or female, seen as organizationally naive and lacking sources of "inside dope" will find his or her own lines of information limited.

Finally, even when women are able to achieve some power on their own, they have not necessarily been able to translate such personal credibility into an organizational power base. To create a network of supporters out of individual clout requires that a person pass on and share power, that subordinates and peers be empowered by virtue of their connection with that person. Traditionally, neither men nor women have seen women as capable of sponsoring others, even though they may be capable of achieving and succeeding on their own. Women have been viewed as the *recipients* of sponsorship rather than as the sponsors themselves.

(As more women prove themselves in organizations and think more self-consciously about bringing along young people, this situation may change. However, I still hear many more questions from women managers about how they can benefit from mentors, sponsors, or peer networks than about how they themselves can start to pass on favors and make use of their own resources to benefit others.)

Viewing managers in terms of power and powerlessness helps explain two familiar stereotypes about women and leadership in organizations: that no one wants a woman boss (although studies show that anyone who has ever had a woman boss is likely to have had a positive experience), and that the reason no one wants a woman boss is that women are "too controlling, rules-minded, and petty."

The first stereotype simply makes clear that power is important to leadership. Underneath the preference for men is the assumption that, given the current distribution of people in organizational leadership positions, men are more likely than women to be in positions to achieve power and, therefore, to share their power with others.

Similarly, the "bossy woman boss" stereotype is a perfect picture of powerlessness. All of those traits are just as characteristic of men who are powerless, but women are slightly more likely, because of circumstances I have mentioned, to find themselves powerless than are men. Women with power in the organization are just as effective —and preferred—as men.

Recent interviews conducted with about 600 bank managers show that, when a woman exhibits the petty traits of powerlessness, people assume that she does so "because she is a woman." A striking difference is that, when a man engages in the same behavior, people assume the behavior is a matter of his own individual style and characteristics and do not conclude that it reflects on the suitability of men for management.

REFERENCES

1. Donald C. Pelz, "Influence: A Key to Effective Leadership in the First-Line Supervisor," *Personnel*, November 1952, p. 209.

2. See my book, *Men and Women of the Corporation* (New York: Basic Books, 1977), pp. 164-205; and David Kipnis, *The Powerholders* (Chicago: University of Chicago Press, 1976).

3. Pehr G. Gyllenhammar, *People at Work* (Reading, Mass.: Addison-Wesley, 1977), p. 133.

4. William E. Fulmer, "Supervisory Selection: The Acid Test of Affirmative Action," *Personnel*, November-December 1976, p. 40.

5. See my chapter (coauthor, Barry A. Stein), "Life in the Middle: Getting In, Getting Up, and Getting Along," in *Life in Organizations*, eds. Rosabeth M. Kanter and Barry A. Stein (New York: Basic Books, 1979).

6. Warren Bennis, *The Unconscious Conspiracy: Why Leaders Can't Lead* (New York: AMACOM, 1976).

7. See my chapter, "How the Top Is Different," in *Life in Organizations*.

8. David C. McClelland, *Power: The Inner Experience* (New York: Irvington Publishers, 1975), p. 263. Quoted by permission.

4

Power Is the Great Motivator

DAVID C. McCLELLAND AND
DAVID H. BURNHAM

What makes or motivates a good manager? The question is so enormous in scope that anyone trying to answer it has difficulty knowing where to begin. Some people might say that a good manager is one who is successful; and by now most business researchers and businesspeople themselves know what motivates people who successfully run their own small businesses. The key to their success has turned out to be what psychologists call "the need for achievement," the desire to do something better or more efficiently than it has been done before. Any number of books and articles summarize research studies explaining how the achievement motive is necessary for people to attain success on their own.[1]

But what has achievement motivation got to do with good management? There is no reason on theoretical grounds why a person who has a strong need to be more efficient should make a good manager. While it sounds as if everyone ought to have the need to achieve, in fact, as psychologists define and measure achievement motivation, it leads people to behave in very special ways that do not necessarily lead to good management.

For one thing, because they focus on personal improvement, on doing things better by themselves, achievement-motivated people want to do things themselves. For another, they want concrete short-term feedback on their performance so that they can tell how well they are doing. Yet a manager, particularly one of or in a large complex organization, cannot perform all the tasks necessary for success by him or herself. Managers must manage others so that they will do things for the organization. Also, feedback on subordinates' performance may be a lot vaguer and more delayed than it would be if they were doing everything themselves.

The manager's job seems to call more for people who can influence others than for those who do things better on their own. In motivational terms, then, we might expect the successful manager to have a greater "need for power" than need to achieve. But there must be other qualities beside the need for power that go into the makeup of a good manager. Just what these qualities are and how they interrelate is the subject of this article.

Author's note: All the case material in this article is disguised.

To measure the motivations of managers, good and bad, we studied a number of individual managers from different large U.S. corporations who were participating in management workshops designed to improve their managerial effectiveness. (The workshop techniques and research methods and terms used are described in the Appendix.)

The general conclusion of these studies is that the top manager of a company must possess a high need for power, that is, a concern for influencing people. However, this need must be disciplined and controlled so that it is directed toward the benefit of the institution as a whole and not toward the manager's personal aggrandizement. Moreover, top managers' need for power ought to be greater than their need for being liked by people.

Now let us look at what these ideas mean in the context of real individuals in real situations and see what comprises the profile of the good manager. Finally, we will look at the workshops themselves to determine how they go about changing behavior.

Measuring Managerial Effectiveness

First off, what does it mean when we say that a good manager has a greater need for "power" than for "achievement"? To get a more concrete idea, let us consider the case of Ken Briggs, a sales manager in a large U.S. corporation who joined one of our managerial workshops. Some six or seven years ago, Ken Briggs was promoted to a managerial position at corporate headquarters, where he had responsibility for salespeople who service his company's largest accounts.

In filling out his questionnaire at the workshop, Ken showed that he correctly perceived what his job required of him, namely, that he should influence others' success more than achieve new goals himself or socialize with his subordinates. However, when asked with other members of the workshop to write a story depicting a managerial situation, Ken unwittingly revealed through his fiction that he did not share those concerns. Indeed, he discovered that his need for achievement was very high—in fact over the 90th percentile—and his need for power was very low, in about the 15th percentile. Ken's high need to achieve was no surprise—after all, he had been a very successful salesman—but obviously his motivation to influence others was much less than his job required. Ken was a little disturbed but thought that perhaps the measuring instruments were not too accurate and that the gap between the ideal and his score was not as great as it seemed.

Then came the real shocker. Ken's subordinates confirmed what his stories revealed: he was a poor manager, having little positive impact on those who worked for him. Ken's subordinates felt that they had little responsibility delegated to them, that he never rewarded but only criticized them, and that the office was not well organized, but confused and chaotic. On all three of these scales, his office rated in the 10th to 15th percentile relative to national norms.

As Ken talked the results over privately with a workshop leader, he became more and more upset. He finally agreed, however, that the results of the survey confirmed feelings he had been afraid to admit to himself or others. For years, he had been miserable in his managerial role. He now knew the reason: he simply did not want to nor had he been able to influence or manage others. As he thought back, he realized that he had failed every time he had tried to influence his staff, and he felt worse than ever.

Ken had responded to failure by setting very high standards—his office scored in the 98th percentile on this scale—and by trying to do most things himself, which was close to impossible; his own activity and lack of delegation consequently left his staff demoralized. Ken's experience is typical of those who have a strong need to achieve but low power motivation. They may become very successful salespeople and, as a consequence, may be promoted into managerial jobs for which they, ironically, are unsuited.

If achievement motivation does not make a good manager, what motive does? It is not enough to suspect that power motivation may be important; one needs hard evidence that people who are better managers than Ken Briggs do in fact possess stronger power motivation and perhaps score higher in other characteristics as well. But how does one decide who is the better manager?

Real-world performance measures are hard to come by if one is trying to rate managerial effectiveness in production, marketing, finance, or research and development. In trying to determine who the better managers were in Ken Briggs's company, we did not want to rely only on the opinions of their superiors. For a variety of reasons, superiors' judgments of their subordinates' real-world performance may be inaccurate. In the absence of some standard measure of performance, we decided that the next best index of managers' effectiveness would be the climate they create in the office, reflected in the morale of subordinates.

Almost by definition, a good manager is one who, among other things, helps subordinates feel strong and responsible, who rewards them properly for good performance, and who sees that things are organized in such a way that subordinates feel they know what they should be doing. Above all, managers should

---

Exhibit I Correlation between Morale Score and Sales Performance for a Large U.S. Corporation

Average percent gain in sales by district from 1972 to 1973

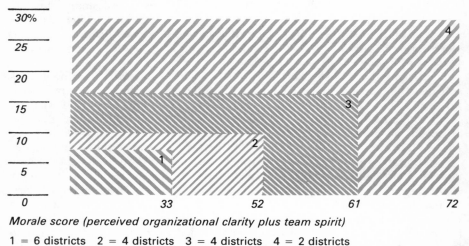

Morale score (perceived organizational clarity plus team spirit)

1 = 6 districts   2 = 4 districts   3 = 4 districts   4 = 2 districts

foster among subordinates a strong sense of team spirit, of pride in working as part of a particular team. If a manager creates and encourages this spirit, the subordinates certainly should perform better.

In the company Ken Briggs works for, we have direct evidence of a connection between morale and performance in the one area where performance measures are easy to come by—namely, sales. In April 1973, at least three employees from this company's 16 sales districts filled out questionnaires that rated their office for organizational clarity and team spirit. Their scores were averaged and totaled to give an overall morale score for each office. The percentage gains or losses in sales for each district in 1973 were compared with those for 1972. The difference in sales figures by district ranged from a gain of nearly 30% to a loss of 8%, with a median gain of around 14%. *Exhibit I* shows the average gain in sales performance plotted against the increasing averages in morale scores.

In *Exhibit I* we can see that the relationship between sales and morale is surprisingly close. The six districts with the lowest morale early in the year showed an average sales gain of only around 7% by year's end (although there was wide variation within this group), whereas the two districts with the highest morale showed an average gain of 28%. When morale scores rise above the 50th percentile in terms of national norms, they seem to lead to better sales performance. In Ken Briggs's company, at least, high morale at the beginning is a good index of how well the sales division actually performed in the coming year.

And it seems very likely that the manager who can create high morale among salespeople can also do the same for employees in other areas (production, design, and so on), leading to better performance. Given that high morale in an office indicates that there is a good manager present, what general characteristics does he or she possess?

A Need for Power

In examining the motive scores of over 50 managers of both high and low morale units in all sections of the same large company, we found that most of the managers—over 70%—were high in power motivation compared with men in general. This finding confirms the fact that power motivation is important for management. (Remember that as we use the term "power motivation," it refers not to dictatorial behavior, but to a desire to have impact, to be strong and influential.) The better managers, as judged by the morale of those working for them, tended to score even higher in power motivation. But the most important determining factor of high morale turned out not to be how their power motivation compared to their need to achieve but whether it was higher than their need to be liked. This relationship existed for 80% of the better sales managers as compared with only 10% of the poorer managers. And the same held true for other managers in nearly all parts of the company.

In the research, product development, and operations divisions, 73% of the better managers had a stronger need for power than a need to be liked (or what we term "affiliation motive") as compared with only 22% of the poorer managers. Why should this be so? Sociologists have long argued that, for a bureaucracy to function effectively, those who manage it must be universalistic in applying rules. That is, if they make exceptions for the particular needs of individuals, the whole system will break down.

The manager with a high need for being liked is precisely the one who wants to stay on good terms with everybody, and, therefore, is the one most likely to make exceptions in terms of particular needs. If an employee asks for time off to stay home with a sick spouse to help look after the kids, the affiliative manager, feeling sorry for the person, agrees almost without thinking.

When President Ford remarked in pardoning ex-President Nixon that he had "suffered enough," he was responding as an affiliative manager would, because he was empathizing primarily with Nixon's needs and feelings. Sociological theory and our data both argue, however, that the person whose need for affiliation is high does not make a good manager. This kind of person creates poor morale because he or she does not understand that other people in the office will tend to regard exceptions to the rules as unfair to themselves, just as many U.S. citizens felt it was unfair to let Richard Nixon off and punish others less involved than he was in the Watergate scandal.

Socialized Power

But so far our findings are a little alarming. Do they suggest that the good manager is one who cares for power and is not at all concerned about the needs of other people? Not quite, for the good manager has other characteristics which must still be taken into account.

Above all, the good manager's power motivation is not oriented toward personal aggrandizement but toward the institution which he or she serves. In another major research study, we found that the signs of controlled action or inhibition that appear when a person exercises his or her imagination in writing stories tell a great deal about the kind of power that person needs.[2] We discovered that, if a high power motive score is balanced by high inhibition, stories about power tend to be altruistic. That is, the heroes in the story exercise power on behalf of someone else. This is the "socialized" face of power as distinguished from the concern for personal power, which is characteristic of individuals whose stories are loaded with power imagery but which show no sign of inhibition or self-control. In our earlier study, we found ample evidence that these latter individuals exercise their power impulsively. They are more rude to other people, they drink too much, they try to exploit others sexually, and they collect symbols of personal prestige such as fancy cars or big offices.

Individuals high in power and in control, on the other hand, are more institution minded; they tend to get elected to more offices, to control their drinking, and to want to serve others. Not surprisingly, we found in the workshops that the better managers in the corporation also tend to score high on both power and inhibition.

Profile of a Good Manager

Let us recapitulate what we have discussed so far and have illustrated with data from one company. The better managers we studied are high in power motivation, low in affiliation motivation, and high in inhibition. They care about institutional power and use it to stimulate their employees to be more productive. Now let us compare them with affiliative managers—those in whom the need for affiliation is higher than the need for power—and with the personal power managers—those in whom the need for power is higher than for affiliation but whose inhibition score is low.

In the sales division of our illustrative company, there were managers who matched the three types fairly closely. *Exhibit II* shows how their subordinates

Exhibit II   Average Scores on Selected Climate Dimensions by Subordinates of Managers with Different Motive Profiles

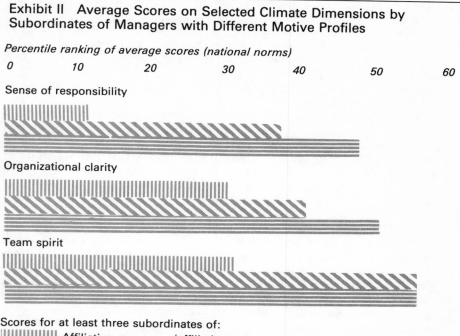

Percentile ranking of average scores (national norms)

| 0 | 10 | 20 | 30 | 40 | 50 | 60 |

Sense of responsibility

Organizational clarity

Team spirit

Scores for at least three subordinates of:

Affiliative managers (affiliation greater than power, high inhibition)
Personal power managers (power greater than affiliation, low inhibition)
Institutional managers (power greater than affiliation, high inhibition)

rated the offices they worked in on responsibility, organizational clarity, and team spirit. There are scores from at least three subordinates for each manager, and several managers are represented for each type, so that the averages shown in the exhibit are quite stable. Note that the manager who is concerned about being liked by people tends to have subordinates who feel that they have very little personal responsibility, that organizational procedures are not clear, and that they have little pride in their work group.

In short, as we expected, affiliative managers make so many ad hominem and ad hoc decisions that they almost totally abandon orderly procedures. Their disregard for procedure leaves employees feeling weak, irresponsible, and without a sense of what might happen next, of where they stand in relation to their manager, or even of what they ought to be doing. In this company, the group of affiliative managers portrayed in *Exhibit II* were below the 30th percentile in morale scores.

The managers who are motivated by a need for personal power are somewhat more effective. They are able to create a greater sense of responsibility in their divisions and, above all, a greater team spirit. They can be thought of as managerial equivalents of successful tank commanders such as General Patton, whose own daring inspired admiration in his troops. But notice how in *Exhibit II* these men are still only in the 40th percentile in the amount of organizational clarity they create, as compared to the high power, low affiliation, high inhibition managers, whom we shall term "institutional."

Managers motivated by personal power are not disciplined enough to be good institution builders, and often their subordinates are loyal to them as individuals rather than to the institution they both serve. When a personal power manager leaves, disorganization often follows. His subordinates' strong group spirit, which the manager has personally inspired, deflates. The subordinates do not know what to do for themselves.

Of the managerial types, "institutional" managers are the most successful in creating an effective work climate. *Exhibit II* shows that their subordinates feel that they have more responsibility. Also, these managers create high morale because they produce the greatest sense of organizational clarity and team spirit. If such a manager leaves, he or she can be more readily replaced by another manager, because the employees have been encouraged to be loyal to the institution rather than to a particular person.

Managerial Styles

Since it seems undeniable from *Exhibit II* that either kind of power orientation creates better morale in subordinates than a "people" orientation, we must consider that a concern for power is essential to good management. Our findings seem to fly in the face of a long and influential tradition of organizational psychology, which insists that authoritarian management is what is wrong with most businesses in this country. Let us say frankly that we think the bogeyman of authoritarianism has in fact been wrongly used to downplay the importance of power in management. After all, management is an influence game. Some proponents of democratic management seem to have forgotten this fact, urging managers to be primarily concerned with people's human needs rather than with helping them to get things done.

But a good deal of the apparent conflict between our findings and those of other behavioral scientists in this area arises from the fact that we are talking about *motives*, and behaviorists are often talking about *actions*. What we are saying is that managers must be interested in playing the influence game in a controlled way. That does not necessarily mean that they are or should be authoritarian in action. On the contrary, it appears that power motivated managers make their subordinates feel strong rather than weak. The true authoritarian in action would have the reverse effect, making people feel weak and powerless.

Thus another important ingredient in the profile of a manager is his or her managerial style. In the illustrative company, 63% of the better managers (those whose subordinates had higher morale) scored higher on the democratic or coaching styles of management as compared with only 22% of the poorer managers, a statistically significant difference. By contrast, the latter scored higher on authoritarian or coercive management styles. Since the better managers were also higher in power motivation, it seems that, in action, they express their power motivation in a democratic way, which is more likely to be effective.

To see how motivation and style interact, let us consider the case of George Prentice, a manager in the sales division of another company. George had exactly the right motive combination to be an institutional manager. He was high in the need for power, low in the need for affiliation, and high in inhibition. He exercised his power in a controlled, organized way. His stories reflected this fact. In one, for instance, he wrote, "The men sitting around the table were feeling pretty good; they had just finished plans for reorganizing the company; the company has been beset with a number of organizational problems. This group, headed by a hard-driving, brilliant young executive, has completely reorganized the company structurally with new jobs and responsibilities. . . ."

This described how George himself was perceived by the company, and shortly after the workshop he was promoted to vice president in charge of all sales. But George was also known to his colleagues as a monster, a tough guy who would "walk over his grandmother" if she stood in the way of his advancement. He had the right motive combination and, in fact, was more interested in institutional growth than in personal power, but his managerial style was all wrong. Taking his cue from some of the top executives in the corporation, he told people what they had to do and threatened them with dire consequences if they didn't do it.

When George was confronted with his authoritarianism in a workshop, he recognized that this style was counterproductive — in fact, in another part of the study we found that it was associated with low morale — and he subsequently changed to acting more like a coach, which was the scale on which he scored the lowest initially. George saw more clearly that his job was not to force other people to do things but to help them to figure out ways of getting their job done better for the company.

The Institutional Manager

One reason it was easy for George Prentice to change his managerial style was that in his imaginative stories he was already having thoughts about helping others, characteristic of people with the institution-building motivational pattern. In further examining institution builders' thoughts and actions, we found they have four major characteristics:

1. They are more organization-minded; that is, they tend to join more organizations and to feel responsible for building up these organizations. Furthermore, they believe strongly in the importance of centralized authority.

2. They report that they like to work. This finding is particularly interesting, because our research on achievement motivation has led many commentators to argue that achievement motivation promotes the "Protestant work ethic." Almost the precise opposite is true. People who have a high need to achieve like to get out of work by becoming more efficient. They would like to see the same result obtained in less time or with less effort. But managers who have a need for institutional power actually seem to like the discipline of work. It satisfies their need for getting things done in an orderly way.

3. They seem quite willing to sacrifice some of their own self-interest for the welfare of the organization they serve. For example, they are more willing to make contributions to charities.

4. They have a keen sense of justice. It is almost as if they feel that if people work hard and sacrifice for the good of the organization, they should and will get a just reward for their efforts.

It is easy to see how each of these four concerns helps a person become a good manager, concerned about what the institution can achieve.

Maturity. Before we go on to look at how the workshops can help managers to improve their managerial style and recognize their own motivations, let us consider one more fact we discovered in studying the better managers at George Prentice's company. They were more mature. Mature people can be

Exhibit III   Average Scores on Selected Climate Dimensions by Over 50 Salespeople Before and After Their Managers Were Trained

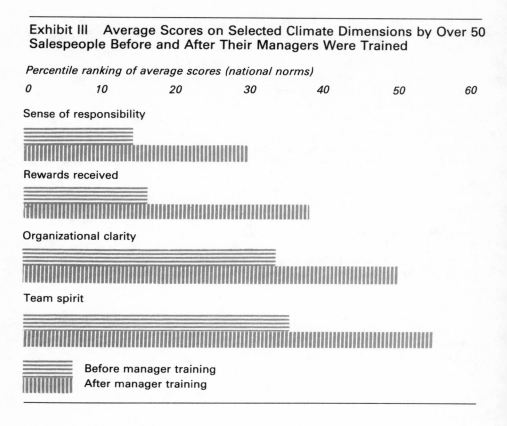

Percentile ranking of average scores (national norms)

most simply described as less egotistic. Somehow their positive self-image is not at stake in what they are doing. They are less defensive, more willing to seek advice from experts, and have a longer range view. They accumulate fewer personal possessions and seem older and wiser. It is as if they have awakened to the fact that they are not going to live forever and have lost some of the feeling that their own personal future is all that important.

Many U.S. businesspeople fear this kind of maturity. They suspect that it will make them less hard driving, less expansion-minded, and less committed to organizational effectiveness. Our data do not support their fears. These fears are exactly the ones George Prentice had before he went to the workshop. Afterward he was a more effective manager, not despite his loss of some of the sense of his own importance, but because of it. The reason is simple: his subordinates believed afterward that he genuinely was more concerned about the company than about himself. Where once they respected his confidence but feared him, they now trust him. Once he supported their image of him as a "big man" by talking about the new Porsche and the new Honda he had bought; when we saw him recently he said, almost as an aside, "I don't buy things anymore."

Changing Managerial Style

George Prentice was able to change his managerial style after learning more about himself in a workshop. But does self-knowledge generally improve managerial behavior?

Some people might ask, "What good does it do to know, if I am a manager, that I should have a strong power motive, not too great a concern about being liked, a sense of discipline, a high level of maturity, and a coaching managerial style? What can I do about it?" The answer is that workshops for managers that give information to them in a supportive setting enable them to change.

Consider the results shown in *Exhibit III*, where "before" and "after" scores are compared. Once again we use the responses of subordinates to give some measure of the effectiveness of managers. To judge by their subordinates' responses, the managers were clearly more effective afterward. The subordinates felt that they were given more responsibility, that they received more rewards, that the organizational procedures were clearer, and that morale was higher. These differences are all statistically significant.

But what do these differences mean in human terms? How did the managers change? Sometimes they decided they should get into another line of work. This happened to Ken Briggs, for example, who found that the reason he was doing so poorly as a manager was because he had almost no interest in influencing others. He understood how he would have to change if he were to do well in his present job, but in the end decided, with the help of management, that he would prefer to work back into his first love, sales.

Ken Briggs moved into "remaindering," to help retail outlets for his company's products get rid of last year's stock so that they could take on each year's new styles. He is very successful in this new role; he has cut costs, increased dollar volume, and in time has worked himself into an independent role selling some of the old stock on his own in a way that is quite satisfactory to the business. And he does not have to manage anybody anymore.

In George Prentice's case, less change was needed. He was obviously a very competent person with the right motive profile for a top managerial position. When he was promoted, he performed even more successfully than before because he realized the need to become more positive in his approach and less coercive in his managerial style.

But what about people who do not want to change their jobs and discover that they do not have the right motive profile to be managers?

The case of Charlie Blake is instructive. Charlie was as low in power motivation as Ken Briggs, his need to achieve was about average, and his affiliation motivation was above average. Thus he had the affiliative manager profile, and, as expected, the morale among his subordinates was very low. When Charlie learned that his subordinates' sense of responsibility and perception of a reward system were in the 10th percentile and that team spirit was in the 30th, he was shocked. When shown a film depicting three managerial climates, Charlie said he preferred what turned out to be the authoritarian climate. He became angry when the workshop trainer and other members in the group pointed out the limitations of this managerial style. He became obstructive in the group process and objected strenuously to what was being taught.

In an interview conducted much later, Charlie said, "I blew my cool. When I started yelling at you for being all wrong, I got even madder when you pointed out that, according to my style questionnaire, you bet that that was just what I did to my salespeople. Down underneath I knew something must be wrong. The sales performance for my division wasn't so good. Most of it was due to me anyway and not to my salespeople. Obviously their reports that they felt very little responsibility was delegated to them and that I didn't reward them at all had to mean something. So I finally decided to sit down and try to figure what I could do about it. I knew I had to start being a manager instead of trying to do everything myself and blowing my cool at others because they didn't do what I thought they should. In the end, after I calmed down on the way back from the workshop, I realized that it is not so bad to make a mistake; it's bad not to learn from it."

After the course, Charlie put his plans into effect. Six months later, his subordinates were asked to rate him again. He attended a second workshop to study these results and reported, "On the way home I was very nervous. I knew I had been working with those people and not selling so much myself, but I was very much afraid of what they were going to say about how things were going in the office. When I found out that the team spirit and some of those other low scores had jumped from around 30th to the 55th percentile, I was so delighted and relieved that I couldn't say anything all day long."

When he was asked how he acted differently from before, he said, "In previous years when the corporate headquarters said we had to make 110% of our original goal, I had called the salespeople in and said, in effect, 'This is ridiculous; we are not going to make it, but you know perfectly well what will happen if we don't. So get out there and work your tail off.' The result was that I worked 20 hours a day and they did nothing.

"This time I approached it differently. I told them three things. First, they were going to have to do some sacrificing for the company. Second, working harder is not going to do much good because we are already working about as hard as we can. What will be required are special deals and promotions. You are going to have to figure out some new angles if we are to make it. Third, I'm going to back you up. I'm going to set a realistic goal with each of you. If you make that goal but don't make the company goal, I'll see to it that you are not punished. But if you do make the company goal, I'll see to it that you will get some kind of special rewards."

When the salespeople challenged Charlie saying he did not have enough influence to give them rewards, rather than becoming angry Charlie promised rewards that were in his power to give—such as longer vacations.

Note that Charlie has now begun to behave in a number of ways that we found to be characteristic of the good institutional manager. He is, above all, higher in power motivation, the desire to influence his salespeople, and lower in his tendency to try to do everything himself. He asks the salespeople to sacrifice for the company. He does not defensively chew them out when they challenge him but tries to figure out what their needs are so that he can influence them. He realizes that his job is more one of strengthening and supporting his subordinates than of criticizing them. And he is keenly interested in giving them just rewards for their efforts.

The changes in his approach to his job have certainly paid off. The sales figures for his office in 1973 were up more than 16% over 1972 and up still further in 1974 over 1973. In 1973 his gain over the previous year ranked seventh in the nation; in 1974 it ranked third. And he wasn't the only one in his company to change managerial styles. Overall sales at his company were up substantially in 1973 as compared with 1972, an increase which played a large part in turning the overall company performance around from a $15 million loss in 1972 to a $3 million profit in 1973. The company continued to improve its performance in 1974 with an 11% further gain in sales and a 38% increase in profits.

Of course not everyone can be reached by a workshop. Henry Carter managed a sales office for a company which had very low morale (around the 20th percentile) before he went for training. When morale was checked some six months later, it had not improved. Overall sales gain subsequently reflected this fact since it was only 2% above the previous year's figures.

Oddly enough, Henry's problem was that he was so well liked by everybody that he felt little pressure to change. Always the life of the party, he is particularly popular because he supplies other managers with special hard-to-get brands of cigars and wines at a discount. He uses his close ties with everyone to bolster his position in the company, even though it is known that his office does not perform well compared with others.

His great interpersonal skills became evident at the workshop when he did very poorly at one of the business games. When the discussion turned to why he had done so badly and whether he acted that way on the job, two prestigious participants immediately sprang to his defense, explaining away Henry's failure by arguing that the way he did things was often a real help to others and the company. As a result, Henry did not have to cope with such questions at all. He had so successfully developed his role as a likeable, helpful friend to everyone in management that, even though his salespeople performed badly, he did not feel under any pressure to change.

Checks and Balances

What have we learned from Ken Briggs, George Prentice, Charlie Blake, and Henry Carter? Principally, we have discovered what motive combination makes an effective manager. We have also seen that change is possible if a person has the right combination of qualities.

Oddly enough, the good manager in a large company does not have a high need for achievement, as we define and measure that motive, although there must be plenty of that motive somewhere in the organization. The top managers shown here have a high need for power and an interest in influencing others, both greater than their interest in being liked by people. The manager's concern for power should be socialized—controlled so that the institution as a whole, not only the individual, benefits. People and nations with this motive profile are empire builders; they tend to create high morale and to expand the organizations they head.

But there is also danger in this motive profile; empire building can lead to imperialism and authoritarianism in companies and in countries.

The same motive pattern which produces good power management can also lead a company or a country to try to dominate others, ostensibly in the interests of organizational expansion. Thus it is not surprising that big business has had to be regulated from time to time by federal agencies. And it is most likely that international agencies will perform the same regulative function for empire-building countries.

For an individual, the regulative function is performed by two characteristics that are part of the profile of the very best managers—a greater emotional maturity, where there is little egotism, and a democratic, coaching managerial style. If an institutional power motivation is checked by maturity, it does not lead to an aggressive, egotistic expansiveness.

For countries, this checking means that they can control their destinies beyond their borders without being aggressive and hostile. For individuals, it means they can control their subordinates and influence others around them without resorting to coercion or to an authoritarian management style. Real disinterested statesmanship has a vital role to play at the top of both countries and companies.

Summarized in this way, what we have found out through empirical and statistical investigations may just sound like good common sense. But the improvement over common sense is that now the characteristics of the good manager are objectively known. Managers of corporations can select those who are likely to be good managers and train those already in managerial positions to be more effective with more confidence.

Workshop Techniques

The case studies and data on companies used in this article were derived from a number of workshops we conducted where executives came to learn about their managerial styles and abilities as well as how to change them. The workshops had a dual purpose, however. They provided an opportunity for us to study which motivation pattern, whether it be a concern for achievement, power, people, or a combination thereof, makes the best managers.

When the managers first arrived at the workshops, they were asked to fill out a questionnaire about their job. Participants analyzed their jobs, explaining what they thought it required of them. The managers were asked to write a number of stories to pictures of various work situations. The stories were coded for the extent to which individuals were concerned about achievement, affiliation, or power, as well as for the amount of inhibition or self-control they revealed. The results were then matched against national norms. The differences between people's job requirements and their motivational patterns can often help assess whether they are in the right job, whether they are candidates for promotion to another job, or whether they are likely to be able to adjust to fit their present positions.

At the workshops and in this article,

we use the technical terms "need for achievement," "need for power," and "need for affiliation" as defined in the books *The Achieving Society* and *Power: The Inner Experience*. The terms refer to measurable factors in groups and individuals. Briefly, these characteristics are measured by coding an individual's spontaneous thoughts for the frequency with which he thinks about doing something better or more efficiently than before (need for achievement), about establishing or maintaining friendly relations with others (need for affiliation), or about having impact on others (need for power). (When we talk about power, we are not talking about dictatorial power, but about the need to be strong and influential.) As used here, therefore, the motive labels are precise terms, referring to a particular method of defining and measuring, much as "gravity" is used in physics, or "gross national product" is used in economics.

To find out what kind of managerial style the participants had, we gave them a questionnaire in which they had to choose how they would handle various realistic work situations in office settings. Their answers were coded for six different management styles or ways of dealing with work situations. The styles depicted were democratic, affiliative, pace-setting, coaching, coercive, and authoritarian. The managers were asked to comment on the effectiveness of each style and to name the style that they prefer.

One way to determine how effective managers are is to ask the people who work for them. Thus, to isolate the characteristics that good managers have, we surveyed at least three subordinates of each manager at the workshop to see how they answered questions about their work situations that revealed characteristics of their supervisors along several dimensions, namely: (1) the amount of conformity to rules required, (2) the responsibility they feel they are given, (3) the emphasis the department places on standards of performance, (4) the degree to which they feel rewards are given for good work as opposed to punishment for something that goes wrong, (5) the degree of organizational clarity in the office, and (6) its team spirit.[1] The managers who received the highest morale scores (organizational clarity plus team spirit) from their subordinates were determined to be the best managers, possessing the most desirable motive patterns.

The subordinates were also surveyed six months after the managers returned to their offices to see if the morale scores rose after the workshop.

One other measure was obtained from the participants to find out which managers had another characteristic deemed important for good management: maturity. Scores were obtained for four stages in the progress toward maturity by coding the stories which the managers wrote for such matters as their attitudes toward authority and the kinds of emotions displayed over specific issues.

People in Stage I are dependent on others for guidance and strength. Those in Stage II are interested primarily in autonomy, in controlling themselves. In Stage III, people want to manipulate others; in Stage IV, they lose their egotistic desires and wish to selflessly serve others.[2]

The conclusions presented in this article are based on workshops attended by over 500 managers from over 25 different U.S. corporations. However, the data in the exhibits are drawn from just one of these companies for illustrative purposes.

1. Based on G.H. Litwin and R.A. Stringer's *Motivation and Organizational Climate* (Boston: Division of Research, Harvard Business School, 1966).

2. Based on work by Abigail Stewart reported in David C. McClelland's *Power: The Inner Experience* (New York: Irvington Publishers, 1975).

REFERENCES

1. For instance, see my books *The Achieving Society* (New York: Van Nostrand, 1961) and (with David Winter) *Motivating Economic Achievement* (New York: Free Press, 1969).

2. David C. McClelland, William N. Davis, Rudolf Kalin, and Eric Warner, *The Drinking Man* (New York: The Free Press, 1972).

5

Clues for Success in the President's Job

JOSEPH C. BAILEY

Is it the role of a company president to do what other members of his organization do not do, cannot do, or should not do? Does he have a special function, or does he merely do *more* of the same things others do—on a far bigger and broader scale? Is there a common denominator among those who successfully handle the "toughest problems" of their organizations that cuts across industries, companies, types of organizations, and even cultures? Must the ability to find solutions to such problems be a requirement of the president's job, inevitable to his role? Is there some largely concealed aspect of his job that is worthy of a serious research undertaking?

The answers to these questions, based on my current sample of company presidents, are decidedly in the affirmative. Yes, there does seem to be a common denominator. There do seem to be clear reasons why the organization's toughest problems demand—and *must* receive—the top man's exclusive attention. Moreover, there seem to be utterly understandable reasons why these problems often remain shrouded in silence and secrecy. And finally, there seems to me clearly to be a challenge for a major research effort of a most difficult and sophisticated character.

The single-common-denominator clue which I have elected to pursue in my current inquiry is one that was alluded to in the "conflict of codes" concept presented by Chester I. Barnard in *The Functions of the Executive.*[1] Essentially, this concept claims that in every formally organized cooperative human activity there will arise from time to time inevitable and inescapable conflict between the codes that control the conduct of different individuals and the groups who are contributing to the overall cooperative purpose.

At the very apex of the executive responsibility, Barnard puts the burden of resolving the recurring conflict of codes that will inevitably arise in every formal organization. He sees this task as the key to successful leadership, and acutely so for the role of the top man. He further contends that the solution to such problems has to be the "creation of a higher moral code"—one that will encompass and reconcile at a higher and more embracing level the interests and values that come into unanticipated, yet still legitimate, conflict as the organization goes about pursuit of its ever-evolving goals.

Clues for Success

This view of the importance and the difficulties of the creative art and skills required in successfully handling serious conflict of codes is offered here because my long experience with such problems, as well as my current inquiry, seems to confirm it.

Should it stand confirmed, then it follows that the hidden key to success in the president's role of final and ultimate decision maker for his organization may rest more on his capabilities in this limited area than in any other single segment of his total presidential task. And should that prove to be the case, then it further follows that this is a less urgent inquiry than the one inevitably linked with it, to wit: What kinds of behavior, and what attitudes, values, skills, and training are characteristic of those chief executives who do relatively better than their peers in handling "conflict" issues? Can any uniformities be discerned among them, or among their problem-handling attributes, that may provide provisional clues for their relatively greater success?

There do seem to be some. In fact, I feel rather certain that there are even though the ones I shall present in this article may turn out to be merely a first approximation of those that are truly indispensable. It is much too soon at this juncture, and my present sample of top men is much too limited, to be confident that anything more than clues for further exploration have made an appearance.

Yet the frequent recurrence of some uncommon patterns of behavior, accompanied and supported by some key values and attitudes the presidents hold toward their jobs and themselves, stand out in sharp contrast to those of a large number of their peers. In my experience, the latter generally have greater difficulties with their toughest problems, are less self-confident of a healing solution, and are clearly more inclined both to minimize the seriousness of and to postpone, ignore, or evade (rather than deliberately and consciously confront) their problems.

It must be kept in mind, then, that the uniformities discussed here are drawn from a random sample of presidents who have learned somehow, somewhere, to do relatively better than their peers with the toughest problems that beset their jobs.

Management of Stress

Of all the individual uniformities common to top men, the most immediately self-evident is their ability to cope with stress. They all have learned to live—and for most of the time alone—with heavy stress. They have learned how to control it, contain it, channel it, offset it, or simply "lock the door" on it, while they rest and refresh themselves to resume their quest for an alternative that will acceptably resolve the conflict of codes.

The practices, devices, habits, and mental and emotional points of view that are utilized in coping with heavy stress are seemingly infinite in their variety and ingenuity. They are strongly influenced by the temperament, the background, and the idiosyncrasies of each individual executive. Yet behind all this seeming diversity is an implicit—and frequently quite explicit—acknowledgement that unless heavy stress is "managed"—that is, held within some tolerable limit—it can quickly become unmanageable, inducing panic and collapse of promising remedies.

To cope with stress, some top executives deliberately turn to a strikingly different kind of problem and immerse themselves thoroughly in it for a few hours. Or they sometimes return to their offices at unconventional hours — late at night or early in the morning — when the building is deserted and they can isolate themselves and think. Often they carefully compose a memorandum to themselves stating the problem as bluntly and concisely as possible and indicating what an adequate solution will require. This practice has a dual purpose:

(1) It forces out the plainest possible statement of the problem and its desired solution. This, when well done, enables them to "forget" the problem or, more accurately, to force it down to the level of their subconscious for attention there.

(2) It forces them to do all they can with the problem at the intellectual level and to signify this to their nervous systems by drafting the most up-to-date résumé of the situation that they can then prepare.

In either case they rid themselves of a persistent nagging from their minds and nerves and win a respite which they can use to renew themselves before resuming the search and struggle.

Further along on the spectrum above, or on one like it, some of these men occasionally seem to find the means to tap serendipity. After prolonged and intensive struggle with the issues at conflict, suddenly they take off for a distant region and a sport or pleasure (such as fishing for rare and prized species or elk hunting high in the Sierras) that is a keen joy in life to them. After two or three weeks out of all old ruts and routines, removed physically and emotionally as far as they can get, they sometimes discover — perhaps on the journey home — that the answer comes to them. They know that this practice is not surefire; but when they are "at wit's end," there is little to lose and, maybe, an inspiration to gain.

One president I talked with secured such a gain on the morning of the day I saw him. Over his wife's demur, he rose at four o'clock, took a long horseback ride in the mountain foothills near his home, and returned jubilantly with the reconciling solution to a problem that had vexed him for months. It was a deep-seated and unyielding conflict of codes that had nearly brought open warfare among members of his board, various groups of stockholders, and a large number of civic leaders whose communities' welfare seemed to them to be involved. He made that story the subject of his toughest-problem narrative.

Self-Expendable Attitude

Another recurring uniformity of belief and behavior among these men is their readiness to view themselves as "expendable." Because this attitude is so clearly the ultimate device employed in standing — and in *withstanding* — stress, it could have been placed under the success clue just discussed. Yet, because of its decisive importance, I have chosen to present it separately.

The readiness to put their jobs on the line over an issue they deem fundamental to their organization's long-range welfare is perhaps the simplest touchstone by which the more successful company presidents are distinguishable.

Sometimes it is utilized directly, virtually in the form of an ultimatum: "If continued, our labor relations policy will incur liquidation or bankruptcy in less than five years. It must be revised and reformulated radically, even at the risk of an immediate strike. Either our current policy goes, or I go."

Far more often, the readiness of the president to put his job on the line is merely latent in crisis situations. Nonetheless, it is clearly present and perceived by those who deal with him on these peak decisions. And it *is* present because when the top man does his utmost in working out a resolution to his conflict issues, he is the one prepared to undertake its implementation and abide by the consequences. No man can do more than shoulder that decisive responsibility —and the moment sometimes comes when a vote of confidence is called for.

Men less sure of themselves—those lacking the opportunity to practice and achieve some preliminary successes with such problems or those unable to face with equanimity the loss or surrender of their job with its power, prominence, and inward gratification—are generally tempted to rationalize away the importance of making such an ultimate decision and to minimize the hazards that they hope to be able to postpone or evade. They find it uncomfortable to view themselves as expendable and to contemplate the disquieting prospect of having to renew their careers in other environments where they might not regain such organizational eminence.

Psychological forces, deeply hidden yet very powerful, are so obviously involved in this ability to view oneself as expendable in the role of president that it is only necessary to call attention to the uniformity with which I find it present among my interviewees. (I leave its further explanation to those better equipped to interpret its psychic importance.) Organizationally, however, its value to a president when he is confronted alone with heavy stress is unmistakable. For him it is the ultimate safety valve, and I think it enables him to labor at his critical decision making well shielded from fears and anxieties about his personal fate. That bridge he has crossed beforehand.

That most of these top men recognize the value of this ability to view themselves as expendable usually comes out when I ask them whom they look to for approval, approbation, or understanding once a serious crisis has been satisfactorily surmounted. Reference groups frequently mentioned include: members of the board, the business community (watching from the sidelines), members of their own executive organization, the investment community (frequently privy to the severity and seriousness of some of these crises), and their whole organization as a total system cognizant in some degree of what has been afoot.

Surprisingly, a near majority of the top men in my sample—after some quiet reflection on my query—named none of the reference groups above. The answer simply was something like this: "Me. I must satisfy myself, above all, that I have done the best I can do. When I can do that, anything else or anyone's approval is pleasant, but superfluous."

When I questioned the top men who named other groups first about the importance of self-approval, it was instantly accepted as being so self-evident that each had taken for granted that I understood its priority and its indispensability to his view of his role in the organization.

Capacity to Concentrate

Another factor, closely related to the one just given, appears with sufficient frequency that I believe it to be a uniformity also. Sometimes it is mentioned early in the interviews, when the presidents feel that a brief résumé of the assignments given them as they rose through the ranks is relevant. Sometimes it is supplied later, when I request a recapitulation of their advancement by rank and increasing responsibility.

Beginning usually with their very first task after entering the organization, they reveal a capacity to immerse themselves with so much zest and with such an uncommon self-forgetfulness in the job assigned that it is completed ahead of schedule—and completed so well that another and a more demanding one is promptly supplied. Not only are these assignments expected, but so are the rewards: more work and more responsibility!

These top executives seem to have risen faster than their peers (and faster than is customary) principally because of a demonstrated capacity or appetite for exacting assignments into which they plunge *for the sake of the challenge* rather than for an opportunity to get ahead of their competitors. None of these men are naive about organizational politics; yet it is displaced—both as a major preoccupation in their minds and as a diversion to their energies—by their preference to get a job well done ahead of anything else. This trait of deep absorption in the task at hand creates, in a manner of speaking, a pull upward in the nature of assignments to ever-increasing responsibilities.

From listening carefully to these executives' stories, by studying the details written down later, and by occasionally hearing about some of them from other people who know them personally, I have formed the opinion that not many of these top men invest much of their time or thought in the race of "getting to the top." They get there, but rather as an afterthought, as it were, or as something secondary and extrinsic to doing well the job at hand. (With several of the men interviewed, I gained the impression that their job as president had come as something of a surprise at the time.)

This ability of the more successful men to concentrate deeply on each day's work not only serves to conserve time and energy that other contenders invest in clique activities, power plays, empire-building pursuits, and so on, but it leaves them largely free of the leftover resentments from old feuds and battle scars that handicap those unsuccessful candidates when the president's position becomes vacant at a time all are ready for consideration. In some cases it may tip the scales in their favor because they are less beholden to others for their advancement; in other cases, the deciding factor may be that they are more acceptable to more of their future subordinates than are their "rivals" who have made numerous enemies on *their* way up.

Influence of "Model"

In my early interviews with top men, it often happened that a leading second executive was soon brought into the conversation and reappeared repeatedly as the discussions unfolded. Although seldom involved directly in the specific cases being presented, he was pictured as being of dominant importance in the president's organization career.

He usually was about 30 years older than the speaker, and most often their acquaintance began soon after the younger man first entered the company and was assigned to the older man's organizational unit. Typically, the rank of the elder man at the time of first meeting was general manager or division vice president. Again, typically, the older man went on to become president, then chairman, and only recently retired or died.

Positive Pattern. I now have come to expect this "model" background figure to appear in my interviews, and in nearly every case he does so.

He frequently threatens to run away with the "case" at hand because the narrator's enthusiasm about him is so evident, as is his admiration and gratitude.

It is common to hear a president say, "You should have known *him*; he was the best executive I've ever known." Or, "He brought me up; he taught me the ropes." Or, "He gave me the chance to show what I could do." Or, "He really made this company." The speaker sometimes has difficulty in returning to the thread of the narrative he is relating and does so with regret and visible reluctance because he plainly feels we are dropping a more engrossing topic — namely, the personality and behavior of the man who "taught me all I know about this job I've got."

A father figure? Probably, as far as that tired phrase can carry us toward any agreed-on significance. At another level of discourse, however, the part this older individual has played in helping his young associate to form, to work out, and to *practice* his own patterns of organizational behavior is unmistakable. Aside from their expressions of admiration, 90% of the material my narrators supply about their older sponsor (tutor? coach? mentor?) are concrete illustrations of *his* organizational behavior that was exceptionally skillful as to morale-building, performance-producing, conflict-reducing, and so forth. And his were the patterns on which the younger man consciously chose to model his own developing organizational behavior. Whatever else the older man may be, he is clearly a model the young associate eagerly copies and to whom he renders tribute and gives predominant credit for most of his accomplishments.

Negative Figure. The very few top men who fail to introduce their model immediately, later invariably bring into their stories a similar background figure who seems to serve the same need in a reverse manner. For want of a better phrase, I have come to see this older man in the same way many presidents do — as an anti-model.

He is usually introduced not only later on in these discourses, but in a different fashion, such as: "Do you know anything about So-and-so, an earlier predecessor of mine? I ask because he was quite well known in his day." From this opening, they then characterize So-and-so as the chief executive who "brought this organization to the brink of ruin" because "he made *all* the decisions." Or, "He trusted no one but himself; he just couldn't delegate." Or, "You couldn't talk to him because he wouldn't listen." Or, he was "arbitrary," "insensitive," "ruthless," "vindictive," "obstinate," "vain."

The refrain about the anti-model is unvarying: "I watched every move he made because I couldn't believe what I saw. I asked myself, doesn't he know what damaging and costly results that move he is making (illustrated with a concrete example of his predecessor's behavior) will have on the people in this organization, or doesn't he care? How could a man be so stupid about organizational matters and ever get to be president?" (In one of these cases, the individual in question had bought control of the company with an enormous fortune made in stock market operations; in another, he had been ensconced through a famous family's influence.)

The lessons these top men draw from their anti-models are vivid and explicit: "I made up my mind that should I ever be a president, I would do exactly the opposite of X, and I could not lose!" Or, "I could hardly wait for a chance to replace him and try to undo the damage he had done." Or, "I wanted to try and see if we could ever catch up with all the opportunities he let slip by."

Again, whether anti-father figure or not, his every move was followed with minute vigilance by his anti-acolytes; his policies and managerial practices were daily scrutinized, analyzed, and criticized by an intent observer who was driven to declare—at least to himself and to a confidant or two from time to time—what he would do differently as the top executive, and in what specific ways the organization would be better, and why. Such resistance to, and disapproval of, the organizational behavior of Mr. Anti produced for these top men nearly the same firsthand knowledge-in-detail about administration-in-detail that was acquired by their counterparts under more agreeable (but scarcely more instructive) circumstances.

Other Attributes

Beyond these four uniformities, there seem to be some others, perhaps of equal or greater relevance. One of these might be the value the presidents clearly attach to having a temperamental opposite—some person available and near their level in the organization—who is a formidable and constructive critic or skeptic on whom they can test out their schemes for innovation. Such loyal opposition is encouraged and rewarded because "he's saved us from some God-awful blunders"; or because "if he can punch holes in it that I can't overcome, I usually drop it."

Most of the other attributes I have discerned, in addition to those I have given as examples, do not recur as frequently or have not been articulated as unmistakably. They must wait for the collection of more data from more top men, although I am inclined now to believe that, fully pursued, enough separate individual uniformities will disclose themselves to reappear as linked indissolubly together in patterns of mutually reinforcing uniformities common to top executives of the caliber I have had the good fortune to listen to.

Innate or Acquired?

The age-old issue of nature versus nurture presents itself at this point. How do men such as these get to be what they are? What aspects of their organizational behavior is learned behavior? What portion rests on natural endowments? How much of it stems from, let us say, a quarter-century of career training opportunities *before* taking over the top job? How much of it is role-induced *after* assuming the presidential task? How much of their fitness for that role was actually present well before they even entered their organizations? Does the constant daily testing on the various jobs they hold tend to sift out and to favor those with some inherent aptitude for the top organizational job?

Literature Inconclusive

Definitive answers to this long-standing issue still elude us. Since even a little light thereon is better than no light at all, readers who share my involvement in this pursuit may welcome a few further comments from the literature now accumulating rapidly on creativity and creative people. I, myself, ventured into this area some time past to see what others have found pertinent to the question of how these men "get that way." To what extent can the relatively better performance of some presidents be traced to their career training? To what extent must it be ascribed to a fortuitous combination of factors, some of them genetic and hence beyond our present ability to duplicate and transmit to others? Specifically, I wanted to find out what the chances are that a sizable segment of top men could have been—and *now* can be—better equipped by experience, training, or any kind of help to deal more constructively and creatively with the conflict of codes inherited with their office.

The views of writers on this topic range the spectrum from a few who hold that "they are born that way" to a larger number who feel that creativity is present as a variable in all healthy humans and can be strongly developed through the efforts of others if such "training" is understood to be the total influence exerted 24 hours a day by all other individuals on the subject in question. This view, of course, identifies education as an individual's total life experience and, for our purposes, begs the issue. In the center of this spectrum of views as to training are found the majority—those who are in doubt or decline to offer an opinion.

My present view is that since the question is currently beyond our reach to settle with certainty, we should follow the lead given us by those who hold that more creativity is available if we seek it. Not *all* creativity. And maybe not creativity for *all*. But more creativity for most of us if we take a culture-wide view of what an individual's total life experience actually does—and does not— "teach" us. This view has been strongly reinforced by my sample of some of the better top men, all of whom insist on pounding home the value and indispensability of (a) the training they received over 25 or 30 years of managing, and (b) having a model figure to emulate—or to repudiate—in terms of specific day-in, day-out episodes of organizational behavior.

Training for "Comers"

If additional data support my present surmise that the attributes I find are indeed uniformities-in-common, then it seems to me that it should be possible to devise tests or screening procedures to locate more quickly and more accurately individuals who possess, or are busy developing, the traits most often associated with the behavior of the more successful presidents. If the improvement in selectivity were to be no more than 5% to 10%, the larger yield would still be an enormous benefit. The most direct beneficiaries, naturally, would be the individuals possessing or acquiring the cluster of special talents required for the president's role.

Of course, other individuals intensely pursuing the job, but plainly lacking some of the essential traits, would also gain by having their drives redirected away from reasonably certain frustration and defeat toward goals more compatible with their capabilities. Their organizations would so palpably gain from better placement of executives for tasks to which their behavior patterns point that the savings from futility, frayed nerves, loss of forward movement, and so on, would simply be monumental. And the general society, in which these corporations' activities occupy an ever-increasing importance, would be the gainer by finding its affairs more often in the most competent hands.

The opportunities to improve, enlarge, and hasten the better training of more promising candidates would multiply the same benefits indicated above. Consider, for example, the manifold ways in which any total organization would flourish if the potential presidential timber within its ranks could be tentatively identified and placed under the skillful and nurturing supervision of some excelling "model" such as most of my sample presidents have had the supreme good fortune to attract! At the very least, another 5% to 10% improvement over our current trial-and-error methods would be another huge source of gain at trifling cost.

Aid for Incumbents

Returning to the present, I feel an obligation to call attention to the crushing character of the burdens—whose weight is often grossly underestimated or is airily dismissed as being overcompensated—the more successful presidents assume on behalf of the whole organization and indirectly on behalf of society-at-large. It does not reduce the seriousness of the point I am making to reply that many of these presidents actually relish opportunities to wrestle with seemingly insoluble problems. I know they do. I am glad they do. But I seriously want to see a far greater number of their peers feel the same way, and this brings me to the very point I most wish to make.

These top men face their most stressful, most important organizational problems alone—too much alone with respect to their own health and/or optimum task performance. And, in my opinion, needlessly too much alone.

They need, most of all, the vast relief of someone to talk with. They need to share, at least in part, the stress—to explore and clarify it, and to speed up the process of identifying the key issues from the more clamorous ones. In short, they need someone to aid them in expediting their search for the jugular.

They do not need a prop, a substitute problem-solver, or a pinch-hitter. They do not need an expert or other specialist in some given area for a problem that embraces a conflict of codes issue; there are no specialists in an area where each problem seldom has an applicable precedent. They do not need either a yes-man or a no-man. Preferably, they need most a noninvolved alter ego who can share their diagnostic search for the core problem—one who can stimulate the seeking for creative alternatives, but who resolutely leaves the ultimate decision to the top man for the simple and all-sufficient reason that he can never share the costs and risks of implementation.

The top executives most in need of the kind of help so roughly outlined are not the relatively more successful presidents that I know. (Being what they are, these successful men would probably be the first to use such expediting assistance!) Rather, the top men most in need of assistance are those whose batting averages are currently at the midpoint. Aid just a few times at critical junctures could possibly tip the scales favorably and put them—and their self-confidence—on a more equal footing with the fortunate sample of company presidents I have come to know.

Conclusion

Where have we gotten to? How can this limited first step of inquiry be summed up? I shall attempt to do this by enumerating the four essential things that I feel I have learned from this preliminary reconnaissance.

1. *Presidents do have to face problems for their organizations that other executives do not—and cannot—handle.* This is a matter of necessity, not of choice. It comes affixed to their role of final decision maker and cannot be evaded. Nor can it be delegated, at least as a totality, although portions—especially some of the technical and financial aspects—can be assigned for study and analysis.

On this part of my query, I feel reasonably confident that further research will confirm and not significantly modify the position stated.

2. *Problems that presidents must handle force their way upward because their resolution demands an ultimate "yes" or "no."* They demand the attention of the man whose authority is the widest and whose responsibility is the broadest in acting for the organization as a whole. These problems demand not only the ultimate in authority, but also the ultimate in overall ability because they are the most fraught with risks to the system. They compel admission to where "the buck stops."

Beyond their potential threat, these problems generally are also confusing in their complexity—cutting across all formal organization structures and frequently being intertwined with unheard-of nonorganizational elements of decisive importance. They are obscure as well as complex; one or more facets that are only dimly glimpsed, or even hidden, may conceal the core issue or contain the king pin to releasing the whole log jam.

Complicated, obscure, freighted with risk, attended by a welter of strong contradictory individual feelings of anger, frustration, anxiety, and fear, it is small wonder that these problems get passed rapidly upward ("Let him solve *this* one! Isn't that his job?").

This part of my quest seems rather clearly established too; namely, that the toughest, most unprecedented, most embracing, and touchiest problems in all organizations unfailingly make their way to the presidential desk. And they rightly are the top man's problems because that *is* his job—to handle the problems that no one else is sufficiently empowered to cope with and to handle these alone, somehow, or see his influence slowly dwindle.

3. *Conflict of codes—and the necessity of reconciling it through the creation of a higher, more embracing code—is inevitably present in every formal organization.* Since this is the interpretation and judgment of only one person, its merit must remain indeterminate pending the accumulation of a much broader sample, but more especially its verification by other investigators and methods.

4. *The patterns of organizational behavior disclosed by the data secured thus far strike me strongly with numerous parallels to the behavior of creative people encountered in the literature.* For those who may wish to look at some of the parallels involved, I suggest for a starter, Abraham H. Maslow's unconventional book, *Eupsychian Management*.[2] His long-pursued interest in those whom he labels "superior people" leads him to identify many of their traits and characteristics as the necessary attributes to make such people outstanding candidates for leadership and management. There is, in fact, a close fit between the uniformities I find common to my subjects and those he ascribes to the superior people. I offer this reference to Maslow's work chiefly to promote—and perhaps to provoke—relevant speculation as to where and how we can increase our supply of such people or, more exactly, the creative behavior they display.

REFERENCES

1. Cambridge, Mass.: Harvard University Press, 1938, Chapter 17.
2. Homewood, Ill.: Richard D. Irwin and Dorsey Press, 1965.

PART THREE

THREE

Managing Others' Careers

As you mature in your career, you will be called upon to supervise, guide, and direct others who will be accountable to you. In addition, you will be expected by those people to act on behalf of their own career pursuits, given their own wish to move toward their ego ideals. The greater an individual's desire to achieve, the greater the pressure he or she feels to move toward the ego ideal. That in turn makes for heavy demand by the subordinate that the boss or manager act in ways that will enhance the subordinate's competence, adaptive capacity, and movement toward career goals. If the manager fails to act in these ways, then subordinates will become demoralized and that can lead to high turnover, lethargy, anger, withdrawal, and other behaviors that are inconsistent with both personal and organizational success.

There is yet another issue. When you mature in your career, you come into what Erik H. Erikson has called the stage of generativity.[1] In this period, you presumably have passed through the middle-age transition, and, with painful awareness of your mortality, tend to shift your focus toward the development of others, whether members of your own family or those who report to you in an organization. So it becomes psychologically important for a manager to become more involved in the development of younger people through whom he or she will be perpetuated, either directly as in the family or symbolically as in the organization.

These same issues hold whether coming into a psychological stage is an evolutionary aspect of your career development or whether you have moved into an alternative career. Your own chronological and psychological stage will be the same in either case.

In "Tailor Executive Development to Strategy," James F. Bolt describes how four major corporations formalize their executive development programs and tie them to the achievement of measurable business results. Also included in these respective training programs are reports from subordinates about executive behavior, which enable managers to reflect on and adapt their behavior where necessary. Although Bolt's description is of corporate programs, you may readily infer a specific aspect of your own managerial behavior that could be focused and strengthened.

In his inimitable way, Peter F. Drucker, in "How to Make People Decisions," speaks of matching people to roles. He spells out the steps in that matching. Readers will find it helpful to turn from his criteria to the first two articles in this book, which discuss the manner in which people perceive themselves and the ego ideal goals toward which they are striving. The reader may first describe a given role and then him or herself in the terms that I outline in "On Choosing a Second Career." The juxtaposition of the descriptions of role and self will narrow the focus of the assessment of individual strengths and weaknesses.

Of course, as Drucker indicates, not all appointments are successful. In "Who Is to Blame for Maladaptive Managers?," I observe that many of the failures are a product of the way higher management manages. I delineate six such ways that will enable the reader to examine more carefully his or her own actions and ideally to avoid some of the problems of supervision.

Arch Patton, in "The Coming Promotion Slowdown," argues that the promotion rate will fall dramatically as more managers compete for fewer executive roles. That's in part a product of the baby boom and in part a product of the consolidation of many organizations. The promotion rate becomes a pressing issue when, as I have noted, the increasing intensity of the drive toward the ego ideal results in more pressure for demonstrated achievement. The issues that Patton discusses necessarily must be dealt with by anyone in a significant managerial role who has to contend with the feelings that result from the facts Patton cites.

Jeffrey Sonnenfeld takes up the issue of managing those who are middle aged and older in "Dealing with the Aging Work Force." He, too, reviews the problems associated with the sense of limited opportunity in middle and post-middle age. He calls attention to the need to observe the decline of morale and performance among many managers, and to pay special attention to the mobility of those in the middle-age range. Part of the decline in morale results from severe frustration and part from the trauma of the loss of youth. He notes that it is especially important to contradict the stereotypes of people in older-age ranges and suggests ways of continuing to make effective use of their contributions. He lays out specific steps that a manager can take to deal with these important issues.

Inevitably, whether because of age or changes in organizational structure or downsizing or business decline, some managers must go. Basil Robert Cuddihy, in "How to Give Phased-Out Managers a New Start," describes how the Aluminum Company of Canada, Limited, attempted to help each dismissed employee find a new job while simultaneously helping that person understand why he had become expendable. He lays out the steps that can be taken, utilizing a given employee's manager as the counselor through whom the constructive phasing-out activity can be conducted. This article will be helpful to the reader who may be in the position of having to phase others out or who finds himself or herself being phased out. The specific steps in the process, together with recognition of the feelings that people experience under such circumstances, can lend themselves to constructive and creative career developments.

Jay Lorsch and Haruo Takagi, in "Keeping Managers Off the Shelf," point out that, despite all the reorganization, most people will be plateaued in the latter halves of their careers. This could easily lead to frustration and futility on the part of the manager and anger on the part of higher management. Therefore, the need to teach such people, to excite them, and to motivate them is important, but even more important is whatever can be done to help avoid plateauing. The authors note that the most important difference between committed and passive managers was whether their early job assignments were connected to the mainstream of the company's activities. They specify actions that will prevent managers from turning off in early career stages and after they have plateaued.

1

Tailor Executive Development to Strategy

JAMES F. BOLT

Leading U.S. corporations are approaching the training and development of their top executives in a fundamentally different way than they did in the past. Professional training staffs are not forcing the change. Chief executives and chief operating officers themselves are in the driver's seat. The shift is a return to basics—training that is more results oriented, programs that are aimed at implementing business strategies and achieving corporate objectives—a move away from training as the development of a manager's administrative potential. Training and development in these companies focus on the corporate boardroom.

Recently, I conducted a survey of many of the nation's most highly regarded corporations. These are my findings:

Senior executives are playing a more directive role in shaping management training and development courses and curricula.

The demand for greater productivity, the threat of worldwide competition, and recognition of the change many corporate cultures need lead to a greater demand for management training and development at the very highest levels of the corporation.

Senior executives—including the chief executive officer—are not only mandating a larger role for management training and development, but are also themselves taking a role in the programs.

At the root of these shifts is management's belief that it has lost its way and that it is now time to regroup and get back on track. In 1980, William J. Abernathy and Robert H. Hayes charged U.S. managers with a plethora of shortcomings: a focus on short-term results, an infatuation with cost reduction for the sake of this year's earnings rather than with long-term innovation and risk taking, and a neglect of long-term strategic goals.[1]

Harsh criticism? Perhaps. But it has been repeated in too many quarters to be taken lightly. Anthony G. Athos and Richard Tanner Pascale underscore the point that vaunted U.S. management practices no longer seem to work.[2] And no less a statesman of corporate America than Reginald H. Jones of General Electric joins the chorus of criticism, writing recently that "the indictment in many cases is justified. It should be taken very seriously."

Apparently, chief executives are doing exactly that. And leaders of many top corporations are finding that one of the strongest weapons in their arsenal is a program that harnesses the energy and directs the talents of their senior executives.

My interest piqued by the survey findings, I looked at programs in four leading corporations—General Foods, Xerox, Motorola, and Federated Department Stores—to learn how they train and develop top managers.

Six common threads stand out:

1. The impetus for a successful, effective executive training and development program comes from the very top of the organization.

2. All four programs have precisely articulated objects.

3. The most important emphasis of the four programs is on the executive's role in implementing the corporation's strategies and achieving goals—including bottom-line business results.

4. The senior management team is involved in the design of the program.

5. Senior executives at three of the four corporations even teach part of the course.

6. Each program is custom designed.

Let's look at each of these findings in detail. The intentions of the four corporations are too similar to be dismissed.

Elements of Top-Level Training Programs

Although it is too early to draw any hard conclusions about the results of these programs, they offer a valuable blueprint for the executives who are trying to find a way to harness the energies of their senior management teams to get them working with a common purpose toward common goals.

Top Management Is the Impetus

At each of the four corporations I examined, the top executive was the force behind the program. President and chief operating officer Philip L. Smith at General Foods, president and chief executive officer David T. Kearns at Xerox, chairman Robert Galvin at Motorola, and chief executive officer Howard Goldfeder at Federated Department Stores all became convinced of the need for a development program for their senior executives. I cannot overemphasize this point. Distinct from the past when most senior executives halfheartedly went along with the recommendations of their staffs, these senior executives did not merely respond to their training professionals' proposals; each planted the seeds that their staffs later nurtured.

At General Foods, Philip Smith became president and chief operating officer in the fall of 1981. Early on, he determined that the company needed a way to focus the energies and efforts of its entire senior management team in a common direction. Thus the business leadership program was born. "Without that commitment from Smith," says one GF staffer, "I don't believe we would have gotten our program off the ground."

The same was true at Xerox. There, the senior management program was born out of some compelling business reasons and the determination of David Kearns that executive development would be a key factor in revitalizing Xerox.

A variety of forces—most notably the emergence of strong competition in an industry that Xerox once owned—combined to slow the growth of the copier giant. In the mid-1970s, market share began to erode. By the early 1980s, the rate of revenue growth had fallen and profits were declining. Kearns, a long-time supporter of management development, saw it as a crucial factor in improving business results. "Our investment in training will help managers deal more effectively with the complex business issues of the eighties and beyond," he wrote, "and will pay long-term dividends in productivity and profitability."

Kearns was determined to put that philosophy to work at the top of the house. In early 1982, Xerox completed a mammoth and detailed overhaul of its strategies and objectives for the coming decade. Kearns already had put in place the senior management team he wanted. He saw a senior management training and development program as the ideal means to introduce his team to the top 250 executives at Xerox, to communicate to them the corporation's strategies and objectives, and to gain their commitment to achieve the corporate goals.

The initiative for an executive development program at Motorola also came from the top of the house. In late 1982, Robert Galvin directed the professional training and development staff to study the feasibility of such a program. He stayed close to its development, and included William Weisz and John Mitchell — the other two members of Motorola's chief executive office — at every stage of the development cycle.

These executives leave no doubt about the importance they attach to the senior executive program. In a letter delivered to each participant at the outset of the program in 1983, the three most senior Motorola executives wrote:

"This program offers an opportunity for each of us to carry on a responsibility that is fundamental to the continued well-being of Motorola. Throughout the week and long after we return to our businesses, we need to relentlessly challenge the assumptions on which we've come to rely while leading this corporation. We have on previous occasions emphasized the absolute necessity of rethinking our approach to success — of finding those fundamental pivot points where our current thinking may not be right. This week is an excellent opportunity for such rethinking. You will be working together in an extended, uninterrupted fashion, stimulated by the finest scholars and focusing on the global issues and realities that confront each of our businesses."

Federated, the largest department store chain in the United States, has a strong financial base and holds an enviable position in most of its markets. But because the industry is going through transformation, and competition has been increasing dramatically, Federated is also a company in transition.

In the summer of 1981, Howard Goldfeder, then newly appointed as Federated's CEO, oversaw an exhaustive study on the role of store general managers — or principals as Federated prefers to call them — in relation to the strategic direction of the corporation.

Goldfeder's plan for continued success included a heavy emphasis on strategic goals, higher financial returns, close scrutiny of expansion decisions, and tighter control of assets. It also included training to give store managers the tools, skills, and authority to control their businesses on a more sophisticated and disciplined basis. The new chief executive was looking for increased professionalism and sophistication in business management practices to complement the professionalism that existed in retailing disciplines.

All four executives were at the forefront in getting their senior management training and development programs off the ground. Without their imprimatur, the programs would have lacked the priority and visibility they needed and deserved.

Objectives Are Clearly Articulated

While in past programs the objectives have often been poorly defined or ill conceived, in the four corporations I studied, management had spelled out in detail anywhere from three to five objectives.

At General Foods, the program developers agreed that the executives who would ultimately complete it should achieve five objectives:

1. Identify more accurately the results their unit or function can achieve.

2. Identify changes necessary for their unit's or function's current environment to produce superior results.

3. Recognize—through subordinates' feedback—his or her impact as a leader of the business unit or function.

4. Identify strategies and opportunities for empowering the unit or function.

5. Identify personal actions that reinforce and reward the values and behaviors required to achieve the goals of both the unit or function and the corporation.

Similarly, at Xerox the senior management program (which will be updated and run again in 1986) had a list of five very specific educational goals that included articulating strategies, giving direction, identifying opportunities and roadblocks, and building teamwork.

Motorola took both a long-term and a short-term approach in setting its objectives. The Motorola program envisions a long-term educational process that will be built around specific annual development programs. This process has two overriding objectives: (1) increase senior executives' knowledge and understanding of future external trends and environments and their potential impact on Motorola and (2) enhance the ability of senior executives to collectively influence Motorola's future in the face of anticipated, sweeping change. About 18 to 25 officers attended the six-day, off-site program.

Specific objectives for the 1984 senior executive program were: identify and understand key emerging Asian competitive threats; understand the factors in Asia that are subject to change and that may affect Motorola's business; and provide a perspective that will be helpful in the development and improvement of strategic plans in the respective business units.

At Federated, too, the four objectives of the Senior Management Institute have been codified in very precise language:

1. Develop participants' understanding as to how Federated is organized and how it operates—at the corporate level and at the division and store levels.

2. Discuss with senior managers a leadership model tailored to Federated's changing market conditions, culture, size, and business.

3. Stimulate participants to assess their strengths and weaknesses and to develop a self-improvement plan.

4. Develop among managers an understanding of the roles and functions of the store general managers.

This last objective has several subsets, among them: to enable participants to run their businesses more strategically, to facilitate collaboration with corporate management and integrate divisional activity with corporate goals, to create a climate that is conducive to achieving strategic objectives, and to create and use information that allows appropriate, efficient, and timely action.

Implementation of Strategy Is the Focus

Far from being "nice-to-do" exercises, the four programs aimed to achieve measurable business results. The business leadership program at General Foods was designed to help participants identify change needed in the unit's current environment in order to produce superior results. It is aimed almost exclusively at the executive's role in achieving GF's overriding objective of becoming the premier food and beverage company.

Personal action planning ensures that each executive internalizes what he or she has learned. Drawing on the discussions held during the program's sessions, the feedback of their subordinates, their understanding of the GF vision, their own aspirations for their units, and a heavy dose of introspection, participants pinpoint the factors critical to their organization's success. The intent is to isolate one major action that each executive is committed to initiating. To build commitment and to galvanize the motivation to stick with its implementation, the executive shows the plan to one other person.

At Xerox the program staff presents a comprehensive overview of the corporate strategy, the financial implications of the strategy (including a workshop on participants' parts in improving return on assets), and an examination of the strategies of each main business sector. Again with an eye toward the participants' role in implementation, the staff goes over key functional strategies like human resources and technology.

The Xerox program also addresses management styles and practices. Participants receive a report on how their subordinates rate them on a series of managerial practices considered important in implementing Xerox's new strategic direction. The feedback provides the basis for each person's plan on how to improve those areas that need the most change.

The senior executive program at Motorola also represents a significant departure. For 12 or more years, the Motorola Executive Institute had brought groups of 16 executives each to an Arizona retreat for a month-long program. The faculty consisted of some of the most renowned and respected teachers of management from around the world. The intent always was to stimulate thinking of senior managers.

In the late 1970s, the program was discontinued. Explains one observer: "The Motorola Executive Institute had served the corporation well, but the environment had changed. Competition had increased and the business had become much more complex. Suddenly, 30 days in the Arizona desert seemed nice, but not necessary."

A six-year hiatus in executive training ensued. The renaissance came as a result of Galvin's initiative. In late 1982, he directed Motorola's training and development staff to study the feasibility of creating a program for senior management. What followed was far more results oriented than previous programs. "Frankly," says one person close to the program's development, "I don't think our top executives would sit still for a week-long program that was not germane to the business in a very practical way. The world has become more competitive. Things have changed. We have to change our approach to things as well."

The Senior Management Institute at Federated has a two-pronged focus: thwart competition in an industry that is going through significant change and emerge a business leader.

Not surprisingly, all four programs give participants feedback on how their subordinates view them, which forces them to reflect on how they behave in the company. This exercise tailors each program to each executive and is very results oriented. It's as if Smith, Kearns, Galvin, and Goldfeder want to perch on the shoulder of each executive and say: "O.K., now that you really understand the strategy, how are you going to change to help me implement it?"

Management Is Involved in the Program Design

At all four corporations, the staff responsible for the program design conducted extensive interviews with 12 to 80 of the company's most senior executives. Data from these interviews altered the objectives, scope, and content of each of the programs that were later put in place.

At the request of Smith, the training and development staff at General Foods interviewed a number of senior executives, officers, and general managers to identify the company's issues and needs concerning leadership. Three needs emerged repeatedly:

To translate a newly adapted corporate mission statement into business actions.

To identify and communicate the parameters of acceptable risk taking so that executives could be more aggressive and innovative and know that they were still acting within corporate boundaries.

To develop personal leadership behavior that supported, reinforced, and rewarded results.

Underlying these issues was a belief that senior management must act in ways that visibly demonstrate and reinforce GF's stated goal of becoming an innovative, aggressive organization that is responsive to opportunity. Armed with the data from the interviews, the staff then proceeded to design a program that met the requirements of the entire senior management team.

At Xerox several themes resulted, without which, says one training and development staffer, "I'm convinced we would have gone astray." Among the needs cited were:

Senior managers of Xerox needed to understand the company's total strategy so that they could develop a unified purpose, common goals, and a consistent management style.

Senior managers needed to be challenged to develop specific actions they would themselves take to implement the strategy.

Senior managers needed to understand the strategies and critical success factors in each major business sector.

Motorola's staff interviewed more than half the company's 150 officers to determine if the managers thought an executive development program was necessary in the first place and, if so, what its focus might be. The consensus was clear. With one exception, each of the nearly 80 officers interviewed strongly supported the need for a new program. Also, many of them thought there should be a program designed for officers. Finally, a clear majority thought that the subject matter should in some way deal with the worldwide competitive threat to Motorola. As we shall see, these and other findings profoundly affected the scope and content of the program that the Motorola staff implemented.

Perhaps the most thorough involvement of a senior management team in the design of an executive development program was achieved at Federated in a series of lengthy one-on-one interviews with Goldfeder, members of his senior management team, and several store principals. The objective was to "identify the critical skills, activities, practices, and personal characteristics required of a store principal to be successful at FDS in the late 1980s."

A major finding of that round of interviews was the need for a management training and development program. At a principals' meeting in October 1981, the concept of a senior management institute was unveiled. The reaction was overwhelmingly positive, and top management gave a green light for futher analysis and development. A wealth of findings was unearthed—findings that affected the design of the institute. Four, in particular, are worthy of note: (1) the program should be realistic and geared to the "real world of Federated," (2) the program should challenge senior managers and force them to work hard, (3) the program should broaden the participants' business perspective, and (4) the institute should offer executives compelling and accurate feedback on their strengths and weaknesses as managers.

The extent to which the senior management team influenced the programs at each of the four companies is important for two reasons. First, top management was responsible for and thus owned the end product. And second, it ensured that the design of the program met executives' needs and would be of real—not just ritualistic—value.

Senior Executives Teach Courses

At General Foods, Smith discusses his personal view of leadership with program participants and leads an informal discussion on his vision of GF. At Xerox, Kearns spends a half-day listening to presentations by program participants and engages them in dialogue. At Motorola, Galvin, Weisz, or Mitchell participate in the last day of each program. Here are the details.

The second phase of the General Foods program, communicating the vision, is aimed at helping participants understand their roles as leaders, the impact of those roles on business results, and how they can enhance their performance. A high point of this segment is a session with Smith who shares his personal vision for General Foods and the crucial role each GF executive must play to make that vision a reality.

I can't do justice here to Smith's view of leadership, but a brief synopsis is in order. It contains five guidelines:

1. Develop a vision that you can communicate to an organization in clear terms.

2. Follow up with clear direction so the organization knows what it has to do to translate the vision into reality.

3. Gain the commitment of the organization to that vision and direction.

4. Establish an environment that is conducive to helping the organization achieve its vision.

5. Develop a sense of trust that flows from integrity at the top and gives the organization confidence to do what's required—even when it is not necessarily in the worker's self-interest.

After dinner on the first day, each participant shares a story about a leader or leaders who have had a profound impact on his or her life and values. Smith guides the discussion. Participants get a strong message: just as they have been influenced by leaders, so too they can have a lasting and compelling impact on the people they manage.

The dialogue with Smith is freewheeling, give-and-take. An observer at one of these sessions says: "You get the feeling early on that there are no sacred cows and nothing is off limits. You also get the impression that although Smith's vision for GF and his views on leadership are clear and run deep, they don't preclude other executives from having a style that is quite different."

Most of the faculty of the Xerox senior management program are senior executives of the corporation: the chief financial officer, the chief strategy officer, the chief human resources officer, and key operating group presidents. Toward the end of the week-long program, participants work in small groups to identify one important issue they can act on to help meet the corporate strategy. The focus is on thinking of actions and solutions whose implementation is within the power of the individual or group.

Each group then presents its recommendations to Kearns, who spends a half-day listening and responding to the presentations. It is no mere exercise: Kearns requests that many of the presentations be given to the Corporate Management Committee or to the member who has responsibility for the issue being addressed. Kearns often acts on recommendations himself or directs others to do so.

Perhaps most important, Kearns uses the sessions as a teaching vehicle. If an idea seems ambiguous, he clarifies it. If a point seems vague, he amplifies it. If a legitimate concern is raised, Kearns makes sure it receives attention and, if justified, action. One participant describes the Kearns performance as "inspirational." Another says, "It developed an openness and an opportunity to share views and have them heard without being concerned that you would be labeled a nay-sayer if you raised an issue or voiced a criticism."

At Motorola, the senior executives play much the same role that Kearns plays at Xerox. On the sixth and final day of the Motorola program, the class breaks into smaller groups. They identify and rank the key issues and then recommend action plans to deal with them. The groups present their recommendations to one of Motorola's three chief executive officers (Galvin, Weisz, or Mitchell).

These three men leave no doubt about the importance they attach to the senior executive program. Each of them has been a student in the full program and each clearly relishes listening to and teaching participants. One person who has observed them remarks: "One of the most lasting impressions people take away from the senior executive program is the view of their leaders instructing, teaching, and expanding the horizons of others. It's quite extraordinary."

Each Program Is Unique

Each company custom designed its program. There was literally no portion of the Xerox program, for example, that could be given to executives in the three other corporations. At General Foods, the management training and development staff developed the program for the company.

The first phase of the General Foods program, owning the vision, is geared toward getting each participant to understand and internalize what it takes to lead his or her GF unit toward higher performance. Each participant spends time alone and in small groups fantasizing about how the company will look and behave when it has achieved its goal of becoming the world's "premier food and beverage company." The staff instructs participants to be specific about their unit's environments, their staff, and their business goals and strategies. Most important, the students rigorously assess their own strengths and weaknesses as leaders in the General Foods environment. The comparison between the world as they would like it to be and the world as it is today provides executives with a powerful way to identify gaps and areas that need change.

Xerox packs a lot into its five-and-a-half-day program — and all of it is tailored to its own needs. The curriculum covers eight areas, beginning with a look at where Xerox has been as well as at the scope of the competitive threat worldwide. Participants are given a look at the world in 1992 and the role that Xerox would like to play in that world. Finally, they are given a feel for the challenges they must overcome, particularly the financial hurdles, to be where they want to be in 1992.

During the next four parts of the program — on corporate strategy, the financial implications of that strategy, the strategies of each major business sector, and the strategies of functional areas — the most senior person in each area presents that section of the program. The chief financial officer, for example, handles the session on the financial strategy and return on assets, while the presidents of all major divisions present and discuss their strategies.

The program section on customer satisfaction may be unique to U.S. industry. Senior representatives of a major Xerox customer — such as Westinghouse Electric Corporation, Digital Equipment Corporation, and Manufacturers Hanover Trust — are invited to give a panel presentation on what they like and do not like about Xerox. The staff encourages customers to concentrate on the latter and asks them to assess Xerox's products in terms of cost, quality, and reliability as well as to recommend what Xerox must do to keep them as customers.

The candid and lively discussions last through a reception and dinner. The senior executives of Xerox, put on the firing line, hear candid criticism from a customer in an environment conducive to openness. The process supports one of Xerox's major goals: to improve customer satisfaction significantly.

The content of Motorola's program is also tied to its unique needs and position in the marketplace. The first day of the 1984 program was devoted to an overview of the position of the United States in a worldwide economy that is becoming increasingly competitive, a discussion of the nature and value of having a global perspective, and an examination of Motorola's activities in Asia.

Day two began an analysis of each Asian country — China, Taiwan, Japan, and South Korea — of special interest to Motorola. The purpose is to give all senior executives a common framework for assessing the strengths and weaknesses of other countries and companies as well as a tool to improve Motorola's ability to carry out its strategies. The participants proceed to examine the leading economic entities in Asia and one of Motorola's main competitors in that part of the world. The participants look at economic, political, and social factors. The object is to answer five questions:

Is a particular country's economic performance in accord with its goals?

Is a country's economic performance in accord with its international context?

Can a country's economic policies bring about change to coordinate economic performance with its goals?

Is it reasonable to expect these policy changes to occur and to influence the economy's performance?

How will the future domestic and international environments look and can the government in each country meet the resulting challenges?

Experts, usually drawn from the academic community, make presentations and lead the discussion on each country. A special aspect of the program ensures that the expert stays on course and does not get too theoretical. While the country expert holds forth in the front of the room, a second expert who has lived in the country for an extended period—usually an officer from the State Department or a consultant—sits in the back of the room. This person plays devil's advocate, challenging the first expert and adding real-world examples. At the end of each country analysis, participants summarize the key conclusions and implications for Motorola.

According to one participant, "The blend of an academic and a seasoned field person adds a special and powerful dimension to the analysis of the country. It opens up a dialogue and adds tremendous credibility to the entire program. You come away with a much richer understanding of the country. The experience takes information out of the textbook and makes it all very real."

After the analysis of each country, the class examines a leading competitor of Motorola in that country. "That's an eye-opener," says an observer. "Suddenly you're not talking about some vague concept like 'the Japanese,' but you're talking about a real company that sells real products to *your* customers."

The country-by-country analysis lasts through the fifth day of the program, followed by the groups' presentations to one of the three top executives in Motorola.

Federated's six-and-a-half-day program opens with a three-day session on strategy formulation. The managers analyze the retail business and formulate a specific competitive strategy. They learn how to communicate the strategy upward and downward throughout the organization and how to implement the strategy over time by making decisions consistent with the strategy and modifying it when and where appropriate. The students gain an awareness of the complexity of and potential impact of this crucial managerial function on the corporation's future success. And they learn to develop strategies that deal not only with internal and external forces but also with the financial requirements of the corporation.

Two of the three days are spent analyzing an imaginary business that closely resembles Federated. Participants learn how to identify and analyze competitive forces as well as how to pinpoint a division's strengths and weaknesses. And they learn to develop strategies that deal not only with internal and external forces but also with the financial requirements of the corporation.

The second segment of the program at Federated focuses on managing the organization through the store principal, who as a manager of managers must achieve the company's goals through other people. During the two-and-a-half-day segment, managers learn how to assess an organization's climate and what impact their activities have on it.

The third and last segment of the Senior Management Institute is a one-day session on Federated's partnership approach to leadership. At Federated, "partnership" normally refers to the collaboration that takes place between the two principals at the top of each division. But for the purposes of the Senior Management Institute, it includes the cooperation and teamwork that ideally exists across functional and organizational lines. The institute uses exercises to develop the ability to articulate a position and stand firm when appropriate, to confront others constructively with a logical case, to resolve conflicts in a constructive and mutually beneficial manner, and to influence others to support a charted action.

Is Such a Program Right for You?

It would be foolhardy to suggest that every corporation needs an executive development program like the ones I've described or that the programs are easy to design and implement. They are decidedly not for everyone, nor are they simple to achieve.

For one thing, the timing has to be right. In three of the four cases described here, the executive who initiated the program was in his position for two years or less. So the environment was right for something new. And in all four cases, the executive involved had a very definite blueprint for the future. Without that, any attempt at an executive development program is probably doomed.

Another critical element is the chemistry between the top executive and the person responsible for executive development. In all four cases, the training person was one of the best in the field, had the confidence of management, and possessed the skills and temperament to launch and sustain such a program. In many—perhaps in most—corporations, this is not the case. Training and development is often only an appendage to the business process. In these situations, the training and development staffs usually possess neither the perspective nor the clout to design and implement programs of the scope examined here.

To launch an executive development program without the commitment of the corporate hierarchy, the right timing, and a capable development staff is to invite disaster. The corporate landscape is littered with programs that were begun but never implemented or—worse yet—were started but fell far short of expectations.

It would be foolhardy to draw any firm conclusions about the impact these executive development programs have on the performance of their companies. The ultimate test, of course, will be how well these four corporations implement their strategies and meet their business objectives in the next several years.

Yet we can glean some sense of their potential from less empirical data. At General Foods, the business leadership program was launched in November 1983. Reaction was so positive that the program is now conducted monthly virtually unchanged. Phil Smith notes that, "The saliency of the issue has been raised enough so that people are thinking and talking about leadership."

Smith was surprised to learn "the degree to which the elements of what General Foods is about and doing were really not understood at all." However effective headquarters had been in communicating these elements, Smith's involvement in the leadership program gives him a chance to reinforce his vision of the company. GF's plans call for the most senior executives—about 350—to complete the course by early 1985.

Between March of 1983 and January of 1984, Xerox conducted twelve senior management programs. In all, 288 senior managers—all officers of the corporation, functional heads, and heads of major operating organizations—attended. The response to the program was extremely positive. One participant seemed to speak for many when he wrote: "The program provided a believable and comprehensible picture of where the corporation is in total and where it is heading. It was frank, to the point, and showed us that our problems will be tough but not impossible to resolve. I understand what I have to do and I am committed to get out and do it." This is the result, of course, that Xerox had hoped for.

Xerox plans to include elements of "Understanding and Implementing Xerox's Business Strategies" in the training of the next lower echelon of its management corps and to bring back the top 275 executives in 1986 for an updated program.

Reaction to Motorola's senior executive program, which all Motorola executives have attended, has also been excellent. The Motorola program is to be continued, with a new topic, on an annual basis. In addition, a similar program is under way for the corporation's director-level managers.

At Federated, some 200 senior vice presidents and executives above that rank have participated in ten sessions of the Senior Management Institute, and their reactions have been very positive.

It is quite likely that over the next five years or so companies will continue to take the nuts-and-bolts approach. More and more companies will move away from broad, educational programs and move toward curricula aimed at meeting more specific business objectives. There is, however, both a need and a place for the perspective-broadening program of the past. The pendulum is likely to swing back toward the center so that companies will use programs that meet the practical as well as the broader needs.

Already, Xerox—which may have led the current trend with its 1982 program—is planning to reinstitute its senior management program so that all top managers attend every two years. The next version will likely include an update on strategic direction and objectives, a discussion of new strategic issues, and a review of progress since the last program—including feedback for participants on their management practices so they can see their progress. It will also include some modules aimed at presenting state-of-the-art thinking on contemporary issues of interest at Xerox.

This blend of hard-hitting, business-oriented content with an external focus on topics of a more general education value may be the wave of the future. But whatever the future holds, one thing is certain. With the CEO taking a more active role, executive training will never be the same again. And that's all to the good.

REFERENCES

1. Robert H. Hayes and William J. Abernathy, "Managing Our Way to Economic Decline," HBR July-August 1980, p. 67.

2. Anthony G. Athos and Richard Tanner Pascale, *The Art of Japanese Management* (New York: Simon and Schuster, 1981).

NOTE

1. Erik H. Erikson, *Childhood and Society* (New York: Norton, 1963).

2

How to Make People Decisions

PETER F. DRUCKER

Executives spend more time on managing people and making people decisions than on anything else—and they should. No other decisions are so long lasting in their consequences or so difficult to unmake. And yet, by and large, executives make poor promotion and staffing decisions. By all accounts, their batting average is no better than .333: at most one-third of such decisions turn out right; one-third are minimally effective; and one-third are outright failures.

In no other area of management would we put up with such miserable performance. Indeed, we need not and should not. Managers making people decisions will never be perfect, of course, but they should come pretty close to batting 1,000—especially since in no other area of management do we know as much.

Some executives' people decisions have, however, approached perfection. At the time of Pearl Harbor, every single general officer in the U.S. Army was overage. Although none of the younger men had been tested in combat or in a significant troop command, the United States came out of World War II with the largest corps of competent general officers any army has ever had. George C. Marshall, the army's chief of staff, had personally chosen each man. Not all were great successes, but practically none were outright failures.

In the 40 or so years during which he ran General Motors, Alfred P. Sloan, Jr., picked every GM executive—down to the manufacturing managers, controllers, engineering managers, and master mechanics at even the smallest accessory division. By today's standards, Sloan's vision and values may seem narrow. They were. He was concerned only with performance in and for GM. Nonetheless, his long-term performance in placing people in the right jobs was flawless.

The Basic Principles

There is no such thing as an infallible judge of people, at least not on this side of the Pearly Gates. There are, however, a few executives who take their people decisions seriously and work at them.

Marshall and Sloan were about as different as two human beings can be, but they followed, and quite consciously, much the same principles in making people decisions:

If I put a person into a job and he or she does not perform, I have made a mistake. I have no business blaming that person, no business invoking the "Peter Principle," no business complaining. I have made a mistake.

"The soldier has a right to competent command" was already an old maxim at the time of Julius Caesar. It is the duty of managers to make sure that the responsible people in their organizations perform.

Of all the decisions an executive makes, none are as important as the decisions about people because they determine the performance capacity of the organization. Therefore, I'd better make these decisions well.

The one "don't": do not give new people new major assignments, for doing so only compounds the risks. Give this sort of assignment to someone whose behavior and habits you know and who has earned trust and credibility within your organization. Put a high-level newcomer first into an established position where the expectations are known and help is available.

Some of the worst staffing failures I have seen involved brilliant Europeans hired by U.S. companies — one based in Pittsburgh; the other, Chicago — to head up new European ventures. Dr. Hans Schmidt and M. Jean Perrin (only the names are fictitious) were hailed as geniuses when they came in. A year later they were both out, totally defeated.

No one in Pittsburgh had understood that Schmidt's training and temperament would make him sit on a new assignment for the first six or nine months, thinking, studying, planning, getting ready for decisive action. Schmidt, in turn, had never even imagined that Pittsburgh expected instant action and immediate results. No one in Chicago had known that Perrin, while a solid and doggedly purposeful man, was excitable and mercurial, flailing his arms, making speeches about trivia, and sending up one trial balloon after another. Although both men subsequently became highly successful CEOs of major European corporations, both executives were failures in companies that did not know and understand them.

Two other U.S. companies successfully established businesses for the first time in Europe during the same period (the late 1960s and early 1970s). To initiate their projects, each sent to Europe a U.S. executive who had never before worked or lived there but whom people in the head offices knew thoroughly and understood well. In turn the two managers were thoroughly familiar with their companies. At the same time, each organization hired half a dozen young Europeans and placed them in upper-middle executive jobs in the United States. Within a few years, both companies had a solid European business and a trained, seasoned, and trusted corps of executives to run it.

As Winston Churchill's ancestor, the great Duke of Marlborough, observed some three centuries ago, "The basic trouble in coalition warfare is that one has to entrust victory if not one's life, to a fellow commander whom one knows by reputation rather than by performance."

In the corporation as in the military, without personal knowledge built up over a period of time there can be neither trust nor effective communication.

The Decision Steps

Just as there are only a few basic principles, there are only a few important steps to follow in making effective promotion and staffing decisions:

1. **Think through the assignment.** Job descriptions may last a long time. In one large manufacturing company, for example, the job description for

the position of division general manager has hardly changed since the company began to decentralize 30 years ago. Indeed, the job description for bishops in the Roman Catholic church has not changed at all since canon law was first codified in the thirteenth century. But assignments change all the time, and unpredictably.

Once in the early 1940s, I told Alfred Sloan that he seemed to spend an inordinate amount of time pondering the assignment of a fairly low-level job — general sales manager of a small accessory division — before choosing among three equally qualified candidates. "Look at the assignment the last few times we had to fill the same job," Sloan answered. To my surprise, I found that the terms of the assignment were quite different on each occasion.

When putting a man in as division commander during World War II, George Marshall always looked first at the nature of the assignment for the next eighteen months or two years. To raise a division and train it is one assignment. To lead it in combat is quite another. To take command of a division that has been badly mauled and restore its morale and fighting strength is another still.

When the task is to select a new regional sales manager, the responsible executive must first know what the heart of the assignment is: to recruit and train new salespeople because, say, the present sales force is nearing retirement age? Or is it to open up new markets because the company's products, though doing well with old-line industries in the region, have not been able to penetrate new and growing markets? Or, since the bulk of sales still comes from products that are 25 years old, is it to establish a market presence for the company's new products? Each of these is a different assignment and requires a different kind of person.

2. **Look at a number of potentially qualified people.** The controlling word here is "number." Formal qualifications are a minimum for consideration; their absence disqualifies the candidate automatically. Equally important, the person and the assignment need to fit each other. To make an effective decision, an executive should look at three to five qualified candidates.

3. **Think hard about how to look at these candidates.** If an executive has studied the assignment, he or she understands what a new person would need to do with high priority and concentrated effort. The central question is not "What can this or that candidate do or not do?" It is, rather, "What are the strengths each possesses and are these the right strengths for the assignment?" Weaknesses are limitations, which may, of course, rule a candidate out. For instance, a person may be excellently qualified for the technical aspects of a job; but if the assignment requires above all the ability to build a team and this ability is lacking, then the fit is not right.

But effective executives do not start out by looking at weaknesses. You cannot build performance on weaknesses. You can build only on strengths. Both Marshall and Sloan were highly demanding men, but both knew that what matters is the ability to do the assignment. If that exists, the company can always supply the rest. If it does not exist, the rest is useless.

If, for instance, a division needed an officer for a training assignment, Marshall looked for people who could turn recruits into soldiers. Every man that was good at this task usually had serious weaknesses in other areas. One was not particularly effective as a tactical commander and was positively hopeless when it came to strategy. Another had foot-in-mouth disease and got into trouble with the press. A third was vain, arrogant, egotistical, and fought constantly with his commanding officer. Never mind, could he train recruits? If the answer was yes—and especially if the answer was "he's the best"—he got the job.

In picking the members of their cabinets, Franklin Roosevelt and Harry Truman said, in effect: "Never mind personal weaknesses. Tell me first what each of them can do." It may not be coincidence that these two presidents had the strongest cabinets in twentieth-century U.S. history.

4. **Discuss each of the candidates with several people who have worked with them.** One executive's judgment alone is worthless. Because all of us have first impressions, prejudices, likes, and dislikes, we need to listen to what other people think. When the military picks general officers or the Catholic church picks bishops, this kind of extensive discussion is a formal step in their selection process. Competent executives do it informally. Hermann Abs, the former head of Deutsche Bank, picked more successful chief executives in recent times than anyone else. He personally chose most of the top-level managers who pulled off the postwar German "economic miracle," and he checked out each of them first with three or four of the person's former bosses or colleagues.

5. **Make sure the appointee understands the job.** After the appointee has been in a new job for three or four months, he or she should be focusing on the demands of that job rather than on the requirements of preceeding assignments. It is the executive's responsibility to call that person in and say, "You have now been regional sales manager—or whatever—for three months. What do you have to do to be a success in your new job? Think it through and come back in a week or ten days and show me in writing. But I can tell you one thing right away: the things you did to get the promotion are almost certainly the wrong things to do now."

If you do not follow this step, don't blame the candidate for poor performance. Blame yourself. You have failed in your duty as a manager.

The largest single source of failed promotions—and I know of no greater waste in U.S. management—is the failure to think through, and help others think through, what a new job requires. All too typical is the brilliant former student of mine who telephoned me a few months ago, almost in tears. "I got my first big chance a year ago," he said. "My company made me engineering manager. Now they tell me that I'm through. And yet I've done a better job than ever before. I have actually designed three successful new products for which we'll get patents."

It is only human to say to ourselves, "I must have done something right or I would not have gotten the big new job. Therefore, I had better do more of what I did to get the promotion now that I have it." It is not intuitively obvious to most people that a new and different job requires new and different behavior. Almost 50 years ago, a boss of mine challenged me four months after he had advanced me to a far more responsible position. Until he called me in, I had continued to do what I had done before. To his credit, he understood that it was his responsibility to make me see that a new job means different behavior, a different focus, and different relationships.

High-Risk Decisions

Even if executives follow all these steps, some of their people decisions will still fail. These are, for the most part, the high-risk decisions that nevertheless have to be taken.

There is, for example, high risk in picking managers in professional organizations—for a research lab, say, or an engineering or corporate legal department. Professionals do not readily accept as their boss someone whose credentials in the field they do not respect. In choosing a manager of engineering, the choices are therefore limited to the top-flight engineers in the department. Yet there is no correlation (unless it be a negative one) between performance as a bench engineer and performance as a manager. Much the same is true when a high-performing operating manager gets a promotion to a staff job in headquarters or a staff expert moves into a line position. Temperamentally, operating people are frequently unsuited to the tensions, frustrations, and relationships of staff work, and vice versa. The first-rate regional sales manager may well become totally ineffective if promoted into market research, sales forecasting, or pricing.

We do not know how to test or predict whether a person's temperament will suit a new environment. We can find this out only by experience. If a move from one kind of work to another does not pan out, the executive who made the decision has to remove the misfit, and fast. But that executive also has to say, "I made a mistake, and it is my job to correct it." To keep misfits in a job they cannot do is not being kind; it is being cruel. But there is also no reason to let the person go. A company can always use a good bench engineer, a good analyst, a good sales manager. The proper course of action—and it works most times—is to offer the misfit a return to the old job or an equivalent.

People decisions may also fail because a job has become what New England ship captains 150 years ago called a "widow maker." When a clipper ship, no matter how well designed and constructed, began to have fatal "accidents," the owners did not redesign or rebuild the ship. They broke it up as fast as possible.

Widow makers—that is, jobs that regularly defeat even good people—appear most often when a company grows or changes fast. For instance, in the 1960s and early 1970s, the job of "international vice president" in U.S. banks became a widow maker. It had always been an easy job to fill. In fact, it had long been considered a job in which banks could safely put "also rans" and could expect them to perform well. Then, suddenly, the job began to defeat one new incumbent after another. What had happened, as hindsight now tells us, is that international activity quickly and without warning became an integral part of the daily business of major banks and their corporate customers. What had been until then an easy job became, literally, a "nonjob" that nobody could do.

Whenever a job defeats two people in a row, who in their earlier assignments had performed well, a company has a widow maker on its hands. When this happens, a responsible executive should not ask the headhunter for a universal genius. Instead abolish the job. Any job that ordinarily competent people cannot perform is a job that cannot be staffed. Unless changed, it will predictably defeat the third incumbent the way it defeated the first two.

Making the right people decisions is the ultimate means of controlling an organization well. Such decisions reveal how competent management is, what its values are, and whether it takes its job seriously. No matter how hard managers try to keep their decisions a secret—and some still try hard—people decisions cannot be hidden. They are eminently visible.

Executives often cannot judge whether a strategic move is a wise one. Nor are they necessarily interested. "I don't know why we are buying this business in Australia, but it won't interfere with what we are doing here in Fort Worth" is a common reaction. But when the same executives read that "Joe Smith has been made controller in the XYZ division," they usually know Joe much better than top management does. These executives should be able to say, "Joe deserves the promotion; he is an excellent choice—just the person that division needs to get the controls appropriate for its rapid growth."

If, however, Joe got promoted because he is a politician, everybody will know it. They will all say to themselves, "Okay, that is the way to get ahead in this company." They will despise their management for forcing them to become politicians but will either quit or become politicians themselves in the end. As we have known for a long time, people in organizations tend to behave as they see others being rewarded. And when the rewards go to nonperformance, to flattery, or to mere cleverness, the organization will soon decline into nonperformance, flattery, or cleverness.

Executives who do not make the effort to get their people decisions right do more than risk poor performance. They risk losing their organization's respect.

3

Who Is to Blame for Maladaptive Managers?

HARRY LEVINSON

By the time a man enters management, many businessmen believe it is too late to change his "character." To a great extent this belief is true; the experiences of childhood and adolescence are indeed crucial. Many of the troublesome attitudes and actions of managers which are typically blamed on "character," however, can be traced to management itself. In other words, although "character" is relatively enduring, many of management's "people problems" are partly products of its own making. Again and again, in my observation of industry, I find that the undesirable behavior of subordinates is precipitated or aggravated by the unintentional actions of their superiors. Such a statement is not news to subordinates — to them it is by now a cliché — but it is often disdained by their bosses as sheer rationalization.

In one sense, this observation is a discouraging commentary on the practice of management today. In another sense, it is a reason to be encouraged. For, to the extent that "people problems" *are* created by management, it has the immediate power to solve them by changing its approach. It does not have to defer the solution until long-range training programs and education have had a chance to work.

In this article I shall discuss six common management actions which lead to troublesome or problematic behavior among subordinates, and suggest supplemental or alternative actions which might be taken to avoid the difficulty. This analysis is based on an examination of 287 cases presented by participants in 15 executive seminars held at The Menninger Foundation.

Problem-creating Actions

The actions that I shall describe frequently seem to make sense at the time they are taken. But while they may be defensible in the short run, in the long run they turn into liabilities. From the standpoint of sound organizational growth, they must be judged as errors.

Error #1: encouragement of power seeking. No single kind of subordinate pleases his superiors more than the man who is able to assume responsibility for a crisis task, jump to his task with zest, and accomplish it successfully with dispatch. Such men become the "jets" of industry, the "comers," the "shining lights."

They are usually bright, energetic managers who have considerable ability and even more promise. Sometimes, as revealed in our cases, they rescue some part of the organization from failure or produce outstanding results in resolving difficult problems almost single-handedly.

Naturally, higher management rewards such men for their capacity to organize, drive, and get results. Management therefore encourages them in their wide-ranging pursuit of personal power. Then what happens? Management abruptly changes the signals. At a certain point, further advancement hinges not on what the men themselves can do alone but on their ability to lead, not drive, others.

Of our 287 cases, 12 revolve around just such men. Although this number is small, the group nevertheless is a highly important one because of the talents the men have. The men are described as problems because they reportedly overdominate their staffs; they are unable to coach and develop subordinates; they concentrate decision making in their own hands while driving their subordinates unnecessarily hard. In short, they are *authoritarian*. Their individual achievements have led to promotion, and the aura of their record has obscured for a considerable time the fact that they are now destroying or failing to build some part of the organization.

These are the very sort of men of whom it is frequently said that they could be outstandingly successful if only they could "work with people." Since they cannot, they will either have to leave their companies or be doomed to the continued frustration of their ambitions. Whether they cannot work well with others because of the kind of people they are, or because of organizational pressures to produce, is not always clear from the cases. It is clear, however, that *both* factors usually are involved.

Possible Alternatives

Top management has several alternatives with such men in those cases where it is not already too late. If management is primarily concerned with building an organization and with making it possible for men to grow into larger organizational responsibilities, then, contrary to popular conceptions, it must provide for close supervision of them. Such supervision must be pointed to helping support subordinates and to rewarding team, rather than individual, productivity. True, some of the "jets" may not be able to work in harness no matter what is done, and may therefore have to leave; but they will do so without having developed expectations that they can succeed in the organization by hard driving alone and before management builds up unrealistic expectations about their future development.

If a situation is such that it calls for heroic rescue or rebuilding efforts by a single person, both he and his superiors should recognize together the unique value of his talents in a particular situation and the likelihood that he may have to find a similar task elsewhere when this one is completed. My own observations suggest that a heroic organizing or rebuilding task takes from three to five years. After that, individual efforts, which by then have resulted in an organizational structure, must give way to group effort. Rarely is it possible for people who have ranged far and wide in an organization to accept increasing circumscription of their behavior. Usually, at the end of the initial building period a whole new group of managers must be introduced whose talents lie less in their own vigorous attack and more in coordinating and supporting the problem-solving abilities of groups. This phenomenon is an old story in many different contexts, ranging from offensive and defensive platoons in football, to guerrilla units in the military and reform movements in politics. It is not yet widely recognized in business.

Error #2: failure to exercise controls. Senior executives, according to some of our cases, often seem to condone behavior which is beyond the bounds of common courtesy. The result is devastating to those who are subject to such behavior and detrimental to the organization. The cost of tolerating this behavior is reflected particularly in that group of 15 cases which I call *the angry ones.* These are executives who reportedly spew their anger about them—at colleagues, subordinates, and superiors. These are the people who are described as being unnecessarily critical, as arguing too long and too much, as being crude and rude to others, and as seeming to flail at their working environment.

Again, it is sometimes difficult to determine how much of this behavior results from what is going on in the organization and how much from the personalities of the men themselves. But what is clear is the fact that they have got away with their outbursts, that the undesirable behavior seems to increase in intensity, that others are hurt by it, and that the angry ones themselves often feel guilty and contrite after their outbursts.

In another group of 20 cases, self-centeredness seems to be the most conspicuous aspect of the problem. The major form this self-centeredness takes is the exploitation of and attack on others as part of the subject's efforts to maintain or increase his own status. He differs from those who are authoritarian and directive in that he is more manipulative. The self-centered man is more clearly out for his own self-aggrandizement and often seems not to care what he does to others in the process; the authoritarian executive more frequently is sympathetic to others in a paternalistic way.

The striking aspect of both the angry and the self-centered executives is the manner in which they are able to intimidate others and get away with it. *Some of them have been permitted to go on in this way for years*, often for the reason that the man in question has some particular skill or talent which the organization needs. Even when the responsible executive knows that such behavior is destructive to the organization, to other subordinates, and to the man himself, he often permits it to go on. He excuses it with such words as "temperamental," or "the problem you have with creative people."

Such behavior may be a way of demonstrating power or a way of getting attention. For some people, any attention, whether criticism from superiors or loving kindness from oneself, is better than none. Anger or self-centeredness may also be an expression of increased insecurity and anxiety, particularly if job burdens are felt to be too heavy and failure threatens. Whatever the reason, as long as higher management condones the behavior or tolerates it, the problem is swept beneath the managerial rug.

What seems to happen in such cases is that the superior is taken aback by the aggressive outbursts or the chronic hostility of the subordinate. The superior may feel afraid of the subordinate's anger, being cowed by it just as lower-level employees are, and may then back away from confrontation or control for fear of precipitating even more anger. Or the hostility of the subordinate may arouse the superior's anger to the point where the superior feels guilty because of his angry thoughts toward the subordinate. If the superior feels inordinately guilty about his own angry feelings and doubts his ability to control them once they are unleashed, he may be paralyzed into inactivity as a way of coping with his own feelings.[1]

In either case, the subordinate is left free to vent his spleen on others. Those who are victims resent both him and the superiors who permit him to behave in this way. Working relationships with colleagues are impaired. The superior feels angry with himself for not stopping the aggressive behavior; and the angry subordinate, whose behavior is really a cry for help, continues to thrash about, to his own detriment and that of the organization. Thus when the responsible executive does not exercise adequate control, he contributes to the malfunctioning of those subordinates who are unable to maintain their own controls.

Asserting Control

The first step in the control process is to define the problem. As long as others put up with an angry one's behavior, he has no reason to stop it; there is no problem. He can easily feel that he must be right in his anger or manipulation if everyone else puts up with it, particularly if his own superiors tolerate it despite the complaints and turnover of lower level personnel.

Once the superior has defined which aspects of the subordinate's behavior are unacceptable and has confronted the subordinate with a statement of the problem as he sees it, then the two need to look at their own relationship. There may be features of the superior's behavior which provoke and sustain the anger of the subordinate. There may be role conflicts among superiors which tear the subordinate apart psychologically. Work stresses may take their toll. It may well be that the subordinate unconsciously is asking for more support from his superior. Whatever the case, the two of them need to examine the situation together for possible causal influences. The superior needs to be alert to possible fears and anxieties which the subordinate cannot express, such as the fear of failure or a sense of inadequacy in the supervision of others.

Regardless of whether there are mitigating circumstances, the superior must draw the line for what is permissible. He simply cannot permit destructive behavior to go on. If environmental circumstances which precipitate anger cannot be altered, if indeed there seem to be no problems of such proportion as to induce such anger, then it is a reasonably safe assumption that the problem is primarily within the individual and therefore he himself must do something about it. The chances are that he will have to seek professional help. If this is the case, bear in mind that the organization does not have to put up with the man's behavior until he solves his problem. If he still cannot control his outbursts after the line is drawn, then he should be removed from his job.

The executive must not assume that undesirable behavior can be stamped out by forbidding it. Discussion of problems means just that—self-critical examination by both parties of their working relationship. It does not mean that the superior tells the subordinate he must stop behaving as he does and that the conversation ends there. Follow-up is needed. For instance, the superior strengthens the structure of the organization by seeing to it that the subordinate makes use of those organizational avenues, policies, and procedures which presumably are the agreed-on ways by which problems are to be dealt with in the company.

When a superior finds himself condoning hostile behavior or procrastinating in doing something about it because the subordinate is "too valuable to lose," the chances are that he is taking an expensive, short-run view of the problem.

More often than not, when pinned down, the senior executive admits that the subordinate is more trouble than he is worth and that his failure to act arises from his own feelings of anger and guilt.

Error #3: stimulation of rivalry. The central problem in a group of 36 cases is rivalry. Sometimes the executive presenting the problem recognizes this, but more often he does not. He may, for example, concentrate his attention on the hostility between two subordinates without recognizing why they became hostile, although the rivalry aspects of the problem often seem clear from his own description. For example:

> A man is promoted to a position in which he becomes a rival of a senior person. He is instructed to "light a fire" under the senior person or is promised the senior man's job, as, for example, when the chairman of the board chooses an executive vice president to prod the president. But the subordinate "freezes" in his job, failing to show the previously successful behavior which brought him his promotion. His seniors cannot understand why.

Frequently the rivalry is between department heads or different functions—for instance, between sales and production; and here again the underlying psychological reasons for the rivalry may not be recognized. Thus:

> A production-minded president sees the need for a strong sales effort and employs a competent sales executive, only to resent his success. He then rejects or sabotages the sales executive without being aware of what he is doing or knowing why.

The destructive effects of rivalry thus stimulated are rarely recognized by the presenting executives, in my experience. Executives are not aware of the deep-seated psychological roots of rivalry and the guilt feelings which immediate personal competition can arouse in many people. Often they have consciously encouraged rivalry on the assumption that all competition is good. They cannot understand why a hard competitor will suddenly stop competing, let alone see the psychological trap in which the subordinate has been placed.

Although executives usually recognize why two colleagues can no longer be friends after one is promoted, or that older subordinates will rebel against a younger boss, generally they do little to prevent or ameliorate such frictions. Some young executives promoted rapidly over the heads of older men have guilt feelings about taking the opportunities of the older men. Such feelings are not recognized by superiors either. *In none of the cases with rivalry problems described in our seminars was the issue of rivalry discussed, either by the rivals themselves or by their superiors, as preparation for dealing with their new jobs.*

Rivalry, by definition, is the essence of competitive enterprise. But in such an enterprise, where the desirable end product is the result produced by the organization, all effort should be focused on the collective attainment of that result. When a superior plays subordinates off against each other, overstimulates rivalry in other ways, or acts competitively with his subordinates, he forces them to divert energies from competition with other organizations into interpersonal rivalry. Less attention is focused on problems which the organization has to solve.

In addition, the subordinates become defensive, or destroy cooperative possibilities by attacking each other, or maneuver for the favor of the boss. The more intensely intraorganizational rivalry is stimulated, the more acute the problem of company politics becomes.[2]

Constructive Discussion

Open discussion of and joint solution of mutual problems make it possible for managers to use much more profitably the energy which might otherwise be dissipated in destructive rivalry. In dealing with this problem the superior needs to take a critical look at his own motivation with possibilities like these in mind:

He may consciously or unconsciously encourage rivalry because he likes to see a good fight, rationalizing his pleasure by believing that the better ideas or the better men will survive.

Men in executive positions have strong feelings of rivalry that are sufficiently aroused by real problems, if the executives are given enough freedom to attack them; the range of ideas in a problem situation is generally wide enough to produce ample differences and critical examination. Playing men off against each other is merely psychological goading. Those who are not moved by the problems themselves will not be moved by goading either. Instead, they will be even more rigidly paralyzed. One can only wonder about the motivation of an executive who has to goad his subordinates into fighting each other, just as one would wonder about a parent who does the same with his children.

He may be angry at one of the rivals and use the other as a weapon to displace his own hostility.

This is a subtle phenomenon which happens frequently. The senior executive can ask himself to what extent he avoids one subordinate, speaks harshly of him behind his back, and disdains his communications. If he finds himself doing these things without clearly being aware of it, his behavior is one clue to what may be influencing the conflict between the two subordinates. He would do better to talk directly to the man with whom he is angry than to get at him by using another man as a weapon.

He may fear the rivalry of subordinates for his own position, and either keep them off balance or permit them to destroy themselves by encouraging their rivalry of each other.

Few men can grow older without envying and fearing the younger men who will take their places, no matter how much they like and respect the younger men. Such fears, though natural, are hard for a man to accept in himself. According to the folklore of our culture, he is not supposed to have them. Why should he not retire in due time without regret or recrimination? He has it made; what more does he want? But our feelings are simply not that logical. Moving up through executive ranks is much like playing the children's game, "King of the Mountain." A man often feels as if he is always pushing the man ahead of him off the top—even if it is only a small hill. Inevitably, it is difficult for him to relinquish his position without feeling he is being pushed, too. If he feels that way and is unaware of it, he will perforce defend his position in many subtle ways. If he can accept such feelings as legitimate, he is then in a better position to control their expression.

The two rivals may well represent his own inner conflicts about his identification with different parts of the business.
Often executives rise through the ranks on the basis of their identification with a particular capacity, skill, or experience. Then, on reaching a high level, they find that new business requirements make their old skill relatively obsolete or compel them to evolve multiple skills. For example, many a production man has risen to chief executive only to discover that we are now in a marketing economy and that he must either shift his own focus from production to marketing or at least become more knowledgeable about marketing.

To change one's focus or to broaden one's perception can also mean that a man has to change his image of himself. A production man who looks on marketing as manipulation, for example, may have considerable conflict within his own conscience about becoming a manipulator. Even though he may well recognize the need for marketing, he may still not want to be a salesman. The conflict within himself between the wish to continue being what he always was and the wish to have the organization compete successfully by competitive marketing may then reflect itself in his inability to make decisions.

It will also reflect itself in conflict between the men who have to carry on the two responsibilities about which he is in conflict. In hardly discernible ways he will support one, then the other, or make an ally of one and then the other. The two subordinates soon find themselves on opposite sides of a fence whose origin is then attributed to "poor communications" or the supposition that "salesmen are always like that." Perhaps only after the third successive sales vice president has been fired might it dawn on the president that something more than a "personality clash" is afoot. The clash within himself clangs loudly in the behavior of those who report to him.

In the promotion or transfer of any executive, careful attention should be given to the rivalry aspects of the situation. These should be *talked about frankly* as problems to be dealt with in the new job. And for those who must accept a new superior or colleague, it can be helpful to reassure them honestly of their own value, to recognize openly with them the inevitable presence of rivalry feelings, and to indicate that, though such feelings exist, the task is still to be done and the new boss has the superior's full support in managing that group toward the required goals of the organization.

Error #4: failure to anticipate the inevitable. Many experiences in life are painful to people. Some, like aging and its accompanying physical infirmities and incapacities, are the lot of everyone. Others are specific to a man's work life, e.g., failure to obtain an expected promotion or the prospect of retirement. We can speak of such painful experiences as *psychological injuries.*
Such injuries are inevitable. Yet there is little in our 287 cases to indicate that companies recognize their inevitability and have established methods for anticipating or relieving them. The result is that those who are hurt in this manner have considerable hostility which is repressed or suppressed. Sometimes the thought of retirement is what hurts. Those men to whom prospective retirement

is a psychological injury often refuse to train subordinates and become obstructionists, displacing their repressed or suppressed hostility on both subordinates and organization. Physical changes such as hearing loss and heart attack also leave residues of resentment as men attempt to deny their incapacity. Other sources of psychological injury are:

Not being promoted to a job one has expected.

Having one's judgment rejected.

Having some of one's responsibilities given to someone else.

Lonesomeness—wishing to be gregarious but being unable to act that way, and therefore feeling rejected by others, with a resulting hypersensitivity to further psychological wounds.

Helpful Steps

Judging from our executive seminars during the past nine years, superiors are more aware of psychological injury than any other form of impairment, and they try to do more about it. Yet they typically have great difficulty dealing with such problems, especially because the older men who are more subject to them are managers of long service. In the many cases where superiors have done a good job of providing support for the "problem people" and have saved their jobs, they have done it by hard work and heroic rescue attempts.

However, such extraordinary measures—and the pain and frustration which usually attend them—can often be made unnecessary by advance preparation in anticipation of possible injury. People not only have a right to know what is likely to happen to them as far ahead as such events can be anticipated, but also *they* can then prepare themselves for the eventuality or choose alternative courses of action. If they are not informed and then experience a sudden blow from higher management, they have every reason to feel manipulated and exploited.

The organization contributes to executive malfunction when it does not—

. . . *systematically prepare people throughout their work careers for the realities which inevitably will come their way;*

. . . *provide shock absorbers, in the form of counseling services, to help people cope with psychological injury.*

Every important change should be discussed with each man involved before it occurs. A major part of such discussion should be the opportunity for him to express his feelings, without embarrassment or fear, about the change. When a man can say to his superior how he feels about the latter's decision or an organizational decision, the acceptance of his feelings conveys to him that he is accepted and respected as an individual. This in turn supports his feelings of self-esteem and makes it possible for him to deal with the change and his feelings more reasonably. No amount of sugarcoated praise will substitute for being heard.

When a person has help in absorbing the shock of injury and support in recovering from it, he is in a much better position to mobilize his resources to cope with what has happened to him. More often than not, a senior executive who would quickly offer a supporting hand to a man with a sprained ankle, and indeed get him medical attention, has difficulty seeing psychological injuries in the same light.

Error #5: pressuring men of limited ability. The characteristic and futile way of trying to deal with men of limited ability is by frontal assualt. Repeatedly the senior executives attempt to persuade a rigid person to stop being rigid, exhort a dependent person to become independent, or cajole an impulsive person to gain better self-control. Although the executives may know in their minds that the subordinate is inflexible or unable to accept responsibility or assume initiative, they tend to *act* as if they could compel or stimulate him to change. Thus:

> It is difficult for most successful executives to understand that grown men can be frightened and dependent. Sometimes, in a misguided effort to stimulate the subordinate, they open up the possibilities of greater responsibility and more active participation in decision making.
>
> Such gestures are even more threatening to men who are already immobilized than exhortation is. Sometimes seniors actually promote the problem man in the vain hope that he will change when he has more responsibility or when he is sent off to a management development course. It is not understood that such pressure on a person who is already devoting so much effort to controlling or protecting himself (which is what the aberrant behavior means) will only increase the intensity of the undesirable behavior. If a man is characteristically rigid, dependent, or impulsive, he is likely to become more so under increasing stress, which is what the pressure exerted by the boss becomes.
>
> Impulsive men present another problem for their superiors. Because so often they are intellectually competent, even gifted, their superiors are reluctant to face the problems of their behavior squarely and thus can only continue to chafe at their episodic failure. Our seminar cases included eight instances of men who do their jobs well "when they want to." However, they are frequently absent, often embroiled in multiple family difficulties, and sometimes irresponsible with respect to getting their work done or doing it thoroughly. Here also are the men who, though not alcoholic, will drink too much in the presence of their superiors, and others whose worst behavior will occur when they are with highest-level superiors. The self-defeating aspects of such behavior are obvious.
>
> Poor impulse control and low frustration tolerance usually reflect considerable anxiety and insecurity. More often than not, such behavior reflects the need for professional counsel. Repeated admonitions usually serve little purpose.
>
> Inflexibility is the most prominent reported behavior of 14 men in our cases. For nearly half of these men, the problem is characterized as an inability to plan for or accept change. Several others seem to resist change not because they are personally inflexible, but because the organization has prepared them poorly and they are angry. In one case, the *organization* was so rigid that the best man available for a given post was not going to be promoted because he did not believe in God! Rigid people find their self-protection in well-ordered lives. Often they have high standards for themselves. Those who become more rigid under stress are in effect building a protective shell for themselves.

Management Action

How should management try to deal with problems of the sort just described?

First, it should so delimit the person's duties that he can confine himself to standardized, detailed work, with clear policy guidance. It should be made clear to him what his responsibilities do *not* include.

Secondly, higher management should consider what demands have made the person more anxious and defensive. As earlier pointed out, change always requires support from superiors if it is to take place with a minimum amount of stress. Much of the time senior management takes it for granted that people can and will change; few can do so without stress. The most effective kind of support lies in joint problem solving—in making changes together step-by-step so that the person can feel he is still master of himself and his fate instead of being arbitrarily buffeted about by anonymous forces over which he has no control.

Thirdly, management should take a hard look at the "climate" of the executive organization. In our seminar cases a frequent corollary of inability to perform as expected is the report by the presenting executives that the problem men were previously suppressed in an excessively authoritarian structure for years. Some are able to function reasonably well as long as they have the close support of their superiors. Some cannot make decisions themselves.

Undoing dependent behavior is no easy task, particularly when the organization continues to demand conforming behavior. Where conformity is the first rule of survival, no amount of exhortation will produce initiative. Where mistakes are vigorously hunted out and held against a person thereafter, few men will take a chance on making a mistake. Therefore, close, minute supervision of a man as he assumes greater responsibility is not an unmixed blessing. There are rewards for such supervision—and costs. This situation often creates great conflict among senior executives—the wish that subordinates demonstrate initiative versus the wish to be in complete control.

Error #6: misplacement. Despite the plethora of psychological consultants, assessment and rating scales, and a wide-ranging literature on promotion, there is little indication in our cases that careful assessments are regularly made to indicate a man's limitations or predict his inability to carry greater responsibility. In cases where men have been outgrown by their jobs, there seems to have been almost no anticipation that such an eventuality would come about. As a result, there has been no continuing discussion of the problem, which might help the man become aware of what he will have to do to keep up with his job. Nor is there support for him in facing his feelings about becoming less competent to do the job or having to give it up. Instead, whatever the reason a man has not grown, often he is left to flounder in his job because superiors recognize it is not his fault that he is failing, but theirs for having placed him in that position. Thus the failure is compounded.

In 47 cases of misplacement, by my interpretation, half of the men placed in the wrong job are unable to function adequately in the face of larger responsibilities. Often these are men who did well in jobs of lesser responsibility and who seemed to have promise of being able to carry on a more responsible job. Some men, however, have been placed in managerial positions despite the fact that their limitations are known, particularly their inability to supervise others. Some have moved up through the ranks because of their technical knowledge at a time when it was thought that technical knowledge was the most important qualification which a leader could have. The remaining men in this group could not consistently meet the demands of their present jobs. Often they could do some aspects of their jobs well, but not others.

About one third of the cases involve men who reportedly cannot keep up with the continuing growth of the organization and the particular jobs they hold. In most of these instances the executive simply does not have the knowledge or the skill for the expanding job. His growing job has gone beyond his training and experiences and beyond his capacity for organizing and making judgments. This problem is even more painful when the incumbent has had long service in the position or when he has made highly significant contributions to organizing and developing an activity, sometimes even the company itself. In these situations the superior bears considerable pain because he feels compelled to take action against a man who has contributed so much to the organization. His anger toward the man who "forces" him into such a situation arouses his guilt feelings, and his conscience punishes him severely.

How much of the failure to keep up with the growth of the company was passive aggression — failure to do what a man was capable of doing as a way of defeating the company — I have no way of knowing. Often rigidity and plateaus in performance are products of passive aggression. One way of being aggressive covertly is by not changing, not doing what is expected of one, letting the boss down in one way or another. Passive aggression is an extremely widespread phenomenon.

Recommended Approach

The single most helpful practice for dealing with misplacement is to have a *continuing and consistent relationship* with a psychological consultant. Psychological testing and evaluation are no better than the person who does them. His judgments and predictions can be no better than his knowledge of the man, the position, and the company. If he is to serve all three, then he must develop a feel for the company, knowledge of specific jobs and the men who supervise them, and, finally, some understanding of the candidate. Standardized batteries given by psychologists who see neither the company nor the probable position of the candidate among others in the company have limited value. Mail-order testing has even less value (apart from the ethical question involved). Occasional referral to a local psychologist is hardly enough to keep the latter in touch with the climate of the organization.

Growth is the essence of living. All of us like to feel that we are becoming wiser as we grow older. Most men seek opportunities for continued growth. Some, however, cannot or do not. This problem is likely to occur with increasing frequency as executive roles become more complex. To avoid failures, companies will have to evolve methods for anticipating and coping with misplacements before they become a painful and destructive fact. In a continuing professional relationship the psychologist can be in contact with executives from day to day, know when they are under particular stress, and provide support and counsel as necessary. In growing companies one of his continuing tasks should be to keep an eye out for those who are not keeping pace.

Conclusion

The contemporary management scene is characterized by frequent complaints about the inadequacies of subordinates and potential executive successors. The validity of such complaints would seem to be verified by the widespread use of management consultants for every conceivable purpose and by the repetitive reorganizations of businesses. These phenomena reflect the chronic pain of management, enormous dissipation of human energy, and the palliative nature of the attempted cures. Dr. Karl Menninger coined the term "polysurgical addiction" to describe people who repeatedly demanded operations to cure their multiple, repetitive complaints.[3] It would not stretch the analogy too far to speak of "polyconsultative addiction" to describe this all too frequent mode of solving managerial problems.

This phrase is not meant to reflect on consultants any more than Menninger's phrase was a criticism of surgeons. Both practitioners serve highly important purposes. Rather, it refers to a characteristic managerial way of looking at problems as caused by someone or something foreign to oneself, and as being resolvable by excision or reconstruction, also by someone else. The tragedy of such a tendency is that the executive, like the patient who wants someone else to cut out the presumably offensive part, often has within himself the power to cope with managerial problems. This is especially true with respect to those problems which are of his own (if inadvertent) making.

In this article I have outlined, from cases reported by executives, six common managerial errors in the supervision of subordinates, and I have suggested ways which may help avoid or correct each error. Most management problems seem to call for increased investment, more experts, and long periods of planning and execution before results can be expected. The problems described in this article do not. Though few managerial difficulties are more troublesome than those which have to do with people, the solutions to them are often relatively simple, given a modicum of attention and sensitivity. The manager needs only to examine more carefully his own actions. Of course, some problems, like those which arouse feelings of guilt, will remain difficult no matter how simple the solutions seem. Even these, however, will be somewhat easier to cope with if the underlying issue is more visible. Perhaps, then, the greatest self-healing managerial talent, as the psalmist would put it, is to "make wise the simple."

REFERENCES

1. See my book, *Emotional Health: In the World of Work* (New York: Harper & Row, 1964), Chapter 18, for further elaboration of this point.

2. See Edgar H. Schein, *Organizational Psychology* (Englewood Cliffs: New Jersey, Prentice-Hall, 1965), pp. 80–87.

3. Karl Menninger, *Man Against Himself* (New York: Harcourt, Brace, 1938).

4

The Coming Promotion Slowdown

ARCH PATTON

A combination of inflation and the aging of the "baby boom" generation promises to create personnel problems in the 1980s such as U.S. industry has never faced before. Furthermore, American business has been slow to recognize the profound changes that these forces are likely to produce in the motivation and productivity of middle-level managers — that vital element in the welfare of our private enterprise system.

The seriousness of these problems and their effect on business will depend to a great degree on the rate of inflation. If it drops to the 2% to 3% level of the Eisenhower years, some problems will evaporate and others will be less difficult to live with. But that is unlikely. In the 1970s inflation averaged 7½% annually. Continuation of that rate during the 1980s will, among other things, almost certainly:

Reverse the trend toward early retirement as more and more managers realize that, because their pensions underfinance future cost-of-living increases, they cannot afford to quit.

Slow the promotion rate among executives as the result.

Sharply increase pension costs as corporations seek to close the rapidly widening pension gap.

But even at a low inflation rate, demographic changes occurring in the 1980s would create knotty problems of their own. Between 1980 and 1990, for example, the 35- to 45-year-old age group will jump from 25.3 million to 36.9 million, an unprecedented 46% rise. In the same period the 55 to 65 age group will actually decline moderately in size. This means that competition for middle-management jobs — the target of most 35- to 45-year-old industry employees — will intensify. The resulting downward pressure on compensation can hardly avoid conflicting with this generation's high expectations. On the other hand, a shortage of experienced managers in the over-55 group will produce upward pressure on compensation at the top.

The most serious personnel issue facing U.S. business in the 1980s is the virtual certainty that the promotion rate will fall dramatically. Executives are likely to stay on the job longer because they cannot afford to retire; at the same time, the number of candidates for their jobs will expand at the highest rate ever.

Promotion, of course, is the most potent motivating force in our industrialized society, for it means prestige as well as money. Any weakening of this incentive for improving productivity can only have a negative influence that must be offset in some way.

The arithmetic of inflation plus demography has been given far less attention than it deserves. In the 1980s attention will be absolutely necessary.

Scary Arithmetic

The low birth rate during the depression years resulted in a scarcity of experienced executives in the 1970s, continuing a trend that started in the prior decade. U.S. business reacted by sharply stepping up the pirating of executive talent from other companies (a gambit that also characterized the 1960s). The paying of front-end bonuses in the millions, even before the newly hired executive came to work, was another characteristic of the 1970s caused by demography.

While industry responded quickly to the highly visible challenges posed by inflation and demographics, during the last decade it largely overlooked one area of major significance to its employees: pensions. Last year McKinsey & Company asked 21 of the 100 largest industrial companies to estimate the pension—including social security—as of October 1979 of an employee who retired in October 1969 at age 65 after 30 years' service, whose salary for the three years before retirement was $25,000.

In 1969 the figure was an average $12,600, or about 50% of salary. Ten years later, the average pension had risen to $18,900. In other words, the average pension—including social security—of these industry executives increased only 50%, while living costs rose 100%.

More important from the standpoint of industry's reaction to its employees' needs, the government contributed $3,700 (through social security) to the 10-year increase of $6,300, while employers contributed only $2,600 by additions to their pension plan payouts.

These are average figures, of course, and differences among the 21 surveyed companies were substantial. Two companies boosted pension payments four times during the decade, the biggest total increase being 45%, while five companies reported no general increase at all. Several made individual adjustments "based on need." (By comparison, pensions of federal employees in the same circumstances were $14,100 in 1969 and $31,500 in 1979—the latter figure being $6,500 more than they had earned at work.)

Obviously, industry has some catching up to do in the 1980s where pensions are concerned. However, these outlays already cost large corporations an average of nearly 30% of profits. Furthermore, according to actuaries, pension costs rise 10% for each percentage point added to the inflation rate. With inflation averaging 7½% a year, even a modest effort to close the "inflation gap" in pensions would substantially affect profits—despite the deductibility of such outlays.

Meanwhile, what of the retirees? Given, among other problems, the chronic federal deficits, our dependence on foreign oil, and a population that continues to look first to the government for financial support, an annual inflation rate of 8% in the 1980s is a distinct possibility.

Project this rate on a pensioner's income. If he or she retires at $50,000 in 1980, purchasing power will have fallen to $23,600 by 1990. Putting the problem another way, to maintain purchasing power under such circumstances the pensioner must have an income of $99,920 by 1990 (a conservative figure because it does not include tax "creep").

A large proportion of pensioners, of course, live at least 20 years after retirement. Projection of the 8% inflation rate an additional decade cuts purchasing power another 50% to $10,400; and the income salary required just to stay even doubles again, to $201,600.

It is unrealistic to regard these figures as a probability. Even a partial fulfillment of this scenario, however, presents an awesome problem for the millions of present and potential retirees in the private sector.

Delaying Retirement

The simplest and theoretically cheapest means of closing the pension gap in industry is to permit employees to postpone retirement. Any other approach has costs so prohibitive—or creates such unacceptable problems for employees—that this method is certain to be adopted widely.

Simply putting off retirement has potent advantages. For the employee it means a longer period of salary increases that keep step with inflation, as well as reduced reliance on the relatively static pension. From the employer's viewpoint, the longer work period lowers pension costs or permits larger pensions at the same cost. Delaying retirement also means retention of managerial skills that only experience provides. Finally, a longer productive life is physically and mentally healthy for the individual and good for the nation.

But delayed retirement poses problems too. When does an aging management begin undermining corporate efficiency? What yardstick would trigger a person's retirement? How would general postponement affect a company's promotion rate?

Administrative organisms prefer policies calling for a uniform retirement age. But individual productivity varies substantially with increasing age. The abilities of some executives start declining in their fifties; these people coast through the final decade of their careers. And then there are those whose physical and mental vigor lasts well into their seventies.

Delayed retirement will almost necessarily substitute judgment for age as the administrative trigger. This shift will put the burden for judgment on fair evaluation of individual performance. Because of their fear of inflation, most eligible employees are likely to regard delayed retirement favorably. So they leave the decision about their departure date until the future.

The impact of postponement on the promotion rate, however, is likely to be devastating. Obviously, the problem will be worst among the upper echelons. It takes time to reach the top; hence, jobholders at this level tend to be fairly close to the historic 65 retirement age. The average chief executive is about five years from retirement, and a high proportion of the upper managerial levels are likely to be only a few years younger than the CEO.

But top executives of large publicly owned companies, with their generous compensation and fringe benefits, are not likely to suffer after retirement at 65. The top managers of smaller companies are often in a less enviable position because pension plans in this large group are often less than adequate.

In all companies, of course, lower executive ranks have fewer incumbents close to retirement. But since their pay levels and accumulated pension reserves are considerably lower than those of senior executives, they need deferral of retirement more.

In the typical organization, retirement delays at the top will block advancement opportunities deep down. I recall that at a major retailer, the departure at age 65 of a vice president resulted in 20 down-the-line promotions. Seldom do retirements at the top produce fewer than six or seven upward moves.

The big question is: How much delay in retirement will be necessary to produce enough funding of the huge pension gap that exists? I suspect that a stretch-out of about five years will prove close to the minimum requirement.

But five additional years are a long time to wait for advancement. Surveys I made some years ago indicated that two-thirds of corporate executives were promoted once or not at all in a seven-year period, while only a third received two or more promotions. On this basis, even a five-year delay in retirement would double the waiting time of a sizable proportion of managerial employees.

Diminished Expectations

What can management do to blunt the motivational loss resulting from a slump in the promotion rate? This will come at a time when companies especially need increased productivity.

Many companies have already acted to "buy" the early retirement of executives who are no longer adequate because the skills required by the job have changed or their ability to handle it has atrophied. This action usually involves a sizable increase in total pension cost, but management considers it cheaper in the long run because it upgrades the talent available to fill the position. The action also clears the road for upward movement.

The long-term cost implications of this approach will depend, in part at least, on the responsibility of companies for inflation's impact on pensioned employees — whether it is moral, as now, or legal. If the federal government decides to call the shots, the outcome could be expensive.

Slow-growing companies, particularly those with large staffs, may be tempted to meet the advancement slowdown by adopting a form of "word change promotion." This is common in the federal civil service, where full-grade promotions may involve nothing more than changing the job description phrase "some responsibility" to "considerable responsibility." No additional employees or other responsibilities need be included in the arrangement, although the organization often makes a slight title change.

The word change promotion may have modest prestige implications in a limited number of corporate cultures. It will have little value, however, in the more competitive environment facing most businesses.

In this decade, the talent shortage in the 55 to 65 age group (due to the depression-created population dip) will necessitate more rapid acceleration of young executives up the corporate ladder. To make such a program successful, many high-level executives will have to improve their ability to judge both current performance and future potential.

Even so, companies are finding that the life-styles and interests of a growing proportion of their outstanding people remove them from the list of promotables. Spouses of these young executives may like *their* jobs, families may balk at moving to a different location, or executives may simply resist risk.

This being the case, business will need to accelerate the development of high-potential managers willing to accept the risk of advancement. Because of the limited availability of outstanding talent, it will probably also be necessary to try changing the life-style aspirations of those with outstanding potential who reject promotion for one reason or another. This effort will require top-level executives to know their young managers much better than most do today. The growing competition for middle-management jobs during the 1980s, however, should strengthen discipline in the corporate culture, making young executives become more realistic about possible life-styles.

To be sure, the need for talent may also force changes in management style along the cooperative lines that have proven so successful in Japan. The older men at the top, however, are likely to change their ideas more slowly than their younger subordinates, who will be under strong competitive pressures.

Whatever else is said, promotion in the lower managerial ranks is still dominated by turnover at the middle levels. Unfortunately, the baby-boom group enjoyed unusually rapid promotion rates during the 1970s and therefore entered this decade with very high expectations. Cooling the expectation level will require time and innovative moves by top management.

Money alone is incapable of spawning the motivational power that a step up the ladder creates. In my experience, money is rarely a match for promotion. So the motivational loss resulting from a slumping promotion rate must be offset by some other emotion-charged symbols of accomplishment.

The armchair strategist who forecasts what these are likely to be as the decade unfolds runs considerable risks. Management will be probing unexplored territory. One thing can be said, however, with reasonable confidence: the excitement generated by the pursuit of a believed-in goal has worked motivational wonders under inspired leadership.

My guess is that these new symbols of accomplishment evolving during the 1980s will stem from the excitement that outstanding leaders bring to their corporate game plans. The shape the symbols take will depend on the individual leader and the conditions facing him or her at the time.

5

Dealing with the Aging Work Force

JEFFREY SONNENFELD

The extension of mandatory retirement to age 70, signed into U.S. law last April, has caught most organizations off-guard and has surfaced latent fears about the general age drift in the work force. Management experts and journalists over the last year or so have become quite vocal in their prophecies about the changing complexion of the work force.

We used to hear predictions about the "greening of America." Now we hear references to impending problems resulting from the "graying of America," as the country belatedly awakens to the composite effects of demographic trends, improvements in life expectancy, and changes in social legislation. Executives are being warned to anticipate changes in employee performance and attitudes, performance appraisals, retirement incentives, training programs, blocked career paths, union insurance pensions, and affirmative action goals, among other worrisome issues.

Business managers have been the target of superficial and conflicting admonitions appearing in the press. As the chief executive of a leading paper company recently complained to me, "At first we were interested in the warnings. Now, they all say the same things. We hear all the fire alarms being sounded, but no one suggests where we should send the engines."

The needs of a very different work force overshadow many of the other issues of the 1980s for which managers must prepare their organizations. Just as other organizational activities must adapt to a changing environment, human resource planning dictates a major overhaul in recruitment, development, job structure, incentives, and performance appraisal. Thus management attention should now be focused on specific problems in mid- and late-career planning.

It is hard enough to comprehend the individual aging process without at the same time assessing the effects of an entire population growing older. If Congress and President Carter had not extended the work years, leaders of America's organizations would still have had to face troublesome human resource changes.

As a consequence of the 43 million babies born in the years immediately following World War II, a middle-aged bulge is forming and eventually the 35- to 45-year-old age group will increase by 80%. By the year 2030, this group will be crossing the infamous bridge to 65, increasing the relative size of that population from 12% of all Americans to 17%, a jump from 31 million to 52 million people.[1]

Some labor analysts point out that even those Department of Labor statistics are conservative, for likely changes downward in the mortality rate due to advanced medical treatment are not reflected in the predictions. Today, the average life expectancy is about age 73, which is 10 years longer than the years of life expected at birth in the 1950s.

On examining the rate of this change, one sees that the size of the preretirement population, between the ages of 62 and 64, will not be affected dramatically until the year 2000. Until that time, this group will expand at an annual rate of 7.6% above 1975 figures. Between 2000 and 2010, however, it will grow by 48%. For one to assume, however, that there are at least 22 years before major problems arise would be incorrect. This population bulge will be moving through several critical career phases before reaching the preretirement years.

One should pause and reflect on how, in just the next ten years, the population bulge will be lodged in the "mid-life crisis" age. This added strain will magnify the traditional work and nonwork problems associated with the sense of limited opportunity at that age. Even sooner, the decline in youth population, which is currently causing the consolidation of secondary schools, will shift the balance of power and the approach in company recruitment.

As a consequence, a dwindling young work force will make it more difficult to fill entry-level positions. Already there are predictions about shortages in blue-collar occupations by the mid-1980s.[2] It is not at all too soon for managers to start investigating their company demographics.

On top of the foregoing, the recent legislation on extending mandatory retirement further heightens the concern about job performance in the later years. Sooner than even the advocates of this legislation dreamed, business managers find themselves faced with contemplating the implications of long-tenured senior employees.

The immediate impact of this legislation depends, of course, on how older workers respond to the opportunity to remain on the job. Many companies are looking at the well-publicized trend toward earlier retirement, and concluding that this trend will counteract the effects of extended tenure possibilities. Labor force participation rates are dropping for workers age 55 and older and for those age 60 and over.

A retirement expert on the National Industrial Conference Board, a business research organization, said, "People want to retire while they are still young and healthy enough to enjoy the activities of their choice."[3] Another Conference Board researcher reported that these younger retirees are interested in education, in traveling, and in spending more and more money on themselves.[4]

Also, Victor M. Zin, director of Employee Benefits at General Motors, commented, "There used to be a stigma to going out. He was over the hill, but now it's a looked-for status. Those retirement parties, they used to be sad affairs. They are darn happy affairs now. The peer pressure is for early retirement."[5]

Research suggests, however, that such a trend reflects worker income, education, job conditions, and retirement security. Dissatisfied workers and those with better pension plans seem to be more likely to opt out earlier. The experience of Sears, Roebuck and Polaroid, and several insurance companies which have already introduced flexible retirement, shows that at least 50% of those workers reaching age 65 remain on the job. In contrast, only 7% of auto workers take advantage of the opportunity to continue past age 65.

Gerontologists also do not support an early retirement trend. They cite the greater political activity of older Americans, the increasing average age of nursing home occupants, and a 1974 Harris Poll survey of retirees over 65 who claimed they would still work if they had not been forced out.[6] Such a reversed trend might be strengthened as age 65 becomes early retirement and workers see extended career opportunities.

Mid-Career Considerations

With the projection of middle-aged workers shortly comprising a large part of the work force, and with greater numbers of older people a certainty later on, executives have good reason to be interested in relationships between age and performance.

Important age and performance considerations are manifest in younger workers well before they ever become established members of the "gray work force." In looking across the occupations of those in their mid-30s to mid-40s, one sees career drops in performance and morale, along with higher rates of turnover. There has also traditionally been higher mobility in these mid-life years as well.

Longitudinal career studies tracking people over ten-year intervals for the past three decades show that, despite growing barriers to employment in certain occupations, there has been an outstanding peak in job mobility for those in their mid-30s to mid-40s. This mobility may vary somewhat across occupations because of exceptionally high turnover rates in some jobs such as sales and service.

Candidates for second careers tend to be in their 40s and report a perceived discrepancy between personal aspirations and current opportunities for achievement and promotion. This gap widens as the opportunity for advancement decreases and results in major career frustration.

Occupational Stagnation

A survey of over one thousand middle-aged men in managerial and professional positions found that five out of every six respondents endured a period of severe frustration and trauma which began in their early 30s. Work performance, emotional stability, and physical health were seriously affected. The study also found that one out of every six middle-aged workers never fully recovered from traumatic realizations that their sense of eternal youth had been replaced by physical deterioration and greater sensitivity to the inevitability of death. The loss of spirit led to lowered goals and diminished self-expectations.

Psychologist Erik Erikson first brought academic attention to this mid-career crisis, characterizing it as the locus of a conflict between feelings of "generativity versus stagnation."[7] The middle-aged worker senses that new starts in life are coming to an end.

Gerontologist Bernice Neugarten, reporting on her research that indicated a new perspective on "time" appears in the mid-to-late 30s, commented:

"Life is restructured in terms of time-left-to-live rather than time-since-birth. Not only the reversal in directionality, but the awareness that time is finite is a particularly conspicuous feature of middle age. Thus 'you hear so much about deaths that seem premature — that's one of the changes that come over you over the years. Young fellows never give it a thought. . . .' The recognition that there is 'only so much time left' was a frequent theme . . . those things don't quite penetrate when you're in your 20s and you think that life is all ahead of you."[8]

Harvard psychiatrist George E. Vaillant likens this period to the stresses of adolescence and rebellion against authority and structure. His original clinical research tracks people through 40 years of life, and provides a valuable in-depth analysis of adult development. Vaillant feels that, by 40, people "put aside the preconceptions and the narrow establishment aims of their 30s and begin once again to feel gangly and uncertain about themselves. But always, such transitional periods in life provide a means of seizing one more change and finding a new solution to instinctive or interpersonal needs."[9]

From his clinical studies of people progressing through their middle years, Yale psychologist Daniel Levinson argues, "This is not an extended adolescence, but a highly formative, evolving phase of adult life." He found that, while a smooth transition is indeed possible, more often dramatic chaos is likely to characterize mid-life transition. One's former life structure (e.g., occupation, marital life) suddenly seems inappropriate and new choices must be made.

According to Levinson, "If these choices are congruent with his dreams, values, talents, and possibilities, they provide the basis for a relatively satisfactory life structure. If the choices are poorly made and the new structure seriously flawed, however, he will pay a heavy price in the next period."[10]

Regardless of the causes of this stressful period, several events in society indicate that the symptoms will soon spread in epidemic proportions:

First, those persons reaching the mid-career period in the next ten years will have achieved far higher educational levels and associated higher aspirations than ever experienced by this group previously. By 1980, one out of four workers will have a college degree.

Second, the pattern of occupational growth suggests increasingly insufficient opportunities for advancement in a narrower occupational hierarchy. Unfavorable predictions of future needs through 1985 by the Bureau of Labor Statistics confirm the cause for distress. Professional positions will remain scarce, and the expanded demands of the 1960s for engineers, scientists, and teachers, which influenced so many young people to undertake higher education, will remain history. Clerical, sales, service, and operative workers are expected to be in demand.

Third, the size of the postwar baby boom means intense competition for whatever opportunities do exist. This competitiveness is due to the bulk of the population being at the same career point rather than being more evenly distributed.

Finally, the new legislation on mandatory retirement threatens to further limit opportunities for advancement.

Organizations should prepare now for the inevitable frustrations of career stagnation in the middle years. Already there are individual and organized complaints from those who say that somehow society has cheated them. After investing valuable years in expensive higher education, following glowing promises held out by society, graduates are entering a stagnant labor market. In many cases, academic degrees have become excess baggage to those recipients who are forced to enter the labor market at inappropriate levels.

Many research studies have warned about the growing expectations for self-fulfillment in work. Poor physical health, mental maladjustment, and social disenchantment are consequences of status conflict.

Some social analysts have suggested that anarchistic tendencies of the terrorists in Italy and other parts of Europe are expressions of rage against betrayal by the social order. The fury that burned college buildings in this country in the last decade may strike again in the coming decade, as that generation reacts in frustration to limited opportunities and a sense of defeat.

Stereotyped Perception

One of the fears of businessmen is that they will no longer be able to ease out older workers. Much of the initial reaction to the recognition of a graying work force has been to try to figure out new ways of "weeding out the deadwood." Pension inducement, less generous and "more realistic" performance appraisals, and other rationalizations for eliminating older, less desirable workers are being developed.

Who should be the target of those designs? Columnist William L. Safire has echoed the fears of many businessmen who link age to performance:

". . . old people get older and usually less productive, and they ought to retire so that business can be better managed and more economically served. We should treat the elderly with respect which does not require treating them as if they were not old. If politicians start inventing 'rights' that cut down productivity, they infringe on the consumer's right to a product at the lowest cost . . ."[11]

The Later Years

It is important to explore how much factual evidence there is to support the stereotyping and the prejudices that link age with senility, incompetence, and lack of worth in the labor market. Age 65 was an arbitrarily selected cutoff age used by New Deal planners who looked back historically to Bismark's social welfare system in nineteenth century Germany.

Certainly, one does not have to look hard to find the elderly among the greatest contributors to current society. The list is long of older citizens who have made major contributions in all fields including the arts, industry, science, and government, and who continue to be worthy and inspiring members of our society.

Age-related Change

Physiological changes are most pronounced and most identified with old age, but vary markedly in degree between individuals of the same age. It is not clear what changes are actually a result of aging and what can be attributed to life-styles. Researchers indicate, however, that after age 50 life-style becomes a less influential factor in physiological change than aging itself.

Among age-related changes are declines in the sensory processes, particularly vision, failures in the immunity system that lead to cardiovascular and kidney problems, and degenerative diseases such as rheumatoid arthritis. While 85% of those workers over 65 suffer from chronic diseases, these are not sudden afflictions. Hence 75% of those 60 to 64 years old suffer from these diseases, many of which can be controlled by modern medical treatment. The major effects of these diseases are loss of strength in fighting off invaders and loss of mobility.

Reaction time seems to be affected by the increase in random brain activity, or "neural noise," which distracts the brain from responding to the proper neural signals. A fall in the signal-to-noise ratio would lead to a slower performance and increased likelihood of error. To correct for this possibility of error, performance is delayed to permit time to gain greater certainty. Research on cognitive abilities shows that older people are more scrupulous in the use of decision criteria before responding or forming associations required for decision making. Older people are less likely to use mnemonic or "bridging" mechanisms to link similar concepts. They require a 75% chance of certainty before committing themselves, while younger people will take far greater risks.[12]

When time pressure is not a relevant factor, the performance of older people tends to be as good, if not better, than that of younger people. In self-paced tests and in self-paced learning situations, older people do not have to make speed versus accuracy trade-offs and, consequently, their performance is higher.

Learning is also inhibited by the delayed signal-to-noise ratio since it interferes with memory. Most of the learning difficulties of older people stem from acquisition and recall rather than from retention. This relates to the two-step process of memory involving an initial introduction and a later retention period. That is, older people have a harder time holding information in short-term memory, awaiting long-term storage, due to neural noise. This is the same sort of problem older people have with recall.

However, once the information reaches long-term storage, it can be retained. The process of inputting the information, and retrieving it, can become blocked for intervals of time. Cognition is perhaps the most important difficulty of older workers and relates to problem solving, decision making, and general learning ability. Training in appropriate mental techniques can overcome many of these short-term memory blockages.

Similarly, intelligence tests often have age biases built in with the inherent speed versus accuracy trade-off. Recent researchers have tried to avoid such a bias and have found problem solving, number facility, and verbal comprehension to be unaffected by age. The ability to find and apply general rules to problem solving are more related to an individual's flexibility and education than to age.

Work Attitude

Research studies on all sectors of the American work force have found that age and job satisfaction seemed to bear positive relationships, but it has become apparent that it is hard to consider job satisfaction without considering what aspects of the work experience are important to the individual.[13] Organizations must carefully consider the type of satisfaction which they are measuring, and try to determine how both the more productive and less productive workers in different age groups vary. Perhaps the types of incentives built into a company's rewards package may encourage the less productive, rather than the more productive, older workers to remain with the company.

Along the same line, increasing monetary benefits but not expanding opportunities for job variety would be a serious mistake if the desired workers are more interested in personal growth and achievement than in financial incentives. Mastery and achievement are closely related to job satisfaction. As such, the need for mastery, or recognized accomplishment, becomes increasingly important.

Thus sudden change in job structure and social networks can be threatening to older workers. Their niche in society is defined largely by their contribution in the work place. The job presents friendship, routine, a sense of worth, and identity. Obsolescence and job change are major fears of older workers.

Job Performance

In reviewing studies of performance by occupation for different age groups, it is important to be aware of biases built into the performance appraisals themselves. On top of this, cross-sectional studies of different age groups are also viewing different individuals. It is quite possible that selection factors in older populations explain much of the difference between older and younger populations. In other words, the older workers staying on the job may be different somehow in their skills or interests in that they have managed to remain on the same job.

Looking first at *managers*, one once again sees the manifestation of the tendency toward caution with age. Victor H. Vroom and Bernd Pahl found a relationship between age and risk taking and also between age and the value placed on risk.[14] They studied 1,484 managers, age 22 to 58, from 200 corporations and used a choice-dilemma questionnaire. It seemed that the older managers were less willing to take risks and had a lower estimate of the value of risk in general.

These findings are supported by another study on determinants of managerial information processing and decision-making performance; 79 male first-line managers with ages ranging from 23 to 57 years (a median of 40 years) were measured by the Personnel Decision Simulation Questionnaire.[15] Older decision makers tended to take longer to reach decisions even when the influence of prior decision-making experience was removed.

However, the older managers were better able to accurately appraise the value of the new information. Hesitancy about risk taking was also supported in this study; older decision makers were less confident in their decisions.

Another study focusing on task-oriented groups also found that older group members once again sought to minimize risk by seeking more reliable direction.[16] Younger members were more willing to shift authority within the group and to make better use of the experience of others. In this way, younger members of the group were more flexible and more tolerant.

Studies of professionals generally concentrate on *scientists* and *engineers*. Perhaps this is because their output is so easy to measure (e.g., publications, patents). Such studies have found bimodal distributions of innovativeness as a function of age. That is to say, there were two peaks of productivity separated by ten-year intervals in research laboratories compared with development laboratories. The first peak in research laboratories occurred by age 40, and the second peak did not appear until age 50. In the development laboratories, the first peak occurred around age 45 to 50, and the second appeared around age 55 to 60.[17] These studies tracked contribution longitudinally over a person's career.

Wider studies of scholarship and artistic contribution revealed a similar first peak at about age 40 and a second peak in the late 50s. Looking more broadly at productivity, it is clear that creative activity was lowest for the 21- to 50-year old group and generally increased with age.[18] It is also a fact, however, that younger scholars and scientists have a more difficult time achieving recognition in the journal networks than do their senior colleagues.

Older people seem to have achieved superior standing among *sales workers* as well and to have remained higher performers. Reports from insurance companies, auto dealers, and large department stores suggest that age is an asset, if a factor at all, in performance.

In a large study of sales clerks in two major Canadian department stores, performance improved with age and experience, the actual peak performance of the sales clerks being about age 55.[19] In several organizations, particularly high technology companies, however, morale plummeted corresponding to length of service. These latter organizations may have used sales as a traditional entry position for managerial development. Those employees remaining on the job over ten years began to perceive frustration in their personal goals of managerial advancement.

Age has had surprisingly little effect on *manual workers*. In several studies, performance seemed to remain fully steady through age 50, peaking slightly in the 30s. The decline in productivity in the 50s never seemed to drop more than 10% from peak performance. Attendance was not significantly affected, and the separation rate (quits, layoffs, discharges) was high for those under age 25 and very low for those over 45.[20]

These findings may not only indicate greater reliability among older workers, but also suggest that those who have remained on the job are, in some way, the most competent. Such a sorting out of abilities may not take place equally well across all industries. While tenure among factory workers within industries is reduced with age, absenteeism rates in heavy industry and construction do increase with age. This may be a more evident consequence of mismatches between job demands and physical abilities.

Finally, the high variation of manual labor performance within age groups, compared with the variation between age groups, suggests that individual differences are much more important than age group differences. The need to evaluate potential on an individual basis, and not by age group, has been convincingly established in these studies.

Considerable variation within age groups is found in studies on *clerical workers* as well. A study of 6,000 government and private industry office workers found no significant difference in output by age. Older workers had a steadier rate of work and were equally accurate. Researchers in many studies found that older clerical workers, both male and female, generally had attendance records equal to that of other workers, as well as lower rates of turnover.[21]

Corporate Experience

Many well-publicized reports identify particular companies in various parts of the country which have never adopted mandatory retirement policies yet have continued to be profitable and efficient with workers well into their 70s and 80s. For example, Thomas Greenwood, president of Globe Dyeworks in Philadelphia, who has retained workers hired by his grandfather, commented, "As long as a man can produce, he can keep his job."[22] The 87-year-old president of Ferle, Inc., a small company owned by General Foods, which employs workers whose average age is 71, commented, "Older people are steadier, accustomed to the working discipline."[23] Sales workers at Macy's department stores in New York have never had to conform to a mandatory retirement age, and have demonstrated no apparent decline in performance attributable directly to age.

Banker's Life and Casualty Company proudly points to its tradition of open-ended employment, retaining top executives, clerks, and secretaries through their late 60s, 70s, and 80s. Of the 3,500 workers in Banker's home office, 3.5% are over 65 years of age. Some have been regular members of the Banker's work force, while others have come after being forced into retirement from other companies. The company reports that older workers show more wisdom, are more helpful and thorough, and perform their duties with fewer personality clashes. Studies on absenteeism at Banker's Life and Casualty show that those over 65 have impressive attendance records.

Large companies that have changed to flexible retirement plans in recent years have had similar satisfactory performance reports. U.S. Steel has permitted more than 153,000 nonoffice employees to continue working as long as they can maintain satisfactory levels of performance and can pass medical examinations.

Polaroid has found that those employees who choose to remain on the job after age 65 tend to be better performers. Company retirement spokesman, Joe Perkins, explained, "If you like to work, you're usually a good worker." He added that attendance is also exemplary as older workers ". . . often apologize for having missed work one day, three years ago because of a cold. There is a fantastic social aspect as people look forward to coming to work." No one is shifted between jobs at Polaroid unless the worker requests a change. Even among older workers whose jobs entail heavy physical demands high performance is maintained.

Performance Appraisal

Generally the companies just mentioned have not had to deal with older workers who remain on the job despite poor performance. There is no guarantee that workers will always be able or willing to perform well, and to relinquish their jobs when they are no longer capable of fulfilling the job requirements. Even if both the company and the individual want to continue their relationship, it is not always possible to effectively match an employee's skills with the company's job opportunities.

This need to identify differences between more and less productive older workers is a difficult distinction to make with current performance measurement techniques. The process must be objective, consistent, and based on criteria that are uniformly applied and which will endure court challenges. Arthur C. Prine, Jr., vice president of R.R. Donnelley & Sons Company, recently explained, "As soon as you pick and choose, you'll scar a lot of people when they are most sensitive. I just dread the thought of calling someone and saying, 'You've worked for forty-five years and have done a wonderful job, but you've been slipping and you must retire.' "[24]

Instead of carrying less productive older workers near retirement on the payroll, employers may begin to weed them out earlier in an effort to deter age-discrimination charges. Richard R. Shinn, president of Metropolitan Life, forecasts that "employers are going to make decisions earlier in careers if it appears that someone is going to be a problem as time goes on."[25]

Thus predictions of future performance will be important criteria in performance appraisal. Even the use of formal standard evaluations does not eliminate age bias or avoid self-fulfilling prophecies which prejudice the evaluation process.

Such a bias was shown in a recent poll of managers. A 1977 questionnaire of HBR readers concluded that "age stereotypes clearly influence managerial decisions."[26] HBR readers perceived older workers as more rigid and resistant to change and thus recommended transferring them out rather than helping them overcome a problem. The respondents preferred to retain but not retrain obsolete older employees and showed a tendency to withhold promotions from older workers compared with identically qualified younger workers.

Part of this discrimination problem is that many companies consider an employee's potential to be an important element in his evaluation. As mentioned in the section on basic abilities, chronological age never has been a valid means of measuring a worker's potential and now is illegal under the Age Discrimination

Employment Act. The strength of various faculties may slightly correlate with age in certain regards, but there is no categorical proof that age has an affect on capabilities. Individuals vary greatly, and useful measures of potential must recognize such differences.

One of the best known functional measures was the GULHEMP system designed by Leon F. Koyl, physician from DeHaviland Aircraft.[27] This system had two dimensions, the first being a physical-mental profile and the second a job-demand profile. Workers were examined on seven factors of general physique, upper extremities, lower extremities, hearing, eye sight, mental features, and personality attributes. These individual factors were plotted on a graph and superimposed on similarly graphed job task profiles. Individuals were then viewed in relation to the job profiles available. While successful in its pilot experience, this federally supported project was not seen as a high priority government expenditure. Thus the project in functional age measurement was terminated.

Functional measures, however, are not the answer to the performance appraisal question. While they can provide the quantifiable "expert" criteria companies might need for age-discrimination suits, their strength lies in largely assessing the potentials of physical labor. The sensitive areas in performance appraisal are evaluations of the more nebulous factors.

Ratings of "mental abilities" and "personality attributes," which were the poorest factors on the GULHEMP scale, are the most sensitive areas in the appraisal process, and the only truly relevant dimensions in most white-collar and managerial jobs. Some consulting firms have been assessing the important elements of successful job performance, appraising corporate personnel, and establishing appropriate organizational recruitment and development programs.

What Managers Can Do

How can companies resolve the kinds of frustration expressed at the beginning of this article by the chief executive of the paper company? Where can they send the fire engines? It is far easier to read about social trends than to perceive ways of preparing for them. It is clear that America's work force is graying. Older workers will tend toward caution, will experience far greater levels of frustration, and will show signs of age individually at very different rates.

However, companies are not fated for stodginess. In this section let us look at six priorities for managers to consider in preparing for the impending dramatic change in their own internal environments:

1. *Age profile*

It has been demonstrated that age per se does not necessarily indicate anything significant about worker performance. Instead, executives should look at the age distribution across jobs in the organization, as compared with performance measures, to see what career paths might conceivably open in the organizations in the future and what past performance measures have indicated about those holding these positions.

2. *Job performance requirements*

Companies should then more precisely define the types of abilities and skills needed for various posts. A clear understanding of job specifications for all levels of the organization is necessary to plan for proper employee selection, job design, and avoidance of age-discrimination suits. For example, jobs may be designed for self-pacing, may require periodic updating, or may necessitate staffing by people with certain relevant physical strengths.

Several companies have looked at the skills needed in various jobs from the chief executive down to reenlisted older and even retired workers who have the needed experience and judgment. For example, as Robert P. Ewing, president of Banker's Life and Casualty, stated, "Our company sets performance standards for each job and these standards are the criteria for employment. Age doesn't count. Getting the job done does."

Such an approach requires careful assessment of needed job competence where traits, motives, knowledge, and skills are all evaluated. When this information is considered in relation to the magnitude and direction of planned company growth, future manpower needs can be predicted. Obsolete job positions can be forecast and workers retrained in advance. Necessary experience cannot be gained overnight, and development programs should be coordinated with precise company manpower needs.

3. *Performance appraisal*

Corresponding with improved job analyses, companies must improve their analyses of individual performance as well. Age biases are reflected in both the evaluation format and the attitudes of managers. Management development programs should be aware of the need to correct these biases. Both Banker's Life and Polaroid have teams that audit the appraisals of older workers to check for unfair evaluations. These units have also been used to redress general age prejudice in the work place.

Companies need a realistic understanding of current work force capabilities for effective human resource planning. A company cannot adjust its development, selection, and job training strategies appropriately without knowing the current strengths and weaknesses of its workers. Additionally, potential courtroom challenges on staffing and reward procedures necessitate evidence of solid decision criteria.

4. *Work force interest surveys*

Once management acquires a clearer vision of the company's human resource needs, and what basic abilities its workers have, it must then determine what the current workers want. If management decides that it wants to selectively encourage certain types of workers to continue with the organization while encouraging turnover of other types, it must next determine what effects different incentives will have on each group.

In addition, management must be well aware of workers' desires and values so that it can anticipate and prepare for morale drops. Understanding work force aspirations is essential in reducing the harmful organizational and personal consequences of mid-career plateauing. For example, companies might offer counseling programs to those who frequently but unsuccessfully seek job changes, or might consider making alterations in the prevailing company culture and in the norms which link competence and mobility.

5. *Education and counseling*

Management may discover that its workers are also confronted with a variety of concerns regarding the direction of their lives after terminating current employment. Counseling on retirement and second-career development are becoming increasingly common to assist workers in adjusting to the major social disengagement following retirement.

IBM now offers tuition rebates for courses on any topic of interest to workers within three years of retirement, and continuing into retirement. Subject matter need not have any relation to one's job and many workers include courses in preparation for second careers (learning new skills, professions, and small business management).

Counseling is also important to address problems of the work force which remains on the job. Career planning to avoid mid-career plateauing, and training programs to reduce obsolescence, must be developed by each company. The educational programs must reflect the special learning needs of older workers. Self-paced learning, for example, is often highly effective. Older workers can learn new tricks, but they need to be taught differently.

6. *Job structure*

A better understanding of basic job requirements and employee abilities and interests may indicate a need to restructure jobs. Such restructuring cannot be done, however, until management knows what the core job tasks are in the organization and what types of changes should be instituted. Alternatives to traditional work patterns should be explored jointly with the work force. Some union leaders have expressed reservations about part-time workers whom they fear may threaten the power of organized labor. Management, too, wonders about its ability to manage part-time workers. Some part-time workers have found that they "lack clout and responsibility" in their jobs in small companies.

Management may have more flexibility than anticipated in changing conditions like work pace, the length or timing of the work day, leaves of absence, and challenges on the job. With a tightened reward structure for older workers, satisfaction with the job may shift increasingly to intrinsic features of one's current job.

America's work force is aging, but America's organizations are not doomed to hardening of the arteries. Older workers still have much to offer but organizations must look at certain policies to ensure that their human resources continue to be most effectively used. Organizations must be alert to changing work force needs and flexible in responding to meet those needs.

REFERENCES

1. U.S. Bureau of the Census, "Current Population Reports," Series P-25, No. 61, *"Projections of the Population of the United States, 1975 to 2050"* (Washington, D.C.: U.S. Government Printing Office, 1975).

2. Neal H. Rosenthal, "The United States Economy in 1985: Projected Changes in Occupations," *Monthly Labor Review*, December 1973, p. 18.

3. Jerry Flint, "Early Retirement Is Growing in U.S.," *New York Times*, July 10, 1977.

4. Jerry Flint, "Businessmen Fear Problems from Later Age for Retirement," *New York Times*, October 2, 1977.

5. Ibid.

6. "The Graying of America," *Newsweek*, February 28, 1977, p. 50.

7. Erik Erikson, *Childhood and Society* (New York: Norton, 1963).

8. Bernice Neugarten, *Middle Age and Aging* (Chicago: University of Chicago Press, 1968), p. 97.

9. George E. Vaillant, *Adaptation to Life* (Boston: Little, Brown, 1977), p. 193.

10. Daniel J. Levinson, "The Mid-Life Transition: A Period in Adult Psychosocial Development," *Psychiatry*, 40, 1977, p. 104.

11. William L. Safire, "The Codgerdoggle," *New York Times*, September 3, 1977, p. 29.

12. For an example of research on cognitive abilities, see A.T. Welford, "Thirty Years

of Psychological Research on Age and Work," *Journal of Occupational Psychology*, 49, 1976, p. 129.

13. See, for example, John W. Hunt and Peter N. Saul, "The Relationship of Age, Tenure, and Job Satisfaction in Males and Females," *Academy of Management Journal*, 20, 1975, p. 690; also, Bonnie Carroll, "Job Satisfaction," *Industrial Gerontology*, 4, Winter 1970.

14. Victor H. Vroom and Bernd Pahl, "Age and Risk Taking Among Managers," *Journal of Applied Psychology*, 12, 1971, p. 22.

15. Ronald N. Taylor, "Age and Experience as Determinants of Managerial Information Processing and Decision Making Performance," *Academy of Management Journal*, 18, 1975, p. 602.

16. Ross A. Webber, "The Relation of Group Performance to Age of Members in Homogeneous Groups," *Academy of Management Journal*, 17, 1974, p. 570.

17. Ronald C. Pelz, "The Creative Years in Research Environments," Industrial and Electrical Engineering, Transaction of the Professional Technical Group on Engineering Management, 1964, EM-11, p. 23, as referenced in L.W. Porter, *"Summary of the Literature on Personnel Obsolescence,"* Conference on Personnel Obsolescence, Dallas, Stanford Research Institute and Texas Instruments, June 21–23, 1966.

18. Wayne Dennis, "Creative Productivity Between the Ages of 20 and 80 Years," *Journal of Gerontology*, 21, 1966, p. 1.

19. *"Age and Performance in Retail Trades,"* Ottawa, Canadian Department of Labor, 1959, as referenced in Carol H. Kelleher and Daniel A. Quirk, "Age Functional Capacity and Work: An Annotated Bibliography," *Industrial Gerontology*, 19, 1973, p. 80.

20. U.S. Department of Labor, *The Older American Worker*, Report to the Secretary of Labor, title 5, sec. 715 of the Civil Rights Act of 1964 (Washington, D.C.: U.S. Government Printing Office, June 1965).

21. See, for example, U.S. Department of Labor, Bureau of Labor Statistics, *Comparative Job Performance by Age: Office Workers*, Bulletin No. 1273 (Washington, D.C.: U.S. Government Printing Office, 1960); and U.S. Department of Labor, Bureau of Labor Statistics, *Comparative Performance by Age: Large Plants in the Men's Footwear and Household Furniture Industries*, Bulletin No. 1223 (Washington, D.C.: U.S. Government Printing Office, 1957).

22. J.L. Moore, "Unretiring Workers, to These Employees, The Boss is a Kid," *Wall Street Journal*, December 7, 1977.

23. S. Terry Atlas and Michael Rees, "Old Folks at Work," *Newsweek*, September 26, 1977, p. 64.

24. Irwin Ross, "Retirement at Seventy a New Trauma for Management," *Fortune*, May 8, 1978, p. 108.

25. Ibid.

26. Benson Rosen and Thomas H. Jerdee, "Too Old or Not Too Old," HBR November-December 1977, p. 105.

27. Leon F. Koyl and Pamela M. Hanson, *Age, Physical Ability and Work Potential* (New York: National Council on the Aging, 1969).

6

How to Give Phased-Out Managers a New Start

BASIL ROBERT CUDDIHY

At one time, only clerical and blue collar workers fell victim to adverse business conditions or financial setbacks. The executive suite and the laboratory were sacrosanct and their occupants secure. But those days are over. Now it is no longer uncommon for executives, professionals, and administrative personnel to suddenly find themselves out of a job. Unlike clerical and blue collar workers, however, these men and women are simply unprepared for this fate. First, they have always belonged to a secure work force that does not anticipate being laid off. Second, they usually have not given much serious thought to their careers.

Although the dismissals experienced by the increasingly large number of high-level personnel are often precipitated by a profit squeeze or some other financial crisis, the crisis itself does not cause these individuals to be chosen for dismissal. They are ousted because for one reason or another they have fallen into a career slump or have become managerially obsolete. When the squeeze comes, they are the ones who feel it.

Traditionally, there have been two ways to deal with the individual who can no longer contribute to an organization's growth. The first is the gentle, "let's be nice" approach: no one mentions what's happening but everyone knows what's going on. A person suddenly finds his responsibilities reduced, his name removed from routing slips, and his presence no longer required at meetings. The second way is to tell someone bluntly that he is fired. For those who can take it, this may be kinder in the long run, since it certainly leaves a person with no illusions about his place within the company. But there are those who cannot take it, those for whom this blunt approach may be the beginning of a serious, even fatal, physical and/or emotional deterioration.

In this article I am going to suggest a different approach to the problem of executive redundancy. It was first tried by my company when over 200 professional and managerial people had to be dismissed because of unalterable business conditions. First, I shall discuss the process by which individuals become expendable and the necessity for sharing the blame for these failures. Next, I shall describe the new, constructive approach my company has taken to make the separation procedure more socially responsible. Finally, I shall recommend steps other companies might follow in order to avoid painful dismissals, with their accompanying bitterness and anxiety.

Crisis by Consensus

Alcan is the short name for Alcan Aluminum Ltd., for many of its subsidiaries, and for the Alcan group as a whole. In this paper, we are concerned with the Montreal head office of Alcan Aluminum Ltd., with the Montreal offices of the Aluminum Company of Canada, Ltd., Alcan's largest subsidiary, and with certain of their plants throughout Canada. At the close of 1971, after a prolonged period of business setbacks, Alcan's management decided that at least 200 employees in the head offices would have to go. In trying to devise a method for dealing with the problem, top management decided that both traditional approaches to cutbacks were unacceptable. Both methods assume that the employee is the only one to blame for his situation, whereas Alcan felt that it is the shared responsibility of the company, the employee's boss, and the organization's culture, as well as of the employee himself.

For many years Alcan had provided a very secure career for its employees; it seemed as difficult for anyone to lose a job as it was to get one in the first place. This attitude naturally led to a sense of complacency which the company saw no reason to undermine.

Another factor contributing to employee stagnation, which Alcan recognized as being present in its own offices, is poor communication between a boss and his subordinates. Many employees had not received a formal performance review or appraisal for the last 15 or 20 years. Of course, some quite comprehensive appraisals did exist, but once compiled they were merely filed away, without any pertinent information being relayed to the individuals concerned. And even though some appraisals of these employees had been done on an informal basis, the individuals concerned did not hear (or choose to understand) the messages that were being given to them. Many employees, therefore, never really knew what the organization, as represented by their bosses, thought of them. Understandably, they assumed that they were doing fine and that their performances were satisfactory.

Also contributing to a lack of equity between performance and rewards are the subcultures that develop in the surrounding social environment. A company's senior management often becomes a cultural and social elite. Membership in this group is based not on job performance alone, but often on an executive's awareness, activities, and participation in "right things" as well. It is clear that many factors unrelated to competence or ability are weighed when considering someone for promotion.

Finally, individual executives are also responsible for their own plight. Many of them have never done any serious, constructive career planning. In some cases, they got into the habit of making haphazard, undirected decisions as early as their college years, and are still following employment paths chosen years ago in that same youthful fashion. Once embarked on a career within Alcan, these people stopped thinking about the future. They assumed, rightly or wrongly, that the company was looking after them and their careers. Most often these men reported that they had received good annual salary increases throughout their working lives and, having no other performance yardstick, had assumed that they were doing a good job.

If effective career planning had been part of their activities, these people would have asked for feedback on their performance when that information was not volunteered. Unfortunately, most of the executives in question had developed in an era in which one did not question or challenge anyone with greater authority.

Thus most of the employees we laid off were members of the executive, managerial, and professional staffs, mainly in the 40 to 60+ age group. Strictly speaking, many of these men were not incompetent, but neither they nor their superiors had identified their real strengths and skills. And even when the employees (or their bosses) finally determined that they needed job changes, it was very difficult to sell them to other departments within the company. Most other managers were not willing to take chances with misfits, even when they were presented as having acquired whole new sets of skills.

Regardless, then, of how it happened or who was to blame, Alcan had a real problem. It had to develop a positive, humanitarian, and socially responsible program to help 200 middle-aged employees embark on new careers outside the organization.

Career Cul de Sacs?

Since neither of the traditional methods of dealing with the redundant employees was acceptable, it was decided that a third-party functional group should be set up to help managers and employees deal constructively with the manpower cutback. This unit included a line manager from personnel, two outside consultants, and the staff psychologist (myself).

The line manager is a crucial member of this unit. Because he is the employee's first point of contact after the termination interview, the success of a program like this depends heavily on his skills. He is a key man because he has credibility within the production end of the organization; not only has he worked as a manager, but his age, years of service, and level in the organization are about the same as those of the people that he will deal with in this kind of termination process.

The traditional professional personnel man would be unable to perform this task very effectively; in protecting the company's interests, he is often tied too closely to the rule book. The job requires a man with a great deal of flexibility, understanding, and common sense. He must be both hard-nosed and empathetic, and he must know the particular organization thoroughly. Although the professional personnel man may be very generous with his sympathy, we have found that this does not help the employee who has just been laid off. Being overly sympathetic or saying such things as "I'll see what I can do for you within the company" will only raise the man's hopes of reversing the "awful mistake" that led to his dismissal.

Because of the unit's freedom from daily administrative requirements, it is able to devote a great deal of individual time to each person, and thus understand particular needs far more thoroughly than the employee's own manager could. It should be mentioned, however, that one of the most important factors in making this whole scheme work is the total commitment, both moral and financial, of the company's senior management. Without this the program will fail.

The Procedure Itself

The actual termination encompasses a great number of steps and in some cases takes up to four months to complete (see ruled insert on page 241).

The program begins when an employee's superior identifies him as redundant, meaning that there is no longer a place for him in that division. The personnel department then makes a thorough search in all other departments and divisions within the company for other possible positions. If nothing is found, the man is considered redundant for the entire company.

The immediate supervisor then discusses with the special unit the terms of financial settlement and any other problems involved. All pertinent information about the effective date of termination, financial settlement, pension, life insurance, and medical insurance are then spelled out in detail in a letter that will be handed to the employee by his boss at the time of the termination interview. This letter (1) advises the man to get in touch with the employee benefits people in the company, tax specialists, and so forth, to discuss any further policy details he may want clarified, (2) lists the members of the special unit, and gives their respective telephone numbers, and (3) instructs the employee to get in touch with the unit as soon as possible.

Before the actual interview, the unit asks the company physician to check the employee's medical history to determine if anything in his background would be aggravated by his termination. If there seems to be some evidence in his file that the news of firing would be exceptionally traumatic, a meeting is arranged between the immediate supervisor (who will conduct the initial interview), a member of the special unit, and the medical officer to discuss an appropriate strategy for the termination interview. This is highly important, for the supervisor as well as for the employee to be dismissed. It is no easier to fire than to be fired. We often role play the interview for the supervisor and, if necessary, write out for him exactly what he ought to say. If there are medical problems, arrangements are then made to have the employee visit the medical center as soon as possible after the interview.

If it is felt that some serious emotional or psychological problem may exist, the executive conducting the termination interview will often make an appointment for the employee with the special unit, without waiting for the employee to make the first contact. This appointment is usually scheduled for the same day as the interview, or, at the latest, for the next morning. An employee should be informed of his dismissal as early in the week as possible so that the unit may begin to help him before the weekend; sitting at home on Saturday and Sunday without any assistance can be enormously upsetting.

The Man in the Machine

At this point I feel that it would be worthwhile to describe the experiences of an individual whom Alcan dismissed, and, at the same time, include some of the relevant dialogue that took place between him and the various members of the special unit during his termination process.

Peter Martin, a 54-year-old electrical engineer, had 28 years of service with our company. He worked his way up through the organization—from junior engineer in power house operations to assistant superintendent and then superintendent of electrical maintenance in one of our smelters, and finally to technical customer representative in wire and cable sales. Peter was declared redundant when it was decided to decentralize all of our customer technical-support functions. At the time, he was earning $24,000 a year. His wife and one of four children were living at home, two other children were attending universities out of town, and his daughter was married.

After his termination interview, Peter was badly shaken. He came almost immediately to see our line manager and said, "I just don't understand how a company can do this to a man after 28 years of hard work. I know lots of people who are less competent than me, and they're still working here because someone cared enough about them to find them a job. Why don't you put yourself to work and find me something?" Our line manager explains to the employee that, no matter what he might think to the contrary, the organization has already been thoroughly searched for other possible positions for him. The termination interview is itself an indication that nothing suitable could be found within the company.

Steps and Timing of the Termination Process

Identification of redundant employee	Informal—usually three to six months before termination
Internal search for alternate job possibilities	One month before termination
Supervisor's initial discussion with special unit, and preparation of termination letter	One to two weeks before termination
Check of employee's medical history	One week before termination
Coaching supervisor on termination interview strategy	One to two days before termination
Termination interview	Should be held from Monday to Thursday *only*, and early in the day—*never* prior to vacation
Meeting of separated employee with line manager of special unit	Immediately after termination interview
Counselling and process of reorientation toward outside world	Same day as termination interview, continuing for one week, with periodic interviews
Initial interviews with outside consultants and with staff psychologist	Within three days of termination
Possible interview with company doctor	Within three days of termination
Beginning of psychological assessment	Within one week of termination
Relocation to new offices	Within one week of termination
Intensive work with consultants to finalize resumés	Within ten days of termination
Consultation with employee benefits staff for advice and clarification of termination policy	Within ten days of termination
Time lag between circulation of resumés and first job interviews	Usually three to four weeks
Counselling with line manager of special unit and with staff psychologist	Continues for two to three weeks and tapers off as the employee gains confidence

Feedback session — results of counselling and assessment	Within two weeks of termination
Time needed for employment interviews	Usually three to four months
New job found	Usually within four months

The line manager has to emphasize to the employee the importance of realizing that the umbilical cord with the company is severed. He recommends immediate action, advising the employee not to waste time worrying about why he was let go. The important thing is to find a new job as soon as possible. Obviously, only a hard-nosed line manager is capable of such blunt statements — someone committed to making the employee face the facts.

The employee is given a package of written material that outlines the basic do's and don'ts of job hunting. This package includes names and addresses of people in reputable management-placement firms in the city and the major personnel-placement people within government agencies. It has basic information about resumé preparation, financial management, and so forth. The line manager then explains to the employee that he will be given a certain amount of money to cover traveling and miscellaneous expenses that he may incur while searching for a new job.

A very important part of the termination policy is the financial settlement, discussed with the employee at his first interview. Alcan has had an extremely generous termination allowance for all of its executive, managerial, and professional personnel. The settlement is usually based on years of service with the company, and generally amounts to one month's salary for the first year of service and two weeks' salary for every year after that. However, the settlement can vary according to age, quality of service, number of years' participation in the pension plan, physical health, and so on.

This financial settlement helps provide a comfortable cushion for the employee searching for a new job, and it also helps relieve some of the isolation, desperation, and stress he may feel, brought on by termination at this critical stage of life.

After dealing with the immediate practical questions, Peter spoke about more personal concerns: "How can I tell my wife and kids that the 'bread-winner' is out on the street?" We always advise employees to inform their families as soon as possible of their termination. We realize that this may be very difficult, and on a few occasions we have helped employees explain the situation to their wives. Women at this age are often suffering from the psychological and emotional problems that may accompany menopause, and the news that a husband has just lost his job can aggravate these difficulties. Children should also be told right away, if they are old and/or mature enough to grasp the situation. We find that, in their willingness to help reduce expenses during this period, children can be a great source of support.

Peter expressed his exasperation and depression by declaring that he was too tired to look for a job: "I think I'll take a few weeks off to collect my thoughts and gather my strength before I go out job hunting. Maybe I should put my house up for sale, too, to consolidate my assets." This is always discouraged: valuable time is lost and important opportunities are missed by taking a break at this strategic point. And selling a home before knowing the new job location can turn out to be a financial drain.

At some point during this interview, most of the employees we see indicate some concern about their physical condition, and usually ask for a thorough medical checkup, even if they've had one earlier in the year. This is easily arranged through the company medical center. As would be expected, the older the employee, the more worried and, therefore, the more likely to request a physical exam.

One of the final things the line manager suggests to the employee is that he change his base of operation within the company as quickly as possible, moving from his present location to a space provided on a floor of the main building. On that floor the employee has an office, shares a secretary, and has free use of stationery, telephones, and printing and duplicating equipment.

This abrupt move from his old office and friends might at first upset the employee but it has definite positive aspects. First, the employees in this temporary office space soon meet and begin to help each other by exchanging information about jobs, contacts, newspaper ads, and so forth. Second, there is a clear psychological advantage for the employee in being able to look for work from a secure job base while not having to cope with his old job's responsibilities or with the embarrassment of his friends. The space is available to the employee until he finds a job, regardless of how long that takes. Third, the move emphasizes that a 180-degree turn has been taken: in this new setting the employee is forced to think positively about the challenge ahead of him instead of focusing bitterly on the past.

Cutbacks Can Be Constructive . . .

During the whole procedure, the company's primary goal is to help the employee become active and assertive on his own behalf. Thus, as soon as possible after the initial interview with the line manager, we introduce the executive to one of our outside consultants. The consultants' responsibilities are separate; one handles technical personnel, such as chemists, physicists, and engineers, and the other deals with management and professional people, such as economists, lawyers, accountants, and employees who, because of moves up the administrative ladder, have been away from a technical field for a number of years.

. . . Creating New Careers . . .

Peter relaxed somewhat when he heard about the consultant help. "Well, I guess they can find a job for me. That's some consolation for a man my age, who's never been on the job market." This notion is dispelled immediately. We try to make it very clear to the employee that the role of these consultants is not to find jobs but to give him the techniques that will enable him to market himself more effectively.

During appointments requested by the employee himself, the consultants spend eight to ten hours with each person, helping him through a series of exercises and trial interviews to pinpoint his job preferences and to strengthen his interviewing weaknesses. They help him prepare his resumés, and occasionally recommend preparing several resumés, each emphasizing different facets of his education or work experience. He is encouraged to follow the local, national, and financial papers and the trade and government publications, where job openings might be advertised. This process has an added advantage, in that it involves a fair amount of activity very soon after the employee's termination, so that he is kept occupied. This is good therapy for that early traumatic period.

. . . and Confidence

An interview with the company's staff psychologist is the next step in the termination procedure. This usually occurs within a day of the employee's first visit to the outside consultant. The role of the psychologist/counselor is one that is different from but complementary to that of the line manager from personnel in the special unit. The line manager "softens" the man up, to a certain extent, in a fairly firm and direct manner. He gives him the facts he needs to know about what the company is prepared to do. The psychologist tries to help the employee understand both the experience he has just been through and the problems that he will have to face during one of the most difficult periods of his life.

Peter did not feel as threatened as we thought he might when it was suggested that he take advantage of the help and services that the company psychologist might be able to provide. When Peter came to see me, he said, "I've been eating alright, but I'm not sleeping very well; I've had such terrible nightmares since I got the news the day before yesterday." I try to explain to the employee that anxiety and tension are normal and entirely understandable during this job-hunting period, and that if he has trouble sleeping or keeping his anxieties under control, some mild medication can be prescribed by the company doctor.

Peter's initial reaction was typical. "I don't believe in that sort of thing. What do you think I am—some sort of pill-popping drug addict?" I point out to the employee that all the physical, mental, and psychological resources available to him will have to be mustered during the next few months for this very demanding phase, and that there are times in life when medication can be very helpful.

Every employee is offered a complete psychological assessment. Although we stress the confidentiality of the assessment and the fact that all information will be shown directly to the individual, it is still considered to be a threatening experience. Peter asked the obvious questions: "What will be involved? What will I have to do? How long will it take? Will it do me any good?" I explain that the process involves an interview followed by intelligence, aptitude, interest, and personality tests that should help the individual assess his strengths and weaknesses and enable him to sell his abilities more realistically.

Peter was doubtful. He said, "I had psychological tests once when I was in high school, and I was told I would never make it to a university. Anyway, what good will it do me now to find out I should have been an accountant rather than an engineer? It's much too late to change." I tell the employee that the purpose of the assessment process is not necessarily to make him change, but to help him get a less biased, more objective, and perhaps even scientific view of himself. The assessment should help the individual see what went wrong in the past so that he can avoid the same errors in the new job. It might even help him become aware of a new marketable talent.

Most of the employees, including Peter, accept this assessment offer—if not initially, then at least after a few days of thinking it over. [To reassure the employee of the process's benefits, we refer him to others (with the latters' permission) who have taken advantage of the assessment offer and have found the information useful in finding a new job.]

To avoid putting the man through any more stress than is naturally generated by such a situation, the actual testing is usually spread over a 2-day period. Once the testing is finished, there is a waiting period of 10 to 14 days to get the results. During this time the employee works with the consultants, sends out resumés and letters, and begins the interviewing process.

The psychologist then meets with the individual to discuss his test results. Like most of the men, Peter was very anxious and nervous at this time, and he had begun to lose his self-confidence. He was quite downcast when he came into my office. "I'm not mad at Alcan anymore, but I guess I'm no good. I was just kidding myself all these years. I must really be incompetent." Because very often the individual has as yet received no replies from his initial contacts or job interviews, this attitude gets reinforced.

Now, seeing a psychologist who, by telling him his test results, will probably further increase his loss of confidence and self-esteem is the last straw. Peter said, "All I need right now is someone like you to drive the final nail in my coffin. But after all, I didn't exactly feel up to par when I was writing those tests, so I probably didn't do very well at all." This defensive attitude is typical. In 99% of the cases, the employee will underestimate his intelligence by a fairly substantial margin. When told just where he stands on a national average, he either cannot or will not accept this information. Peter responded, "You're just trying to make me feel good because you know I'm out of work." (We found, incidentally, that just about all of the employees Alcan dismissed fell within the top 8% to 10% of the population in terms of measurable intelligence.)

During a session lasting from three to five hours, the test results are explained in great detail. The psychologist should explain what the test was designed to measure as well as how the individual actually performed on it.

Another very important part of the feedback is the dialogue generated between the psychologist and the employee. The employee is encouraged to question, challenge, and discuss what he hears. Very often he himself will give very good illustrations from his experience to explain something that has been mentioned. When this feedback process is finished, the individual is given a verbal summary of the psychologist's findings and recommendations. Some people find it helpful to bring a tape recorder to the session for later reference.

We have found that the most important thing to come out of the assessment process is the restoration of self-esteem and confidence. The employee knows that the psychologist is being as straightforward and objective as possible, and (perhaps for the first time in his working life) he is hearing—and facing—the good and the bad about himself, told honestly. He finds out that he is not as bad as he had begun to think he was; that he is a relatively stable, intelligent, worthwhile human being who has some very valuable, marketable skills to offer, even at age 50 or 55.

There is a metamorphosis in attitude from the time an employee enters the psychologist's office as a hand-wringing, apprehensive individual to the time he leaves. When Peter left, he was in a much happier frame of mind, "Well, I guess

I'm not all that bad after all. Too bad I didn't go through a session like this 25 years ago. Maybe I wouldn't be in this jam today if I had been through something like this earlier in my career."

The employee is now in a state of mind to turn his back on the company and move forward in a new direction. He can tell himself that they were wrong, that they missed their chance to use his valuable executive know-how, and that now he will show them by using his new-found enthusiasm to find a job elsewhere.

Conclusions

Our experience with this program taught us two basic lessons: (1) that middle-aged executives do have marketable skills and can find new jobs if they look for them, and (2) that the cost of running such a program is great, both in terms of money and emotion, and that if a few guidelines are put into use, these costs might be lowered.

1. Middle-age skills are marketable

It became so evident to us during this staff cutback that the old, "if you are over 40, you can't get a job" cry is nothing but a myth. Men and women ranging in age from 40 to 62 were able to find jobs. About 90% to 95% of the people who used our relocation services found new jobs in less than four months. Most found employment at salaries equivalent to or better than those of their previous positions. Those who did take a cut in salary usually had the same or more take-home pay for the initial new-employment period because of the generous termination allowance.

It is too early to assess whether all these people will be better off in their new jobs, but early feedback is very encouraging. Many of them have told us that they are pleased with the change, some even admitting that it was the best thing that ever happened to them. Some have expressed great new confidence in themselves, because they feel that, on their own, they found more challenging jobs under adverse conditions.

According to firsthand reports from our outside consultants, the new employers are also very pleased with their new personnel. We hope to be able to do follow-up research to see how the individuals and their new employers feel about each other after the halo effect has worn off.

2. Once is enough

It also became abundantly clear to us that the need for the cutback could have been avoided if our manpower-planning personnel were more systematic and conscientious. It was fortunate that our program worked as well as it did, but the cost—in money and in emotional energy of the people involved—was enormous. And this high cost is unnecessary.

Although we still use the same termination procedure when we have to fire someone, there are ways it might be improved. Perhaps in the future the termination settlement policy will come under review, and other approaches costing less money will turn out to be more beneficial to both the individuals and the company. But it is my view that the most beneficial step is to prevent the recurrence of situations for which mass cutback is the only answer.

Alcan's managers and employees now see that the development of the individual is a lifelong process, and that they share responsibility for it. To help out from the management side, we have instituted a system whereby managers from all locations who are functionally responsible for certain areas (such as production or maintenance) meet at least twice a year to discuss all their employees. This system helps the managers identify an employee's problems early in his career and helps develop action plans on which they must act before the next meeting is convened. Therefore, group pressure forces the boss to sit down with his subordinates and discuss their career plans.

Alcan has also instituted career-planning programs for its personnel, for groups and individuals. These programs help employees understand their strengths and weaknesses while they are still young and flexible, and they force employees to think seriously and constructively about their careers and to communicate these concerns to their superiors. It is hoped that these two programs will help break down the communication barriers that exist between employees and managers.

Finally, even though they did not personally go through this bitter experience, the employees who are still with our company also learned a lesson that cannot but help them—and Alcan—in the future. They learned that their first responsibility is to themselves and that company loyalty does not guarantee a successful career. How to make use of what one has to offer is a personal decision. Of course, an employee may never realize his full work potential, but if so, it should be for reasons over which neither he nor the corporate system has any control.

7

Keeping Managers Off the Shelf

JAY W. LORSCH AND HARUO TAKAGI

We may not call it lifetime employment, but still the vast majority of managers in large U.S. companies stay with one employer throughout their careers, and most of them spend the last 10 to 20 years plateaued. The hard truth is that while many managers at a plateau are still productive, many are not. Consider the following contrasting cases.

At 53, Ralph Franklin finds coming to work a drag. The best part of the week is the Friday lunch with his underwriting buddies from other departments. He's worried, though, about the extent to which the lunches have become boozy occasions. He knows they aren't good for either his health or his reputation in the insurance company, where he is a vice president.

But why care about the company anymore? While he's just gotten his 25-year pin and carries the lofty title of regional underwriting vice president, nobody who matters wants his opinions or ideas—despite the underwriting problems galore that he could solve. As long as he gets his job done to minimal standards, no one asks for his advice.

Harold Wyman is a vice president and regional sales manager for an investment firm, a position he's held for the past 11 years. At 51, he is involved in the day-to-day direction of 15 salespeople. In addition, he sees himself as an important member of the regional office's management team. He talks frequently with the partner in charge of tactics and strategy. Along with other sales managers, he also recruits, selects, and trains new sales personnel. Harold particularly enjoys the contact with these bright young people and their contagious enthusiasm. He smiles when remembering a conversation he overheard between two trainees who said that Harold's excitement and commitment inspired them.

Obviously, most top executives want managers like Harold who are committed and very motivated, but instead they see many who feel the frustrations and bitterness that Ralph expresses. Just how many potential Ralphs are there? A large number. At IBM, for instance, 80% to 90% of the managers are long-term employees. At General Electric, the problem's dimensions are huge. Of 83,000 GE managers and professionals, more than 11,000 have been with the company more than 30 years, almost 26,000 have been there more than 20 years, and more than 48,000, 10-plus. Thus about a third of these employees are in the second halves of their careers. Also, as the baby boomers age, more and more managers will reach the point of no progress.

After a brief flirtation, perhaps, with another career or employer, most people who become managers enter a company in their twenties and stay until they retire. Even in a company like Bethlehem Steel, which has experienced a big restructuring in recent years, the proportion of "lifetime" managerial employees is still high—about 80%.

Of course, especially in the United States, some managers and professionals leave voluntarily for greener pastures, but they are a small minority. Others— also a small number—are asked to leave because of poor performance. Regardless, the general broad adherence to long-term employment leads inevitably to many executives reaching a plateau. As employees progress up the organization, the structure narrows, limiting opportunities for advancement.

It is not exaggerating, therefore, to say that at some point in the latter halves of their careers most managers, like those at GE, will be plateaued; they will not be promoted again. This happens to both the Harolds and the Ralphs. But reaching a plateau doesn't have to mean retiring on the job.

Too often senior executives see plateaued managers who have quit emotionally as pariahs to eliminate. What these administrators forget is that these long-service employees may form the cores of their organizations that produce the day-to-day results. Instead of considering how to eliminate such people, top executives must address different questions. How can they keep them turned on, excited, and motivated in the second halves of their careers? Can anything be done earlier to avoid their getting turned off?

The issues we cover here are first, what causes a career to derail, and second, what can top management do to ensure that it develops more Harolds than Ralphs?

First, let's look at a study of a Japanese company that helps us see why some plateaued managers stay committed while others merely go through the motions.[1]

Committed or Turned Off

The Tokyo-based manufacturing company hired its future managerial employees directly out of universities with the understanding that they would stay with the company until retirement. The 30 engineering managers who were the focus of the study entered the company in "annual classes" between 1957 and 1966. They were selected for study both because they were typical of the company's managers and because by 1982, the date of the research, they had moved through three career stages: early (21 to 30 years old), middle (31 to 40 years old), and plateaued (41 years old and up).

By 1982, these managers had from 16 to 25 years of service and had evolved into two distinct groups with very different attitudes toward their jobs and the company. Some managers were exceptionally committed to their work and the company's future. They were actively involved in and enthusiastic about the organization. A department manager's comment is typical:

"I have developed my career with this company through performing mostly tasks that contribute to the company. I have always been aware of the significance my performance had on the corporate results, and my efforts have led to successful product lines in this division. My way of thinking and my actions coincide exactly with the values of the company."

In contrast, the second group of managers was passive. Although not extremely dissatisfied with their lot, they expressed no particular interest or enthusiasm for either their work or the company. Here is a typical comment:

"When I look back over what I have been doing in the laboratory, I don't find I have any technological specialty that has given me self-confidence and career identity. I have conducted many technologically different research and development projects, and all of them have been undemonstratable and minor. I am satisfied with my current status and salary level, and there is no new job I want to do."

What causes these differences in attitude? Since the chances of further advancement for managers in both groups was practically nil, an important part of the answer must lie in the things they had experienced during the early and middle stages of their careers.

Being in the Mainstream

The most important difference between the committed and passive managers was whether their early job assignments were connected to the mainstream of the company's activities. A committed manager recalls his beginning experiences as an engineer:

"I was first placed in a product division. A year later, I was transferred to the laboratory in order to join an important new product development project, in which I took charge of the development of an electric component. I had created its basic idea when I was in the division.

"I reported my progress directly to the top manager of the laboratory any time I felt necessary. I reported to the division general manager every week; I have to consider costs, investments, and so on in addition to technologies. I was developing an important component that would create profit for the company."

A turned-off manager describes his earliest experience this way:

"The product improvement I was working on was minor to the division, and I worried that I would not make a visible contribution. I envied my friends who joined the company at the same time as I did and whose jobs were the development of the main products of the division."

As they progressed from engineers to section managers, the employees found that working on mainstream activities became even more essential to feeling committed. A department manager remembers his experience:

"The laboratory's top manager assigned me to a joint project with several product divisions to develop a new electrical device. At that time, the company was implementing a strategy to compete with the major leaders in the market. The new device was expected to be a key competitive product.

"At last, we developed the new device. Customers really appreciated the product. It turned the expected profit contribution figure I forecast at the beginning of the project into a reality. I felt that I was creating the future of the company."

Contrast this with the experience one of the unmotivated managers reports:

"My task as a laboratory section manager was leading projects that measured electrical characteristics of materials and products that were developed in other parts of the laboratory. The purpose of these projects was simply to filter out materials and products with imperfections but not to improve them. In essence, I was cleaning up technological troubles made by other people.

"My interest in these projects quickly decreased. In fact, the technological problems I dealt with were often very difficult, and the original engineers could not have handled them.

"I continued the job simply because that was my assignment, but I was using only physical energy to do it."

A significant determinant of the enthusiastic managers' commitment to the company in the later stage of their careers is their early job experiences. In a Japanese company where financial rewards are entirely based on seniority, and career advancement largely so, it is not surprising that the most salient feature for these managers was their job assignments.

But there is more to it: these assignments also answered their needs at each career stage. When they joined the company, all the recruits were well trained technically, and like young people everywhere, they were anxious to use and develop their abilities. Those who had the chance to do so early on felt important to the organization and, consequently, felt good about both themselves and the company.

Most significant, as they entered the middle stages of their careers, as section managers in their thirties, if they had held challenging positions earlier, they were confident of their technical abilities and were ready for new hurdles. For those who wound up committed, what they called "mainstream assignments" provided the challenges. As the term *mainstream* suggests, both in terms of their work and their relationships, they were at the heart of the organization.

Their passive colleagues had had different experiences. During the early stages of their careers, they had not had such satisfying assignments. They had not been evaluated as less competent than their peers, but chance matchings of people to available assignments had not gone in their favor. They felt left out —on the periphery of things. They responded by coming to work and doing what was expected, but they lacked enthusiasm and commitment. That they were not more openly critical of their lot and of the company is probably a reflection of the Japanese culture; employees are expected to be loyal to and not complain about their employers.

Importance of Being Candid

What do the Japanese managers' experiences tell us about Harold and Ralph? One must, of course, first recognize important differences between Japanese and U.S. human resource practices. In most U.S. companies, salary increases and promotions are ostensibly related to performance, whereas in Japan, as we've seen, they aren't. Also, U.S. managerial and professional employees, unlike those in Japan, are supposed to receive annual performance reviews. At first glance, such differences might seem to diminish the important roles that job assignment and the accompanying sense of worth played at the Japanese company. But closer examination indicates that the key to turning on U.S. managers is the same: give them a mainstream role. We want to return to Ralph and Harold's contrasting experiences to illustrate the point.

Ralph's history in the insurance company provides insight into how his unhappy feelings developed. At age 27, having been to college and served in the army, he joined the company. By age 34, he had moved up the ranks of underwriters to become a branch underwriting manager. And there he stayed for ten years. After five years in the branch, he had asked several senior officers about his chances of becoming a branch manager. Like his own branch manager in performance review sessions, however, they were evasive. Nobody said he wasn't going to get the job, but no one offered much encouragement. Finally, when he was 44, Ralph became a regional underwriting manager; a few years later he was given the added title of vice president. All the way along he had been given regular salary increases.

Unfortunately for both Ralph and the company, the regional underwriting vice president position was out of the mainstream. Nobody planned it that way. Senior management had expected that Ralph and several others with similar experiences could play a central role in setting national underwriting policy and developing younger professionals. But as the market developed and the company's organization evolved, it turned out that the main action was in the branches. Ralph and his colleagues were on the periphery. Unkindly, those in the field referred to them as "dinosaurs."

In interviewing plateaued U.S. managers like Ralph, we have learned that they are a lot like their Japanese counterparts. They feel they've been treated fairly financially and have got high enough formal titles. But they miss a sense of importance, of being in a position that counts. On the shelf, they become passive and uninterested and make a contribution to the company that is far below their potential.

The importance of his mainstream jobs is evident in Harold's commitment as a regional sales vice president. After completing his navy service during the Korean War, Harold joined the firm in his first full-time job as a securities salesperson in New York. In the early years, he enjoyed not only the work but also the high income. He occasionally wondered what it might be like to work for another company, but he never was seriously tempted even to look around.

At 35, Harold was made a vice president and put in charge of a small specialty sales group in New Jersey. He held this job for six years. During this period, he learned that he was good at leading others and he enjoyed the added responsibility. In fact, the group did so well that Harold began to dream that he might some day become a partner. Since only one of the firm's 65 partners had come from the selling side, this achievement would have been remarkable. Harold's toughest time at the firm came when he failed to make partner. When he was 40, he still had secret hopes, even though his then boss as well as several other partners were very frank in telling him that he was unlikely to make it. When he was asked to take his present job, he knew that any hope he still retained was totally unrealistic.

As disappointed as he had been at the time, he now retains several positive memories of that period, the strongest being that several partners, including the division manager, had taken the time to explain the partnership decision to him. In the process, they had emphasized his importance in the regional office to the success of the firm. In retrospect, he realizes that this support was not smoke but the way they really felt. And he knows from their comments and from the way he has been treated in general that he has been a strong contributor to the firm's success.

As he looks to the future, Harold really wants more of the same. It is exciting to come in to work, to build the business, and to see the younger people develop. In fact, his only nagging concern is whether he will be able to tolerate retirement.

Two points are striking about Harold's and Ralph's situations. While each had climbed as high as he could up the organizational hierarchy, one felt unused and unwanted while the other felt important and committed. Like the committed Japanese managers, Harold was still in the mainstream, which kept him turned on. Further, his bosses, unlike Ralph's, while still emphasizing his potential contribution to the firm, had told him about his limited future prospects; their candor had helped him to get through his disappointment without bitterness.

Keeping the Torch Lit

It is unrealistic to expect that all plateaued managers can be kept motivated. Because of their superiors' failure to be candid in their evaluations, some will be foundering in the wrong positions. Others may have had their spirits so damped by past grievances, real or imagined, that nothing can reignite them.

We assume, however, that most executives whose careers have stopped have the ability to carry out their responsibilities and have had a satisfactory performance record. While they may not be candidates for higher management, they have been and are completely satisfactory in their contributions. They are neither psychological nor ability misfits.

Clearly, early career experiences have a big impact on how managers view both themselves and the company before they reach the plateau. While many early events can affect such perspectives, two are critical: the first is candor about a person's career prospects. The second important factor is challenging job assignments.

Some of the actions we recommend here are geared to preventing managers from turning off in early career stages, including the time during which they learn they have plateaued. Others are intended to keep managers committed and involved after they have reached the plateau.

Tell the Truth

The need for candor starts at the very beginning when company recruiters tell prospective managers on university campuses about their career possibilities. Moreover, if someone is in a sideline position for a while, he or she must know why and realize it will only be for a short time. Understandably, in their enthusiasm to convince fledgling managers about the merits of their companies, recruiters create unrealistic expectations about how far most of them will go. These expectations form a kind of psychological contract and stay with people for many years. If the "contract" is broken, the company may lose the person's trust. Supervisors, of course, also shape a young person's aspirations.

In one company we know of, a manager brought three bright young stars into a division and promised them that they would have lots of resources for working on special projects. As time went by, the newcomers found that they were handling more and more of the division's routine functions. When their boss eventually retired, his replacement disavowed any commitment to special projects and the three stars stopped shining. Eventually two of them left.

All too often senior managers are unwilling to give subordinates clear and honest feedback about their performance and prospects. As Ralph's reactions demonstrate, failure to get such data can lead to feelings of unfair treatment.

Even worse, we have observed many managers who long after their superiors have passed them over still believe they will advance. As they gradually recognize that advancement is unlikely, they become embittered and resentful because no one has leveled with them. Contrast such situations with Harold's. Although disappointed at not being named a partner, because his own boss and other partners had frankly explained why and had emphasized his continued importance to the firm, Harold felt that he'd had fair treatment.

It is especially important for top managers to be candid with employees at the midpoints of their careers, a time when people are also dealing with other mid-life issues like their own mortality, the increasing independence of children, and so forth. Although senior executives can't deal with all these issues, they can and should help subordinates face up to the reality that their careers are leveling off.

In one case, the general manager of a small division in a large consumer products company was feeling restless. After 28 years of service and a history of rapid career progress, he began to worry that he would not be made a corporate vice president of a larger division. His frustration and disappointment ultimately led him to approach an executive search firm, which eventually turned up an attractive offer in another company. Feeling very ambivalent about whether to accept, he went to the group vice president who was his boss to tell him of the dilemma.

His boss remembers it this way:

"I was scared to death when I realized what the situation was. I didn't want to lose him. But I was terrified to tell him that he wouldn't make vice president here because we had concluded that he couldn't handle a bigger job even though he was doing well in his current one. I finally screwed up my courage and told him. We then talked at length about the pros and cons of the offer, but what we both didn't realize at the time was that my candor with him had solved his dilemma.

"I learned this the next day when he called and asked if I'd join his wife and him for dinner. They both thanked me for calling a spade a spade and explained that he wanted to stay in the company. Once he understood how I and others saw him, he realized he felt so much a part of our company that he didn't want to leave, and he understood that his search for alternatives was out of frustration with not knowing where he stood."

Candor helps people face and accept the reality that they are not going to advance further, but the results are not usually so dramatic. As a rule, senior executives need to be persistent during a period of several months and patient in giving the subordinate time to accept the facts.

Also, such frankness is not easy to come by. Senior managements find it difficult to derail employees. No one likes to make definitive judgments about another person's prospects. As Harry Levinson has pointed out, people feel guilty about communicating such appraisals.[2] Also, as in the last case, many top executives are afraid that subordinates will respond to such honesty by leaving. Some may go, of course, but the greater danger is that lack of candor will lead managers to lose their motivation to contribute even though they're still on board.

It's much easier to be open with people at critical points in their careers if you've had sound relationships with them from the beginning. Senior executives need to have routine, frank conversations with their subordinates about performance, prospects, and the expectations on both sides. If the two people maintain such a dialogue over several years, sufficient mutual trust is likely to grow so that when difficult things need to be said, they will be easier for the boss to deliver and for the subordinate to accept. Such a relationship can be an important preventive against the loss of a manager's commitment.

Challenge with Good Jobs

To understand more clearly why challenges are so important, consider what we know about the psychological states of employees as they reach their forties and fifties. Since they have by then accepted the idea that they won't advance further, the challenge for them will have to come from their current work. This means they will want to use the skills and expertise that they have developed throughout their careers.

Besides, if they've spent 15 to 20 challenging mainstream years with their companies, they identify closely with them. And it's when people identify with their organizations that they care about the development of the next generations of professionals and managers.[3] It is one way they can deal with what Erik Erikson has labeled the generativity issue — that is, "What will I leave behind for the next generation?"

With this perspective, three broad guidelines seem useful:

Continue to provide meaningful work. While this is the same thing that we suggested for the early career stages, it now involves a different emphasis. For one thing, it is important to provide assignments where the person can apply professional or technical skills as well as managerial talents. Ralph would have been much more engaged if he could have used his underwriting skills. Similarly, the passive Japanese managers would have felt more committed if their accumulated engineering knowledge had been put to use. The problem is that in many companies it's the management jobs that provide the hierarchical status and the involvement in mainstream activities.

We suggest that senior executives recognize and reward the professional contributions plateaued managers have made. For example, one big aerospace company uses older engineering managers as consultants to its engineering groups.

A way to offer new challenges, albeit not necessarily more important tasks, is to rotate jobs at the same level.[4] For example, a district sales manager who moves to a new territory gets a fresh set of customers to understand and new subordinates to lead and develop. The challenge of learning and dealing with a new situation can make the same responsibilities more exciting. Whatever management considers for providing meaningful work, the guiding principle must be finding ways to enable experienced employees to use their skills and knowledge to contribute.

Encourage involvement in decisions and activities. Here we have in mind two things. First, give managers as much autonomy as possible to carry out their responsibilities. Allow them to make decisions using their accumulated experience and knowledge. Be unobtrusive with the controls you place on their activities.

Second, find ways to use managers' experience and knowledge in ways that go beyond their jobs. Serving on task forces or committees is one example. Perhaps you're considering building a new facility. Why not let plateaued managers serve on the planning group? Their experience and wisdom may be useful, and participation will build their feeling of commitment. At one commercial bank, executives who have stopped progressing in their careers work with other employees and outside directors on a corporate responsibility committee. But the particular task is not the critical factor. What is important is that senior management search for innovative ways to enable experienced executives to make a real contribution to the organization.

Foster teaching and coaching. Because older executives identify with the company and are concerned about the next generation, they can serve as teachers and coaches of new professionals and managers. The benefits to the development of the younger people are obvious. But more important to our concerns, such roles meet important psychological needs of plateaued managers. Contributing in this way makes them feel necessary to the future of the company to which they have devoted so much of themselves.

REFERENCES

1. Haruo Takagi, *The Flaw in Japanese Management* (Ann Arbor, Mich.: UMI Research Press, 1985).

2. Harry Levinson, "Appraisal of *What* Performance?" HBR July–August 1976, p. 30.

3. Daniel J. Levinson et al., *The Seasons of a Man's Life* (New York: Alfred A. Knopf, 1978).

4. See Gordon E. Forward, "Wide-Open Management at Chaparral Steel," HBR May–June 1986, p. 96.

PART

FOUR

Handling Career Stress

S tress is a universal phenomenon, a significant product of the gap between the self-image and the ego ideal. That gap is exacerbated by organizational and managerial activities that either lower the self-image or raise the ego-ideal demands to inordinate proportions. Stress is costly. It drains energy and, if chronic enough, contributes to the incidence and prevalence of physical illness. Much has been written about stress in recent years. A good deal of it is naive and simplistic but the whole topic is now widely covered. Not much of the discussion has been directed to career stress with the exception of discussions that have to do with losing your job or managing the trauma of demotion, downsizing, mergers, and other such overt changes. There are, however, certain stresses that relate to career progress. Some of these have to do with stages in your development. Others have to do with issues of judgment and conscience. Still others have to do with the price that you pay, the kinds of sacrifices you have to make on behalf of your career.

In this section, these issues are taken up in considerable detail. In the first article, "On Being a Middle-Aged Manager," I summarize the career transition issues that arise in middle age and review the underlying psychological conflicts and themes that are at play. The suggestions I make for coping with the middle-aged transitions should be helpful to the reader.

Albert Z. Carr takes up one of the focal issues of stress in "Can an Executive Afford a Conscience?" In it he recalls that many of the positive steps now taken by managements were once bitterly opposed by most business people. These came to be part of the ethical foundation of the American private enterprise economy. He calls our attention to the moral position of an executive who is responsible for both his or her personal ethics and for the social practices of the organization. Carr's discussion, given widely publicized events in the contemporary business world, is apropos. These issues are important for the person who is pursuing a professional career, starting a new business, moving off in a different direction in middle age or after, or holding significant power in an organization.

257

In "Why 'Good' Managers Make Bad Ethical Choices," Saul W. Gellerman cites the experience of three major companies whose employees did not act clearly on their real interests and those of their organizations. When people overlook the ethical questions associated with the choice of means, they ultimately hurt themselves and their organizations. Gellerman's examples and discussion alert readers to the potential dangers for themselves and their organizations. When these issues are ignored, there's significant stress for both the individual and those in the organization who bear the collective responsibility for what has happened.

These issues are compounded for the person who is operating a small business, as David E. Gumpert and David P. Boyd point out in "The Loneliness of the Small-Business Owner." That's largely because such a person usually has no one to talk to, becomes terribly preoccupied with his or her own business and own problems, is isolated, and suffers from loneliness. They note that the loneliness can never be eliminated for owners of small organizations, but that entrepreneurs can take steps to combat those problems and ameliorate the stresses they precipitate.

In the next article, "When Executives Burn Out," in effect I combine many of the issues from the previous four pieces and illustrate what happens when people, because of their intense and unrelenting pursuit of their ego ideals and values, including their sense of obligation to their organizations, simply work themselves into exhaustion. I argue that the complexity of the modern organization increases the threat of burnout and that it's important to recognize the possibility that burnout can and does occur. Therefore, it is important for organizations and their managers to act on behalf of themselves and their subordinates.

Fernando Bartolomé and Paul A. Lee Evans raise the question, "Must Success Cost So Much?," as they look at the impact on the family of commitment to the pursuit of a career. They contend that one major problem in the pursuit of career is the impact of negative emotional feelings aroused at work that spill over into the family's activities. They ask what happens when a manager is unhappy on the job and point out that a well-functioning professional life is a necessary but not sufficient condition for a well-functioning private life. They examine the prices managers pay and suggest ways in which both the individual and the organization can reduce the inordinate cost to the family of some of the strains in career pursuit.

1

On Being a Middle-Aged Manager

HARRY LEVINSON

For most men, attainment of executive rank coincides with the onset of middle age, that vast gulf which begins about 35 and endures until a man has come to terms with himself and his human fate (for no man matures until he has done so). It is the peak time of personal expansion, when a man lives most fully the combined multiple dimensions of his life. He has acquired the wisdom of experience and the perspective of maturity. His activity and productivity are in full flower; his career is well along toward its zenith. He is at the widest range of his travels and his contacts with others. He is firmly embedded in a context of family, society, career, and his own physical performance. His successes are models for emulation; his failures, the object lessons for others. He has become a link from the past to the future, from his family to the outside world, from those for whom he is organizationally responsible to those to whom he owes responsibility. In a word, he has it made.

And need it all come to a harsh and bitter end? *No.*

A man cannot alter his inevitable fate. But he can manage the way he comes to terms with it. If he does so, rather than simply letting events take their course, he can do much to prolong the richness of his life as well as his years.

Sophocles, who lived to be more than 90, wrote *Oedipus Rex* at 75 and *Oedipus et Colonus* at 89. Titian completed his masterpiece, "The Battle of Lepanto," at 95; he began work on one of the most famous paintings in the world, "The Descent from the Cross," when he was 97. Benjamin Franklin invented bifocals at 78. Benjamin Duggar, Professor of Plant Physiology and Botanical Economics at the University of Wisconsin, was removed at age 70 by compulsory retirement; he then joined the research staff of Lederle Laboratories and several years later gave mankind Aureomycin. At 90, Pablo Casals still played the cello as no other man ever had. Santayana, the philosopher, wrote his first novel, *The Last Puritan*, at 72. Carl Sandburg wrote *Remembrance Rock* at 70. Freud's activities continued into his 80's.

These men are the exceptions, of course. But the fact that many people can mature creatively indicates that there is indeed hope for all of us who are closer to 35. In this article I propose to examine some of the experiences of middle age and suggest ways of maintaining creative potential.

First, however, permit me a brief qualification. I am not arbitrarily splitting businessmen into under 35 and over 35. That would be unrealistic. The figure

35 is not fixed. It will waver, because I am using it here in the sense of a stage of life, not a birthday.

Indexes of Health

Behind the flowering of middle age, a critical physical and psychological turnaround process is occurring. This is reflected in indexes of health. Statistics from Life Extension Examiners indicate that specific symptoms—such as extreme fatigue, indigestion, and chest pains—rise sharply among young executives just moving into top management. Only one third of the symptoms found in the 31- to 40-year-old management group can be traced to an organic cause, the examiners report.[1] They suggest that these problems come about because of both the manner in which the men live and the state of mind in which they work.

Psychological Factors

While some explanations for this increase in symptoms are no doubt a product of the aging process itself, there are more pressing psychological forces. The British psychoanalyst, Elliott Jaques, contends that a peak in the death rate between 35 and 40 is attributable to the shock which follows the realization that one is inevitably on a descending path.[2] This produces what for most men is a transitory period of depression. Depression increases a person's vulnerability to illness. There is much medical evidence to indicate that physical illness is likely to occur more frequently and more severely in people who feel depressed.

Lee Stockford of the California Institute of Technology reports from a survey of 1,100 men that about 5 out of 6 men in professional and managerial positions undergo a period of frustration in their middle 30's, and that 1 in 6 never fully recovers from it. Stockford attributes the crisis to a different kind of frustration: "This is the critical age—the mid-30's—when a man comes face to face with reality and finds that reality doesn't measure up to his dreams."[3]

A number of factors in executive work life contribute to the intensification of these feelings and the symptoms which result:

Increasing contraction of the hard work period—The average age at which men become company presidents is decreasing. As it does, the age span during which success can be achieved becomes narrower. The competitive pace therefore becomes more intense. It is further intensified by devices such as management by objectives and performance appraisals which give added impetus to the pressures for profit objectives.

Inseparability of life and career patterns—For managerial men in an intensely competitive career pattern, each year is a milepost. Time in job or level is a critical variable. If one does not move on time, he loses out on experience, position, and above all, the reputation for being a star. This means there necessarily must be repetitive subpeaks of anxiety around time dimensions.

Continuous threat of defeat—When both internal and external pressures for achievement are so high, the pain of defeat—always harsh—can be devastating, no matter how well a man seems to take it. Animal research indicates that when males are paired in combat, up to 80% of the defeated ones subsequently die although their physical wounds are rarely severe enough to cause death. We cannot generalize from animals to humans, but we can get some suggestion of the physical cost of the experience of personal defeat. When we turn back to the management pyramid and the choices which have to be made, obviously many men experience defeat, and all must live with the threat.

Increase in dependency — To cope with competition, the executive, despite his misgivings, must depend on specialists whose word he has to accept because of his lack of specialized knowledge. In fact, John Kenneth Galbraith advanced the thesis in *The New Industrial State* that the technical infrastructure of an organization really makes the decisions, leaving only pro forma approval for the executive.[4] The specialists have their own concepts, jargon, and motivation which often differ from those of the executive. Every executive wants to make good decisions. He is uneasy about decisions based on data he does not fully understand, gathered by people he does not fully understand, and presented in terms he does not fully understand. He is therefore often left to shudder at the specter of catastrophe beyond his control.

Denial of feelings — Commitment to executive career goals requires self-demand and self-sacrifice, and simultaneously inhibits close, affectionate relationships. One cannot allow himself to get close to those with whom he competes or about whom he must make decisions, or who are likely to make decisions about him. Often he bears a burden of guilt for the decisions he must make about others' careers.[5] No matter how strongly a man wants the achievement goals, he still has some feelings of anger, toward both himself and the organization which demands that sacrifice, for having to give up other desirable life goals. He must hold in tightly these feelings of anger, together with the feelings of affection and guilt, if they are unacceptable to him or in his business culture. Repressed feelings must continuously be controlled, a process which requires hyper-alertness and therefore energy.

Constant state of defensiveness — The pursuit of executive success is like playing the children's game, "King of the Hill." In that game, each boy is vying for the place at the top of the stump, fence, barrel, or even literally, the hill. All the others try to push the incumbent from his summit perch. Unlike the game, in executive life there is no respite. Given this state of affairs, together with the other conditions to which I have just referred, one must be always "at the ready," as the military put it. To be at the ready psychologically means that one's whole body is in a continuing emergency state, with resulting greater internal wear and tear.

Shift in the prime-of-life concept — Western societies value youth. It is painfully disappointing to have attained a peak life stage at a time in history when that achievement is partially vitiated by worship of youth, when there is no longer as much respect for age or seniority. This is compounded by one's awareness of the decline of his physical capacities. Thus, at the height of a manager's attainment, he is likely to feel also that he has only partly made it, that he has already lost part of what he sought to win. Since only rarely can one have youth and achievement at the same time, there is something anticlimactic about middle-age success.

Subtle Changes

The issues having to do with health are only one facet of the middle-aging process. There are also subtle, but highly significant, changes in (1) work style, (2) point of view, (3) family relationships, and (4) personal goals. Let us look at each of these in turn.

1. Work Style

Both the mode and the content of the work of creative men differ in early adulthood, or the pre-35 stage, from that of mature adulthood, or the post-35 stage. Jaques pointed this out when he observed:

"The creativity of the 20's and early 30's tends to be a hot-from-the-fire creativity. It is intense and spontaneous, and comes out ready-made. . . . Most of the work seems to go on unconsciously. The conscious production is rapid, the pace of creation often being dictated by the limits of the artist's capacity physically to record the words or music he is expressing. . . . By contrast, the creativity of the late 30's and after is sculptured creativity. The inspiration may be hot and intense. The unconscious work is no less than before. But there is a big step between the first effusion of inspiration and the finished creative product. The inspiration itself may come more slowly. Even if there are sudden bursts of inspiration they are only the beginning of the work process."[6]

Jaques adds that the inspiration for the older man is followed by a period of forming and fashioning the product, working and reworking the material, and acting and reacting to what has been formed. This is an experience which may go on for a period of years. The content of work changes, too, from a lyrical or descriptive content to one that is tragic and philosophical, followed by one that is serene. Jaques recalls that Shakespeare wrote his early historical plays and comedies before he was 35, his tragedies afterward.

Contrary to popular misconception, creativity does not cease at an early age. It is true that creative men have made major contributions before 40, but it is equally true that those who demonstrated such creativity continued to produce for many years thereafter. In fact, both in the arts and in the sciences, the highest output is in the 40's.

Executives have many of the same kinds of experiences as artists and scientists. Executives report the greatest self-confidence at 40. Though their instrumentality is the organization, younger and older men do different creative work with organizations. The younger man is more impulsive, flashy, and star-like with ideas; the older man is more often concerned with building and forming an organization. A conspicuous example is the hard-hitting company founder who, to the surprise of his organization, becomes less concerned with making money and more preoccupied with leaving an enduring company. Suddenly, he is talking about management development.

2. Point of View

Concurrent with the shift in work style or orientation is a shift in point of view. This occurs in political and social thinking as well as in business. It is a commonplace that most people become more conservative as they grow older. It is an unspoken commonplace that they are more bored.

True, many activities are intrinsically boring and become more so with repetition, but others no longer hold interest when one's point of view has changed.

Disillusionment: Some of the boredom results from disillusionment. Early idealism, the tendency toward action, and the conviction of the innate goodness in people are in part a denial of the inevitable. Young people in effect say, "The world can be rosy. I'll help make it that way. People can be good to each other if only someone will show them how or remove the conditions which cause their frustration."

But in mid-life it becomes clear that people are not always good to each other; that removing the conditions of frustration does not always lead to good, friendly, loving behavior; and that people have a capacity for being ugly and self-destructive as well as good. One evidence for the denial of disillusionment is the effort in so many companies to keep things "nice and quiet." Such companies are characterized by the inability to accept conflict as given and conflict resolution as a major part of the executive's job.

Obsolescence: Another factor in change in point of view has to do with the feeling of becoming increasingly obsolescent. The middle-ager feels himself to be in a world apart from the young — emotionally, socially, and occupationally. This is covered today by the cliché "generation gap." But there is something real to the distance because there is a tendency to feel that one cannot keep up with the world no matter how fast he runs. Thus the sense of incompetence, even helplessness, is magnified. Some of this is reflected in an attitude that middle-aged executives often take.

For example, I once addressed the 125 members of the upper management group of a large company. When I finished, I asked them to consider three questions in the discussion groups into which they were going to divide themselves:

1. Of what I had said, what was most relevant to their business?
2. Of what was most relevant, what order of priority ought to be established?
3. Once priority was established, who was to do what about the issues?

They handled the first question well when they reported back; none had difficulty specifying the relevant. They had a little more difficulty with the second. None touched the third; it was as if they felt they were not capable of taking the action with which they had been charged.

Vocational choice: This incident might be excused on a number of bases if it were not for other unrelated or corroborative evidence which reflects a third dimension in our consideration of change in point of view. Harvard psychologist Anne Roe did a series of studies on vocational choice in the adult years. In one study she was trying to find out how people make decisions about selecting jobs.

"The most impressive thing about these interviews," she reports, "was how few of our subjects thought of themselves as considering alternatives and making decisions based on thoughtful examination of the situation. . . . They seemed not to recognize their role as chooser or their responsibility for choices. It was, indeed, this last aspect we found most depressing. Even among the executives, we find stress on contingencies and external influences more often than not."[7]

Pain of rivalry: The sense of being more distant from the sources of change, from the more impulsive agents of change, and of not being a chooser of one's fate spawns feelings of helplessness and inadequacy. This sense of remoteness is further magnified, as I have already noted, by feelings of rivalry. For boys, playing "King of the Hill" may be fun. For men, the greater the stakes and the more intense the motivation to hold one's place, the more threatening the rivals become. Yet, in the midst of this competitive environment, one is required to prepare his rivals to succeed him and ultimately to give way. The very name of the game is "Prepare Your Successor."

I recall a particular corporate situation in which the president had to decide who was to be executive vice president. When he made his choice, some of his subordinates were surprised because, they said, the man he picked was the hottest competitor for the president's job and usually such men were sabotaged. The surprising part of the event, as far as I was concerned, was not the choice, but the fact that the subordinates themselves had so clearly seen what tends to happen to rivals for the executive suite. It is indeed difficult to tolerate a subordinate when the executive senses himself to be, in any respect, on a downward trail while the subordinate is obviously still on his way up and just as obviously is demanding his place in the corporate sun.

This phenomenon is one of the great undiscussed dilemmas of the managerial role. Repeatedly, in seminars on psychological aspects of management, cases refer to executives who cannot develop others, particularly men that have nothing to fear, in the sense that their future security is assured and they still have upward avenues open to them. What is not seen, let alone understood, in such cases is the terrible pain of rivalry in middle age in a competitive business context that places a premium on youth. This paragraph from Budd Schulberg's *Life* review of *Thalberg: Life and Legend* captures the rivalry issue in one pointed vignette:

"There was to be a dramatic coda to the Irving Thalberg Story: the inevitable power struggle between the benevolent but jealous L.B. Mayer and the protégé he 'loved like a son.' Bitter was the conflict between Father and Son fighting over the studio's Holy Ghost. They fought over artistic decisions. They fought over separation of authorities. They fought over their division of the spoils, merely a symbol of power, for by now both were multi-millionaires. It was as if the old, tough, crafty beachmaster L.B. was determined to drive off the young, frail but stubborn challenger who dared ask Mayer for an equal piece of the billion-dollar action."[8]

In this case, the rivalry was evident in open conflict. It could be with men at that level and in that culture. However, in most cases, if the rivalry does not go on unconsciously, it is carefully disguised and rationalized. Executives are reluctant to admit such feelings even to themselves. Therefore, much of the rivalry is unconscious. The parties are less aware of why they are quarreling, or perhaps they are more aware of the fact that they never seem to settle their quarrels. Every executive can test such feelings in his own experience by reviewing how he felt when a successor took his place, even though he himself moved up, particularly when that successor changed some of his cherished innovations.

Thus it is difficult for each of us to see the unconscious battle he wages with subordinates, now wanting them to succeed, now damned if they will. Subordinates, however unable they are to see this phenomenon in themselves, can usually see it quite clearly in the behavior of the boss. But then there are few upward performance appraisals to help make such behavior conscious, and the behavior itself indicates to the subordinate that the rival would do well to keep his mouth shut.

Dose of anger: The change in point of view which throws such problems into relief and intensifies fear (though rarely do executives speak of fear) is compounded further by a significant dose of anger. It is easy to observe the anger of the middle-aged executive toward today's youth—who have more money, more opportunity, and more sex than was available yesterday. There is anger, too, that the youngsters are free to "do their thing" while today's executives, pressed by the experiences of the depression and the constraints of their positions, sometimes find it hard to do what they really want to do.

The anger with youth is most often expressed as resentment because "they want to start at the top" or "they aren't willing to wait their turn or get experience" or "they only want young ones around here now." It is further reflected in such simultaneously pejorative and admiring descriptive nouns as "whiz kids," "jets," and "stars." These mixed-feeling phrases bespeak self-criticism and betrayal.

Every time the middle-aged manager uses such a phrase, he seems also to be saying that he has not done as well or that he has been undercut. He who had to learn how to size up the market from firsthand contact with customers finds that knowledge now useless, replaced by a computer model constructed by a man who never canvassed a customer. He who thought business to be "practical" and "hardheaded" now finds that he must go back to school, become more intellectual, think ahead conceptually, or he is lost. The kids have outflanked him. They have it so good, handed to them on a platter, at his expense.

Older generations have always complained that the youth not only are unappreciative of their efforts, but take for granted what they have struggled so hard to achieve. Nevertheless, management has never taken seriously the impact of such feelings on executive behavior. The result is an expensive loss of talent as it becomes apparent to young people that managements promise them far more than companies deliver.

I am certain in my own mind that it is the combination of rivalry and anger which makes it so difficult to create challenging ways to use young people in management. (Certainly it is not the dearth of problems to be tackled.) That in turn accounts for much of the astronomical turnover of young college graduates in their first years in a company and also for much of their subsequent disillusionment with managerial careers.

3. Family Relationships

The same narrowing which occurs in the cycle of achievement in business has also been taking place within the family. People are marrying at earlier ages, children are being born earlier in the marriage and therefore leaving their parents earlier. In turn, the parents live alone with each other longer (according to latest census figures, an average of 16 years). This poses several problems which come to a head in middle life. By this point in time one usually has lost both his parents. Though he may have been independent for many years, nevertheless for the first time he feels psychologically alone.

Because an executive can less readily establish close friendships at work, and his mobility makes it difficult for him to sustain them in his off-work relationships, he tends to have greater attachment to his children. He therefore suffers greater loss when they leave home, and he usually does not compensate for these losses any more than he actively compensates for the loss of old friendships through death and distance.

His heavy commitment to his career and his wife's to the children tend to separate them from each other—a problem which is obscured while their joint focus is on the children. When the children leave home, he is left with the same conscious reasons for which he married her as the basis for the marriage (attractiveness, charm, liveliness) and often the same unconscious ones (a substitute for mother, anything but like mother, a guaranteed nonequal, and other, similarly unflattering, reasons).

But she is no longer the young girl he married. She has aged, too, and may no longer be her ideal sylph-like self of twenty years before. If, in addition, his unconscious reasons for marrying her are now no longer as important as they were earlier, there is little left for the marriage unless the couple has worked out another basis for mutual usefulness.

Meanwhile, for most couples there has been a general decrease in satisfaction with each other, less intimacy, a decline in frequency of sexual intercourse, and fewer shared activities. Wives become more preoccupied with their husbands' health because age compels them to unconsciously rehearse for widowhood. Husbands sense this concern and the reasons (which sometimes include a wish for widowhood) for it, and withdraw even more. This is part of what increases the sense of loneliness mentioned earlier, in the context of the need for greater closeness. These factors contribute to the relatively new phenomenon of the "twenty-year" divorce peak.

4. Personal Goals

Up to approximately age 45, creative executive effort is largely self-centered. That is, one is concerned with his achievement and his personal needs. After age 45, he turns gradually to matters outside himself. As psychologist Else Frenkel-Brunswik has shown, he becomes more concerned with ideals and causes, derived from religious or parental values.[9] He also becomes more concerned with finding purpose in life.

For example, a young executive, a "jet" in his company, became a subsidiary president early. And while in that role he became involved in resolving racial problems in his community. Although still president, and likely to be promoted to head the whole corporation, his heart is now in the resolution of community problems. Similarly, another executive has retired early to become involved in conservation. Still others leave business for politics, and not a few have become Episcopal priests.

As part of this change (which goes on unconsciously), there are periods of restlessness and discomfort. There appears to be a peak in travel between the ages of 45 and 50, and also a transitory period of loneliness as one leaves old, longstanding moorings and seeks others.

The restlessness and discomfort have another source. When the middle-aged manager is shifting his direction, he must necessarily use psychological energy for that task. As a consequence, it is more difficult to keep ancient, repressed conflicts under control. This is particularly true when the manager has managed to keep certain conflicts in check by promising himself he would one day deal with them. As he begins to feel that time is running out and that he has not delivered on his promises to himself, he begins to experience intense internal frustration and pressure. Sometimes he will try to hide such conflicts under a contemporary slogan like "identity crisis."

Not long ago, a 42-year-old executive told me that despite his age, his professional engineering training, and his good position, he was still having an identity problem. He said he really did not know what he wanted to do or be. A few questions quickly revealed that he would prefer to be in his own business. However, the moment we touched that topic, he was full of excuses and wanted to turn away from it. He did indeed know what he wanted to do; he was simply afraid to face it. He wanted to be independent but he could not break away from the security of his company. He had maintained the fantasy that he might some day, but as the passing years made that less likely, his conflict increased in intensity.

Most men will come nowhere near doing all they want to do with their lives. All of us have some degree of difficulty and frustration as a result. We become even more angry with ourselves when the prospect arises that time will run out before we have sampled, let alone savored, much of what there is in the world. But most of us subtly turn our efforts to meeting those ideal requirements.

The important point in all this is that, as psychologist Charlotte Buhler points out, it relates directly to survival.[10] The evidence indicates that a person's assessment as to whether he did or did not reach fulfillment has more to do with his old-age adjustment than literal loss of physical capacities and insecurity. Put another way, if a man has met his own standards and expectations reasonably well, he adapts more successfully to the aging process. If not, the converse holds: while experiencing the debilitation of aging, he is also simultaneously angry with himself for not having done what he should have. Anger with self is the feeling of depression. We have already noted the implications of depression for physical illness.

Significant Implications

Up to this point, we have been looking at the critical physical and psychological symptoms of the aging process. Now let us turn to the personal and organizational implications in all this.

Facing the Crisis

First, all of us must face up to the fact that there is such an event in men's lives as middle-age crisis. It is commonplace; it need not be hidden or apologized for. It frequently takes the form of depressive feelings and psychosomatic symptoms as well as increased irritability and discontent, followed by declining interest in and efforts toward mastering the world.

There is a premature tendency to give in to fate, to feel that one can have no choice about what happens to him, and, in effect, to resign oneself to the vagaries of chance. This period is essentially a mourning experience: regret, sorrow, anger, disappointment for something which has been lost—one's precious youth—and with it the illusion of omnipotence and immortality. It is necessary to be free to talk about the loss, the pain, and the regret, and even to shed a tear, literally or figuratively. We do indeed die a bit each day; we have a right to be shaken by the realization when we can no longer deny it.

When a middle-aged manager begins to experience such feelings, and particularly if they begin to interfere with his work or his enjoyment of life, he should talk to someone else about them, preferably a good counselor. This kind of mourning is far better than increasing the intense pace of running in an effort to escape reality. In the process of talking, the wise man reworks his life experiences and his feelings until he is all mourned out and no longer afraid of being mortal.

When a manager can take his own life transitions and his feelings about them seriously, he has the makings of maturity. In the course of making wine, after the grapes are pressed, the resulting liquid is left to age. In a sense, it continues to work. In the process of aging, it acquires body, color, and bouquet—in short, its character.

Like wine, people who work over their feelings about the aging process acquire a certain character with age. They deepen their awareness of themselves and others. They see the world in sharper perspective and with greater tolerance. They acquire wisdom. They love more, exploit less. They accept their own imperfection and therefore their own contributions. As Jaques has put it, "The successful outcome of mature creative work lies thus in constructive resignation both to the imperfections of men and to shortcomings in one's work. It is this constructive resignation which then imparts serenity to life and work."[11]

The middle-aged manager who fails to take himself, his crises, and his feelings seriously keeps running, intensifies his exploitation of others, or gives up to exist on a plateau. Some managers bury themselves more deeply in their work, some run after their lost youth with vain cosmetic efforts, others by chasing women, and still others by pursuing more power. A man's failure to mature in this sense then becomes a disease that afflicts his organization. He loses his people, his grasp of the realities of his life, and can only look back on the way it used to be as the ideal.

The executive who denies his age in these ways also denies himself the opportunity to prepare for what is to come, following some of the suggestions I shall discuss in the next section. He who continues to deny and to run will ultimately have to face emptiness when he can no longer do either and must still live with himself. The wise man will come to terms with reality early: he will take seriously the fact that his time is limited.

Taking Constructive Action

Second, a man must act. Only he who acts on his own behalf is the master of himself and his environment. Too many people accept what is for what will be. They most often say, "I can't do anything about it." What they really mean is that they won't do anything. Check your own experience. How often do you mean "won't" when you say "can't"? Much of psychotherapeutic effort is directed to helping people see how they have trapped themselves this way. There are indeed alternatives in most situations. Our traps are largely self-made.

There are a number of fruitful avenues for action in both personal and business life. In personal terms, the most important efforts are the renegotiation of the marriage and the negotiation of new friendships. Husband and wife might wisely talk out their accumulated differences, their disappointments and mutual frustrations as well as their wishes and aspirations. As they redefine their marriage contract, they clarify for themselves their interdependence or lack of it. If they remain silent with each other or attack in their frustration, they run the danger of falling apart in their anger at the expense of their need for each other.

In social terms, the executive must make a formal effort to find and cultivate new friends with a particular emphasis on developing companionship. We know from studies of concentration camp survivors and of the process of aging that those who have companions cope most effectively with the traumas of life. Those who do not almost literally die of their loneliness. As a man becomes less self-centered, he can devote more energy to cultivating others. When he individualizes and cultivates the next person, he creates the conditions for others' recognition of him as a person.

In public terms, the executive must become future oriented, but this time in conceptions that go beyond himself and his job. He invests himself in the future when he becomes actively involved in some on-going activity of social value which has enduring purpose. Hundreds of schools, colleges, hospitals, and community projects — most of them obscure — await the capable man who gives a damn and wants that damn to matter. Most executives need not look more than a few blocks beyond their offices for such opportunities.

In business terms, the executive should recognize that at this point in time he ideally should be exercising a different kind of leadership and dealing with different organization problems. In middle age, the stage Erik Erikson has called "the period of generativity," [12] if he opts for wisdom, he becomes an organizational resource for the development of others. His wisdom and judgment give body to the creative efforts of younger men. They help turn impulse into reality, and then to shape and reshape it into a thousand useful products and services. They offer those characteristics in an executive to be admired and emulated. He shifts from quarterback to coach, from day-to-day operations to long-range planning. He becomes more consciously concerned with what he is going to leave behind.

Organizing for Renaissance

Third, organizations must take the middle-age period seriously in their thinking, planning, and programming. I know of no organization — business, university, church, or hospital — which does. No one knows how much effectiveness is lost.

If one of the needs for coping with middle-age stress is the opportunity to talk about it, then part of every supervisory and appraisal counseling should be devoted to some of the issues and concerns of this state. Company physicians or medical examining centers should provide time for the patient to talk with the doctor about the psychological aspects of his age and his life. Sessions devoted to examining how groups are working together should, if they are middle-aged groups, have this topic on the agenda. Company educational programs should inform both men and their wives about this period and its unique pressures. Personnel counselors should give explicit attention to this issue in their discussions.

Obviously, there should be a different slant to executive or managerial training programs for men over 35 than for those under 35. Pre-35 programs should be geared to keeping the younger men "loose." They should be encouraged to bubble, to tackle old problems afresh. This is not the time to indoctrinate men with rules and procedures, but rather to stimulate them toward their own horizons. Training challenges should be around tasks requiring sparkle, flashes of insight, and impulsive action.

Developmental programs for men over 35 should be concentrated largely on refreshment, keeping up, and conceptualization of problems and the organization. Tasks and problems requiring reorganization, reformulation, refining, and restructuring are tasks for men whose psychological time it is to rework. Brilliant innovative departures are unlikely to come from such men, except as they are the fruition of a lifetime of ferment, as was the *aggiornamento* of Pope John XXIII.

For them, instead, more attention should be given to frequent respites from daily organizational chores to get new views, to examine and digest them in work groups, and to think of their application to organizational problems and issues. When they move toward the future, they are likely to go in protected steps, like the man crawling on ice who pushes a plank before him. Pushing them hard to be free of the plank will tend to paralyze them into inaction. Rather, training programs should specifically include small experimental attempts to apply new skills and views with minimum risk.

Much of managerial training for these men should be focused on how to rear younger men. This means not only emphasis on coaching, counseling, teaching, and supporting, but also time and opportunity to talk about their feelings of rivalry and disappointment, to ventilate their anger at the young men who have it so good—the whole world at their feet and no place to go but up. Finally, it should include the opportunity for them to recognize, understand, and accept their uniquely human role. Instead of rejecting the younger men, they can then more comfortably place their bets and cheer their favorites on. In the youngsters' winning, they, too, can win.

For the executive, his subordinates, and the company, middle age can truly be a renaissance.

REFERENCES

1. "Clinical Health Age: 30–40," *Business Week*, March 3, 1956, p. 56.

2. Elliot Jaques, "Death and the Mid-Life Crisis," *The International Journal of Psychoanalysis*, October 1965, p. 502.

3. Unpublished.

4. Boston: Houghton Mifflin, 1967.

5. See "Management by Guilt" (Chapter 18) in my book *Emotional Health: in the World of Work* (New York: Harper & Row, 1964).

6. Jaques, op. cit., p. 503.

7. Anne Roe and Rhoda Baruch, "Occupational Changes in the Adult Years," *Personnel Administration*, July-August 1967, p. 32.

8. *Life*, February 28, 1969, p. 6.

9. "Adjustments and Reorientation in the Course of the Life Span," in *Middle Age and Aging*, edited by Bernice L. Neugarten (Chicago: University of Chicago Press, 1968), p. 81.

10. Quoted in Raymond G. Kuhlen, "Developmental Changes in Motivation During the Adult Years," in Bernice L. Neugarten, op. cit., p. 134.

11. Jaques, op. cit., p. 505.

12. *Childhood and Society* (New York: W.W. Norton, 1964), p. 13.

2

Can an Executive Afford a Conscience?

ALBERT Z. CARR

Ask a business executive whether his company employs child labor, and he will either think you are joking or be angered by the implied slur on his ethical standards. In the 1970's the employment of children in factories is clearly considered morally wrong as well as illegal.

Yet it was not until comparatively recently (1941) that the U.S. Supreme Court finally sustained the constitutionality of the long-contested Child Labor Act, which Congress had passed four years earlier. During most of the previous eight decades, the fact that children 10 years old worked at manual jobs for an average of 11 hours a day under conditions of virtual slavery had aroused little indignation in business circles.

To be sure, only a few industries found the practice profitable, and the majority of businessmen would doubtless have been glad to see it stopped. But in order to stop it the government had to act, and any interference with business by government was regarded as a crime against God, Nature, and Respectability. If a company sought to hold down production costs by employing children in factories where the work did not demand adult skills or muscle, that was surely a matter to be settled between the employer and the child's parents or the orphanage.

To permit legitimate private enterprise to be balked by unrealistic do-gooders was to open the gate to socialism and anarchy — such was the prevailing sentiment of businessmen, as shown in the business press, from the 1860's to the 1930's.

Every important advance in business ethics has been achieved through a long history of pain and protest.[1] The process of change begins when a previously accepted practice arouses misgivings among sensitive observers. Their efforts at moral suasion are usually ignored, however, until changes in economic conditions or new technology make the practice seem increasingly undesirable.

Businessmen who profit by the practice defend it heatedly, and a long period of public controversy ensues, climaxed at last by the adoption of laws forbidding it. After another 20 or 30 years, the new generation of businessmen regard the practice with retrospective moral indignation and wonder why it was ever tolerated.

A century of increasingly violent debate culminating in civil war had to be lived through before black slavery, long regarded as an excellent business proposition, was declared unlawful in the United States. To achieve laws forbidding racial discrimination in hiring practices required another century. It took 80 years of often bloody labor disputes to win acceptance of the principle of collective bargaining, and the country endured about 110 years of flagrant financial abuses before enactment of effective measures regulating banks and stock exchanges.

In time, all of these forward steps, once bitterly opposed by most businessmen, came to be accepted as part of the ethical foundation of the American private enterprise economy.

Jesse James vs. Nero

In the second half of the twentieth century, with the population, money supply, military power, and industrial technology of the United States expanding rapidly at the same time, serious new ethical issues have arisen for businessmen — notably the pollution of the biosphere, the concentration of economic power in a relatively few vast corporations, increasing military domination of the economy, and the complex interrelationship between business interests and the threat of war. These issues are the more formidable because they demand swift response; they will not wait a century or even a generation for a change in corporate ethics that will stimulate businessmen to act.

The problems they present to business and our society as a whole are immediate, critical, and worsening. If they are not promptly dealt with by farsighted and effective measures, they could even bring down political democracy and the entrepreneurial system together.

In fact, given the close relationship between our domestic economic situation and our military commitments abroad, and the perils implicit in the worldwide armaments buildup, it is not extreme to say that the extent to which businessmen are able to open their minds to new ethical imperatives in the decade ahead may have decisive influence in this century on the future of the human species.

Considering the magnitude of these rapidly developing issues, old standards of ethical judgment seem almost irrelevant. It is of course desirable that a businessman be honest in his accountings and faithful to his contracts — that he should not advertise misleadingly, rig prices, deceive stockholders, deny workers their due, cheat customers, spread false rumors about competitors, or stab associates in the back. Such a person has in the past qualified as "highly ethical," and he could feel morally superior to many of those he saw around him — the chiselers, the connivers, the betrayers of trust.

But standards of personal conduct in themselves are no longer an adequate index of business ethics. Everyone knows that a minority of businessmen commit commercial mayhem on each other and on the public with practices ranging from subtle conflicts of interest to the sale of injurious drugs and unsafe automobiles, but in the moral crisis through which we are living such tales of executive wrongdoing, like nudity in motion pictures, have lost their power to shock.

The public shrugs at the company president who conspires with his peers to fix prices. It grins at the vice president in charge of sales who provides call girls for a customer. After we have heard a few such stories, they become monotonous.

We cannot shrug or grin, however, at the refusal of powerful corporations to take vigorous action against great dangers threatening the society, and to which they contribute. Compared with such a corporation or with the executive who is willing to jeopardize the health and well-being of an entire people in order to add something to current earnings, the man who merely embezzles company funds is as insignificant in the annals of morality as Jesse James is compared with Nero.

The moral position of the executive who works for a company that fails in the ethics of social responsibility is ambiguous. The fact that he does not control company policy cannot entirely exonerate him from blame. He is guilty, so to speak, by employment.

If he is aware that the company's factories pollute the environment or its products injure the consumer and he does not exert himself to change the related company policies, he becomes morally suspect. If he lends himself to devious evasions of laws against racial discrimination in hiring practices, he adds to the probability of destructive racial confrontations and is in some degree an agent of social disruption. If he knows that his company is involved in the bribery of legislators or government officials, or makes under-the-table deals with labor union officials, or uses the services of companies known to be controlled by criminal syndicates, he contributes through his work to disrespect for law and the spread of crime.

If his company, in its desire for military contracts, lobbies to oppose justifiable cuts in the government's enormous military budget, he bears some share of responsibility for the constriction of the civilian economy; for price inflation, urban decay, and shortages of housing, transportation, and schools; and for failure to mitigate the hardships of the poor.

From this standpoint, the carefully correct executive who never violates a law or fails to observe the canons of gentlemanly behavior may be as open to ethical challenge as the crooks and the cheaters.

"Toxins of Suppressed Guilt"

The practical question arises: If a man in a responsible corporate position finds that certain policies of his company are socially injurious, what can he do about it without jeopardizing his job?

Contrary to common opinion, he is not necessarily without recourse. The nature of that recourse I shall discuss in the final section of this article. Here, I want to point out that unless the executive's sense of social responsibility is accompanied by a high degree of realism about tactics, then he is likely to end in frustration or cynicism.

One executive of my acquaintance who wrote several memoranda to his chief, detailing instances of serious environmental contamination for which the company was responsible and which called for early remedy, was sharply rebuked for a "negative attitude."

Another, a successful executive of a large corporation, said to me quite seriously in a confidential moment that he did not think a man in a job like his could afford the luxury of a conscience in the office. He was frank to say that he had become unhappy about certain policies of his company. He could no longer deny to himself that the company was not living up to its social responsibilities and was engaged in some political practices that smacked of corruption.

But what were his options? He had only three that he could see, and he told me he disliked them all:

If he argued for a change in policies that were helping to keep net earnings high, he might be branded by his superiors as "unrealistic" or "idealistic"—adjectives that could check his career and might, if he pushed too hard, compel his resignation.

Continued silence not only would spoil his enjoyment of his work, but might cause him to lose respect for himself.

If he moved to one of the other companies in his industry, he would merely be exchanging one set of moral misgivings for another.

He added with a sigh that he envied his associates whose consciences had never developed beyond the Neanderthal stage and who had no difficulty in accepting things as they were. He said he wondered whether he ought not to try to discipline himself to be as indifferent as they to the social implications of policies which, after all, were common in business.

Perhaps he made this effort and succeeded in it, for he remained with the company and forged ahead. He may even have fancied that he had killed his conscience—as the narrator in Mark Twain's symbolic story did when he gradually reached the point where he could blithely murder the tramps who came to his door asking for handouts.

But conscience is never killed; when ignored, it merely goes underground, where it manufactures the toxins of suppressed guilt, often with serious psychological and physical consequences. The hard fact is that the executive who has a well-developed contemporary conscience is at an increasing disadvantage in business unless he is able to find some personal policy by which he can maintain his drive for success without serious moral reservations.

Distrustful Public

The problem faced by the ethically motivated man in corporate life is compounded by growing public distrust of business morality.

The corporation executive is popularly envied for his relative affluence and respected for his powers of achievement, but many people deeply suspect his ethics—as not a few successful businessmen have been informed by their children. Surveys made in a number of universities across the country indicate that a large majority of students aiming at college degrees are convinced that business is a dog-eat-dog proposition, with which most of them do not want to be connected.

This low opinion is by no means confined to youngsters; a poll of 2,000 representative Americans brought to light the belief of nearly half of them that "most businessmen would try anything, honest or not, for a buck."[2] The unfairness of the notion does not make it less significant as a clue to public opinion. (This poll also showed that most Americans are aware of the notable contributions of business to the material satisfactions of their lives; the two opinions are not inconsistent.)

Many businessmen, too, are deeply disturbed by the level of executive morality in their sphere of observation. Although about 90% of executives in another survey stated that they regarded themselves as "ethical," 80% affirmed "the presence of numerous generally accepted practices in their industry which they consider unethical," such as bribery of government officials, rigging of prices, and collusion in contract bidding.[3]

The public is by no means unaware of such practices. In conversations about business ethics with a cross-section sampling of citizens in a New England town, I found that they mentioned kickbacks and industrial espionage as often as embezzlement and fraud. One man pointed out that the kickback is now taken so much for granted in corporations that the Internal Revenue Service provides detailed instructions for businessmen on how to report income from this source on their tax returns.

The indifference of many companies to consumers' health and safety was a major source of criticism. Several of the persons interviewed spoke of conflicts of interest among corporation heads, accounts of which had been featured not long before in the press. Others had learned from television dramas about the ruthlessness of the struggle for survival and the hail-fellow hypocrisy that is common in executive offices.

Housewives drew on their shopping experience to denounce the decline in the quality of necessities for which they had to pay ever-higher prices. Two or three had read in *Consumer Reports* about "planned obsolescence."

I came to the conclusion that if my sample is at all representative—and I think it is—the public has learned more about the ways of men in corporate life than most boards of directors yet realize.

These opinions were voiced by people who for the most part had not yet given much thought to the part played by industrial wastes in the condition of the environment, or to the inroads made on their economic well-being by the influence of corporation lobbyists on military decision makers. It is to be expected that if, as a result of deteriorating social and economic conditions, these and other major concerns take on more meaning for the public, criticism of business ethics will widen and become sharper.

If the threats of widespread water shortage in the 1970's and of regional clean air shortages in the 1980's are allowed to materialize, and military expenditures continue to constrict civilian life, popular resentment may well be translated into active protest directed against many corporations as well as against the government. In that event, the moral pressure on individual executives will become increasingly acute.

Regard for public opinion certainly helped to influence many companies in the 1950's and 1960's to pledge to reduce their waste discharges into the air and water and to hire more people with dark skins. Such declarations were balm for the sore business conscience.

The vogue for "social responsibility" has now grown until, as one commentator put it, "pronouncements about social responsibility issue forth so abundantly from the corporations that it is hard for one to get a decent play in the press. Everybody is in on the act, and nearly all of them actually mean what they say!"[4] More than a few companies have spent considerable sums to advertise their efforts to protect a stream, clean up smokestack emissions, or train "hardcore unemployables."

These are worthy undertakings, as far as they have gone, but for the most part they have not gone very far. In 1970 it has become obvious that the performance of U.S. corporations in the area of social responsibility has generally been trivial, considering the scope of their operations.

Behind the Boardroom Door

No company that I have ever heard of employs a vice president in charge of ethical standards; and sooner or later the conscientious executive is likely to come up against a stone wall of corporate indifference to private moral values.

When the men who hold the real power in the company come together to decide policy, they may give lip service to the moral element in the issue, but not much more. The decision-making process at top-management levels has little room for social responsibilities not definitely required by law or public opinion.

Proposals that fail to promise an early payoff for the company and that involve substantial expense are accepted only if they represent a means of escaping drastic penalties, such as might be inflicted by a government suit, a labor strike, or a consumer boycott. To invest heavily in antipollution equipment or in programs for hiring and training workers on the fringe of employability, or to accept higher taxation in the interest of better education for the children of a community—for some distant, intangible return in a cloudy future—normally goes against the grain of every profit-minded management.

It could hardly be otherwise. In the prevailing concept of corporate efficiency, a continual lowering of costs relative to sales is cardinal. For low costs are a key not only to higher profits but to corporate maneuverability, to advantage in recruiting the best men, and to the ability to at least hold a share of a competitive market.

Of the savings accruing to a company from lowered costs, the fraction that finds its way into the area of social responsibility is usually miniscule. To expend such savings on nonremunerative activities is regarded as weakening the corporate structure.

The late Chester A. Barnard, one of the more enlightened business leaders of the previous generation and a man deeply concerned with ethics, voiced the position of management in the form of a question: "To what extent is one morally justified in loading a productive undertaking with heavy charges in the attempt to protect against a remote possibility, or even one not so remote?"[5] Speaking of accident prevention in plants, which he favored in principle, he warned that if the outlay for such a purpose weakened the company's finances, "the community might lose a service and the entrepreneur an opportunity."

Corporate managers apply the same line of reasoning to proposals for expenditure in the area of social responsibility. "We can't afford to sink that amount of money in nonproductive uses," they say, and, "We need all our cash for expansion."

The entrepreneur who is willing to accept some reduction of his income— the type is not unknown—may be able to operate his enterprise in a way that satisfies an active conscience; but a company with a competitive team of managers, a board of directors, and a pride of stockholders cannot harbor such an unbusinesslike intention.

Occasionally, statesmen, writers, and even some high-minded executives, such as the late Clarence B. Randall, have made the appeal of conscience to corporations. They have argued that, since the managers and directors of companies are for the most part men of goodwill in their private lives, their corporate decisions also should be guided by conscience.

Even the distinguished economist A.A. Berle, Jr. has expressed the view that the healthy development of our society requires "the growth of conscience" in the corporation of our time.[6] But if by "conscience" he meant a sense of right and wrong transcending the economic, he was asking the impossible.

A business that defined "right" and "wrong" in terms that would satisfy a well-developed contemporary conscience could not survive. No company can be expected to serve the social interest unless its self-interest is also served, either by the expectation of profit or by the avoidance of punishment.

"Gresham's Law" of Ethics

Before responsibility to the public can properly be brought into the framework of a top-management decision, it must have an economic justification. For instance, executives might say:

"We'd better install the new safety feature because, if we don't, we'll have the government on our necks, and the bad publicity will cost us more than we are now saving in production."

"We should spend the money for equipment to take the sulfides out of our smokestacks at the plant. Otherwise we'll have trouble recruiting labor and have a costly PR problem in the community."

It is worth noting that Henry Ford II felt constrained to explain to stockholders of the Ford Motor Company that his earnest and socially aware effort to recruit workers from Detroit's "hard-core unemployed" was a preventive measure against the recurrence of ghetto riots carrying a threat to the company.

In another situation, when a number of life insurance companies agreed to invest money in slum reconstruction at interest rates somewhat below the market, their executives were quick to forestall possible complaints from stockholders by pointing out that they were opening up future markets for life insurance. Rationally, the successful corporate manager can contemplate expense for the benefit of society only if failure to spend points to an eventual loss of security or opportunity that exceeds the cost.

There can be no conscience without a sense of personal responsibility, and the corporation, as Ambrose Bierce remarked, is "an ingenious device for obtaining individual profit without individual responsibility." When the directors and managers of a corporation enter the boardroom to debate policy, they park their private consciences outside.

If they did not subordinate their inner scruples to considerations of profitability and growth, they would fail in their responsibility to the company that pays them. A kind of Gresham's Law of ethics operates here; the ethic of corporate advantage invariably silences and drives out the ethic of individual self-restraint.

(This, incidentally, is true at every level of the corporate structure. An executive who adheres to ethical standards disregarded by his associates is asking for trouble. No one, for example, is so much hated in a purchasing department where graft is rife as the man who refuses to take kickbacks from suppliers, for he threatens the security of the others. Unless he conforms, they are all too likely to "get him.")

The crucial question in boardroom meetings where social responsibility is discussed is not, "Are we morally obligated to do it?" but, rather, "What will happen if we don't do it?" or, perhaps, "How will this affect the rate of return on investment?"

If the house counsel assures management that there will be no serious punishment under the law if the company does not take on the added expense, and the marketing man sees no danger to sales, and the public relations man is confident he can avoid injury to the corporate image, then the money, if it amounts to any considerable sum, will not be spent—social responsibility or no social responsibility.

Even the compulsion of law is often regarded in corporate thinking as an element in a contest between government and the corporation, rather than as a description of "right" and "wrong." The files of the Federal Trade Commission, the Food and Drug Administration, and other government agencies are filled with records of respectable companies that have not hesitated to break or stretch the law when they believed they could get away with it.

It is not unusual for company managements to break a law, even when they expect to be caught, if they calculate that the fine they eventually must pay represents only a fraction of the profits that the violation will enable them to collect in the meantime. More than one corporate merger has been announced to permit insiders to make stock-market killings even though the companies concerned recognized that the antitrust laws would probably compel their eventual separation.

What Can the Executive Do?

One can dream of a big-business community that considers it sound economics to sacrifice a portion of short-term profits in order to protect the environment and reduce social tensions.

It is theoretically conceivable that top managers as a class may come to perceive the profound dangers, for the free-enterprise system and for themselves, in the trend toward the militarization of our society, and will press the government to resist the demand for nonessential military orders and overpermissive contracts from sections of industry and elements in the Armed Services. At the same level of wishfulness, we can imagine the federal government making it clear to U.S. companies investing abroad that protection of their investments is not the government's responsibility.

We can even envisage a time when the bonds of a corporation that is responsive to social needs will command a higher rating by Moody's than those of a company that neglects such values, since the latter is more vulnerable to public condemnation; and a time when a powerful Executive League for Social Responsibility will come into being to stimulate and assist top managements in formulating long-range economic policies that embrace social issues. In such a private-enterprise utopia the executive with a social conscience would be able to work without weakening qualms.

In the real world of today's business, however, he is almost sure to be a troubled man. Perhaps there are some executives who are so strongly positioned that they can afford to urge their managements to accept a reduced rate of return on investment for the sake of the society of which they are a part. But for the large majority of corporate employees who want to keep their jobs and win their superiors' approbation, to propose such a thing would be inviting oneself to the corporate guillotine.

He Is Not Powerless

But this does not necessarily mean that the ethically motivated executive can do nothing. In fact, if he does nothing, he may so bleach his conception of himself as a man of conviction as to reduce his personal force and value to the company. His situation calls for sagacity as well as courage. Whatever ideas he advocates to express his sense of social responsibility must be shaped to the company's interests.

Asking management flatly to place social values ahead of profits would be foolhardy, but if he can demonstrate that, on the basis of long-range profitability, the concept of corporate efficiency needs to be broadened to include social values, he may be able to make his point without injury—indeed, with benefit—to his status in the company. A man respected for competence in his job, who knows how to justify ethically based programs in economic terms and to overcome elements of resistance in the psychology of top management, may well be demonstrating his own qualifications for top management.

In essence, any ethically oriented proposal made to a manager is a proposal to take a longer-range view of his problems—to lift his sights. Nonethical practice is shortsighted almost by definition, if for no other reason than that it exposes the company to eventual reprisals.

The longer range a realistic business projection is, the more likely it is to find a sound ethical footing. I would go so far as to say that almost anything an executive does, on whatever level, to extend the range of thinking of his superiors tends to effect an ethical advance.

The hope and the opportunity of the individual executive with a contemporary conscience lies in the constructive connection of the long economic view with the socially aware outlook. He must show convincingly a net advantage for the corporation in accelerating expenditures or accepting other costs in the sphere of social responsibility.

I was recently able to observe an instance in which an executive persuaded his company's management to make a major advance in its antipollution policy. His presentation of the alternatives, on which he had spent weeks of careful preparation, showed in essence that, under his plan, costs which would have to be absorbed over a three-year period would within six years prove to be substantially less than the potential costs of less vigorous action.

When he finished his statement, no man among his listeners, not even his most active rivals, chose to resist him. He had done more than serve his company and satisfy his own ethical urge; he had shown that the gap between the corporate decision and the private conscience is not unbridgeable if a person is strong enough, able enough, and brave enough to do what needs to be done.

It may be that the future of our enterprise system will depend on the emergence of a sufficient number of men of this breed who believe that in order to save itself business will be impelled to help save the society.

REFERENCES

1. For amplifications of this view, see Robert W. Austin, "Responsibility for Social Change," HBR July-August 1965, p. 45; and Theodore Levitt, "Why Business Always Loses," HBR March-April 1968, p. 81.

2. Louis B. Harris and Associates, in a survey reported at a National Industrial Conference Board meeting, April 21, 1966.

3. Raymond C. Baumhart, S.J., "How Ethical Are Businessmen?" HBR July-August 1961, p. 6.

4. Theodore Levitt, "The Dangers of Social Responsibility," HBR September-October 1958, p. 41.

5. *Elementary Conditions of Business Morals* (Berkeley: Committee on the Barbara Weinstock Lectures, University of California, 1958).

6. *The Twentieth Century Capitalist Revolution* (New York: Harcourt, Brace, 1954), pp. 113–114.

3

Why "Good" Managers Make Bad Ethical Choices

SAUL W. GELLERMAN

How could top-level executives at the Manville Corporation have suppressed evidence for decades that proved that asbestos inhalation was killing
their own employees?

What could have driven the managers of Continental Illinois Bank to pursue
a course of action that threatened to bankrupt the institution, ruined its reputation, and cost thousands of innocent employees and investors their jobs and
their savings?

Why did managers at E.F. Hutton find themselves pleading guilty to 2,000
counts of mail and wire fraud, accepting a fine of $2 million, and putting up an
$8 million fund for restitution to the 400 banks that the company had system-
atically bilked?

How can we explain the misbehavior that took place in these
organizations—or in any of the others, public and private, that litter our newspapers' front pages: workers at a defense contractor who accused their superiors
of falsifying time cards; alleged bribes and kickbacks that honeycombed New
York City government; a company that knowingly marketed an unsafe birth
control device; the decision-making process that led to the space shuttle Challenger tragedy.

The stories are always slightly different; but they have a lot in common
since they're full of the oldest questions in the world, questions of human behavior and human judgment applied in ordinary day-to-day situations. Reading
them we have to ask how usually honest, intelligent, compassionate human beings
could act in ways that are callous, dishonest, and wrongheaded.

In my view, the explanations go back to four rationalizations that people have relied on through the ages to justify questionable conduct: believing
that the activity is not "really" illegal or immoral; that it is in the individual's or
the corporation's best interest; that it will never be found out; or that because
it helps the company the company will condone it. By looking at these rationalizations in light of these cases, we can develop some practical rules to more
effectively control managers' actions that lead to trouble—control, but not eliminate. For the hard truth is that corporate misconduct, like the lowly cockroach,
is a plague that we can suppress but never exterminate.

280

Three Cases

Amitai Etzioni, professor of sociology at George Washington University, recently concluded that in the last ten years, roughly two-thirds of America's 500 largest corporations have been involved, in varying degrees, in some form of illegal behavior. By taking a look at three corporate cases, we may be able to identify the roots of the kind of misconduct that not only ruins some people's lives, destroys institutions, and gives business as a whole a bad name but that also inflicts real and lasting harm on a large number of innocent people. The three cases that follow should be familiar. I present them here as examples of the types of problems that confront managers in all kinds of businesses daily.

Manville Corporation

A few years ago, Manville (then Johns Manville) was solid enough to be included among the giants of American business. Today Manville is in the process of turning over 80% of its equity to a trust representing people who have sued or plan to sue it for liability in connection with one of its principal former products, asbestos. For all practical purposes, the entire company was brought down by questions of corporate ethics.

More than 40 years ago, information began to reach Johns Manville's medical department—and through it, the company's top executives—implicating asbestos inhalation as a cause of asbestosis, a debilitating lung disease, as well as lung cancer and mesothelioma, an invariably fatal lung disease. Manville's managers suppressed the research. Moreover, as a matter of policy, they apparently decided to conceal the information from affected employees. The company's medical staff collaborated in the cover-up, for reasons we can only guess at.

Money may have been one motive. In one particularly chilling piece of testimony, a lawyer recalled how 40 years earlier he had confronted Manville's corporate counsel about the company's policy of concealing chest X-ray results from employees. The lawyer had asked, "Do you mean to tell me you would let them work until they dropped dead?" The reply was, "Yes, we save a lot of money that way."

Based on such testimony, a California court found that Manville had hidden the asbestos danger from its employees rather than looking for safer ways to handle it. It was less expensive to pay workers' compensation claims than to develop safer working conditions. A New Jersey court was even blunter: it found that Manville had made a conscious, cold-blooded business decision to take no protective or remedial action, in flagrant disregard of the rights of others.

How can we explain this behavior? Were more than 40 years' worth of Manville executives all immoral?

Such an answer defies common sense. The truth, I think, is less glamorous—and also less satisfying to those who like to explain evil as the actions of a few misbegotten souls. The people involved were probably ordinary men and women for the most part, not very different from you and me. They found themselves in a dilemma, and they solved it in a way that seemed to be the least troublesome, deciding not to disclose information that could hurt their product. The consequences of what they chose to do—both to thousands of innocent people and, ultimately, to the corporation—probably never occurred to them.

The Manville case illustrates the fine line between acceptable and unacceptable managerial behavior. Executives are expected to strike a difficult balance—to pursue their companies' best interests but not overstep the bounds of what outsiders will tolerate.

Even the best managers can find themselves in a bind, not knowing how far is too far. In retrospect, they can usually easily tell where they should have drawn the line, but no one manages in retrospect. We can only live and act today and hope that whoever looks back on what we did will judge that we struck the proper balance. In a few years, many of us may be found delinquent for decisions we are making now about tobacco, clean air, the use of chemicals, or some other seemingly benign substance. The managers at Manville may have believed that they were acting in the company's best interests, or that what they were doing would never be found out, or even that it wasn't really wrong. In the end, these were only rationalizations for conduct that brought the company down.

Continental Illinois Bank

Until recently the ninth largest bank in the United States, Continental Illinois had to be saved from insolvency because of bad judgment by management. The government bailed it out, but at a price. In effect it has been socialized: about 80% of its equity now belongs to the Federal Deposit Insurance Corporation. Continental seems to have been brought down by managers who misunderstood its real interests. To their own peril, executives focused on a single-minded pursuit of corporate ends and forgot about the means to the ends.

In 1976, Continental's chairman declared that within five years the magnitude of its lending would match that of any other bank. The goal was attainable; in fact, for a time, Continental reached it. But it dictated a shift in strategy away from conservative corporate financing and toward aggressive pursuit of borrowers. So Continental, with lots of lendable funds, sent its loan officers into the field to buy loans that had originally been made by smaller banks that had less money.

The practice in itself was not necessarily unsound. But some of the smaller banks had done more than just lend money—they had swallowed hook, line, and sinker the extravagant, implausible dreams of poorly capitalized oil producers in Oklahoma, and they had begun to bet enormous sums on those dreams. Eventually, a cool billion dollars' worth of those dreams found their way into Continental's portfolio, and a cool billion dollars of depositors' money flowed out to pay for them. When the price of oil fell, a lot of dry holes and idle drilling equipment were all that was left to show for most of the money.

Continental's officers had become so entranced by their lending efforts' spectacular results that they hadn't looked deeply into how they had been achieved. Huge sums of money were lent at fat rates of interest. If the borrowers had been able to repay the loans, Continental might have become the eighth or even the seventh largest bank in the country. But that was a very big "if." Somehow there was a failure of control and judgment at Continental—probably because the officers who were buying those shaky loans were getting support and praise from their superiors. Or at least they were not hearing enough tough questions about them.

At one point, for example, Continental's internal auditors stumbled across the fact that an officer who had purchased $800 million in oil and gas loans from the Penn Square Bank in Oklahoma City had also borrowed $565,000 for himself from Penn Square. Continental's top management investigated and eventually issued a reprimand. The mild rebuke reflected the officer's hard work and the fact that the portfolio he had obtained would have yielded an average return of nearly 20% had it ever performed as planned. In fact, virtually all of the $800 million had to be written off. Management chose to interpret the incident charitably; federal prosecutors later alleged a kickback.

On at least two other occasions, Continental's own control mechanisms flashed signals that something was seriously wrong with the oil and gas portfolio. A vice president warned in a memo that the documentation needed to verify the soundness of many of the purchased loans had simply never arrived. Later, a junior loan officer, putting his job on the line, went over the heads of three superiors to tell a top executive about the missing documentation. Management chose not to investigate. After all, Continental was doing exactly what its chairman had said it would do: it was on its way to becoming the leading commercial lender in the United States. Oil and gas loans were an important factor in that achievement. Stopping to wait for paperwork to catch up would only slow down reaching the goal.

Eventually, however, the word got out about the instability of the bank's portfolio, which led to a massive run on its deposits. No other bank was willing to come to the rescue, for fear of being swamped by Continental's huge liabilities. To avoid going under, Continental in effect became a ward of the federal government. The losers were the bank's shareholders, some officers who lost their jobs, at least one who was indicted, and some 2,000 employees (about 15% of the total) who were let go, as the bank scaled down to fit its diminished assets.

Once again, it is easy for us to sit in judgment after the fact and say that Continental's loan officers and their superiors were doing exactly what bankers shouldn't do: they were gambling with their depositors' money. But on another level, this story is more difficult to analyze—and more generally a part of everyday business. Certainly part of Continental's problem was neglect of standard controls. But another dimension involved ambitious corporate goals. Pushed by lofty goals, managers could not see clearly their real interests. They focused on ends, overlooked the ethical questions associated with their choice of means— and ultimately hurt themselves.

E.F. Hutton

The nation's second largest independent broker, E.F. Hutton & Company, recently pleaded guilty to 2,000 counts of mail and wire fraud. It had systematically bilked 400 of its banks by drawing against uncollected funds or in some cases against nonexistent sums, which it then covered after having enjoyed interest-free use of the money. So far, Hutton has agreed to pay a fine of $2 million as well as the government's investigation costs of $750,000. It has set up an $8 million reserve for restitution to the banks—which may not be enough. Several officers have lost their jobs, and some indictments may yet follow.

But worst of all, Hutton has tarnished its reputation, never a wise thing to do—certainly not when your business is offering to handle other people's money. Months after Hutton agreed to appoint new directors—as a way to give outsiders a solid majority on the board—the company couldn't find people to accept the seats, in part because of the bad publicity.

Apparently Hutton's branch managers had been encouraged to pay close attention to cash management. At some point, it dawned on someone that using other people's money was even more profitable than using your own. In each case, Hutton's overdrafts involved no large sums. But cumulatively, the savings on interest that would otherwise have been owed to the banks was very large. Because Hutton always made covering deposits, and because most banks did not object, Hutton assured its managers that what they were doing was sharp—and not shady. They presumably thought they were pushing legality to its limit without going over the line. The branch managers were simply taking full advantage of what the law and the bankers' tolerance permitted. On several occasions, the managers who played this game most astutely were even congratulated for their skill.

Hutton probably will not suffer a fate as drastic as Manville's or Continental Illinois's. Indeed, with astute damage control, it can probably emerge from this particular embarrassment with only a few bad memories. But this case has real value because it is typical of much corporate misconduct. Most improprieties don't cut a corporation off at the knees the way Manville's and Continental Illinois's did. In fact, most such actions are never revealed at all—or at least that's how people figure things will work out. And in many cases, a willingness to gamble thus is probably enhanced by the rationalization—true or not—that everyone else is doing something just as bad or would if they could; that those who wouldn't go for their share are idealistic fools.

Four Rationalizations

Why do managers do things that ultimately inflict great harm on their companies, themselves, and people on whose patronage or tolerance their organizations depend? These three cases, as well as the current crop of examples in each day's paper, supply ample evidence of the motivations and instincts that underlie corporate misconduct. Although the particulars may vary—from the gruesome dishonesty surrounding asbestos handling to the mundanity of illegal money management—the motivating beliefs are pretty much the same. We may examine them in the context of the corporation, but we know that these feelings are basic throughout society; we find them wherever we go because we take them with us.

When we look more closely at these cases, we can delineate four commonly held rationalizations that can lead to misconduct:

A belief that the activity is within reasonable ethical and legal limits—that is, that it is not "really" illegal or immoral.

A belief that the activity is in the individual's or the corporation's best interests—that the individual would somehow be expected to undertake the activity.

A belief that the activity is "safe" because it will never be found out or publicized; the classic crime-and-punishment issue of discovery.

A belief that because the activity helps the company the company will condone it and even protect the person who engages in it.

The idea that an action is not really wrong is an old issue. How far is too far? Exactly where is the line between smart and too smart? Between sharp and shady? Between profit maximization and illegal conduct? The issue is complex: it involves an interplay between top management's goals and middle managers' efforts to interpret those aims.

Put enough people in an ambiguous, ill-defined situation, and some will conclude that whatever hasn't been labeled specifically wrong must be OK—especially if they are rewarded for certain acts. Deliberate overdrafts, for example, were not proscribed at Hutton. Since the company had not spelled out their illegality, it could later plead guilty for itself while shielding its employees from prosecution.

Top executives seldom ask their subordinates to do things that both of them know are against the law or imprudent. But company leaders sometimes leave things unsaid or give the impression that there are things they don't want to know about. In other words, they can seem, whether deliberately or otherwise, to be distancing themselves from their subordinates' tactical decisions in order to keep their own hands clean if things go awry. Often they lure ambitious lower level managers by implying that rich rewards await those who can produce certain results—and that the methods for achieving them will not be examined too closely. Continental's simple wrist-slapping of the officer who was caught in a flagrant conflict of interest sent a clear message to other managers about what top management really thought was important.

How can managers avoid crossing a line that is seldom precise? Unfortunately, most know that they have overstepped it only when they have gone too far. They have no reliable guidelines about what will be overlooked or tolerated or what will be condemned or attacked. When managers must operate in murky borderlands, their most reliable guideline is an old principle: when in doubt, don't.

That may seem like a timid way to run a business. One could argue that if it actually took hold among the middle managers who run most companies, it might take the enterprise out of free enterprise. But there is a difference between taking a worthwhile economic risk and risking an illegal act to make more money.

The difference between becoming a success and becoming a statistic lies in knowledge—including self-knowledge—not daring. Contrary to popular mythology, managers are not paid to take risks; they are paid to know which risks are worth taking. Also, maximizing profits is a company's second priority, not its first. The first is ensuring its survival.

All managers risk giving too much because of what their companies demand from them. But the same superiors who keep pressing you to do more, or to do it better, or faster, or less expensively, will turn on you should you cross that fuzzy line between right and wrong. They will blame you for exceeding instructions or for ignoring their warnings. The smartest managers already know that the best answer to the question, "How far is too far?" is don't try to find out.

Turning to the second reason why people take risks that get their companies into trouble, believing that unethical conduct is in a person's or corporation's best interests nearly always results from a parochial view of what those interests are. For example, Alpha Industries, a Massachusetts manufacturer of microwave equipment, paid $57,000 to a Raytheon manager, ostensibly for a marketing report. Air force investigators charged that the report was a ruse to cover a bribe: Alpha wanted subcontracts that the Raytheon manager supervised. But those contracts ultimately cost Alpha a lot more than they paid for the report. After the company was indicted for bribery, its contracts were suspended and its profits promptly vanished. Alpha wasn't unique in this transgression: in 1984, the Pentagon suspended 453 other companies for violating procurement regulations.

Ambitious managers look for ways to attract favorable attention, something to distinguish them from other people. So they try to outperform their peers. Some may see that it is not difficult to look remarkably good in the short run by avoiding things that pay off only in the long run. For example, you can skimp on maintenance or training or customer service, and you can get away with it—for a while.

The sad truth is that many managers have been promoted on the basis of "great" results obtained in just those ways, leaving unfortunate successors to inherit the inevitable whirlwind. Since this is not necessarily a just world, the problems that such people create are not always traced back to them. Companies cannot afford to be hoodwinked in this way. They must be concerned with more than just results. They have to look very hard at how results are obtained.

Evidently, in Hutton's case there were such reviews, but management chose to interpret favorably what government investigators later interpreted unfavorably. This brings up another dilemma: management quite naturally hopes that any of its borderline actions will be overlooked or at least interpreted charitably if noticed. Companies must accept human nature for what it is and protect themselves with watchdogs to sniff out possible misdeeds.

An independent auditing agency that reports to outside directors can play such a role. It can provide a less comfortable, but more convincing, review of how management's successes are achieved. The discomfort can be considered inexpensive insurance and serve to remind all employees that the real interests of the company are served by honest conduct in the first place.

The third reason why a risk is taken, believing that one can probably get away with it, is perhaps the most difficult to deal with because it's often true. A great deal of proscribed behavior escapes detection.

We know that conscience alone does not deter everyone. For example, First National Bank of Boston pleaded guilty to laundering satchels of $20 bills worth $1.3 billion. Thousands of satchels must have passed through the bank's doors without incident before the scheme was detected. That kind of heavy, unnoticed traffic breeds complacency.

How can we deter wrongdoing that is unlikely to be detected? Make it more likely to be detected. Had today's "discovery" process—in which plaintiff's attorneys can comb through a company's records to look for incriminating evidence—been in use when Manville concealed the evidence on asbestosis, there probably would have been no cover-up. Mindful of the likelihood of detection, Manville would have chosen a different course and could very well be thriving today without the protection of the bankruptcy courts.

The most effective deterrent is not to increase the severity of punishment for those caught but to heighten the perceived probability of being caught in the first place. For example, police have found that parking an empty patrol car at locations where motorists often exceed the speed limit reduces the frequency of speeding. Neighborhood "crime watch" signs that people display decrease burglaries.

Simply increasing the frequency of audits and spot checks is a deterrent, especially when combined with three other simple techniques: scheduling audits irregularly, making at least half of them unannounced, and setting up some checkups soon after others. But frequent spot checks cost more than big sticks, a fact that raises the question of which approach is more cost-effective.

A common managerial error is to assume that because frequent audits uncover little behavior that is out of line, less frequent, and therefore less costly, auditing is sufficient. But this condition overlooks the important deterrent effect of frequent checking. The point is to prevent misconduct, not just to catch it.

A trespass detected should not be dealt with discreetly. Managers should announce the misconduct and how the individuals involved were punished. Since the main deterrent to illegal or unethical behavior is the perceived probability of detection, managers should make an example of people who are detected.

Let's look at the fourth reason why corporate misconduct tends to occur, a belief that the company will condone actions that are taken in its interest and will even protect the managers responsible. The question we have to deal with here is, How do we keep company loyalty from going berserk?

That seems to be what happened at Manville. A small group of executives and a succession of corporate medical directors kept the facts about the lethal qualities of asbestos from becoming public knowledge for decades, and they managed to live with that knowledge. And at Manville, the company — or really, the company's senior management — did condone their decision and protect those employees.

Something similar seems to have happened at General Electric. When one of its missile projects ran up costs greater than the air force had agreed to pay, middle managers surreptitiously shifted those costs to projects that were still operating under budget. In this case, the loyalty that ran amok was primarily to the division: managers want their units' results to look good. But GE, with one of the finest reputations in U.S. industry, was splattered with scandal and paid a fine of $1.04 million.

One of the most troubling aspects of the GE case is the company's admission that those involved were thoroughly familiar with the company's ethical standards before the incident took place. This suggests that the practice of declaring codes of ethics and teaching them to managers is not enough to deter unethical conduct. Something stronger is needed.

Top management has a responsibility to exert a moral force within the company. Senior executives are responsible for drawing the line between loyalty to the company and action against the laws and values of the society in which the company must operate. Further, because that line can be obscured in the heat of the moment, the line has to be drawn well short of where reasonable men and women could begin to suspect that their rights had been violated. The company has to react long before a prosecutor, for instance, would have a strong enough case to seek an indictment.

Executives have a right to expect loyalty from employees against competitors and detractors, but not loyalty against the law, or against common morality, or against society itself. Managers must warn employees that a disservice to customers, and especially to innocent bystanders, cannot be a service to the company. Finally, and most important of all, managers must stress that excuses of company loyalty will not be accepted for acts that place its good name in jeopardy. To put it bluntly, superiors must make it clear that employees who harm other people allegedly for the company's benefit will be fired.

The most extreme examples of corporate misconduct were due, in hindsight, to managerial failures. A good way to avoid management oversights is to subject the control mechanisms themselves to periodic surprise audits, perhaps as a function of the board of directors. The point is to make sure that internal audits and controls are functioning as planned. It's a case of inspecting the inspectors and taking the necessary steps to keep the controls working efficiently. Harold

Geneen, former head of ITT, has suggested that the board should have an independent staff, something analogous to the Government Accounting Office, which reports to the legislative rather than the executive branch. In the end, it is up to top management to send a clear and pragmatic message to all employees that good ethics is still the foundation of good business.

4

The Loneliness of the Small-Business Owner

DAVID E. GUMPERT AND DAVID P. BOYD

When Daniel C. chose to abandon his 20-year career as a corporate executive and acquire a small structural steel company, he assumed that his prime concerns would be financing the venture and marketing his wares. Certainly these have been challenges, but they paled beside the unexpected demon that surfaced in his new life and for which he was totally unprepared. Its name, for want of a better, is loneliness.

Daniel reflects: "I'd never thought about loneliness before because I'd never met it. In corporate life, there was always someone to share ideas with—my boss or another colleague. They knew what I was saying because they had been there. In my former post, there were 15 fellow general managers and any number of junior managers to talk to.

"Now it seems I have no one. Sure, there is an association of structural steel people, but they are my competition. I learned early on that pricing talk is resolutely avoided at association meetings, but even if we don't talk about prices, there are tensions between us simply because we're competitors."

Daniel's new career also affected his personal relationships: "My wife just doesn't understand business. Sometimes I get impatient. She asks questions that are hard to answer without getting mad. If I complain that sales are slow, she tells me, 'Go out and sell more.' At times, despite myself, I snap at her. She asks the wrong question at the wrong time. She can't help it; she just doesn't understand."

Even friendships became a problem: "Old friends seemed to fade away. It wasn't in my makeup to work at building friendships in or out of business hours."

Daniel's difficulties are understandable. The long hours he devotes to business inhibit nonwork contacts, and at work he has no equals in stature or responsibility. But the loneliness of entrepreneurship takes its toll. To his surprise, Daniel realized that his new role as business owner aggravated the headaches and the ulcer that were his usual signs of stress.

Daniel's feelings and experience are common among small-company owners. In an earlier survey of this group we found a high incidence of physiological symptoms associated with stress.[1] Our present survey shows a strong correlation between stress and loneliness as well.

289

Of 210 owners who expressed an opinion when asked whether they "frequently feel a sense of loneliness," 109, or 52%, said they do. Moreover, this same group reported a much higher incidence of stress symptoms than those who said they do not feel lonely. In fact, we found that a respondent's perception of loneliness was closely correlated with his or her total stress score, which was derived by multiplying the number of symptoms by their frequency. Not surprisingly, loneliness was also strongly correlated with each of the disorders — back pain, chest pain, headache, impaired digestion, and insomnia — the entrepreneurs commonly exhibited.

In view of recent research on the interrelations among loneliness, stress, and poor health, this is a sobering finding. One review of clinical studies and published data, for example, concludes that loneliness contributes to premature death and is especially implicated in heart disease.[2]

While only a slight majority of respondents were aware of a recurring sense of loneliness, the percentage seems high to us given the stigma attached to the term. Because our society puts a premium on popularity, friendship, and gregariousness, acknowledging loneliness often implies inadequacy or even failure. In addition, many people assume that the lonely are responsible for their own situations and that resolution requires nothing more than making the effort. As a result, the lonely often find it embarrassing to discuss their plight until, or unless, it becomes overwhelming. Thus, it is surprising that so many achievement-oriented entrepreneurs would express an emotion with such negative connotations.

What accounts for the sense of isolation that so often besets small-company owners? What can they do to prevent and relieve it? We sought answers to these questions in follow-up interviews with a dozen respondents drawn from a mail survey. What we found relates directly to the pressures of small-business ownership.

On the one hand, loneliness reflects objective or environmental factors, such as the special nature of a small business and value conflicts between owners and those close to them — chiefly family and friends. On the other, it is also a response to internal or subjective pressures, including the need to project a strong image and a proclivity for individual achievement rather than group dynamics.

One or more of these variables can trigger or exacerbate an owner's sense of isolation. External and internal pressures may also interact: start-up ventures attract solitary persons who may, in turn, find that the need to be a strong leader isolates them even more.

Not all entrepreneurs with a marked sense of loneliness will have problems in all these areas, of course. But acknowledging and assessing loneliness are important for at least two reasons. First, based on the correlation we have shown between loneliness and stress, it is reasonable to assume that diminishing the loneliness entrepreneurs feel will reduce stress and improve the quality of their lives.

Second, without input from peers, friends, or family, entrepreneurs are unlikely to consider all relevant options and risks in their decision making. Reducing loneliness should improve decision making, therefore, and this, in turn, should improve financial results. One respondent underscored the advantage of discussing business problems openly when he noted: "Holding a business too close to yourself can make it die from lack of fresh air and thought. You need help."

Me, Myself and I

Smaller ventures have little room at the top. At the beginning, the people in charge and those at the bottom are usually one and the same. And even after the survival stage has passed, small companies tend to run lean because their limited resources are typically used to maximize sales and production rather than to recruit managerial talent. Founders fill in the lower levels through hiring, while keeping authority in their own hands.

As a consequence, entrepreneurs often lack colleagues with whom to share experiences, explore ideas, and commiserate. Among respondents to our survey, 68% reported that they had no confidant with whom they could share their deep concerns. Also, owners become more and more sequestered as demands on their time isolate them from others.

Ironically, the presence of partners does not necessarily change this pattern. In fact, it can make things worse. Our first survey showed that more than two-thirds of the respondents who began with partners eventually split up. Conflict among principals was the chief reason. Understandably, therefore, these owners approach the idea of a subsequent partnership reluctantly.

They also tend to regard later partnerships as inherently unequal because they have already invested so much time in their businesses. Impelled by a strong proprietary sense, they can become emotionally entangled in their companies. This tendency may explain why one respondent warned: "Treat the business like a public company."

The phenomenon of loneliness is perhaps most striking among those who exchange large organizations for the brave new world of small business. "It's a big change," recalls Jack F., who left a large employment agency after four years to start his own executive placement service. "It's definitely nicer to have someone around. For five minutes you take a break and talk about the Red Sox or the Celtics. Or you share your frustrations about the business."

Even when a one-person business begins to hire, loneliness may not abate. Indeed, for Jack, the loneliness intensified when his venture passed the survival stage and he hired two job placement counselors to handle the rising work load. For one thing, "there's this distance you have to maintain as manager," he observes. For another, the financial burden of his expanded payroll created unbearable stress: "I suddenly got my asthma back, and I suspect stress was a good portion of it. . . . I had it last when I was five years old and was told later that when you get rid of it at that age, you usually don't have it again for the rest of your life. The last two years I have been going for allergy shots."

While some entrepreneurs worry about the physiological effects of excessive isolation, others are more concerned with its adverse effect on decision making. Alan C., owner of a company that manufactures electrical parts, questions the notion of making decisions without consultation: "All you're getting is your own feedback. The best way to make important decisions is to talk to somebody else. I can remember when I left my job at Texas Instruments to start this company. One thing that really hit me was how lonely it was. I was used to sitting down with a bunch of guys who knew the problems I was facing and drawing from their knowledge. Suddenly there was no one I could do that with."

When isolation replaces brainstorming, the pressure of decision making increases. Owners like Alan want to feel that they have made the right decisions.

But evaluating their own performance in the absence of trusted peers is stressful in its own right and becomes more so when comparative standards are also lacking. Competitive persons crave benchmarks to measure success. But the owner of a young business is likely to have few.

Closing Out Family and Friends

When owners and those close to them subscribe to different values, the loneliness inherent in running a small business is intensified. It is therefore disturbing to note that the demands of entrepreneurship may actually foster divergent values.

Spouses and children want to share their problems and accomplishments, and friends of long standing may wish to maintain social contact. But entrepreneurs, predictably, are preoccupied with venture survival and growth—business-oriented values. They are apt to view any respite from work as lost business. As the parties grow apart, relationships that once were close and supportive become distant and strained.

Worse yet, when entrepreneurs find themselves marooned in their business pursuits, they often become angry and resentful.

For Joseph S., the owner of a three-year-old collection agency, separation from family and friends has provoked feelings verging on desperation. "I carry this business with me," he says. "I went to a doctor recently for a checkup because I felt the stress was affecting me. I had a complete examination and there was nothing physically wrong. But I seem to experience a lot of anxiety. I'm relating to the business practically 24 hours a day. I carry a calculator with me everywhere I go. When I sit at home at night, I'm figuring things out."

Family and friends give Joseph scant relief. "I've tried my family on some things. We have light conversations at home—how is the business, and that sort of thing. But we don't get into specifics. They know I have problems, but they're not in a position to do anything about them." As for friends, "They're people who don't own a business. They're not aware of the problems, and they don't really care about them."

Estranged and isolated, Joseph says, "I feel alone and lonely. I have difficulty enjoying the fruits of my labor."

His remedy, unfortunately, is far from ideal. "If I want to come up with a new marketing plan, I'm not going to talk to my competition. I can't do that. There is no one else, so I discuss these things with customers, which really isn't right. I end up giving them a lot of inside information about the business."

Judy K.'s experience with personal relationships contrasts sharply with Joseph's. The owner of a files-on-microfilm service, she has been subject to chronic migraine, heart palpitation, insomnia, and an ulcer for most of her 11-year business career. In the past year, however, her symptoms have subsided. This change coincides with her marriage to a man who is "very interested in what I do, so I have someone to talk to. That's been a big help."

Judy's participation in a peer group of six business owners from noncompeting professions also helped her reduce stress. "We get together once a month for lunch. If I've heard some promising information, I pass it along. Someone else might tell me where to sell my microfilm service. Also, when I've been trying a sales approach that doesn't work, someone might help me rewrite my package or tell me what I'm doing wrong. It's a good support group—sort of a misery-loves-company thing."

The Marlboro Man

Poker players soon learn to contain their emotions lest frowns, smiles, sighs, or chuckles give away their cards. Small-business owners are like poker players except that their "opponents" are suppliers, bankers, competitors, and employees.

Robert M., owner of a company making accoustic materials, observes: "If I have something as simple as an upset stomach, I can't let people know, because they will construe it as weakness. Suppliers, competitors, and customers are all looking for signs of something. They are trying to read me, and an upset stomach means 'He must have a rough business.' They don't know that pizza the night before was a factor. So I have to be cautious about what I say."

Robert believes that his approach is especially important with employees, who "want to know that they have an income today, tomorrow, next week, next year. They want to know that they have a chance for growth and that things will be comfortable for them. Threaten that and they do irrational things. Their work quality may fall off and they may lose interest in the job. So if I come in with a nervous stomach, the employees think something has happened to the business. They wonder what it's going to do to them, and they're scared."

Robert summarizes his attitude this way: "I don't want anybody to know my weaknesses. They might regard them as worse than they are, and this perception could work against me." Moreover, he believes that he should appear to have all the answers because he's the boss.

Robert's way of dealing with his employees hasn't been entirely successful, however. Recently he spent several years prosecuting two senior managers whom he suspected of embezzlement. Being out of touch with his employees cost the company thousands of dollars and seriously aggravated his health problems. Now 58, Robert has a chronic heart condition as well as recurring indigestion and insomnia.

Robert's reluctance to admit difficulties was common among our interviewees. It certainly makes sense for start-up entrepreneurs, who must mobilize assorted individuals and project unwavering faith in their ventures. But over time, the need to be a tower of strength may lose its usefulness and become a burden. Our study shows that this attitude exaggerates an owner's feeling of loneliness and heightens the symptoms of stress.

Those who act less defensively find the results rewarding. Betty G., the owner of a company that makes specialty housing supplies, has always made a point of "having a lot of fun" with her 35 employees, most of whom are less than half her age. Until last year, when her business passed the $1 million sales mark and she hired a plant and office manager, she worked alongside them. "They're a great bunch and I've stayed friends with them all, even the ones I laid off."

Solitary Pursuits

A composite profile of the entrepreneur is difficult, perhaps impossible, to draw, as research yields conflicting results about such individuals' needs and aspirations. Having conducted studies, however, we can safely state that small-company principals lean toward solitary activities. At work and play, they favor environments free from involvement with others.

Independence and the opportunity for unimpeded creativity are the factors that give owners the greatest satisfaction, we find. Entrepreneurs like to make decisions about critical matters without the blessing of superiors. They scorn bureaucracy, shun milieus where pyramidal power and the politics of patrons determine success, and they seek to manage their own lives totally.

Thus, although Daniel bemoans the loneliness that is part of his new life, he would rather continue as sole helmsman than return to the corporate world. "I'm not competing with anyone here. In corporate life, I was competing with everybody. If one of my decisions didn't work out, you'd better believe there were six other guys in the company saying it was my fault. In my own business, the only competition is outside." Work is so much fun now that he would cheerfully skip vacations if he could: "The only reason I go on vacation is to take my family away."

Our respondents also preferred solitary pursuits outside business hours. Activities that emphasize individual accomplishment, such as sailing, flying, mountain climbing, and swimming, ranked high among their avocations. In contrast, they showed little interest in team sports such as basketball or softball.

Douglas E., the owner of an 11-year-old commercial printing business, likes flying for the sheer solitude it imposes. This all-engaging hobby "takes the place of" his real business and lets him jettison marketplace concerns. "There is nothing like flying and being 'lonely at the top,' if you will. It's truly an exhilarating experience. My nerve problems started soon after I sold that plane back in 1976."

His nerve problems were attacks of panic during which he was certain he was having a heart attack or stroke. He would experience a feeling of impending doom, sweat profusely, and suffer chest pain. After medical consultation, Douglas decided to resume flying and pursue sports more actively. In addition to flying, he now skis, hang-glides, and climbs mountains. Most recently, he has taken on a new pursuit, climbing trees. "I just bought tree-climbing gear," he says. "I have an acre and a quarter, all wooded, so I have trees to climb and prune."

Alan feels similarly about hang-gliding. "It's something you can do where you're really alone. You depend on yourself. It's like mountain climbing, but for those of us who don't want to crawl our way up mountains."

Avocations need not be sports. For Joseph, the collection agency owner who complained about alienation, the stock market is an outlet. "The time I don't spend on the business, I spend investing," he says. "That's why I have the TV here, so I can watch the stock market during the day. I enjoy that. I can get on the phone and buy or sell. When it works out, it shows I made the right decision and did my homework."

Solo activities are satisfying for the immediate feedback on performance and the sense of control they provide. Yet pursued too keenly, they further reduce the personal ties that might relieve loneliness.

Taming the Demon

Loneliness does not disappear with time. Experienced owners report its presence as often as do start-up entrepreneurs. Thus it seems that small-company owners are prepared to accept loneliness as a pervasive irritant in an otherwise satisfying life.

And yet, isolation has real costs that should not be minimized. Its effects spill over onto family and friends.[3] It heightens stress and hampers decision making. It even appears to adversely affect the bottom line. Indeed, our survey suggests that people holed up in the office do not set the pace financially. On the contrary, companies run by "lonely" managers performed below those run by their "non-lonely" peers on the basis of five-year sales revenues and returns on investment.

Unfortunately, loneliness cannot be completely eliminated from an entrepreneur's life. Small-business ownership is isolating and tends to attract people inclined toward individual pursuits. Nevertheless, owners can exercise some control over their environment and behavior if they so choose. On the basis of the survey and follow-up interviews, we suggest the following strategies for reducing loneliness and stress:

Rearrange the work environment. Richard D., for example, formalized interaction with others by building it into his organization chart. He established a board of directors drawn from people outside his company and regularly discusses business concerns with them and his three vice presidents. Since company activities no longer revolve exclusively around him, he necessarily interacts with others.

Participate in peer groups. Several owners cited contact with managers of noncompeting companies as an antidote to the inherent loneliness of running a business. Business organizations, such as Rotary Clubs and the Young Presidents' Organization, foster these contacts and are easy to join.

Alan, for example, finds his involvement with the Smaller Business Association of New England very satisfying: "Anytime you go to an SBANE meeting, you'll find people talking—not about their skiing or flying—but about business. Everybody just loves to have the chance to talk to somebody else who's not a threat. There's no concern about confidentiality or anything like that. I do a lot of talking and it helps." The ideal confidant, of course, is someone who has already gone through the problems of start-up.

Be attentive to family and friends. Because Alan keeps his wife informed about business affairs, he gets worthwhile feedback that wards off loneliness. "Though she has no business experience, I count on her for overall judgment," he says. "She may not understand a lot of the technical details, but she has the ability to say, 'Well, it sounds like the right thing to do,' or, 'Maybe that's sticking your neck out a little too far. What do you do if that fails? Can you recover?' She channels my thinking. She's always been good at that."

Similarly, Betty sought new companions when she discovered, after a few years in her building materials business, that she had little in common with former friends. During the start-up years, she remembers, "Our social life went by the boards. Most of the time we just turned everything down—no weddings, no funerals, no Saturday nights. Now I find that most of our old friends have gotten too old for me. Aches and pains. So I've made new friends, most of them in business and most of them a good deal younger than I am. They are customers and suppliers and business people in the area. We get together to talk about things that interest me—business conditions, cost of materials—but we also have fun and enjoy ourselves."

Modify attitudes that reinforce job-related isolation. Dealing with internally generated loneliness is particularly difficult because it requires introspection, objectivity, and persistence. Nevertheless, entrepreneurs should recognize the counterproductive effects of "Marlboro man" habits and accept the fact that they need not be towers of strength.

The workplace is not a confessional, of course. But owners who clear the way to a middle ground may find that social interaction relieves their loneliness. In addition, it is likely to improve their relationship with the very people on whom their business success depends. Breaking out of isolation may thus bring economic dividends as well as personal rewards.

Owners can also alleviate loneliness by checking their bent toward individual activity. We doubt that entrepreneurs will ever give up solo pursuits entirely—nor should they. Valuable insight can come from solitude. And individual activities are often an excellent remedy for stress, as one respondent recognized when he observed: "After I have done strenuous sports, most problems have diminished in scope, or else I have found a solution."

Yet, in view of our findings, we think it essential that entrepreneurs also enter into group activities with family and friends. The energy and determination they show in the marketplace must be directed toward emotionally satisfying relationships as well.

Too often small-business owners become trapped in a self-destructive cycle. Because they have no one to confide in, they lack a ready way to vent the stress that builds with their job. By breaking free from this isolation, small-business owners can improve their health and enhance the quality of their lives. In the process, they may also improve their business performance.

REFERENCES

1. See our article "Coping with Entrepreneurial Stress," HBR March-April 1983, p. 44.
2. James J. Lynch, *The Broken Heart* (New York: Basic Books, 1977).
3. See Fernando Bartolomé and Paul A. Lee Evans, "Must Success Cost So Much?" HBR March-April 1980, p. 137.

5

When Executives Burn Out

HARRY LEVINSON

"I just can't seem to get going," the vice president said. He grimaced as he leaned back in his chair. "I can't get interested in what I'm supposed to do. I know I should get rolling. I know there's a tremendous amount of work to be done. That's why they brought me in and put me in this job, but I just can't seem to get going."

Eighteen months before making these comments, the vice president had transferred to company headquarters from a subsidiary. His new job was to revamp the company's control systems which, because of a reorganization, were in disarray. When the vice president reported to headquarters, however, top management immediately recruited him to serve as a key staff figure in its own reshuffling. Because he was not in competition with line executives, he was the only staff person who interviewed and consulted with both the line executives and the chief executive officer. And because the top managers regarded him as trustworthy, they gave his recommendations serious attention.

But his task was arduous. Not only did the long hours and the unremitting pressure of walking a tightrope among conflicting interests exhaust him, but also they made it impossible for him to get at the control problems that needed attention. Furthermore, because his family could not move for six months until the school year was over, he commuted on weekends to his previous home 800 miles away. As he tried to perform the unwanted job that had been thrust on him and support the CEO who was counting heavily on his competence, he felt lonely, harassed, and burdened. Now that his task was coming to an end, he was in no psychological shape to take on his formal duties. In short, he had "burned out."

Like generalized stress, burn-out cuts across executive and managerial levels. While the phenomenon manifests itself in varying ways and to different degrees in different people, it appears, nonetheless, to have identifiable characteristics. For instance, in the next example, the individual changes but many of the features of the problem are the same:

A vice president of a large corporation who didn't receive an expected promotion left his company to become the CEO of a smaller, family-owned business, which was floundering and needed his skills. Although he had jumped at the opportunity to rescue the small company, once there he discovered an unimaginable morass of difficulties, among them continuous conflicts within the family. He felt he could not leave; but neither could he succeed. Trapped in a kind of psychological quicksand, he worked nights, days, and weekends for months trying to pull himself free. His wife protested, to no avail. Finally, he was hospitalized for exhaustion.

As in the previous example, the competence of the individual is not in question; today he is the chief executive of a major corporation.

Quite a different set of problems confronted another executive. This is how he tells his story:

"In March of 1963, I moved to a small town in Iowa with my wife and son of four weeks. I was an up-and-coming engineer with the electric company—magic and respected words in those days.

"Ten years later things had changed. When we went to social gatherings and talked to people, I ended up having to defend the electric company. At the time we were tying into a consortium, which was building a nuclear generating plant. The amount of negative criticism was immense, and it never really let up. Refusing to realize how important that generating plant was to a reliable flow of electricity, people continued to find fault.

"Now, nearly ten years later, we are under even greater attack. In my present role, I'm the guy who catches it all. I can't seem to get people to stand still and listen, and I can't continue to take all the hostility that goes with it—the crank calls, being woken up late at night and called names. I don't know how much longer I can last in this job." Before looking in depth at what the burn-out phenomenon is, let's look at the experience of one more executive who is well on his way to burning out:

"I have been with this company for nearly 15 years and have changed jobs every 2 to 3 years. Most of our managers are company men, like me. We have always been a high-technology company, but we have been doing less well in marketing than some of our competitors. Over the past 10 years we have been going through a continuous reorganization process. The organization charts keep changing, but the underlying philosophy, management techniques, and administrative trappings don't. The consequence is continuous frustration, disruption, resentment, and the undermining of 'change.' You don't take a company that has been operating with a certain perspective and turn it around overnight.

"With these changes we are also being told what we must do and when. Before, we were much more flexible and free to follow our noses. These shifts create enormous pressures on an organization that is used to different ways of operating.

"On top of that, a continuous corporate pruning goes on. I am a survivor, so I should feel good about it and believe what top management tells me, namely, that the unfit go and the worthy remain. But the old virtues—talent, initiative, and risk taking—are *not* being rewarded. Instead, acquiescence to corporate values and social skills that obliterate differences among individuals are the virtues that get attention. Also the reward process is more political than meritocratic.

"I don't know if we're going to make it. And there are a lot of others around here who have the same feeling. We're all demoralized."

Burn-Out—A Slow Fizzle

What was happening to these executives? In exploring that question, let's first look at what characterized the situations. In one or more cases, they:

Were repetitive or prolonged.

Engendered enormous burdens on the managers.

Promised great success but made attaining it nearly impossible.

Exposed the managers to risk of attack for doing their jobs, without providing a way for them to fight back.

Aroused deep emotions—sorrow, fear, despair, compassion, help-lessness, pity, and rage. To survive, the managers would try to harden outer "shells" to contain their feelings and hide their anguish.

Overwhelmed the managers with complex detail, conflicting forces, and problems against which they hurled themselves with increasing intensity—but without impact.

Exploited the managers but provided them little to show for having been victimized.

Aroused a painful, inescapable sense of inadequacy and often of guilt.

Left the managers feeling that no one knew, let alone gave a damn about, what price they were paying, what contribution or sacrifice they were making, or what punishment they were absorbing.

Caused the managers to raise the question "What for?"—as if they'd lost sight of the purpose of living.

Those who study cases like these agree that a special phenomenon occurs after people expend a great deal of effort, intense to the point of exhaustion, often without visible results. People in these situations feel angry, helpless, trapped, and depleted: they are burned out. This experience is more intense than what is ordinarily referred to as stress. The major defining characteristic of burn-out is that people can't or won't do again what they have been doing.

Dr. Herbert J. Freudenberger of New York evolved this definition of burn-out when he observed a special sort of fatigue among mental health workers.[1] Freudenberger observed that burn-out is followed by physiological signs such as the inability to shake colds and frequent headaches, as well as psychological symptoms like quickness to anger and a suspicious attitude about others.

Christina Maslach, who is a pioneer researcher on the subject at the University of California, Berkeley, says that burn-out "refers to a syndrome of emotional exhaustion and cynicism that frequently occurs among people who do 'people work'—who spend considerable time in close encounters."[2]

People suffering burn-out generally have identifiable characteristics: (1) chronic fatigue; (2) anger at those making demands; (3) self-criticism for putting up with the demands; (4) cynicism, negativism, and irritability; (5) a sense of being be-sieged; and (6) hair-trigger display of emotions.

Although it is not evident from these examples, frequently other destructive types of behavior accompany these feelings—including inappropriate anger at subordinates and family and sometimes withdrawal even from those whose sup-port is most needed; walling off home and work completely from each other; diffuse physical symptoms; efforts to escape the source of pressure through illness, absenteeism, drugs or alcohol, or increased temporary psychological escape (meditation, biofeedback, and other forms of self-hypnosis); increasing rigidity of attitude; and cold, detached, and less emphatic behavior.

Most people, even reasonably effective managers, probably experience a near burn-out at some time in their careers. A 20-year study of a group of middle managers disclosed that many of them, now in their forties and with few prospects of further promotions, were tolerating unhappy marriages, narrowing their focuses to their own jobs, and showing less consideration to other people.[3] Despite outward sociability, they were indifferent to friendships and were often hostile. They had become rigid, had short fuses, and were distant from their children.

Personality tests disclosed that these men had a higher need to do a job well for its own sake than did most of their peers, and they initially had a greater need for advancement as well (although this declined over time). They showed more motivation to dominate and lead and less to defer to authority than other managers. While they still could do a good day's work, they could no longer invest themselves in others and in the company.

When people who feel an intense need to achieve don't reach their goals, they can become hostile to themselves and others as well. They also tend to channel that hostility into more defined work tasks than before, limiting their efforts. If at times like these they do not increase their family involvement, they are likely to approach burn-out.

The Breeding Ground

Researchers have observed this exhaustion among many kinds of professionals. As the previous examples indicate, it is not unusual among executives and managers, and under very competitive conditions it is more likely to occur than in a stable market. Managerial jobs involve a lot of contact with other people. Often this contact is unpleasant but has to be tolerated because of the inherent demands of the job.

And one problem with managing people lies in the fact that such a focus creates unending stress for the manager. The manager must cope with the least capable among the employees, with the depressed, the suspicious, the rivalrous, the self-centered, and the generally unhappy. The manager must balance these conflicting personalities and create from them a motivated work group. He or she must define group purpose and organize people around that, must resolve conflicts, establish priorities, make decisions about other people, accept and deflect their hostility, and deal with the frustration that arises out of that continuing interaction. Managing people is the most difficult administrative task, and it has built-in frustration. That frustration, carried to extremes beyond stress, can — and does — cause managers to burn out.

Many contemporary managerial situations also provide the perfect breeding ground for cases of burn-out.

Today's managers face increasing time pressure with little respite. Even though benefits such as flexible working hours and longer vacation periods offer some relief, for the most part the modern executive's workday is long and hard. Also, as more women join the work force, the support most men used to receive at home is lessening, and women at work get as little, if not less, than the men. To many managers, the time they spend with their families is precious. It is understandable if managers feel guilty about sacrificing this part of their life to the demands of work and also feel frustration at being unable to do anything about it.

Adding to the stress at work is the complexity of modern organizations. The bigger and more intricate organizations become, the longer it takes to get things done. Managers trying to get ahead may well feel enormous frustration as each person or office a project passes through adds more delays and more problems to unravel before a task is finished.

Along with the increase in complexity of organization goes an increase in the number of people that a manager has to deal with. Participative management, quality of worklife efforts, and matrix structures all result in a proliferation in the number of people that a manager confronts face to face. Building a plant, developing natural resources, or evolving new products can often mean that a manager has to go through lengthy, and sometimes angry and vitriolic, inter-action with community groups. Executives involved in tasks that entail contro-versial issues can find themselves vilified.

As companies grow, merge with other companies, or go through reorgani-zations, some managers feel adrift. Sacrifices they have made on behalf of the organization may well turn out to have little enduring meaning. As an organi-zation's values change, a manager's commitment and sense of support may also shift. Another aspect of change that can add to a person's feeling burned out is the threat of obsolescence. When a new job or assignment requires that managers who are already feeling taxed develop new capacities, they may feel over-whelmed.

These days change can also mean that managers have to trim jobs, cut back, and demote subordinates—and maybe even discharge them. Managers whose job it is to close a plant or go through painful labor negotiations may feel enraged at having to pay for the sins of their predecessors. Also, a fragmented market-place can mean intense pressures on managers to come up with new products, innovative services, and novel marketing and financing schemes.

Finally, employees are making increasing demands for their rights. Managers may feel that they cannot satisfy those demands but have to respond to them.[4] And if inflation gets worse, so will these kinds of pressures.

Prevention Is the Best Cure

Top management can take steps to keep managers out of situations where they are likely to burn out. Of course, something as subtle as psychological exhaustion cannot be legislated against completely, but the following steps have been known to mitigate its occurrence:

First, as with all such phenomena, recognize that burn-out can, does, and will happen. The people in charge of orientation programs, management training courses, and discussions of managerial practice ought to acknowledge to em-ployees that burn-out can occur and that people's vulnerability to it is something the organization recognizes and cares about. Personnel managers should be candid with new employees on the psychological nature of the work they are getting into, especially when that work involves intense effort of the kind I've described. The more people know, the less guilt they are likely to feel for their own perceived inadequacies when the pressures begin to mount.

Keep track of how long your subordinates are in certain jobs and rotate them out of potentially exhausting positions. Changes of pace, changes of demands, and shifts into situations that may not be so depleting enable people to replenish their energies and get new and more accurate perspectives on themselves and their roles.

Change also enables people to look forward to a time when they can get out of a binding job. Long recognizing this need, the military limits the number of combat missions Air Force personnel fly and the duration of tours ground personnel endure.

Time constraints on a job are crucial to preventing burn-out. Don't allow your people to work 18 hours a day, even on critical problems. Especially don't let the same people be the rescuers of troubled situations over and over again. Understandably, managers tend to rely on their best people; but best people are more vulnerable to becoming burned-out people.

Overconscientious people, in particular, need to take time off from the role and its demands and to spend that time in refreshing recreation. The military has long since learned this lesson, but for some reason management has not. One way to make sure people break from work would be to take a whole work group on a nominal business trip to a recreational site.

Some companies have set up regular formal retreats where people who work together under pressure can talk about what they are doing and how they are doing it, make long-range plans, relax and enjoy themselves, and, most important, get away from what they have to cope with every day. When managers talk together in a setting like this, they can make realistic assessments of the problems they are up against and their own responsibilities and limits.

I think, for example, of the extremely conscientious engineers in many of the small electronics companies on Route 128 in the Boston area, of those in the research triangle in North Carolina, or in the Palo Alto, California area who have reported feeling that they simply are not developing new products fast enough. They are convinced they aren't living up to the extremely high standards that they set for themselves. Such people need to talk together, often with a group therapist or someone else who can help them relieve some of the irrational self-demands they frequently make on themselves as groups and as individuals.

Make sure your organization has a systematic way of letting people know that their contributions are important. People need information that supports their positive self-images, eases their consciences, and refuels them psychologically.

Many compensation and performance appraisal programs actually contribute to people's sense that their efforts will be unrecognized, no matter how well they do. Organizational structures and processes that inhibit timely attacks on problems and delay actually produce much of the stress that people experience at work. If top executives fail to see that organizational factors can cause burn-out, their lack of understanding may perpetuate the problem.

It is also important that top managers review people's capacities, skills, and opportunities with their employees so that, armed with facts about themselves and the organization, they can make choices rather than feel trapped.

During World War II, the Army discovered that it was better to send soldiers overseas in groups rather than as single replacements. It may be equally effective for you to send groups of people from one organizational task to another rather than assemble teams of individually assigned people. When Clairol opened a new plant in California, it sent a group of Connecticut-based managers and their spouses, who were briefed on the new assignment, the new community, and the potential stresses they might encounter. They discussed together how they might help themselves and each other, as well as what support they needed from the organization.

Some construction companies also create teams of people before undertaking a new project. People who have worked together have already established various mutual support systems, ways to share knowledge informally, and friendly alliances. These can prevent or ameliorate potential burn-out that may occur in new, difficult, or threatening tasks.

Provide avenues through which people can express not only their anger but also their disappointment, helplessness, futility, defeat, and depression. Some employees, like salespeople, meet defeat every day. Others meet defeat in a crisis—when a major contract or competition is lost, when a product expected to succeed fails, when the competition outflanks them. When people in defeat deny their angry feelings, the denial of underlying, seething anger contributes to the sense of burn-out.

If top executives fail to see these problems as serious, they may worsen the situation. If the company offers only palliatives like meditation and relaxation methods—temporarily helpful though these may be—burn-out victims may become further enraged. The sufferers know their problem has to do with the nature of the job and not their capacity to handle it.

Those managers who are exposed to attack need to talk about the hostilities they anticipate and how to cope with them. Just as sailors at sea need to anticipate and cope with storms, so executives need to learn how to cope with the public's aggression. Under attack themselves, they need to evolve consensus, foster cohesion, and build trust rather than undermine themselves with counterattacks.

Another way to help is to defend publicly against outside attacks on the organization. In recent months a prominent chief executive raised the morale of all of his employees when he filed suit against a broadcast medium for false allegations about his company's products. Another publicly took on a newspaper that had implied his organization was not trustworthy. A visible, vigorous, and powerful leader does much to counteract people's sense of helplessness.

As technology changes, you need to retrain and upgrade your managers. But some people will be unable to rise to new levels of responsibility and are likely to feel defeated if they cannot succeed in the same job. Top management needs to retrain, refresh, and reinvigorate these managers as quickly as possible by getting them to seminars, workshops, and other activities away from the organization.

As Freudenberger commented after his early observations, however, introspection is not what the burned-out person requires; rather, he or she needs intense physical activity, not further mental strain and fatigue. Retreats, seminars, and workshops therefore should be oriented toward the cognitive and physical rather than the emotional. Physical exercise is helpful because it provides an outlet for angry feelings and pent-up energy.

Managers who are burning out need support from others from whom they can get psychological sustenance. Ideally, those others should be their bosses—people who value them as individuals and insist that they withdraw, get appropriate help, and place themselves first.

In times of unmitigated strain it is particularly important that you keep up personal interaction with your subordinates. To borrow from the military again, generals valued by their troops, like George Patton and James Gavin in World War II, make it a practice to be involved with their frontline soldiers.

Freudenberger points out that the burn-out phenomenon often occurs when a leader or the leader's charisma is lost. He notes that people who join an organization still led by the founder or founding group frequently expect that person or group to be superhuman. They were, after all, the entrepreneurs with the foresight, vision, drive, and imagination to build the organization. "As they begin to disappoint us, we bad-rap them and the result, unless it is stopped, is psychic damage to the whole clinic," he comments.[5] The issue is the same whether it is a clinic, a hospital, a police department, or a business.

Executives who are idealized should take time to publicly remove their halos. They can do that by explaining their own struggles, disappointments, and defeats to their subordinates so that the latter can view them more accurately. They need also to help people to verbalize their disappointment with the "fallen" executive hero.

When the leader leaves, either through death or transfer, when a paternalistic, successful entrepreneur sells out, or when an imaginative inventor retires, it is important for the group that remains to have the opportunity to go through a process of discussing its loss and mourning it. The group needs to conduct a psychological wake and consider for itself how it is going to replace the loss.

Frequently, the group will discover that, though the loss of the leader is indeed significant, it can carry on effectively and contribute to the success of the organization. Failing to realize its own strengths, a group can, like the Green Bay Packers after the death of coach Vince Lombardi, feel permanently handicapped. To my knowledge, few organizations effectively deal with the loss of a leader. Most respond with a depression or slump from which it takes years to recover. Also, and more crippling, is the way people in the organization keep yearning and searching for a new charismatic leader to rescue them. As part of a national organization, Americans have been doing this searching ever since the death of John Kennedy.

REFERENCES

1. Herbert J. Freudenberger, "Staff Burn-Out," *Journal of Social Issues*, vol. 30, no. 1, 1974, p. 159; see also his recent book, *Burn-Out: The Melancholy of High Achievement* (Garden City, N.Y.: Doubleday, 1980).

2. Christina Maslach, "Burn-Out," *Human Behavior*, September 1976, p. 16.

3. Douglas W. Bray, Richard J. Campbell, and Donald L. Grant, *Formative Years in Business* (New York: John Wiley, 1974).

4. Opinion Research Corporation reports a recent survey that confirms this point.

5. Freudenberger, "Staff Burn-Out," p. 160.

6

Must Success Cost So Much?

FERNANDO BARTOLOMÉ AND
PAUL A. LEE EVANS

A good number of executives accept the cliché that success always demands a price and that the price is usually deterioration of private life. This cliché does not always reflect reality, however—some executives seem to be exempt. What distinguishes the executives who pay a heavy personal price for their success from those who are able to maintain and develop fulfilling private lives?

In studying the private and professional lives of more than 2,000 managers for nearly five years, we've seen that some very successful executives have meaningful private lives. One thing that does *not* distinguish these executives is professional commitment. (To succeed, individuals have to give their jobs a high priority in their lives.) Nor is it easier for these executives to develop a private life. For everyone, it is difficult.

What *does* distinguish the two groups is this: the executives whose private lives deteriorate are subject to the negative effects of what we call emotional spillover; work consistently produces negative feelings that overflow into private life. In contrast, the other group of executives have learned to manage their work and careers so that negative emotional spillover is minimized, and thus they achieve a balance between their professional and private lives.

After countless exchanges with managers and their wives and after careful analysis of research data, we concluded that the major determinant of work's impact on private life is whether negative emotional feelings aroused at work spill over into family and leisure time. When an executive experiences worry, tension, fear, doubt, or stress intensely, he is not able to shake these feelings when he goes home, and they render him psychologically unavailable for a rich private life. The manager who is unhappy in his work has a limited chance of being happy at home—no matter how little he travels, how much time he spends at home, or how frequently he takes a vacation.

When individuals feel competent and satisfied in their work—not simply contented, but challenged in the right measure by what they are doing—negative spillover does not exist. During these periods executives are open to involvement in private life; they experience positive spillover. When work goes well, it can have the same effect as healthy physical exercise—instead of leading to fatigue, it is invigorating.

If things go right at work, a feeling of well-being places people in the right mood to relate to others. They open up, they are available, they may search for contact. That, of course, does not guarantee that such contact will be successful. A person may not be skillful at it, or there may be deep conflicts from the past that make contact difficult. But when the executive feels good at work, contact at home is at least possible.

We can summarize our findings this way: for an ambitious person, a well-functioning professional life is a necessary though not sufficient condition for a well-functioning private one.

For the time being, our study has focused on male managers only. We have not yet studied female executives, but our exchanges with some women and our reading of the literature on women managers lead us to believe strongly that the ideas we present apply to them as well.

The dilemmas and conflicts women face in trying to manage the relationship between their professional and private lives may be even more difficult than those faced by men. While in many cultures it is acceptable for men to specialize in their professional roles and delegate the main responsibility for private life to their wives, our impression is that even in the more liberal and advanced cultures the married woman who chooses to pursue a career is still expected to be responsible for the quality of the couple's private life.

Women are under more pressure to manage skillfully the boundaries between professional and private life. They are probably more aware of what causes the conflicts than many men. As increasing numbers of women join the work force, these issues are being more openly considered at work.

The Price Some Managers Pay

Even though we recognize that positive spillover exists, for the most part in this article we're going to be concerned with the negative emotions that spill over from work into executives' private lives. What are its sources? How can individuals manage it, and what can companies do to minimize the likelihood that people will suffer from it?

The experience of this 36-year-old manager typifies the spillover phenomenon: "When I started working for my boss four years ago, that affected my family life. He was very different from my previous boss. He was a bit of a tyrant. From working with someone who was terribly easygoing to someone who's an absolute dynamo—that certainly had an influence on my family life. It made me slightly—how can I put it? Well, I'd come home to my wife talking about him, about decisions he had reversed on a certain proposal I'd made. I'd talk it over with my wife, but I couldn't get it out of my mind, because it was such a different way of operating from my previous boss."

All of us have experienced spillover at one time or another in our careers. The problem is that some executives lead life-styles that pave the way for never-ending spillover. Such an executive's wife is likely to react with this sort of comment: "What annoys me is when he comes home tense and exhausted. He flops into a chair and turns on the TV. Or else he worries, and it drives me up the wall."

Work spills over into private life in two ways: through fatigue and through emotional tension, like worry. Fatigue is the natural consequence of a hectic day at the office. But curiously enough, a hectic day—if it has gone well—can make us feel less worn out, often almost energetic. On the other hand, a boring day at the office, when the executive feels he has not accomplished anything, is exhausting. He comes home tired. Home is not a place for private life; it simply becomes a haven—a place to rest, relax, and recharge batteries to survive the next day.

Worrying, the other symptom of negative emotional spillover, is caused by frustration, self-doubt, and unfinished business. One wife puts it this way: "Yes, his mind is often on other things. Yes, he often worries and it *does* disturb the family life. When he is like that he can't stand the noise of the children. . . . He can't stand the fact that the children are tired. In general we have dinner together so that he can be with them. And obviously they chatter, they spill things, they tease each other—and he blows his top. He is tense and uptight—it's disturbing; I can't stand it. I have to try to mediate between them and cool things down. The only thing is to finish everything as soon as possible and get everyone quickly off to bed."

The feelings that spill over from work are acted out at home. Sometimes they are expressed through psychological absence, sometimes through acts of aggression. One loses one's temper with the children. One explodes in fury if one's wife makes a minor mistake. Such aggression is visible and painful, but withdrawal is equally damaging to family relationships. As one wife said:

"My husband is not one of those men who vents all his frustrations on the family. One cannot reproach him for being aggressive or for beating his wife. Instead he closes up like a shell. Total closure. The time he thinks he spends here isn't spent here."

Because psychological withdrawal can make a person blind to what is going on at home, it can have very serious consequences. A 40-year-old executive described the most painful period of his marriage this way:

"It was just after the birth of the third child, eight years ago. The birth coincided with a move to another part of the country and with a complete change in job. And there I have to admit that I was completely unaware of the consequences that all this had for my wife. She was overloaded with work and worries. It went on for some time, and I just wasn't aware of what was happening. Finally she fell ill and had to be hospitalized. It was only then that it began to dawn on me. I was quite unconscious of everything I was doing."

"You were overloaded in your work?"

"Yes. Well, not really overloaded. I was worried about my work. I didn't feel very sure of myself and so was very worried. . . . It was the time of a merger between two companies and a period of great uncertainty. That had led to my new job and the move. And I just couldn't get my work out of my mind. I think back even today—the uncertainties of the time were real. It was normal, but anyway I couldn't get the work out of my mind. Today I'm much more sure of myself. I find it a lot easier to switch off."

When negative emotions spill over, managers often express dissatisfaction with their life-styles and complain of wanting more time for private life. But because their minds are numbed by tension, these people cannot use even their available time in a fulfilling way. Some report needing a double martini just to summon the energy to switch on the television. Many read the newspaper, not because they're interested in world events, but to escape into personal privacy. Some mooch around in the basement or the garden as a way of just getting through the day.

Again and again, the wives of these executives express the same idea: "I don't really mind the amount of work he has to do. That is, if he is happy in his work. What I resent is the unhappiness that he brings home."

Or sometimes they agree with this 42-year-old wife: "The very best moment in our marriage is, without any doubt, right now. We have never before had such a complete life together. The children are interesting to my husband and he is very happy with his work. On the other hand, the most difficult moments have been when he wasn't happy with what he was doing."

Managing Spillover

To have a healthy private life, one must manage the negative emotions that arise at work. When we began our investigation into the work lives and private lives of managers five years ago, we held the biased belief that these two sides of life are in fundamental conflict with each other. During these five years we have gathered more and more evidence suggesting that, among managers at least, individual and organizational interests can be in harmony. Moreover, a healthy professional life is a precondition for a healthy private one.

Job and home can be in harmony and mutually reinforce each other if—and only if—one avoids various pitfalls in the management of self and career and one copes satisfactorily with the emotions that arise at work. Conversely, executives who fail to manage the emotional side of work achieve professional success at the expense of private life.

Let's look now at what the executive can do to manage the emotional side of work better. We single out three major causes of negative emotional spillover: the problems of adapting to a new job, the lack of fit between a person and his job, and career disappointments.

Coping with a New Job

Without doubt, the most common trigger of spillover tension is the process of settling into a new job following promotion, reorganization, or a move to another company. Since all of us change jobs from time to time, we all experience spillover caused by the problems of adaptation. Having to familiarize ourselves with a new task, learn to work with new people, settle in a different town and environment, and establish new relationships with superiors, subordinates, and peers—all at the same time—overloads our emotional systems.

That work dominates the emotional life of a person adapting to a new job is natural and necessary. It allows him to master major changes. Once that is done, the spillover effects begin to fade away.

What is vital is that the individual assess and recognize how important a change he (and his family) face when he changes jobs. The more new skills the job requires and the more radical the change in environment, the longer the adaptation period is likely to be and the longer the negative spillover is likely to last. To deny this reality in an attempt to persuade a reluctant family that the job change will also be good for them is risky.

Top managers often fail to assess correctly the magnitude of the changes and adaptations they ask of executives and their families. Often individual executives, driven by their own ambition, also fail to assess accurately the difficulty of tasks they accept. Only a realistic evaluation of the degree of change executives and their families will face allows them to come through the process of adaptation relatively unscathed.

In talking to executive couples, we have found too often the case of the ambitious executive who accepted an exciting job in a developing country that sounded like a wonderful opportunity and a major career step. His wife was unhappy about it, but there was no heart-to-heart discussion about the decision. The wife felt that her husband's mind was made up and was reluctant to hold him back. Her fears were half-assuaged by his assurances that the move would be challenging and exciting and that he would be there to help out. They moved.

What executives do not realize is that the change to a new and important job, to a new locale, and to a new culture will create massive amounts of tension. The negative spillover into private life will be immense. For a year or more, they will have minimal psychological availability for private life. If their wives expect and need that availability, its absence will aggravate the adaptation problems that they are undergoing themselves. Far too often, the story ends catastrophically for all concerned.

And yet it doesn't need to happen this way. We have heard executives describe enthusiastically how similar moves brought their families together and how dealing with the difficulties of adaptation as a family was a most positive experience.

What accounts for the difference in experiences? These latter executives analyzed the change carefully with their families before the move, negotiated the decision with them, openly expressed the problems they would all confront, and did not promise what they could not deliver.

Most wives will understand and accept that for some time their husbands will be preoccupied with the job and won't be readily available. If they recognize this in advance and as long as they know that emotional spillover will fade away, they may even support him at this difficult time. But sometimes spillover does not fade away. The new job turns out to be beyond the person's talents or capacities.

If after a reasonable period of time—say, one year—negative spillover is increasing rather than fading away, a misfit situation (where the only way of mastering the job is through sheer brute energy rather than skill) could be in the making. Because wives experience the spillover consequences directly, they are good judges as to whether it is increasing or decreasing. If it's increasing, the time has come to negotiate a move out.

Taking the Right Job

The lack of fit between an individual and a job is the second most common source of negative spillover. Judgments on the "shape" of people and jobs are difficult to make; square pegs are often put in round holes. Top managers may overemphasize skills and experience while ignoring the very important factors of personality and individual goals. Consider the experiences of Jack and Melinda:

Three years ago, Jack was a computer company's research manager, content in his job and very ambitious. Top management offered him a promotion to a job as manager of administrative services. While at first Jack didn't like the position offered him, management persuaded him to accept it by arguing that it would be an important step in his career development. Since Jack's ambition was to become research director, the argument seemed logical. The new job would give him administrative experience that would help qualify him for the post he wanted. Jack accepted the job.

Jack has already spent three years in this job, yet spillover tension is not on the wane. On the contrary, during the past three years it has increased steadily and is now an almost inextricable part of his life. But while he is hurting, his wife Melinda and his two children are hurting even more.

Melinda talks of how Jack has brought nothing but sadness and tension into the family's life since he undertook his new job. Since then, she says, "He hasn't even been interested in talking about our problems." In fact, she has often considered divorce.

For his part, Jack finds it difficult to say anything positive about his job. "You meet interesting people and a wide variety of situations," he says, "but one part of the work consists of acting as the office boy to deal with everyone's banal problems." The other part consists of negotiating with trade union officials on grievances, a duty that Jack finds tiring and frustrating. "You have no authority over anyone," he says, "and what I didn't realize at the beginning is that one doesn't have any real contact with the people in research."

The tension and doubt that Jack feels—and which his wife experiences even more strongly—are growing. At the end of a two-hour interview, he spoke of the feeling of being trapped: "I'm not really content in this job, but if I do well it will help me in my next job in research. It's a thankless task, being at everybody's beck and call. The trouble is that it's getting to me. I can't take the strain much longer. I went to my boss last month and told him that I want to move back to research. He told me that they would take care of that in due time, that I was doing a grand job now, and that they needed me here.

"The trouble is—did he really mean it that I was doing a grand job? I feel that things can only go downhill from here. And I'm drifting further and further away from research."

Lack of Fit

Jack is a misfit. However valid or invalid his reasons for accepting his present job, the work does not suit his personality. It makes him permanently tense without satisfying him. Yet because he took the job as a "stepping stone," he *must* perform.

Lacking deep interest and natural skill for the work, the misfit can only compensate with an over-investment of energy. This investment may lead to success—but at the price of enormous internal tension, reinforced fear of failure, and the suspension of an investment in private life.

Tension and deep fear of failure are the natural consequences of going against one's grain. People who take jobs for which they are ill-fitted are often afraid that their weaknesses will show, that they will be found out. These inner doubts can be so intense that no amount of external recognition or acknowledgment of success can eliminate them.

For misfits the ultimate irony is that, instead of decreasing with each new success, fear of failure increases. Outward success does not reassure them. Instead, their successes trap them in jobs they do not enjoy. With their bridges burned behind them, they feel snared in situations that create permanent and increasing tension.

Let us define what we mean by the fit between individual and job. A perfect fit occurs when you experience three positive feelings at the same time: you feel competent, you enjoy the work, and you feel that your work and your moral values coincide. To express this in another way, a job should fit not only with skills and abilities but also with motives and values.

A misfit situation occurs whenever one of these three conditions is absent. In the case of the *total misfit*, none of the conditions is fulfilled: he is not particularly competent at what he does, he enjoys few aspects of his work, and he feels ashamed doing things that go against his values or ideals. Jack, the manager we just described, is an example.

Absence of skill. The *competence misfit* enjoys his work and is proud of what he does. He works hard enough to keep his job, but he is not sure of his ability to really master the work. For example, a manager in a line position may find it difficult to make decisions, or someone taking a personnel administrator's job hoping to broaden his skills may not work well with people. For the time being, those executives may manage well, but they live with the persistent fear that things will get out of hand. This sense of insecurity tends to diminish their enjoyment of the job and spills over into their private lives.

This "competence misfit" most typically happens to people in the early stages of their careers, when they haven't yet found out what they are good at doing. It is the type of misfit that organizations are most sensitive to, which they try hardest to avoid. But two other kinds of misfit, which most organizations fail to recognize, are equally important. We call them the "enjoyment misfit" and the "moral misfit."

Dislike for the job. An *enjoyment misfit* occurs when an individual is competent at his job and proud of doing it but does not like it. One executive had the necessary qualities to be a manager and was promoted to a managerial job even though he would have rather remained in a technical position. Despite his preference for individual challenge over the laborious process of working through other people, he succumbed to a sense of duty and to unanimous pressure and accepted the job. He is unhappy in his new job and consequently suffers from negative spillover.

The most frequent cause of "enjoyment misfit" is intrinsic dislike of various work characteristics, but other causes are common as well. Staying in a job for too long can transform enjoyment into boredom; persons can be competent but see what they do as predictable variations of a humdrum theme. Having too much work to do can also destroy enjoyment: some people, finding it very difficult to say no to challenges and tasks they enjoy doing, agree to do too much. The consequent stress gradually erodes the intrinsic pleasure of the tasks.

Different values. The last type of misfit, *moral misfit*, results when individuals enjoy their work and are competent but do not feel proud of what they do, when they feel they compromise their values. A sales manager we met, for example, was good at his job, but he did not believe in the merits of the product he was selling. He would not have bought it himself and could not wholeheartedly recommend it to others. He used to reassure himself by saying that "as long as there is a market for it, it must be O.K." After a successful and important sale, rather than feeling proud of himself he would come out feeling "thank goodness that's over."

The negative spillover created by going along with unethical business practices (such as bribing foreign officials) has two additional painful twists to it. The person fears potential legal consequences, and he cannot vent his feelings by expressing them to others because the position dictates secrecy.

Each of these ways of not fitting a job is dangerous. If individuals accept tasks for which they lack the competence, they risk feeling continual self-doubt. If they accept jobs for which they are skilled but which they do not like doing, they will be bored. If they accept jobs in which they do not feel pride, they will not feel at peace with themselves.

The incompetent misfit may be the only type of misfit the organization is able to spot; whatever the cause of the misfit, however, the individuals and their families will suffer. For an individual in top management to avoid putting the wrong person in the wrong job, it is essential to understand what causes some of the mistakes.

Why People Take the Wrong Job

We find four main reasons why people are in the wrong jobs: the strong attraction of external rewards, organizational pressure, inability to say no, and lack of self-knowledge or self-assessment. Let's examine each one of these issues in turn.

External rewards. We all like and need money and have some healthy needs for status and recognition as well. But because in our Western society having these things implies that one is a "good" person, we sometimes put too much value on them. As a result, many people end up doing what will bring rewards rather than what fits them. They are seen as good members of society but don't feel good about themselves.

Executives we spoke with often justified accepting jobs they didn't really want on the ground that the material rewards the jobs provided were essential to realizing a fulfilling private life. They fail to realize (except in hindsight) that no matter how much they earn, no matter how much status is attached to the position, their private lives will suffer through emotional spillover if the job doesn't fit them.

Organizational pressures. When management approaches an individual in the organization or outside it to offer him a job, in most cases it does so after carefully analyzing available candidates. The person chosen is usually the one management deems most competent for the job.

But management pays little if any attention to the two other dimensions of fit—will the person enjoy the job and will he be proud of it? If it assesses these dimensions at all, management will often dismiss any problem as an individual or personal concern. A person's capacity to do the job well is all that counts. Some managers assume that if he does not feel he will like it or be proud of it, then he will say no; some also assume that if he doesn't say no, the personal issues don't exist.

But here is the problem. When management reaches its final decision and offers the person the promotion or the new job, he is no longer simply a candidate for that job. Management has made a statement that he is the best person available. To refuse is to deny management what it wants. Of course, he is free to say no on emotional grounds; but is he really? The pressures to accept are considerable.

Management often adopts a selling attitude that manifests itself in a variety of ways. The rewards and incentives are expressively described, the fact that this is a "unique opportunity" is stressed, and the argument that "this will be good for your career" is emphasized. If the individual points out that he may lack some of the necessary skills for the job, management is likely to say that this is "an exceptional opportunity to develop such skills," expressing vague doubts about the future otherwise. At the end of the process, management often brings the ultimate pressure to bear. It makes it clear that a decision has to be reached quickly, that an answer is expected "let's say, in 72 hours."

By this time many executives will have succumbed to the appeal of external rewards or to the fear of saying no or of showing hesitation. Nevertheless, the best of them will indeed insist on enough time to analyze as thoroughly as possible the intrinsic characteristics of the job and the extent to which it fits them.

These people are deeply aware that their decisions will influence not only every working hour in the years ahead but also every hour of their private lives. And these are the people most likely to avoid becoming misfits and suffering from massive spillover. In most cases, their attitudes are reinforced by a real concern for their families and a deep understanding of the impact that changing jobs may have on them.

Above all, such executives realize that they hold the main responsibility for managing their careers and are unwilling to transfer that responsibility to anybody else.

The ability to say no. If learning to ask for sufficient time to think over accepting a job is difficult, learning to say no is even more difficult, particularly in times of economic crisis.

Learning to say no requires, first of all, the ability to estimate realistically the consequences of refusal. Many people assume fearsome consequences that they often are too afraid to test. But one also has to estimate realistically the negative effects of acceptance. Executives we spoke to mentioned they had sometimes made the decision easier by minimizing the difficulties they would face.

Ability to assess consequences realistically is one of the characteristics of highly successful people. They can do this because they have the final and most important quality of people who want to avoid spillover — namely, self-knowledge and the ability to assess themselves accurately.

Self-assessment. Much of our behavior is rooted in unconscious motives, and it is difficult to know that part of ourselves. Also, as we age we are continually changing and acquiring new experiences. So, even under the best of circumstances, to assess whether one will fit with a new job is difficult.

Self-assessment implies that one can accurately recognize one's competences — acknowledging limitations as well as strengths, identifying what brings pleasure or pain, and knowing what elicits pride or guilt in different work situations. It requires admitting to feelings rather than masking them.

The raw data for self-assessment are past experiences. Because of limited experiences, the task is especially difficult for the younger manager. During one's 20s and early 30s, the only way to assess oneself is to take different jobs in different companies to find out what kind of work one does best, enjoys most, and finds most meaningful. Our research indicates that foreclosing this phase of exploration too quickly may have negative consequences later in one's career.[1]

This exploration, however, does not need to be a blind process. Under ideal circumstances, a mentor successfully guides the younger person in the trial and error stages of his career. The mentor—an older, experienced, and trusted guide (often a boss with whom one enjoys an open and special relationship)—does more than simply provide new challenges and experiences. This mentor also helps the younger manager learn from those experiences what his skills, needs, and values are, and thus speeds up the process of self-assessment.

No matter how well this process of starting one's own career and finding one's professional identity goes, the individual will suffer from considerable tension and stress. Managers at this stage in life are predominantly oriented toward launching their careers, and emotional spillover often pervades private life.

After such a period of exploration and with better knowledge of themselves, some individuals in their mid-30s eventually find jobs or positions that fit them in the three dimensions outlined earlier. The young man assessing a job asks himself above all "Can I do it?" But the more mature man asks two other questions as well: "Will I enjoy doing it?" and "Is it worth doing?" He is likely to accept the job only if all three answers are positive.

People at this stage in their careers turn more toward their private lives. They are no longer content simply with the competence fit. They aim for total fit that ensures minimal spillover and full availability for private life. They can achieve this if they have developed sufficient self-knowledge to guide their careers. This knowledge will also allow them, after having benefited from a mentor in their early careers, to become mentors themselves.[2]

For some people, self-knowledge grows with experience, and consequently they are able to manage their careers and avoid spillover. Others, however, fail to learn from experience and as a result are likely to suffer from the third main cause of spillover—namely, career disappointment.

Learning from Disappointments

Prevention is better than cure. Individuals skilled at self-assessment run a smaller risk not only of finding themselves in the wrong job but also of suffering serious disappointments. But all of us face disappointment at one time or another in our careers. It can have immense psychological impact, especially if work is an important part of our lives.

The most frequent type of disappointment that we have found in our research is experienced by the older manager whose career flattens out below the level he expected to reach. More or less consciously, he recognizes that he has plateaued. Individual signals of the end—a turned-down promotion, a merit raise refused, a bad appraisal, or a shuffling aside in a reorganization—are bitter blows.

When deeply hurt, most of us will automatically react in a defensive way. While some individuals can eventually react healthily and learn from a painful experience, many become disillusioned and turn into bitter, plateaued performers. Often such executives disengage from activity. Abraham Zaleznik suggests that two things are necessary to cope well with disappointment: the ability "to become intimately acquainted with one's own emotional reactions" and the capacity to "face the disappointment squarely." And, he adds, "The temptation and the psychology of individual response to disappointment is to avoid the pain of self-examination. If an avoidance pattern sets in, the individual will pay dearly for it later."[3] In all cases, the danger is distortion of reality.

In our contacts with executives, we have found ample confirmation of Zaleznik's observations. It is indeed difficult for people to face disappointment squarely. The experience often triggers in them strong feelings of loss that they turn into anger against themselves, which sometimes manifests itself as depression or withdrawal. But people cope with such situations in diverse ways. After a short period of mourning their losses, some bounce back (having learned something) and adapt successfully; others get permanently stuck in bitter and self-destructive positions.

Those who do not recover from severe disappointment often find themselves stuck in no-exit jobs that they do not enjoy and are not particularly proud of. They find it difficult to accept that their careers have plateaued in this way. They feel cheated. The emotional tension of an unenjoyable job, now aggravated by bitterness, often spills over into their home lives, where everyone else also pays for their sense of failure. Private life, as well as professional life, becomes hollow and empty. The injury to self-esteem they received in the professional world seems to color their whole experience of life.

Other plateaued managers recover their enthusiasm for their professional and private lives in a constructive way. They may compensate for their disappointment by enriching their present jobs—for example, adopting a role as mentor.

Often this positive compensation comes through developing leisure activities. These activities have, however, a professional quality to them rather than being mere relaxation. One man transformed his hobby of riding into a weekend riding school. Another got involved in community activities. A third broadened his home redecorating pastime into buying, redoing, and selling old houses. In these examples, work became more meaningful in that it helped to finance an active leisure interest; family life benefited since the man recovered his sense of self-esteem.

We can add a nuance to Freud's idea that the main sources of self-esteem and pleasure in an individual's life are work and love. Failure at work cannot be fully compensated by success in love. Failure at work has to be compensated by success in worklike activities. Only when work and love coexist in parallel and appropriate proportions do we achieve happiness and fulfillment.

What Organizations Can Do

We have suggested that the main responsibility for managing a career, reducing negative spillover, and achieving a good balance between professional and private life lies with the individual executive. It makes more sense for individuals to feel responsible for managing their own professional lives (taking care that career does not destroy private life) than to expect the organization to do this for them. Management in organizations, however, bears the responsibility for practices and policies that may make it unnecessarily difficult for the individual executive to manage the relationship between his professional and private lives. We see four things top managers can do to reduce the work pressures.

Broaden Organizational Values

Our first recommendation to managers is likely to be the most heretical. Managers can help their people by encouraging them not to be devoted solely to career success. Many managers attach too high a value to effort, drive, dedication, dynamism, and energy. Managers often take long hours at work and apparent single-minded dedication to professional success as indicators of drive and ambition. Attachment to private life and efforts to protect it by working "only" 45 hours a week are interpreted as signs of weakness in today's middle aged; in younger managers, this pattern signifies an erosion of the work ethic, a symptom of what is wrong with the younger generation.

We find little evidence in our research, however, of an erosion of the work ethic among younger managers. Their professional commitment is strong, but it represents a commitment to what interests them rather than a blind commitment to their companies. They resist simply doing what has to be done and conforming to organizational practices, even if they are compensated by incentives. They are aware that a lot of office time is wasted by engaging in ritualistic, nonproductive "work" and that few people make a real success of activities that fail to excite and interest them. Above all they appreciate that the quality of an individual's work life has an enormous impact, positive or negative, on his private life.

Paradoxically, organizations do not necessarily work better when they are full of highly ambitious, career-centered individuals striving to get to the top. As a matter of fact, these "jungle fighters" are often ostracized by their colleagues and superiors because they have too much ambition and too little ability to work with others. What organizations ideally need are a few ambitious and talented high achievers (who fit with their jobs) and a majority of balanced, less ambitious but conscientious people more interested in doing a good job that they enjoy and are adequately rewarded for than in climbing the organizational pyramid.

Organizational practices that overvalue effort and climbing and undervalue pride in one's job and good performance are counterproductive. Economic recessions in years to come will make this even more apparent. As the growth rates of organizations stabilize, the possibilities for advancement and promotion will diminish. People will be productive only if they enjoy the intrinsic value of what they are doing and if they draw their satisfaction simultaneously from two sources — work and private life — instead of one.

Create Multiple Reward and Career Ladders

Since external rewards often pressure people into accepting jobs they don't fit, our second recommendation concerns the reward policies and ladders of organizations.

The reward ladder of most organizations is a very simple, one-dimensional hierarchy; the higher, the more "managerial" one is, the more one is rewarded. People come to equate success with the managerial ladder, which would be appropriate if skilled managerial people were the only skilled people we need. But this is far from the case. Most organizations have relatively few general managerial positions and, while these are important posts, the life blood of the company is provided by people who fit with their jobs in other ways. To encourage these people, reward ladders need to be far more differentiated than they are at present.

Edgar H. Schein shows how managers fit with their work and careers in at least five different ways that he calls "career anchors."[4] While some people indeed have managerial anchors (that is, they aspire to positions in general management), others are oriented toward expertise in a technical or functional area. A desire to be creative is the central motive in the careers of a third group. (And do we not need more entrepreneurs in our large organizations today?) The fourth and fifth groups are anchored in needs for security and autonomy, respectively.

The obvious implication is that organizations must create multiple career and reward ladders to develop the different types of people required for their operations. Some high-technology companies that rely heavily on technical innovation have indeed experimented with offering both managerial and technical reward ladders. In the future, we will probably see the development of reward ladders that reinforce creativity and entrepreneurship as well.

The problem with the simple structures of many organizations is that they channel ambition and talent in only one direction, creating unnecessary conflict for the many individuals who are ambitious or talented but do not walk the single prescribed path. We can warn individuals against being blinded by ambition to the emotional aspects of fit; yet we must also warn organizations, not against fostering ambition, but against channeling it into a single career path.

Give Realistic Performance Appraisals

Our third recommendation is that managers help individuals in their own self-assessment, thus reducing the chances that they will either move into positions that do not fit them or be promoted to their "Peter Principle" level of incompetence. To do this, managers need to pay greater attention to their subordinates' performances and also to be honest in discussions of the subordinates' strengths and weaknesses. Managers should also encourage self-assessment. Contrary to standard assessment practices that only emphasize skills and competence, self-assessment should focus as well on the extent to which the individual enjoys his job — both as a whole and in its component parts.

Many researchers have called for accurate and realistic feedback in performance appraisal.[5] We also ask that managers be as concerned and realistic about enjoyment and value as about competence.

Of all managerial omissions, lack of candor about a subordinate's chances for promotion can be most destructive. At one time or another, to one degree or another, most managers have agonized over trying to motivate an individual with the lure of promotion while knowing that the individual does not have much of a chance. Candor may result in employees' short-term unhappiness and even in their leaving the company, but we suggest that the long-run effects of dissembling are far worse. Eventually truth will out, and the negative effects of disappointment are likely to harm not only the individual's performance at work but also, through the spillover effect, his private life — at a time when perhaps it's too late for him to change jobs.

Reduce Organizational Uncertainty

Uncertainty is an increasingly frequent fixture of today's world. Sudden, unpredictable events — like an oil shortage or the taking of hostages in Iran — can have massive impact on the lives of managers in Dallas, Paris, or Bogotá. Economic recession lurks in the background, and no one feels entirely safe. The jobless executive next door makes many a manager aware that "it could also happen to me." Reorganization and restructuring of companies have become almost annual events; and sudden policy changes have vast repercussions on people's lives that create worries and preoccupations and lead to emotional spillover.

Managers can help reduce unnecessary stress and uncertainty by protecting their subordinates from worry about events over which they have no control. A good example of this is the young manager of a foreign exchange department in a large bank. It is difficult to imagine a more uncertain, hectic, anxiety-ridden job. When we asked him how he managed, he answered: "I protect my subordinates and I trust them. When my superiors drop by to tell us how stupid what we did yesterday was and ask who did it, I tell them that it's none of their business. I offer them my job if they want it. That shuts them up quite fast."

We asked him how he could trust his subordinates in a department that could lose millions in a day. He answered: "I trust them because I have to. And I have learned to show them that I trust them by leaving them alone to do their jobs and helping them only when they ask for help."

Here we have a "shock-absorbing" manager. However, the price for his courage is enormous. He absorbs a lot of the anxiety around him, acting as a buffer against many pressures. He has an ulcer and no nails, but his subordinates love him.

Top managers cannot expect to have many people like this in their ranks. But they clearly need people who can absorb as many shocks for others as possible. And they owe it to such people to relieve them from positions where uncertainty is too high by systematically rotating these jobs after a certain time. People can protect others from uncertainty and anxiety (to some extent this is part of a manager's job), but only for so long.

Whose Life Is It Anyway?

In managerial circles, there's something almost sacred about the separation between private and professional life. The respect for an individual's privacy is one of our fundamental values. However, no one can deny that work has a powerful effect on private life. The issue is where does responsible behavior stop and where does interference begin?

The individual executive adheres to the principle that his private life is none of the organization's business. But today he does expect the organization asking him to accept a big new job in Latin America to consider as legitimate his concerns about, say, his three children and his wife with her own career. In the interest of his future performance, the corporation is well advised to listen and respond to his concerns.

We do not need to invoke altruism to recommend that organizations make sure their people are in jobs that fit them, that they can cope with the changes the organization may ask of them, and that they have the tools for realistic self-assessment. Doing this is essential to the morale and productivity of the organization.

Responsible behavior on the part of the organization is simply behavior that is in its own best interest. This means recognizing the emotional aspects of work and career. A person's capacity to enjoy doing a job is as important a consideration as his potential competence.

Even if organizations choose not to deal with these issues, the changing values and life-styles of younger managers—especially those in dual-career marriages—may eventually force top management to face the impact work has on private life.

REFERENCES

1. See our article, "Professional Lives Versus Private Lives—Shifting Patterns of Managerial Commitment," *Organizational Dynamics*, Spring 1979, p. 2.

2. Ibid.

3. Abraham Zaleznik, "Management of Disappointment," HBR November-December, 1967, p. 59.

4. Edgar H. Schein, *Career Dynamics* (Reading, Mass.: Addison-Wesley, 1978).

5. See, for example, Harry Levinson, "Emotional Health in the World of Work" in *Management by Guilt* (New York: Harper & Row, 1964), pp. 267–291.

PART
FIVE

Retiring with Grace

All things necessarily must come to an end. With respect to careers, retirement can be an especially difficult time. To many it means giving up power, prestige, position. To others it means potential loss of contact with stimulating activity with which they have been engaged for a long time. For some it means they're free at last to do what they had long postponed. In effect, for the last group, retirement becomes a potential for yet another career.

There are a good many issues that need to be dealt with as you approach this time. If you are in an organization, there is the issue of succession and the feelings that are attendant on both choosing a successor and turning over the reins to that person. There's also the issue of coming to terms with your own ego ideal and the degree to which you feel comfortable about your achievements as you must pull away from them. For so many in managerial and executive roles in our culture, work has been the means of justifying oneself to oneself and to others. The move into retirement is often thought of as being accompanied by a sense of uselessness and potential demoralization. As one senior person in a retirement community put it to me, "In retirement, every day is like Saturday afternoon." Of course, every day need not be like Saturday afternoon. The point, however, is that this phase of your life, like all the others, needs anticipation, consideration, and action. It calls for the exercise of the same good judgment that a person has been carrying out up to this point.

To help the executive reader think of one of the most fundamental issues with respect to retirement, I have described in "Don't Choose Your Own Successor" some of the major struggles that prominent chief executives have as they come close to leaving their organizations and then have to leave them in the hands of others. I note that we are all caught up in the wish to demonstrate that nobody can do our job better than we can and sometimes we don't want somebody to even try to do so. That means that it's important to understand yourself and your motivations, as indicated in the first chapter, in order to exercise good judgment at this particular time. I suggest some ways that you might cope with the problem, as both a potential successor as well as a significant executive in top management.

Thomas H. Fitzgerald, in "The Loss of Work: Notes from Retirement," describes what happened to him when he was suddenly forced into retirement. He speaks of the isolation and the absence of the wish to do anything. He points out that perhaps only in retirement people discover much of whom they have become. When we abandon work, we leave part of ourselves behind. He raises the important question, "Do we decide to go on and become something else?" He makes it clear that you can't put off thinking about your postretirement years.

Leland P. Bradford describes what happened to him when he retired in "Can You Survive Your Retirement?" He speaks of the first terrible year and the weeks of talking with his wife and others. He asks why this transition period was so difficult and so different from others he had negotiated. Then he elaborates on his conclusions, particularly the recognition that you can carry on in retirement a second or third career. His ideas complement Fitzgerald's. Both come to the appropriate conclusion that of necessity we all are in charge of our own careers and that we ourselves must take the initiative with respect to them.

Wheelock Whitney and William G. Damroth, in "Don't Call It 'Early Retirement'," describe how they took charge of themselves and their careers. Whitney moved from a CEO role to teaching management and chairing a public service organization. Damroth turned from finance to wildlife photography. Each describes the forces that led to his new career and the gratifications that each is now able to enjoy.

However, giving up, in the sense of yielding your previous work connections and obligations, isn't necessarily easy. It's particularly difficult when what you are giving up is your own company. Michael G. Berolzheimer talks about the intensity of that struggle in "The Financial and Emotional Sides of Selling Your Company." He walks us step by step through the problems of making the decision to sell and then, from his experience, draws conclusions that will be important for anyone who has started his or her own organization to consider. But even selling the company is not the end for him. He, too, turns to a new career in venture capital support of consumer companies.

Coda

That's the panorama. In every stage in our lives, we are necessarily concerned with what we are doing with ourselves and what we will be doing with ourselves when today becomes tomorrow or even only yesterday. Much of what is in these articles says, one way or another, that all of us can make our lives more poetic. We can do that if we think more about ourselves and what we want to do with ourselves in the extremely limited amount of time represented by a life. We may well achieve additional pleasure, gratification, and a different kind of success, as we examine the psychological nooks and crannies of our experiences that we seem to ignore so often while we concentrate so heavily on the big issues, whatever they may be. Centrally what these articles say is that life is to be lived, not merely to be worked. If a farmer doesn't understand his soil, it doesn't take long for the soil to become barren. If he doesn't allow it to lie fallow, then it loses its capacity for regeneration. So it is with human beings. Unlike other creatures, we have the capacity for introspection, retrospection, and prospection; the ability to examine ourselves, to learn about ourselves, to choose a direction, to change directions, and to take advantage of all that is around us. We have many ties to the world that give us a continuing flow of affection and support. These, as we have seen from these articles, provide stability and foster our growth. Though our physiological aging may impair our functioning, it is nevertheless a fact that we have the capacity to think and to feel and to act on both feelings and thoughts. That capacity enables us to establish a course and to change it when we think it needs changing. These pieces, then, are like maps. After telling us something about how to determine a course, they lay out some of the currents and cross-currents, the rocks and the shoals, and the shallow places. They point out those forces that move us along if we know how to use them. They call our attention to the varieties of human association and human existence and repeatedly point to the moorings and the anchorings that provide protection when it's time to pause and rethink our course. They speak of storms and calm. The maritime metaphor is most apropos. One is either a helmsman or simply flotsam.

1

Don't Choose Your Own Successor

HARRY LEVINSON

According to good managerial practice, every CEO, executive, and manager ought to select and prepare his own successor. My contention, however, is that this hallowed practice often creates more problems for an organization than it solves. Taken separately or together, there are four reasons why a CEO may select a successor who will fail:

1. A hindsighted incumbent may be oblivious to the changing business conditions that dictate a different role for the organization's new leader.

2. The process of choosing a successor can founder on the CEO's unawareness of the qualities that made him a success, and that may therefore be necessary in the man who replaces him.

3. Unconscious feelings of rivalry toward anyone able to fill his shoes can blind the CEO in his choice.

4. Obligations to tradition can so circumscribe the selection process that innovators and outsiders are not even considered for the job.

In short, for a CEO to choose his own successor is an organizationally hazardous activity that might better be abolished.

The failures due to this practice are sometimes difficult to spot. They are too easily explained away by clichés such as the Peter Principle or obscured by highly rationalized management shuffles. The failures, however, are very conspicuous in that position most open to public observation: the post of chief executive officer. Recall the following widely publicized incidents:

William A. Patterson, the longtime head of United Airlines, named George E. Keck as his successor. In short order, Keck, who had been with the company for 24 years, was replaced by Edward E. Carlson, a hotel company executive.

After leading American Airlines into first place in its industry, Cyrus R. Smith selected George A. Spater as his successor. Spater lasted five years, and Smith was asked to return.

When David Rockefeller became chairman and chief executive of Chase Manhattan Corporation in March 1969, he named Herbert Patterson, a 20-year veteran of the bank, as president. In October 1972 Rockefeller fired Patterson.

Between 1968 and 1971, 11 key officers and directors, including executive vice president E. P. Reid, who was thought to be a potential successor to Chairman Armand Hammer, left Occidental Petroleum. In December 1973, Joseph E. Baird was chosen over two other "probables," who had come and gone in as many years, to become Hammer's fifth hand-picked successor.

In 1964 Augustus Long retired as chairman and chief executive officer of Texaco. He was succeeded by I. Howard Rambin, who retired in 1970 and was in turn succeeded by Long. According to people in the industry, Long continues to run the organization, although he has been officially replaced by Maurice F. Granville.

In February 1973, I. John Billera, chairman of U.S. Industries, named Charles E. Selecman, who had come up through the ranks, as vice chairman and chief executive officer, and Arthur S. Nicholas as president. By September 1973 Nicholas had gone; by November Selecman had gone. Billera was once again chief executive officer. In August 1974 Billera named C. Russell Luigs as the fourth president of U.S. Industries in 11 months.

In 1969 there was another spectacular—when Henry Ford II fired Semon E. Knudsen as president of Ford Motor Company. Although Knudsen had never before worked for Henry Ford, the two men had known each other for many years. Knudsen's father had worked for the first Henry Ford.

These executive selection failures might be attributed to a wide range of reasons: external events, the wrong man (or woman, and throughout, inclusion of the female sex is understood) in the wrong job at the wrong time, or combinations of other forces. But I would like to advance another hypothesis: *all failed because they were chosen by the person whom they were supposed to replace.*

Before arguing this hypothesis, let me first interject a cautionary note. I have never met any of the executives mentioned in the examples, nor do I have direct knowledge of them or their companies. I have chosen these examples because the experiences are public knowledge, the companies are familiar to most managers, and the circumstances exemplify the discussion that follows. Nor am I asserting that *all* executives who choose their successors are bound to choose wrongly, only that many do.

These cases are a small sample of failures at top and lower management levels in large companies. In small companies it is easy to see how bad choices can be made; the resources for evaluating personnel and jobs are limited, and there are far fewer people to choose from.

Such reasoning, however, would hardly seem to apply to the examples listed, which concern some of the nation's largest companies. Such large businesses have at their disposal unlimited evaluative resources. Their managements have had years to observe the executives who have been promoted into these positions. Moreover, the success of these enterprises attests to the accumulated wisdom of executives who, because they have made their own organizations leaders in their industries, clearly know the requirements of their jobs.

But even though a company may have access to all the expertise it needs to evaluate executives, it is not uncommon for an organization to have problems in establishing a good line of succession. Since 1966, 30% of all new presidents and CEOs have been brought in from the outside, and nearly half of all the top executives promoted into these positions had less than ten years' prior experience with their organizations.[1]

Given that choosing a successor is a problem for any executive, we still have no way of knowing how frequently CEOs or other executives and managers unconsciously select successors who are bound to fail. Nevertheless, I am certain that it happens in a high proportion of situations where the CEO himself does the choosing or is the single dominant voice in the selection.

Of course, some CEOs have done a good job of choosing their successors or many organizations would long since have disappeared. But since so many executives are preoccupied with finding the best person to succeed them, and since so many have failed, I am concerned here to pinpoint why failure occurs, to describe who some of the likely candidates for failure may be, and to discuss what can be done to sidestep the successor problem.

Forces Behind Failure

To varying degrees we are all caught up in the wish to demonstrate that nobody can do our job better than we can. To varying degrees we are also determined that nobody is going to supplant us and that our contributions will endure. These inner pressures sometimes blind us to what we are actually doing. They may lead us to make choices which, despite apparent rationality, can be subsequently characterized as "stupid." When the behavior of an intelligent person, such as a successful CEO, seems "stupid," it may be a clue that the behavior is motivated by unconscious, irrational forces. In the CEO, psychological forces likely to be destructive to him and the organization are probably at work.

At the outset I mentioned four reasons why a CEO might choose incorrectly and ensure that his successor will fail.

Hindsighted Incumbent

Every executive is already doing what he thinks should be done. In effect he has already discounted the future. He has his own perceptions, his own behavior patterns, his own limits of experience, and his own blind spots. He can choose only within that framework. It is therefore frequently difficult for an incumbent to know what other tasks the future will require of his successor, what different talents the job will demand, and what new problems will in time arise.

Because they dealt successfully with the problems they faced, many incumbents make the mistake of assuming that new problems will never occur. It is, however, more than likely that a successor will have to give attention to issues not within the range of his predecessor's strengths or vision. In a world characterized by changing social and economic trends, a successor will have to deal with problems his predecessor could not foresee.

The vigorously entrepreneurial president of the largest bank in a middle-sized community designated a quiet man of great dignity as his successor. The entrepreneur was a man of considerable force who had built his bank into the largest in his community, and whose influence extended to the rest of the state. He was a kingmaker in politics; leading citizens sought his financial advice. Thinking the world would always be the same as he found it, and that he had licked it, the president assumed his quiet successor would play only an integrative role. The obscure successor was, however, faced with an increasingly diverse competitive situation. There was the need to develop branch banks, multiple forms of extending credit, and an active marketing program to protect the bank against encroaching newer banks with younger leadership. The quiet, diplomatic successor was not the person to develop competitive strategy or lead an aggressive counterattack.

Choosing someone who will act on his own, indeed perhaps in a way completely opposite to what was done before, runs afoul of the predecessor's psychology. Fred C. Foy, former chairman of Koppers Company, argues that after any man has been chief executive officer for about ten years, he should fire himself.[2] Foy contends that the cumulative effect of the boss's decisions is likely to be a bosslike corporate pattern by the end of ten years. This pattern of decision, however good it may have been, does not satisfy a changing society or key people in the organization. Unfulfilled executives will depart, leaving behind those who are in greater agreement with the boss and who, therefore, tend to have an inadequate grasp of alternative possibilities. Being human, Foy says, a CEO promotes these favorites.

Furthermore, the longer anyone occupies a given position, the more it becomes psychologically his. Like the entrepreneur who marries the organization, a long-term incumbent marries his job. He and it are almost synonymous (a perfect illustration was the relationship between J. Edgar Hoover and the FBI).

Limited Self-Understanding

Even if the predecessor really wants to select a successor who can maintain the same thrust, there is another problem. It is almost impossible for the incumbent to recognize, let alone fully appreciate, what unique and subtle aspects of his own personality have been instrumental in his success. Consequently, it is unlikely that he can perceive those qualities in others.

Few executives are as self-confident as most people believe them to be. Like the rest of us, they rarely do as well in their own eyes as they would like. Often they do not really know the reason for their success. They have great difficulty tolerating failure; indeed, they are usually their own harshest critics. In short, their ego ideals—their images of themselves as they would like to be—are considerably beyond their self-images—their present view of themselves.

Constantly concerned about doing better, they tend to discount what they have already done. "That was yesterday" is a frequent executive statement. More action-oriented than introspective, most do not know their inner thoughts and feelings very well; frequently, they do not want to know. They tend to belittle their competence and take it for granted.

The chairman of a discount chain was neither an accountant nor an expert in finance. Nevertheless, his financial acumen was held in high esteem by those who lent him money, and his word as well as his judgment was valued by loan officers. Although he did not think very highly of himself and failed to recognize his own strengths and abilities, others valued him greatly. When people told him of his strengths and competence, he laughed them off saying, "Oh, anybody can do it." Indeed, he thought his competence was very limited and that somebody who was more professionally specialized than he would do better in banking circles. Recognizing that a crucial aspect of his work had to do with getting lines of credit, he appointed a financial officer as crown prince. The CEO was astonished to learn that the bankers did not want to do business with the man he had chosen to succeed him.

Unconscious Rivalry

Even if executives are able to perceive their own competence accurately, most are unable to tolerate another person like themselves in their own organization. The process of selecting an executive successor may psychologically recapitulate particular problems of rivalry that stem from experiences in early life.

Rivalry starts with the wish of the small child to grow out of its helplessness and incompetence by emulating the parent of the same sex, thereby seeking to take this parent's place in the other parent's eyes. If the child is abnormally frustrated in these attempts, he may become an inordinately rivalrous adult. Or it may be the case that children who are heavily pressured by their parents to mature will turn against their siblings, whom they do see as competitive but defeatable. Such situations are often reenacted in adult life between peers in an organization whose leader thwarts their progress.

Just as few parents appreciate feelings of rivalry between their children, few executives appreciate the intensity of the same feelings between their subordinates. Having made it to the top, executives tend to forget how consciously rivalrous they were before they got there. By definition, they are still unaware of their unconscious rivalry. So they assume losers will not be hostile and will take their losses with good grace. Dreams of never-never land notwithstanding, organizations, like ancient kingdoms, are often racked by continuing conflicts for power. Long after the original protagonists have gone, individuals and departments still fight with one another without really knowing why.

The more dominant the executive, the more powerful he is in his organization and the more likely he is to have problems appointing a successor. The reasons are self-evident. First, if he is truly rivalrous, he simply cannot stand to appoint someone who may do the job as well or better. And, second, the greater the power the executive attains, the more likely it is that he has defeated his rivals unequivocally. Some of those contenders leave the organization. Others, passive in their defeat, lose motivation and fall back on sinecures. The executive's dominance over his subordinates teaches them to be dominant over theirs, forcing the more enterprising ones to leave. In a short time, the organization contains few promising young executives with either the ability or the desire to make a bid for the top spot.

Obligation to Tradition

Simultaneously, however, such a manager or executive, particularly one in an organization that promotes from within, will feel an obligation both to his people and to the methods by which power and position have traditionally been attained in the organization. He will therefore most likely choose somebody who will carry on the organization's policies and traditions, many of which have become his own. He feels he must balance everyone's interests by retaining the prevailing paths to success. A person who becomes a chief executive officer of a highly bureaucratized organization, where those who follow him and are loyal to him obey the rules and expect to succeed according to those rules, will rarely change the structure of the organization significantly.

The president of a large, traditional organization realized that a massive restructuring was necessary to cope with new trends in the marketplace. He also saw, however, that to revitalize the company he would have to allow younger, stronger men to bypass older employees who were "serving time" in their present positions and who were expecting to be rewarded by advancement to higher office. The president understood his executives' assumptions, as he himself had advanced through the same procedure. So although he saw the need for change, he could not bring himself to make it and disappoint his loyal followers, many of whom he knew personally. His chosen successor, a man of similar pattern, sees the same problem but feels equally obligated to maintain the tradition. It will be only a few years before adherence to this pattern creates a crisis situation in that company.

A CEO's obligation to tradition, reinforced by potential feelings of guilt should he betray his followers, poses a painful problem for an organization needing a leader who will change the rules and redirect the organization to new business circumstances and responsibilities.

In family organizations there is a different kind of tradition problem: one must take into account how a successor will fit in among the family members. Where there are significant family conflicts, an organization needs a combination Solomon and Moses to build bridges between the factions and lead the company forward.

As I pointed out in a previous article, family organizations have always had a difficult time with succession.[3] Regardless of their own lineup, family members will ultimately unite against anyone, including trusted insiders, who pushes views, however constructive, that oppose those of the family.

The founding head of a national distributor of food products was succeeded by his son-in-law. The son-in-law, a kind, gentle, thoughtful man, vowed to make up for the impulsive harshness of his father-in-law, and was widely respected in the organization for his intentions. But even with the urging of his professional managers, it soon became clear that the son-in-law had great difficulty making decisions. As a consequence, the organization became increasingly demoralized. When consultants proved useless, the professional managers sought to obtain the support of the retired chief. They soon found, however, that he and his successor were allied in the path they were following, even if it meant the ultimate death of the organization. Though the two relatives were constantly at each other's throat because of the differences in their managerial approach, when outsiders realistically pointed to the consequences of organizational drifting and pushed for action, the two presented a solid front in the face of what they saw as threats.

In family companies like this one or in organizations where the chief executive officer has served for a long time, the board of directors is characteristically weak and "belongs" to the CEO. Here the chances of a good successor being chosen are slim. The choice is likely to be the CEO's altogether.

The considerations I have discussed individually and collectively create a hazard in those organizations where the CEO chooses his own successor. And to the degree to which incumbents "own" their roles, managers are mysteries to themselves, rivalry is stimulated, or traditions and/or families are strong, there are similar problems at all managerial levels. These forces together produce classic circumstances of ambivalence, the resolving of which nearly guarantee that the CEO will choose a successor who will fail.

The Faces of Failure

Ambivalence occurs when positive and negative feelings, one of which is usually unconscious (most often the negative feeling) are simultaneously felt in connection with the same object. Every person has experienced ambivalence. Think of managerial positions that you have held, particularly those in which you made significant changes or restructured the managerial role. How did you feel when your successor took over, even though his doing so was the necessary precondition for your own upward mobility? And particularly, how did you feel when your successor changed some of your most cherished innovations?

Although ambivalence occurs at all managerial levels, its results are seen most vividly in the selection of the CEO. The need to resolve the conflicts of ambivalence leads a CEO to choose one of four typical candidates as his successor. Each choice is meant to demonstrate that no one can run the organization like the retiring executive.

The Loyal Servant

The easiest unconscious way for a CEO to resolve his ambivalent feelings is to choose a successor who is a loyal and conscientious servant of unquestionable integrity and dedication. The servant will, however, have long ago denied his rivalrous feelings, either because he reacted against them or because he could not compete with his predecessor. If such an heir apparent is also a person who has neither the ability nor the competence to do what the CEO does, especially in a structure tailormade to the CEO's own mode of operation, he is bound to fail. By choosing such a man, the CEO appeases his conscience, repays loyalty, and maintains traditional organizational pathways. By this choice, however, the CEO also makes sure that his influence will persist in the organization and that no one will be able to fill his shoes. Under the loyal servant the company is likely to go downhill until a competent rescuer stops the slide.

The chief executive officer of a gas distribution company named as his successor a man whose single claim to fame was the fact that he was the first person the CEO met when he joined that company many years before. At the time the successor was a clerk. He moved into the executive suite as, in effect, a servant of the boss. When the boss became terminally ill, his chosen successor took over. Before long it became apparent that the crown prince was indeed still a clerk and that the organization was falling apart. The board sought an external rescuer whose competence had been demonstrated in other situations.

The rescuer did manage to pull the organization back together again but not without the continual backbiting of the interim CEO, who sat on the board and was determined to maintain his own predecessor's traditions.

A variant of the loyal servant is the assistant or protégé whom the CEO believes to be so young or so old that that person cannot possibly succeed him. What follows is an interregnum leader, who presumably is to be a caretaker until a new succession evolves.

The Watchful Waiter

If by his unconscious defeat of strong (or support of weak) people, the CEO has made certain that there is no one in the organization to succeed him, he goes to the outside for a stellar performer. It is not unusual for college presidents, generals, or officials at certain levels of government to be recruited into such roles. Then, although everybody in the organization recognizes the heir apparent, he is given no real power despite his title. He merely waits.

The watchful waiter's life is usually not a placid one. He soon discovers that his crown prince role also entitles him to be chief scapegoat. Having wooed and won him, the CEO turns on him. Most often around petty matters, the boss attacks and manipulates the heir. One such crown prince suddenly discovered that his long-planned and previously announced vacation was arbitrarily canceled by his boss.

As his prospective retirement time approaches, the boss's criticisms rise in intensity. In fact, he often either postpones retirement, stops talking about it, or both. He indicates that he is no longer confident in his crown prince and creates doubt in the mind of the latter about whether he ever will succeed. By undermining him with board members, the CEO builds support for his own continuation. The crown prince is left to agonize between sticking it out and leaving. If he leaves, he is a defeated man and a less likely candidate for succession elsewhere. If he stays, he runs the risk of losing face in the organization.

Under pressure from his bankers to find a successor, the retiring CEO of a chemical manufacturing company chose the company lawyer to take his place. The lawyer was reluctant to give up his practice to take on this managerial role but, under continuous pressure from the CEO, finally did so. For nearly ten years the successor lived in the shadow of the CEO, who became increasingly disenchanted with his protégé, and who, at renewed "requests" from his board, stayed on and on. The boss eventually succumbed to a coronary and the lawyer succeeded him. Having adopted his predecessor's view that his own subordinates were inferiors, the successor turned to another company for his potential successor, whom he now treats in much the same way as he himself was treated.

If by some chance a person from within the organization thought to be a weak rival turns out to be stronger than anticipated, the CEO is prone to turn on him in the same way. This is likely to happen if the potential successor is around 38 to 40 years old, a time when, according to Daniel Levinson of Yale University, one wants to throw off his mentor and stand on his own feet.[4] The assertion of greater independence is likely to incur accusations of ingratitude, disloyalty, and rebellion from the CEO.

At lower levels, when potential successors are repeatedly brought in either from the outside or other areas, the same phenomenon is evident. The successors are just as frequently put down by the boss. Managers who tend to make scapegoats of their subordinates are likely to become even more blatant in their attacks on potential successors.

The False Prophet

A person whose area of competence is unrelated to the leadership role for which he is chosen, and who therefore cannot deliver what is unrealistically expected of him, ends up being a false prophet. Often he is somebody's else's second-in-command who has never himself been in a number-one role. Or he may simply be the wrong man at the wrong time. When Howard W. Johnson was made president of M.I.T., he was chosen for a mediative role. His task was to integrate and maintain peace among a number of academic power centers. By way of contrast, when John R. Silber became president of Boston University, his task was to take charge of a demoralized institution and give it a sense of purpose. Johnson would have been an unlikely candidate for Silber's job, and vice-versa. In the other's role it is likely that each would have been a false prophet and that each, therefore, would have failed.

Sometimes candidates are chosen for top executive responsibility because of a spectacular achievement. Dwight D. Eisenhower's military record influenced his being chosen as president of Columbia and of the United States. S.I. Hayakawa became president of San Francisco State College as a result of his forthright action in the face of student disturbances. Some top executives are chosen for their conceptual thinking, which is expected to bring either a desired performance or an imaginative approach to an organization. Two such examples are George W. Beadle, a Nobel prize-winning biologist, who was for a short time president of the University of Chicago, and James P. Dixon, a public health officer who is president of Antioch College. These men could be viewed as false prophets in management. By way of contrast, Father Theodore Hesburgh seems to have brought both a new model and skillful management to Notre Dame.

The Empty Nest

One way to defeat a successor is not to have one. Despite pressures from his board, from financial institutions, and from others, the chief executive officer may designate none. The same procrastination may also occur at lower levels. At any level, this kind of behavior perpetuates and magnifies the rivalry among subordinate executives, leads to defensiveness, disappointment, intraorganizational hostility, and empire building—all of which enlarge the task of any potential successor.

A newspaper publisher structured the succession in his newspaper chain so that his employees would own the chain, but so that no one would have effective financial and therefore administrative control. Multiple conflicting forces thus operate within both the board and management. The resulting compromise management makes it impossible for a decisive leader to arise and give significant direction to the enterprise, which is afflicted by continuous internecine warfare, high turnover among managing executives, and great frustration for others.

If subordinates have a leadership vacuum for some time, they are likely to evolve mutual protective pacts to defeat or limit an incoming boss. If the board or superiors feel dependent on them, the subordinates may even force the successor out. This, according to newspaper reports, was what happened to Knudsen at Ford.[5] Such a cycle can go on until severe deterioration occurs.

Is a "Successor" Possible?

A few chief executives, but not as many as I would like to see, cope with the succession problem effectively. These are the men who, sufficiently secure in their own self-image as capable executives, do not need to defeat somebody else to prove themselves. Their self-images do not hinge on building monuments to themselves or perpetuating their names. They can comfortably take pride in the success of their subordinates and the continued momentum of their organizations. Like Philip Sporn of American Electric Power, who successfully turned over his reins to Donald C. Cook, they permit solid succession. But such CEOs are rarer than most chief executive officers would like to believe.

Some men step back from the process of selecting their successors, as did Nathan Pusey when he retired from the presidency of Harvard University. When an executive does that, most often a committee (from the board if he is a CEO, or from among other executives if he is at a lower level) assesses the organization's needs and evaluates likely candidates. Recently the board of Emerson Electric Company screened 150 candidates for a successor to its CEO, Wallace R. Parsons.[6] In academic circles, students and alumni are increasingly involved in both processes. Similar procedures for wider company involvement are likely to develop in industry.

A person who is chosen under these circumstances has a better chance to win a supportive constituency and the mantle of leadership. He is therefore more apt to be a solid citizen, already well on his way to being integrated into the organization.

But for most executives and CEOs the successor problem is not easy to deal with, particularly as it touches so deeply on their psyches. In my opinion, however, there is one sure sign that CEOs and their boards might look for to indicate whether the CEO or executive is going to have difficulty appointing an heir. And if the sign is apparent, there are some questions a company can ask itself to help solve the successor problem.

Clues and Questions

I hold it to be an axiom that the degree of difficulty any executive is going to have with the succession problem will be reflected in the speed and intensity with which he rejects the thesis of this article. If a CEO is sufficiently dismayed at his reactions to my arguments and if he is willing to discuss his ambivalent feelings with someone in an attempt to resolve them, there might not be a difficult problem. But if the CEO rejects the notion that he might be unconsciously bound to sabotage a successor, there is a problem indeed, and not just for the CEO. Then the successor problem is clearly the responsibility of the whole organization.

If the chief executive officer is unwilling to act on this problem, the board of directors may have to take the initiative. This is, in fact, the ideal. Replacements for all important management posts, including supervisors, subordinates, executives, and even board members themselves, should be decided by a committee which includes several levels. When a position is about to become vacant, the committee should evaluate what demands the position makes on the incumbent. The members should ask themselves what combination of crises in the marketplace, consumer reactions, conservation problems, and economic issues will confront a person in this position. And they should consider what the role itself will require for the organization's continued evolution.

Only after the board can answer these questions should the next one arise, "Who has the talents and abilities to deal with the foreseen problems?" The board or committee should insist on seeing a detailed performance appraisal begun early in the candidate's managerial career. Such an appraisal should include an exact description of what he did. That is, it should include specific responses to given situations. Only from such specific descriptions of behavior in context can inferences be made about how a person is likely to operate in a future context.

The performance appraisal should also give particular emphasis to a candidate's capacity for independent action. That is, what can this manager do by himself? It should also include information about what a person's subordinates think of him. No one knows a person as well as those reporting to him.

What criteria should be used in selecting a chief executive officer, or any senior manager for that matter? An increasingly diverse marketplace, a rapidly changing environment, the continuing erosion of reward-punishment motivational methods and rigid organizational structures—they all combine to require new talents of the executive. Some of the most obvious are:

The ability to conceptualize strategically in order to chart a comprehensive map of the organization's needs and a way of moving toward the goals he has defined.

The ability to define where he himself is going and how being chief executive officer of his organization contributes toward that goal. A strongly defined individual will be able to give support to the people in his organization, thus minimizing the pecking order as the major style of life.

The ability to develop a range of talent in his subordinates and to indicate, in order to support interdependence rather than rivalry, that he values two-way communication between them, and between them and himself.

Whether he should be conservative or liberal, young or old, hinges on the nature of the marketplace. Generally speaking, the more volatile the marketplace and the greater the creativity required to cope with it, the younger the CEO is likely to have to be. A demoralized organization will usually require someone older who can take charge and display the charisma to enlist his followers in their collective cause.

Concluding Note

Each of us in his own unconscious way seeks omnipotence and immortality. To varying degrees, each wants his achievements to stand as an enduring monument to himself; each wants to demonstrate that he was necessary to his organization, that it cannot do without him. This pressure is particularly strong for entrepreneurs and those who hold their positions for long periods of time. As a result, although executives consciously seek to perpetuate their organizations through the wise choice of successors, unconsciously they also seek to demonstrate that no one can succeed them. The way to avoid disaster is not to court it in the first place. Reliance on a committee to select successors for important managerial positions can reconfirm the old truth of safety in numbers.

REFERENCES

1. A.C. Croft, "Editor to Reader," *Personnel Journal*, December 1973, p. 1027.
2. "Why Bosses Should Fire Themselves," *Forbes*, April 15, 1970, p. 93.
3. "Conflicts That Plague Family Businesses," HBR March–April 1971, p. 90.
4. D.A. Sanche, "What Happens—Emotionally and Physically—When a Man Reaches 40," *Today's Health*, Vol. 51, 1973, pp. 40–43.
5. "Bunkie's Downfall—Palace Revolt Forced Henry Ford to Remove Knudsen as President," *Wall Street Journal*, September 17, 1969.
6. "The Successor," *Forbes*, March 15, 1974, p. 68.

2

The Loss of Work: Notes from Retirement

THOMAS H. FITZGERALD

After a lifetime of work, the career was over. The news came suddenly one afternoon. An organizational consolidation would eliminate my position in middling executive ranks and permit my early retirement. First, disbelief, then gratitude: "I won't ever have to work again!" The endless weekend. A pardon from the governor, after so many years.

But soon after the door clicked shut behind me, I felt unexpectedly disoriented. It was like a traffic accident, I've come to think: one minute you're just driving along and the next you're looking up from the pavement. One day I had a wide office, a big desk and management-level chair, my own secretary, even a walnut credenza to hide junk in. The next day I was sitting home in a sweater and corduroys watching the snow fall outside.

The isolation intensified. Weeks passed, and never a call from any of the people I had so often worked with, traveled with, lunched with. Incredible. Until I realized that I had done exactly the same to those who had retired before me. Nothing personal; they merely became the disappeared. Occasionally, one of them would turn up at the office to check on his benefits or whatever, and then we'd remember, "There's old Charlie!" Well, I would not display myself as another of those has-beens.

Nor, in fact, was there much of anything I wanted to do. Now that the demands, expectations, implicit rules — the pushes and pulls of organizational life — had been removed, I was curiously disabled. It was as if my capacity for having intentions had atrophied by long attention to the wishes of others. Images came to mind of the old family servant, finally let out with a small pension, who sits about waiting for the pub to open; or the long-term con who at last stands outside the gates, suitcase in hand, but with no place he can think of to go. Now that freedom was here, it was without content. For someone who had valued it as I had, the experience was chastening.

Considering how I started out, my years in a blue-chip corporation would have seemed unlikely. I was a boy during the Great Depression and grew up in New Jersey with a working-class outlook. In those days, most work was hard, unsafe, and it wore men out. Yet the loss of work was a terrible event, especially to men with large families. Few women worked outside the house, and people had to be destitute to get on relief. My parents' families were mostly clerks—none of your computer excitement then—and they used to urge us to learn a trade so as not to slip down into the poorer world of navvies, or "ditch diggers" as they were called. No one ever spoke of having a career but rather of having work or of their hopes for getting employment. Priests sometimes talked of having a vocation, but we understood that meant a calling to religious life.

From my father I learned to see work as security. He worried so, in the 1930s, about losing out the next time the employer's roll was cut. A captive of the tradition in which fathers did not share their responsibility for the family's welfare, he was baffled and chronically discouraged by the cruelties of the economic system.

He got by with various jobs during much of that long decade. But at dinnertime he talked of this or that fellow who had been laid off or of hungry people in other cities who he'd heard were picking scraps out of garbage cans. During a long strike at the shipyard there was no paycheck for some months, and the main meal every day was a pot of soup. "You can *live* on that," he would say, as if living itself was a small victory—which I suppose it was.

All this made us rather serious children, grateful for kindnesses and aware of our vulnerability. On summer nights, workmen in knit undershirts would sit together on the steps of tenements drinking beer from tin pails. On Sundays, Italians raced pigeons from rickety cages on high flat roofs, while my German grandfather played pinochle through the afternoon with his cronies in the back of his penny-candy store. I knew even then there was life beyond that shabby neighborhood. My father used to bring home old issues of the *National Geographic* bought for a few cents at second-hand book stands, and I would look at the pages of pictures over and over, hoping to go some day to those faraway tropical places (now known as LDCs).

To be sure, the parochial schools I attended helped form my view of the adult world, as schools always do in one way or another. The nuns would tell their small charges of our fallen condition, of the need to be forgiven; they implied that grace was earned, not universally bestowed. The Seven Deadly Sins—a litany now forgotten—included a condemnation of sloth. Occasionally, there was a whipping or verbal shaming of a child, a far cry from the self-expression now promoted in middle-class schools. That training in obedience and docility —the hidden curriculum—was not without future value in getting a job and pleasing the boss enough to keep it.

I dropped out of school at 16 to help support the family. I was, after all, the eldest son. Although I had been delivering newspapers and groceries, my first real job was as a messenger in the financial district of downtown New York. There, in a silly uniform and cap, I walked the streets in any kind of weather to bring cablegrams to the outer offices of white-collar America. Because I was a polite, helpful sort of lad, someone eventually brought me inside where I was able to better myself. The company was steady and secure, and I might have been stuck there forever had not the army found me.

Military service did not improve my attitude toward work. If anything, it brought out all my latent doubts. Recruits, however patriotic, were ordered about by arrogant noncoms; the latter reminded me of my worst bosses and foreshadowed some of the factory foremen I would meet later on. They had that same style of command: the way to get work done was to order people about.

In the army I learned that when we labor under coercion and disparagement, we do so grudgingly and infect each other with the resentment of the indentured.

By chance, after shipment to Europe, I found an obscure corner in military government where I spent months without having to work seriously. It seemed not only luxury but also a successful evasion of the system.

The time lost during the war was recovered in a subsidy for attending college, which I supplemented with a series of jobs. But by then a stiff-spined independence showed through my clerky veneer. My home, and being away from home, had strengthened my character but left me ambivalent toward authority. This ambivalence I've never been able to shake, though eventually it hit me that there is a better freedom than escaping the demands of others; that freedom *from* is not the same as freedom *to*. After the army, I failed to see beyond the negative kind—freedom from the direction of officers and bosses. The alternative freedom is the ability to cultivate and use one's unique talents. That is possible only in the company of others.

Two events helped to change my course. While in graduate school in the Midwest, I finally ran out of savings. There was a recession, and I could not find work anywhere; I was broke and, for a while, actually cold and hungry. I had to get serious.

Not long thereafter I met my first wife. Her father was a self-made man, a real-life entrepreneur who ran a prospering business. He was a great bundle of energy and enterprise, immune to any of the equivocal feelings I've described. His example inspired me to look for a good job, one with "a future." (Later, when I got to know him better, I saw how he could play the tyrant at his factory and again at home, but was not, for all of that, happy.)

The false starts were not quite over. I lost a promising job when the agency where I spent my next year was shut down. Coincidentally, it provided an introduction to General Motors, which took me on as a management trainee—a ticket to ride on the mobility escalator.

During the period of my internship, I was able to move about and see a good deal of the company's operations. I was also able to spend time with a good number of its employees, who had worked for years in one plant or another, sometimes at the very same tasks. They came mostly from small towns or the rural South. I can barely speak of them without sounding either patronizing or sentimental, but they had a certain gritty integrity and an understanding of their situation that the labor statistics did not convey.

Nevertheless, it did not take very long for me to acquire a certain snobbishness. And after a lengthy tour in the field, I was invited into the officers' club. A management position meant I did not become stranded in the many backwaters of the organization. New and different assignments were offered me: fly out somewhere and let us know what's going on; give an address to one group or negotiate with another; look at the pieces of a problem and put things back together. I did my job well enough, and further opportunities followed.

Each time I learned something new, but I also became more cautious and controlled. That kind of experience alters not only the person visible to others but the sense of who you are. On the other hand, it was easy to forget that the stage, costumes, script—the house itself—belonged the whole time to somebody else.

During the 1950s, the idea of pursuing a career had not yet replaced "getting ahead." For most of us, success in very large organizations was not primarily a matter of brilliance and daring or, certainly, of displaying the traits found on employee appraisal forms. It resulted from astute attention to detail, from thinking ahead to offset threats to one's hegemony. It was the reward for deference to and getting along with the level just above, being trustworthy when out on the road, staying visible back at the office—for looking like a person with "potential." I am tempted to add that I did a lot of hard work. But then, legions of men and women work hard and never get anywhere.

These thoughts were not exactly reassuring for someone in human resource management, which is where I landed and remained for several years. At first, HRM appeared rational and professional compared with the creaking antiquities who ran personnel, and I was one of its early evangelists. Besides, it gave me a chance to show off my education (college graduates had not yet taken over). In any case, my faith in HRM did not survive my tenure. Its language tended toward high-minded slogans; its buried assumptions presented the work force as a sort of recalcitrant object requiring both mobilization and pacification. By the time I moved on, I saw HRM types as far less attractive than their promises—outwardly friendly handshakers, privately gossipy and petty backbiters. Blandly they denied the existence of conflict, but you didn't forget that they kept the files on each employee.

My evolving disillusionment with HRM would be of little more than anecdotal interest here were it not for the way it prompted me to think through the deeper connections between work and self. HRM trivialized what I now realize is so positive about work: the way it can bring out the best in us, not as human resources but as human beings.

Work, I've learned, provides the ground for standing in the world. It is a vehicle for transcending our adolescent dependency, to achieve the confidence of self-reliance. We gain the respect of others by showing we can earn our own way through visible competence of one sort or another. We cannot be shaped in isolation. Work provides the necessary audience for trying out new hats and different voices. It is the arena for being tested against the expectations of others and for finding our own comfortable balance between initiative and compliance. Crafts that survive do so because apprentices have come to accept for themselves the standards of workmanship set down by older members of the craft.

For myself, work was a place where I became occupied with others and their tasks, and I accepted responsibility for both. Such involvement with others in work can bring an escape from the self. This is not a calculated payoff but for a while it can seem a blessing: I managed to become a moderate success during the 1960s and lived quite well, having everything my parents would have admired.

And yet my confusion of security with plenty—my over-valuing of both— now seems an incredible lack of imagination. Not that my restlessness faded. I continued to resent being locked up during the best part of the day, with little time left when I came home at night to the family. For years, work ate up the center of my life, leaving only crusts. In spite of this—perhaps because of it— I bound myself even tighter to the organization.

In that same era, a few others on the inside were turning away from the single-minded dedication to success and were even, sometimes noisily, dropping out. I blame only myself for the hardening wall that separated my private self from the public one, but back then, who knew what or whom to blame? My marriage did not survive those days, although I declined to dissolve the union with my corporate spouse. It did not occur to me that, inevitably, the company would divorce me.

Most people think of work as what they do for a living, yet perhaps only in retirement they discover it is much of whom they have become. When we abandon work, or it abandons us, we always leave part of ourselves behind; but if we have allowed work to absorb most of ourselves and our days, we leave even more. The problem then is this: Do we simply continue as a "former manager" or do we decide to go on and become something else? A famous novelist once observed: "There are no third acts in American lives." An unacceptable conclusion, surely, for some of us who are standing around in full costume, feeling unfinished, and wanting to go on — even if our lines must be improvised.

And yet I remain skeptical of the popular remedies for the retired worker's fate — mental health counseling, for example, with its professional aplomb and ready answers. A support group is often suggested, but such meetings imply hasty comforting and solicitude when one might do better to confront past choices. Nor would I ask government to fund recreational specialists to instruct us in "creative leisure" for our many free hours. Perhaps my sympathies remain with the people of my earlier life who didn't have hobbies, who didn't "recreate."

Some companies now offer preretirement seminars. While these efforts may be well-intentioned and can review necessary information like insurance coverages, pensions, and so on, the package programs I have looked into are mindlessly cheerful, with pep talks about becoming a "lifetime learner." Isn't it unreasonable to expect the consultants who design such materials to solve the inner dislocations, the predicament of leaving behind the central piece of our former selves? Whether we jump or are thrown overboard, what if not our condition is our own problem?

In what turned out to be my last assignment for the company, I was asked to head up a large program to promote participation in job improvements by both salaried and blue-collar employees. I welcomed the opportunity to get back in contact with people in the broad base of the organization, and to show that tapping their energy makes good business sense. By that time, too, others had begun to realize that pushing workers around resulted in shoddy work; that rigidly hierarchical structures had become, in the context of our populist society, a source of enervation and failure, robbing work of its spontaneity and generosity.

Anyway, in working on the project I got a preview of the paradox that plagues us in retirement: that the worse work is the more we need it. Jobs that used none of those blue-collar workers' creative powers were dulling and flattening. So when work was lost, they were lost.

That cliché about how our sense of community is eroded in big cities obscures a true loss — loss of generational linkages, of neighbors, friends, and relations who help make the world appear to be personal. Without these people the job becomes one of the last places to nourish an adult identity. What you don't anticipate when you lose your job is that you also lose membership in a community. Shut out of the circle you took for granted, you miss not only those others but your old self as well.

Once while driving to a business meeting, I missed a turn in the back streets of an industrial district and stopped at a tavern to ask directions. Inside, on all the seats along the bar and at many of the tables, were older men. It was barely 10 o'clock in the morning. I recall Barbara Pym's *Quartet in Autumn*: retired workers, she writes, are "swept away as if they had never been."

Many who read this will not be eligible to retire for years, yet might wonder about it. Where to go for answers? How to prepare? I would not recommend that you attempt to discuss these matters with the personnel department.

Talking to people who are already retired is a possibility, but the question, "What do you *do* with all your spare time?" sounds like prying into another's subsidized idleness. Besides, our separate lives cannot be collected into tidy piles. We may share a common situation, but each life is as different as our faces. The best that one can expect from another's account of retirement are questions with which to await one's own impending crisis — in short, my intention here.

And so consider how your day goes there in Marketing, or Engineering, or Finance, or Distribution: conferring endlessly, making recommendations to solve problems and having them listened to, seeing joint projects through to completion, flying around to check on activity at the branches. The density of these days easily discourages thinking about what it will be like when all is lost at a stroke, when no one (except perhaps your spouse) cares what you think about anything — you who were once well-paid for your views.

Even in the public sector, as a citizen with legitimate claims on official attention, you will find yourself of less consequence without letterhead and affiliation. Some of those retirees from my old company, knowing more intuitively than I that the game was really over, just gave up all claims to attention. They are reported to be living in quiet corners like Scottsdale where there's golf every day, or Longboat Key where one can putter endlessly with fishing gear. Not a small achievement on this crowded and dangerous planet.

Do I overstate? Possibly. But if you expect to make good use of your postretirement years, you cannot put off thinking about them until the week or month before you are awarded the gold watch. Now is the time to ask, "How might one live? What do I really care about? What is of value and worth?" These are not easy questions to ponder in the company of burly utilitarians crowding around the big buffet. If you attempt to escape them, however, these questions will return with a peculiar intensity when, with time running out, you are severed from all those who confirm your powers.

Start with a simple assertion of yourself, however symbolic. Take off some time to pursue an adventure wholly your own. Get connected with other people whose exotic skills you admire, people with a different outlook. For me, today, living means doing something of no greater importance — and no less — than mending a broken chair, speaking up at a public meeting, or, indeed, writing this article. The point is to learn to do something for its own sake.

For those who have recently retired, I feel a special affinity, and I want to extend an invitation. Imagine this time as one of life's border crossings, one that brings you to a small clearing — an open space — between arrival and departure. It is a place for quiet conversation with a circle of attentive listeners. Is it too late to reawaken desire after it has been numbed? Is there still opportunity — and courage — to pursue a calling, a project of one's own?

Indeed, we have much to talk about.

3

Can You Survive Your Retirement?

LELAND P. BRADFORD

I was the chief executive of an organization I had helped found, as well as a professional behavioral scientist, and I should have known better. But I didn't. After 25 years of working under the strain of building an organization, of interweaving the ideas and needs of the key staff with a multiplicity of outside forces, I was ready for the beautiful promised land of retirement. I persuaded my wife to leave our lovely Georgetown home and move to North Carolina, where I could golf to my heart's content and enjoy relief from the stress of having to make daily decisions. I thought it would be just wonderful.

How wrong I was! The first year was awful. The organization moved on without me. Important decisions I had made were reversed. No one called for advice. As far as I could see, no one cared. I even felt that my professional reputation had vanished. It hurt.

At times I thought with empathy of a friend who had been president of a large multinational company. He had told me, before he retired, that he had everything planned carefully. A year after his retirement, some of his former vice presidents told me he came to the office at least twice a week seeking someone who was free to lunch with him.

I found that golf did not fill a day. The consultation and volunteer work I did was not satisfying. Other interests paled before the challenges I had faced. Life felt empty. I was not aged, just a little older. I had plenty of energy and I felt just as competent as I had been.

When for the umpteenth time I complained to my wife about the emptiness of my life, Martha exploded, "I've heard enough of your complaining! You dragged me away from the city and home I loved best. Do you know why I don't like it here? Do you know why I've gone to the hospital twice this year for checkups, only to find nothing wrong? It was because I'm unhappy. Did you consider my life in retirement when you retired?" I hadn't, though I thought we had talked everything over. Maybe I had just talked about *my* retirement. What she said woke me up, and I listened.

Then we talked for days, for weeks, it seemed like months—at breakfast, teatime, the cocktail hour, during evenings when there were no parties. We came to know each other's feelings and problems better. We asked ourselves if we were the only ones to react this way, so we looked about us and talked to many others on the golf course and at small parties. We found we weren't alone, although people usually covered up at first before acknowledging the empty hours they dreaded and their sense of futility and uselessness. (We learned later of a census study showing that many persons die four to five years after retirement, seemingly out of a sense of uselessness. And according to a famous French physician, people can indeed die of boredom.)

Only after we had talked through our own difficulties to our satisfaction did we begin to question why this transition period was so very difficult and so different from others we had negotiated. Was it because it marked an ending or were there other causes? Here are our conclusions.

What One Loses in Retirement

As we thought about what had happened to us and to others, we began to see how organizations inadvertently fulfill a number of basic psychological needs for people. The loss of these gratifications on retirement can be devastating unless effectively accommodated to or replaced.

Acceptance and socialization: The organization, for almost all positions, provides colleagues, work groups, teams, committees, units, or departments. Members perforce feel a sense of belonging that they share with others, whether the cohesive factor is task completion or antagonism within groups or the company. Conflict adequately handled is energizing. Task accomplishment is a mutual gain. Work provides the contacts vital for psychological well-being. Otherwise there are no correctives for perceptual distortion, no antidotes for loneliness.

I found all this out. I felt the alienation of no longer being a part of groups I had belonged to for 40 or more hours a week for more years than I cared to remember. Even in my childhood, when I had been temporarily ostracized by playmates, I had not felt so keenly excluded, bereft, outside, disposable.

I thought again of my friend who had returned hungrily to the office to seek the companionship of his past subordinates. What was different for him, and now for me, was the apparent lack of an arena offering equal challenges and companionship. I found it harder than I ever expected to say a permanent good-bye to a lifetime work career. It took time and suffering to find an adequate solution.

Goals, achievement, and affirmation: Organizations provide goals and tasks to be formulated and accomplished. During the middle years these are interwoven with personal financial aims and family responsibilities. Goals make achievement possible, sometimes with soul-warming results. Achievement brings affirmation from others and from one's self. Without this periodic affirmation, self-esteem and self-worth diminish. They are intricately interdependent and, oh, how important!

To be without goals is to be purposeless, to have no reason to arise in the morning; for some, even to live. I teetered on the brink of goallessness and it took Martha to awaken me. Also, a perceptive club member said to me, "Do you realize the purpose of our club is to keep useless people alive?" That helped wake me too.

Not long ago I had lunch with a man whom I had known for years. Highly successful in the positions he had held, he was generous, sensitive to others, and a good companion. He had been retired for a couple of years. During the two

Retiring with Grace

hours of lunch, I don't think I got in three sentences. He didn't tell me what he was doing, because he wasn't doing anything to talk about, but he did talk about the well-known people who sought him out and the artists and musicians who wanted his company. I left our luncheon saddened. He who had achieved so much was now reduced to seeking affirmation from others in superficial ways. How had retirement so drastically stripped him of his sense of achievement?

Power and influence: Companies provide for most employees some degree of power and influence. For top executives, of course, the degree is great, though most would admit to various constraints. Power conveys importance to the person and aids the formation and perception of identity. Power increases the areas in which accomplishment can occur and leads to the gaining of more power.

For executives and others who have known considerable power, its sudden loss at retirement can be an acute deprivation. The shock for many is not only great but also bewildering. Events are less under one's control, and the importance in others' eyes that power gives has evaporated. Must the person who has lost power continue to vie for it, or can the individual find power and importance within himself?

On the board of directors of a local organization of not much significance sit some former executives of well-known companies. The board meets periodically for a stated two hours each meeting. For 5 to 10 minutes real work is accomplished. These executives, before retirement, would have ended a meeting in no more than 15 minutes. Now they are content to spend the two hours. Why? One might guess that, since they have little else to do, two hours fill a portion of a day. One might also hazard a guess that for those two hours power and influence are again theirs.

Support systems: Individuals need a variety of support systems for psychological and emotional health. Colleagues, friends, neighbors, clubs, community responsibilities, family, and others serve as support systems providing recognition, admiration, assurance of abilities, reality testing, feedback on behavior, and encouragement.

When retirement comes, and particularly if the couple moves away, many support systems disappear. I wish I had thought to list all my support systems before I retired, then crossed off those I would miss. I could then have gone on more than just intuitive feeling in deciding which ones were crucial to replace.

Routines and time: The busy executive with wide-ranging interests and multifaceted decisions to make seldom realizes the stabilizing force of set routines — regular staff meetings, daily agendas on the desk each morning, planned luncheon engagements, organized trips, prearranged social events.

When retirement comes, most of these routines stop. At first it seems heavenly: no clock ruling you, no secretary reminding you of your luncheon appointment, no hurried breakfast, no train to catch. So I found it; but not for long, because habit is strong. Besides, inasmuch as my day no longer had its ready-made structure, I was left with the aggravating necessity of making many small decisions. Therefore, routines need to be set; else why should one get out of bed at all? This is a small but significant change in the transition to retirement.

Where we now live there is no postal delivery. Sometime during the morning, everyone goes to the post office to meet friends, exchange gossip, make golf dates, and sometimes arrange parties. Gradually routines like this become established, but only if the person deliberately develops them; no longer does the organization create them.

Before retirement, the expenditure of time, like routine, is primarily under the control of the organization, and time spent on nonwork activities is fitted into the slots remaining. During the driving, challenging, responsible work years, time becomes a scarce and precious commodity: it is the duty of secretaries and assistants to ensure that this precious resource is effectively used.

In retirement the reverse is too frequently true. Time must be filled, somehow, to pass the day. Time can lead people into the dangerous wasteland of empty time, where no purpose is present to stir any interest or desire. If empty time recurs each day, the will and motivation to seek new interests dwindle. Boredom joins with apathy to reduce the joy of living and speed psychological if not physical deterioration.

In my early days of retirement I would become irritated on the links if a slow foursome in front held up our play. My partners, longer retired, would say, "What's your hurry? What else do you have to do today?"

For many of us, golf was followed by time at the bar, perhaps some bridge, more cocktails at home or at a party, followed by a dull evening. The intense preoccupation with work and community responsibilities had precluded leisurely reading in former years. Interests and new skills not developed before retirement were difficult to cultivate after retirement.

So the challenging hours of yesterday become empty hours today, often with disastrous consequences.

Problems of the Retired

The very different conditions of retirement create new problems stemming from existing situations. Two are sufficiently common and serious to be critical in a misery-free transition to retirement.

Marital Difficulties

Marriage, as a dynamic process, alters of course with changing conditions. The abrupt passage from work to retirement should require consideration of possible marital adjustments. There are a number of factors leading to this necessity.

The rights of each: I never realized that my work career, title, status, job responsibilities, office, secretary, even desk represented my turf, or territory, and thus largely defined my identity to others and to myself. When I thought of turf I thought of the way animals fight to secure or defend a bit of space. It was only at retirement, when all aspects of my turf were given to another, that the dreadful realization of being turfless struck home. For an awful moment, I became uncertain of my identity. I knew who I had been, but I was not certain who I was. The sudden movement from "I am" to "I was" was difficult to adjust to.

I had always thought of the home as mine as well as Martha's. But now I found that it was her turf. It had been her territory to manage, where she had made and implemented decisions and dealt with a host of people. I had never thought of the time and knowledge she had put into managing the home.

It was not long before it occurred to me that I was intruding on her turf. I managed to be in the wrong place at the wrong time—for example, we kept bumping into each other in the kitchen. It was her domain and I was obviously curtailing her freedom of action. We talked it through and worked out accommodations that gave me some turf without depriving her and allowed us time alone as well as shared time.

We observed how turf-loss and intrusion problems beset other retired couples. Once we were looking at clothes in the downstairs section of a store. Sitting on the steps leading downstairs was a gray-haired man. A woman standing near us saw us glance at him and she felt impelled to speak. "Since he's retired he goes wherever I go. I can no longer shop in peace," she said, with a hostile look toward the stairs. "It's like having a child with you all day long. I don't know how long I can stand it!"

Then there is the extreme where intrusion means control. An acquaintance of ours had always been restless, but his nervous energy had fit well with the demands of his high-level corporate position. He did not slow up even in retirement. No sooner did he and his wife return from one cruise or plane trip, with stops at various cities, than he was planning another. His wife grew more weary with each trip.

Finally she spoke up, saying she couldn't take it any longer. He brushed her feelings aside. "Nonsense," he said. "Travel is broadening. It's good for you." That silenced her; she couldn't stand up to his strong (and insensitive) personality. But finally, for the first time, she complained openly and bitterly to her friends.

Unless the couple can undertake a conciliatory review of their turf-loss and intrusion problem and make adjustments to it, irritations will grow, bitterness will mount, and conflicts will continue. But such a marital review is not easy to make. Talking through the problem requires a sense of self-worth on the part of each so that feedback can be openly given and nondefensively received. It requires respect of each by the other and sufficient self-understanding so that each feels secure.

The turf-intrusion problem is typical of the mutually affecting strains that become especially stressful in retirement, when husband and wife find themselves spending much more time together. The turmoil that one of them experiences upsets the other. Unless each can share the problems and can accept help and support from the other, relations that before were calm become potentially explosive.

Sex role questions: Particularly for the man who has lost his turf, the fear of losing a masculine image is bothersome. He has had an identity as the family provider, the family head, the ultimate judge on major issues. Title and position in the eyes of others bolster one's self-image, and a man tries to project himself to others as a strong and competent person worthy of their respect.

Because a man cannot overtly assert his macho drives, he directs them into various innocent and socially acceptable channels. The individual may only be dimly aware of these drives, but they are strong.

Not long ago Martha and I attended a small dinner party with four other couples, all friends or acquaintances. The host had always appeared to us to be a quiet, unobtrusive man. That night, however, he was assertive and extremely aggressive toward his wife. If she broke in on his conversation, he told her to wait until he was finished talking. He corrected her and instructed her not to talk unless she knew what she was saying. She made no protest, out of good manners or perhaps for other reasons. The other guests looked as embarrassed as we were.

Martha and I talked the matter over when we arrived home. What we had seen was not the couple's normal pattern of relationship. One hypothesis stood out in our thinking: the husband, without realizing it, was endeavoring to show the other men at the party that, though long since retired, he was still a man and master of his home.

Growing apart: Over the years sharp differences in work responsibilities may have brought first imperceptible and then palpable differences in the levels of growth of the partners. Because so much of the day was spent apart, these differences may not have been important. But with the closer living of retirement, they become almost unbearable.

One man we know rose far in his company through sheer ability. His frequent new contacts, coupled with his absorbing mind, brought continual expansion of his interests. His wife stayed home and socialized with a tight circle of friends. Then he retired, and he suddenly found they had little in common and even less to communicate about. It seemed they had come out of different worlds, and there was nothing they could do but to live out their lives as best they could. My wife and I agreed that both were to blame — he because he had done nothing to help her grow, and she because she had insulated herself and had made no effort to develop.

So at retirement, couples need to undertake a marital review. Those who have negotiated this transition successfully probably made sensitive adjustments as needs arose without waiting for problems to become serious. But those who think that their relationship will remain the same and make no accommodations are in for trouble.

Societal Attitudes

Formerly individuals retired only when they were incapacitated or too old to work. The myth that this is so persists. To be retired, think many younger people, is to be aged. To be aged is somehow obscene; it is a disease to be avoided. Television advertising tells us so — advertising promotes products and devices to make people appear younger. One advertisement asks, "Why look as old as you are?"

A person who is retiring finds it very easy to accept this attitude and feel disposable, unneeded, and useless. It takes effort and will to reject that attitude and project the true picture — to oneself and others — that vast numbers of retired persons are still energetic and competent.

To counteract society's attitude, the individual must not only reject the concept of aging before the fact, he must also change his own attitudes about himself, recognizing the particular psychological and emotional needs which his work formerly satisfied but which he now (together with his partner) is obliged to satisfy himself. My wife and I agree: many years went into preparing us to enter the world of work but nothing was done to prepare us to leave it.

One day we were having a leisurely lunch with a couple who had been longtime friends of ours. He was retiring soon from a key executive post, so Martha and I asked them what they had done in anticipation of that event. He replied that lawyers had worked out family trusts and special accounts for his wife. We pursued the point. She added that they were already looking for the right place to live. We pursued again. They looked puzzled. We explained some of the emotional problems and their causes that we had encountered. They were surprised; they hadn't thought of those.

What Can Be Done

There is no cookbook recipe for retiring. Some may find it a release from hated work and strain; others, whose focus has been the job, may find it a deprivation. Personalities and needs differ. The answer to successful retirement seems to lie in self-understanding, a feeling of self-worth, and the will and ability to survive emotionally.

Census studies indicate that persons reaching 65 can expect, on the average, 15 more years of life—almost one-fifth of the total life span. That is too big a chunk to waste or to endure without purpose or meaning.

Today well over 400 companies reportedly hold preretirement training programs, compared with only a few dozen five or six years ago. Unfortunately, few of these programs deal seriously, if at all, with emotional problems; they merely stress the importance of remaining active and maintaining a healthy outlook. But some enterprising companies are expanding their traditional preretirement sessions to include extra dimensions. Here is a sample of some programs:

Connecticut General Insurance Co. conducts a program over an eight-week period offering a package developed by the American Association for Retired Persons and called AIM (Action for Independent Maturity). Among other aspects, it deals with marital difficulties and emotional problems. The program's focus is new-career planning, whether that means sitting in a rocking chair or embarking on a different type of job.

This insurance concern offers its 13,000 employees a flexible arrangement by which a person can retire as early as age 55 (or leave as early as 45 with vested pension benefits). The employee can participate in the preretirement sessions up to five years before scheduled retirement.

Moog, Inc., which employs 2,500 has taken the initiative to expand its program covering the "classic" matters of health and safety, finances, legal issues, and recreation. For the last two years, this manufacturer of electrohydraulic controls has conducted a pilot program examining emotional adjustments that retirees and their spouses must make. Each group includes about a dozen employees plus their spouses. Some of the sessions are group affairs, and some involve only a single couple.

The participants are in their last year before leaving employment. To help workers make a smoother transition, Moog management plans eventually to start the program for employees in the 50-to-55 age range. The company will encourage "refresher courses" when the employee reaches age 60 and each year thereafter until he or she retires.

Exxon Corporation's giant U.S. affiliate (40,000 employees) recently launched a pilot program in Houston; the first participants were employees retiring in 1979 or early 1980. The company plans to continue the sessions, scheduled for about two dozen persons at a time, and modify them as experience dictates. Each session starts one evening and lasts the next three days.

Exxon's previous preretirement program had stressed the economic factors and—to an extent—physiological factors of retirement. The new program covers psychological elements, particularly how the person can replace the satisfactions and rewards formerly provided by his work. Developing and sustaining relationships with others is a focus of the program (spouses are invited to join the group in this portion).

As the Connecticut General program stresses, retirement can be the beginning of a new career, and the employer can aid the individual in planning and preparing for it. The reward from a new career need not be money; it can be satisfaction, self-affirmation, and achievement of meaningful goals.

Recent research on adult development stresses that growth and learning can continue throughout the life span. The tremendous increase in continuing education courses offered by colleges, community organizations, and high schools is based on this premise. Acceptance of the concept of a new career, increasingly supported by organizational and societal expectations, makes retirement merely a time when careers change. A career, lest the word seem pretentious, can be any sustained activity whose purpose or goal is meaningful to the person, where motivation is maintained, and where achievement brings affirmation from self or others.

Steps to Take

There is much that organizations can do to help employees to make the transition from the organization to a new kind of life in retirement:

1. Employees can be encouraged to widen personal interests that can be carried on in later years and to develop the skills necessary for a second or third career, which need not be for monetary gain. A physician friend, for example, had taught woodworking at night while going through medical school. Today, long retired, he joyously spends his time as an expert cabinetmaker for the benefit of relatives and friends.

2. Training programs can be conducted through the early and middle years of employment for persons who have settled in at the organization. Particularly if such training stresses greater self-awareness and self-acceptance, this can help prepare them for retirement. Many companies offer training programs designed to help each person look backward at accomplishments, assess himself, and look forward to his future life.

3. Preretirement programs, one to two years ahead of the event, should be the focal point of the organization's efforts. It is very important that spouses attend, particularly during sessions dealing with emotional and marital issues. These sessions can be designed in such a way to permit husband and wife to discover gradually for themselves the problems that may be encountered, test some solutions in small groups, and then reach their own decisions in private. Carefully designed sessions permit the person who is retiring to treat realistically the problems of empty time, loneliness, and feeling useless—then to formulate and discuss practical rather than impossible solutions.

But ultimately the development of a successful retirement plan lies with the individual or couple, whether the retiree is a chief executive or a clerk. The will and initiative to seek new activities and socialization patterns—and awareness that saying "I can't" is a way of saying "I choose not to"—are imperatives for the major achievement of the retired: emotional survival.

4

Don't Call It "Early Retirement":

Interviews with Wheelock Whitney and William G. Damroth

Wheelock Whitney

HBR: Mr. Whitney, before we talk about why you decided to retire from your position as chief executive officer of Dain, Kalman & Quail, could you tell us something of what your career path had been up to that point?

Whitney: Yes, but first I want to say I always feel a little bit squeamish about the words "retire" or "early retirement." When I hear them, they send off a little signal; I feel my gut tighten. The reason I get so sensitive about the word "retirement" is that right after I left Dain, I'd walk down the street and these old gentlemen—70, 75 years old—would come up to me, put their arm around me, and say, "Wheelock, welcome to the club. You're going to love it. I wish I'd done it 25 years before I did." After all, I was only 45. I didn't have any intention of "retiring," just shifting my career, doing something different with my life.

What had that career been?

I got out of the Navy in 1946, went four years to Yale, then started work in Minneapolis in the bus business in 1950. After three and a half years of that, I was thinking life was too easy for me. I became restless and curious, and, yes, dissatisfied. I asked myself, "Am I being accepted because of the fact that I'm Wheelock Whitney, and my parents live here in Minneapolis, and I belong to all the good clubs, and I have all of these nice things? What would happen if I went into a community where we didn't know anybody? I wonder if I could hack it." And it weighed on me so heavily that I finally decided, to hell with it, I'm going to do something just to see what would happen if Irene, myself, and the children were on our own.

Were you conscious at the time of this being a big risk, a gamble?

I looked on it more as an adventure. It was an honest effort to try to see if we could make it. What kind of life would it be for us, having to make new friends and having to be taken in as total strangers? So I looked around and got a job in Jacksonville, Florida in the bus business. I started working for them in January 1954.

the company. I decided that if I was going to leave, I'd better leave while business was still good. But basically I was motivated to leave to develop a different life style and a different career.

There wasn't time to develop these interests while you were CEO at DKQ?

Exactly. I simply couldn't do it. There were two interests I had that I knew I wanted to pursue. One was politics. I wanted to take a look realistically as to whether I might like to go back into politics again. There was a governor's race coming up in 1974, and this was 1972.

I also had a tremendous interest in the Johnson Institute. After Irene had been well for a couple of years we said to Vern Johnson, "What about starting an institute whose purpose would be to try to help families, individuals like us who had suffered and waited too long for help?" We wanted to teach principles of intervention for people who are chemically dependent. We started in 1966 with one employee, and by 1971 we had 25 employees. I was chairman, Vern was president. By 1972 I was getting more and more fascinated with what was going on at the Johnson Institute and anxious to spend more time there. But I simply couldn't because I was so tied down in business.

Were there personal interests as well?

Oh, yes. I had three goals. I wanted very much to learn how to speak a foreign language, which I had never had time for, and to learn how to play a musical instrument. I also wanted to travel. I had been a successful businessman and you would think that I had seen the world, but I hadn't. And I wanted to spend more time with my family, and to teach management principles to college students.

Was the question of business values versus your individual life an issue for you at that time?

Well, partly. I have to admit that I was getting turned off by what I thought were absolutely ludicrous, unrealistic amounts of compensation that were being made by people in our business. When a young person could come into our business at the age of 26 and make $75,000 a year, it was . . . well, it got to me, finally. It wasn't just that they made that kind of money, but that they thought they were worth that kind of money. They not only expected that, but they expected that they should even make more than that.

And this was occurring with some people that I was pretty close to and that I really cared for. I guess I was getting grouchy about it, and I think that was one of the negative reasons I wanted to change.

So it wasn't disenchantment with the business world per se?

No, it had nothing to do with respect for the business world, or the business community, or the securities industry, because I believe in all of those. I have a great abiding faith in the business world.

When you left, were you aware of wanting to shed responsibility?

I think that I enjoy responsibility. I enjoy being a leader. I thrive on it. I did not think how nice it would be if I could just be one of the boys and not have to have all these people counting on me. I was very much aware, though, at the same time, of something I wanted to correct in my life, something I would call excessive loneliness. I think it's very lonely to be at the top of anything; it prevents people from sharing with you, from being honest with you, and from getting close to you. And I missed the closeness. I really didn't have many close friends, people that I confided in, people that I saw a lot of, people that I felt comfortable with.

Was that because there was not time for them?

That was certainly a factor. I had so many interests and I was so busy that it was hard for me to take the time, or I did not choose to take the time, to have close relationships with people. Also, I think it was partly the fact that I was the head of a company. I think that you develop a certain place where people don't avoid you, but either through your choice or theirs they don't get close. In any event, during the 1960s my wife got interested in groups as a part of her therapy and she got interested in feelings. I really didn't know much about that and I pooh-poohed it a lot.

And she persisted?

She kept telling me that I wasn't in touch with my feelings, that I operated strictly out of my head. I used to say, "Sometimes I wish you'd never gone into treatment—you come in with all this crap about feelings and all this strange lingo. I think I'm in touch with my feelings." And she said, "Well, I don't," and back and forth we went. In fact, since we didn't have alcohol to argue about anymore, we picked on this. Finally, she persuaded me to go to the Esalen Institute with her for a week in 1967. I'd never done anything like that before. I operated strictly in the straight world.

This was when T-groups and sensitivity groups were at the height of their popularity.

They were just beginning. I spent a week at Esalen in an encounter group. I can point to that as the beginning of opening up a whole new phase of my life. I became aware of how isolated I was from people. Also, I had a lot of anger in me that I had never gotten out. The next year I went to Esalen on my own, and I have been going for one week a year ever since.

Being at the top doesn't make dealing with anger any easier.

No. For so many years, I was trained to keep it cool. Everyone else can lose his head, but the boss has to keep the peace—pour oil on the troubled waters and stay calm, not rock the boat but bring all these dissident forces together. That was my image of a leader, and my image of myself, and I know that I felt you can't trust somebody who can lose his temper or get angry. I mean, Lord, that's unstable. I didn't realize that I was myself suppressing all kinds of anger.

It sounds like Kipling: "If you can keep your head when all about you/Are losing theirs. . . . . . . you'll be a Man, my son!"

Absolutely. I had to keep my feelings in check both in the office and at home. At home I had to be Mr. Stability because when Irene was sick, the kids looked to me as the cool, clear stream of reason. While their mother was in trouble, I had to be the strong man.

So your interest and concern in the human potential movement was actually growing at the same time you were feeling more dissatisfied with your working life?

Yes, I'm sure that some of the things that I learned there and in subsequent years had a lot to do with my willingness to change, to try something new in my life, to experiment more with different fields so that I could be more expressive and freer.

To get back to when you left Dain, what did your associates think? Did they regard your leaving as odd?

I had every kind of reaction. Some said, "Well, you might expect that of Wheelock—he's eccentric—you don't know what he's going to do; I'm not surprised." Some were angry. "What does he mean by turning his back on business—did he forget what got him where he is today?" I remember I was quoted in the Minneapolis Tribune as saying that "the thrill of reaching up isn't there." Some people took great offense at that. They felt that business was having enough trouble without one of its members turning his back on it.

What do you think they thought was so threatening?

I think some were quite threatened for two reasons; one, secretly they would have liked to do it themselves, but for one reason or another hadn't gotten up their courage; or secondly, their wives were going to start nagging them and saying, "For God's sake, why don't you do that? You're in a rut, you know." Of course, some were very, very supportive. They'd say, "Good, I'm glad you did it" and "By gosh, it will make it easier for the rest of us who want to do it."

What about the organization? Was it traumatized?

I think the people there were surprised. I am sure that some people were delighted. I said I was getting grouchy, and certainly some people might have felt I was impeding their progress in the company and said, "Now, I'm going to have a chance." Other people who really thought that I was a good leader and that the firm would suffer, were angry, sad, and really disappointed.

Had you made a general announcement?

I did not choose to go around and share it with everybody in advance; I told the two people in the company who were closest to me in authority what I was going to do, and then I just upped and did it at our annual stockholders' meeting.

Was one of the incentives to get to the top that you had some concept of what you wanted the firm to be? In other words, was it an intellectual as well as a personal issue?

I see myself perhaps more as a creative kind of person than an administrative one, and when I said that "the thrill of reaching up" wasn't there, I meant it. I'd reached up as far as I could and created the thing that I had envisioned. I really felt that the company should go through a period of digestion rather than increased growth and size, and I'm sure that a large part of the measure of fun that I'd had was not only building a concept, but also an organization and people. Just managing that organization wasn't fun anymore.

Can you identify what it is that makes you go at full-tilt or what made it necessary for you to go to the top?

Well, I think curiosity has been a big motivator for me. Curiosity to find a better way to do something. Curiosity to try a new idea, to take a new direction. And I guess I'd have to say I enjoy power. In a position of power I often feel very powerless, but that's not the point. I obviously must enjoy power. I think I have a lot of confidence in my judgment, and I feel as though I am instinctively going to do the right thing. I don't know why that would motivate one to take on more and more responsibility, but I think it does.

But is it so much power over people as it is power to realize a conception or an ideal that you're trying to accomplish?

I don't think that the power over people is it. It is power to change things, the power to make, to create something better, whether it be a business or a social service or a community activity. I'm not aware of enjoying having power over somebody's life—whether I can fire him or hire him. Power has certainly been a motivating factor for me in politics. Politicians are the most powerful of all. One, they have the money and two, they make the laws. And if you have those two things, you have an awful lot of power.

When you left DKQ, you were quoted as saying that you were afraid of wandering, of not finding anything new and meaningful. Did you sink in your own estimation?

I said that mostly for publication. I said that because I thought it would seem more humble. Inside I was as confident as I could be that I had done the right thing. I had made the money that I needed in order to enjoy life. I had achieved what I wanted in my business life. I felt confident that I really was together. I had all kinds of things that I was interested in, so I was extremely confident about being able to make the switch.

At the time you changed, had you discussed it with your wife? What were your family's reactions?

I had a lot of support—from my kids and from my wife. I learned a lot from my kids, too, about risk taking. I think my kids had a lot to do with helping me be more expressive and more open. And my wife was very encouraging and supportive. So there was no concern about, "Gee, what is going to happen to Dad?" or "What will he do?" But they were 100% wrong. I was 100% wrong, too.

What happened to you when you left? How were you 100% wrong?

Well, I soon developed a high degree of insecurity, which I never expected would happen to me. Maybe it was because I had so many things I wanted to do that I couldn't decide which I wanted to concentrate on. Maybe I didn't realize how much the security of an office and a large organization and a staff had meant to me. I had taken it for granted, and suddenly I was on my own. I didn't have power anymore. Suddenly I didn't feel effective. It was as though home plate had just been uprooted and I'd gotten lost. I did in fact become temporarily disconnected. I did lose my bearings. I became depressed and anxious. I had problems with my wife that were reasonably serious during this period of time when my security blanket was removed.

There were no financial problems?

No financial problems at all. It was an identity crisis, not a financial crisis. Certainly one of the things that contributed to it was that at almost precisely that time, my wife took on a full-time job. Suddenly I was confronted with a wife with working hours and all the problems that go with that, and I was free. The way it came home to me was that I would be home, we would have planned dinner for 7:00, and at 7:15 the phone would ring. I knew damn well what was going to happen. It would be Irene and she'd say, "Dear, I'm sorry, you're going to have to eat without me." And I'd say, "What do you mean? I've been waiting here!" And I'd just get absolutely livid with rage.

You were used to having things revolve around your own life?

Lord, yes. It was very hard on me. Just at the time I was losing my own identity, she was really finding hers. It was coincidental, but nevertheless, it was bad for me personally. I probably went for as much as nine months or a year before I finally got things into perspective.

You were not yet working full-time for the Johnson Institute during the bad period?

No, but I was spending a lot of time there. I was also teaching. I was taking guitar lessons. We went on a trip to Scandinavia and on one to South America. I was doing some of the things I wanted to do, but I wasn't zeroed in on anything. What happened was just what I'd said I was afraid of. But I didn't really expect it to happen.

Do you think the feeling of drifting was inevitable?

I would say that part of shifting gears, changing your life style or career goal, or altering your priorities will undoubtedly involve a period of insecurity. I think that if you are prepared for it, it might not hit you as hard as it did me. But I do think that if it hit me, with the financial security that I had and my diverse number of interests, that anybody making a shift like this would have to go through a period of doubting whether or not he had made the right decision. I was very anxious about my life and very distressed about it. It worried me that I should be so unhappy, or that I should need what I had had before.

What brought you out of it?

I think that several things helped me break out of it. I was asked to take and accepted the general chairmanship of the United Way campaign for the Minneapolis area—a huge job. I knew that at some time in my life I'd have to do it, so it was sort of like the sword of Damocles hanging over my head. When they finally asked me to do it, I felt a sense of relief in that now I'd be able to get this behind me. That started in the fall of 1972, and gave me a mission, something clear cut that I wanted to achieve. It required all the skills that I had in organization and leadership to pull off, and I think that helped a lot.

What about politics—weren't you considering running for governor in 1974?

This is a kind of crazy thing to say, but I was in a sense aided and abetted in getting out of politics by Nixon's tragedy. It was so obvious—it became increasingly obvious during 1973 as it wore on—that Nixon's leadership was destroying the Republican Party and with it any chance that I might have of running for public office. And for the future, well, I am getting older. I mean, that's a fact of life. And in Minnesota we like our politicians young.

Do you think that the community spirited atmosphere of Minneapolis has influenced the road you've taken? Would you have worked for the United Way or the Johnson Institute in any event?

I can't answer that honestly. As an adult, I have never lived in any other place except Jacksonville for a brief period. Otherwise I've lived my whole life here. But I think two things would be true of Minneapolis. Number one: this is what we call a home-office town. This is the headquarters of many large corporations. As a result this is where the top executives live, and they want it to be an attractive place. And how do you make it attractive? By making it a well-rounded community. They all pitch in, and in that sense it's a lot different from a branch-office town.

The second thing is that Minnesota is small enough so that people somehow believe they can get their arms around its problems. Whether it's drugs, prison reform, or minorities, whatever the problem, somehow or other it seems manageable in Minnesota.

Are the rewards you are finding now qualitatively different from the ones you found in business?

Yes. And that's one of the things that I still to some degree wrestle with. How do you measure your impact? How do you measure your results in the world, let's say, that I'm now in as opposed to the one I was in? I liked and appreciated the accountability of business. I knew what the rules were. I knew you were measured in terms, simplistically, of earnings per share. I think profit is an excellent discipline.

You don't have measuring sticks in social service?

In social service work you do not have that discipline, and it is very hard to get realistic measurements. You always think that your cause is the most important, you always feel as though you are doing enormously good things, but it is much harder to judge your results honestly. When I teach my course at the University of Minnesota, I really don't know what kind of impact I'm making on the lives of those students who are taking my class. There ought to be better yardsticks to measure social service work because there is so much of our money and activity, and so many people, going into this field.

Have the personal rewards been what you thought they'd be? Have you found the less frantic way of life that you thought you might?

No. My life has not been less frantic. But I'm happier because I'm doing what I really want to do, and there's a difference. I'm feeling fulfilled in my life now. I don't know how long that will last. I mean, who is to know? In some ways I'm perhaps busier than I was before. I don't have an organization to assign people tasks. Oh, I have the Johnson Institute, but everyone there is so busy that I couldn't assign a task anyway, and if I did, they'd probably tell me to go to hell.

You don't run it the same way that you ran Dain?

Quite differently. There's much more group process in decision making. It's painful for me because it takes so much longer. But I think that the people—because they have participated—are more satisfied with the decisions. I don't know if the decisions are better. It's new for me, and I think that in some ways it's better and in some ways it isn't.

Are you still curious about what comes next for you? Or has that curiosity been channeled?

I see myself as a curious person, but I don't feel curiosity about what I'll be doing three years from now. When I say curious, I'm curious about finding a better way to help people cope with chemical dependency. I'm curious about finding a better way to help raise the money that we need for the United Way. I'm curious about a better way to teach students about the business community and about management techniques. And I'm curious about whether I can learn a new tune on my guitar. I really live mostly in the here and now, which I have learned to do through my activities in and exposure to the human potential movement.

A return to business in the future is out of the question for you then?

It would be a remote possibility that I would consider going back into business. I have felt I owed it to myself to take a look at whether the old competitive and earnings-per-share world would be attractive to me again, and whether the unstructured sort of blue-skied, beautiful, helping professional world might not look as good if I got back into business. But I am beginning to realize more and more that that isn't what I want to do. I am so committed to the field of chemical dependency and so optimistic about what is possible to do in this field that I see a long number of years ahead for me in realizing the dreams that I have for what's possible.

And you don't expect yourself ever to feel that loss of identity again?

That wouldn't be true; I'm sure that if I made a shift again in my life, I would be pretty darn confident—but not as confident as last time. Having had it happen to me before, it wouldn't surprise me if I went through a period of insecurity. Again, I'd warn myself next time to watch out for it. I think the transition is one of the things that if you have a little bit more knowledge about, maybe you can handle more easily.

And there is no looking back?

No. Sometimes my ability to pull a curtain down on things that I have done worries me. When I left the bus business, I never gave it another thought. I haven't been back to Yale. I'm going back for my 25th reunion, but I haven't been at all active in the alumni group. I was mayor of my hometown for six years. I put a lot of my life into that. I was a good mayor. But the night I left the council chambers I never went back. When I left DKQ, I never returned. I left the board—I have not taken any active interest in it. I don't know if that's a good or bad trait, but I know it's me. I burn myself out, putting all I have into something, and when it's over, it's over. It's like snuffing out a candle.

William G. Damroth

HBR: Mr. Damroth, you ran your own company, and now you're on your own as a wildlife photographer and conservationist. Did you always want to work for yourself?

Damroth: Yes. A lot of my independent ways stem from an attitude of my father's. He was a very Germanic guy who never went beyond the sixth grade. I loved him but I never pleased him; things were never good enough. No matter what I showed him, such as a footstool I'd made in his basement shop, he'd say, "It's all right, but that joint isn't very good. Make it light-tight." Or if I brought home a report card with an eighty he'd say, "What's the matter? Can't you get a hundred?" When I was eight and proud of my grades, he would say things like that, and I would lock myself in the bathroom and cry. I don't like criticism and never did. I tried to avoid it by making myself boss.

Do you think this affected your career path?

Yes. I'd say I had a need to please myself, and a need to overcome financial insecurity. My father was the superintendent of a building on East Ninth Street in Manhattan. We lived on the top floor. My parents had very little money, and that was what bothered me most as a kid. I'd fantasize, "Someday I want to put my hand in my pocket and say, 'I'll buy it, and I don't care what it costs.' " I wanted to reach that point. I wanted to be a millionaire. I started working as a teenager in Macy's stockroom. After the Air Corps, I ran my own promotion agency, then a small sales consulting firm, and finally the Lexington Corporation. All my life I've really worked for myself.

You started Lexington Corporation yourself?

Not exactly. I had a partner. It was in the late 1950s. I was married by that time. I had three boys, and a good family life. When I was 34 or 35, still with the marketing business, I decided to write a book on "How to Win Success Before Forty." I interviewed about 70 successful people for that, tying each one into some ideas I had about success. The third man I interviewed was John Templeton, who was a Rhodes Scholar and a financial genius. He was about six years older than I. After the book interview, he took me to supper and finally asked me what I did. I explained that I was a marketing consultant and he said, "Maybe we could get together because I've got a financial organization and staff. You can market; basically, mutual funds are a combination of these two. Why don't you think about it. Perhaps we could set up a business." Two months later we formed Templeton, Damroth Corporation, the forerunner of the Lexington Corporation. It took 13 years and a lot of sweat, but it was a success.

What size firm was it?

By 1968 we had assets of $150 million in four mutual funds and $300 million in private investment accounts, 100 employees, and 360 salesmen.

Why did you want to leave, when you were clearly a success, chairman of the board after having been president?

That has a lot to do with my own philosophy. My own values had changed over the past years. You have to know what you want personally — to focus your own drive. You've got to like what you're doing to work 80 and 90 hours a week. When you begin to dislike your work, you'd better quit the job.

What was it you didn't like at Lexington?

Business got to be a bore. For me the fun is not in arriving at the goal, but in the creative process . . . in the doing. It's the conceiving of something, and finally watching the thing start to fall into place. It's the early stages of a concept that are exciting. After ten years at Lexington, things were routine. To me when work becomes repetitious, it becomes a bore. Salesmen were always wanting a little better commission. Managers wanted better branch offices, more expense money, and someone's shoulder to cry on. I finally said to myself, "What am I doing here? What's the fun of this?" I looked ahead 10 years and all I could see was a 10% increase in profits per year and more of the same gripes. What the hell, I could see the future and I didn't like it.

When did you know you actually wanted to leave?

Well, my itch to leave began about five years before I really did. I had joined the Young Presidents' Organization several years earlier and immediately became very active. I guess I was about 40 or 41 at the time. One of the things I can thank YPO for was that it helped overcome my feeling of inferiority about not having gone to Harvard and not having gotten that brilliant business education. Once I met and worked with my peer group, I realized many weren't any sharper than I was. But most significant, it helped me clarify my inner feelings. The group used to hold a week-long annual meeting at which there would be educational courses on business, philosophy, family relations, religions of the world—quite a mix. You could pick whatever subjects interested you. I took the philosophy and religion courses. I didn't attend a single business course.

This decision to leave, then, came in stages?

It built up. I would say it started when I was 42 in 1962, and then grew. At that point I didn't have my financial security. I'd just gone public with my little company. I couldn't sell my stock. The corporation had little value. I had no choice but to hold on in order to build the machine up so I could walk away from it one day. That was my idea from the start.

You were actually trying to build yourself financial security to make yourself an exit?

I've always had the exit in mind. Acquiring financial security opened the door. Not that I knew where I wanted to go with the exit. I only knew I wanted my freedom.

Freedom from what?

From the box. I became a prisoner of my own creation. Business takes away your freedom of mobility. You're obliged to your personnel. You're obliged to your investors, your clients. You're always obliged to something.

What exactly was the burden?

Well, to me the main thing was that I couldn't continue doing what I enjoy the most, which is the creative role, the intense bringing together of all factors, saying, "It ought to look like this." For instance, what I'm doing today is much more satisfying than the long-range planning you have to do for a company. Today's satisfaction is immediate. When I take a trip through the sanctuary and photograph a spoonbill, I can get that proofsheet right away and say, "Really, that's a beauty."

For someone like yourself, who has a conceptual frame of mind, would government intervention, regulations, and consumer boards be a cause of disenchantment?

To a degree. Creating a new fund, or whatever your particular business is, gets to the point where you can conceive of how it *should* be. Then it's nitpicked to death for two years by government agencies, lawyers, and everybody else. By the time an idea would come to reality, I couldn't even recognize my brainchild. Regulation takes a lot of fun out of creativity in business. The reason why you are doing things, why you are driving yourself so hard, is because you enjoy the game. If some nitpicker pulls all the fun out of it, you might as well say, "I'll do something else—I'll sit back and take my blue eyes someplace else." Overregulation does impede. But, then again, in each case you find ways to go along with the rules. It's like choices in life; it is not always, "Which am I going to do—this or that?" The alternatives are thousands, and you pick an alternative that fits with whatever your ideas and your restrictions are.

So what really was bothering you was that you liked creating and not managing.

Yes. I don't like managing people. I like dealing with people when it's on a small, more intimate basis. I like having a viable project in mind and trying to convince somebody to move with me on it. I love that, or a committee, or a whole tableful of people. This is fine. Another thing I didn't like in business was the tension.

What kind of tension?

Oh Lord, every morning I commuted from Tarrytown with an 8 × 13-inch pad. Everyone else was reading his paper, but I was working out all the things I wanted everybody else to be doing. By the time I'd get into the office I'd have ten pages, which I'd hand to the male secretary I had and say, "Get this down to accounting," "Get this down to so-and-so," "Get this down to so-and-so." Then I'd be left with a splitting headache. Everyday it was the same damn thing.

Do you think not liking to manage, liking ideas, is characteristic of most people who make it to the top of their organizations?

Not necessarily, but I think it's a characteristic, to a great extent, of many first-stage entrepreneurs. Usually, though, they have, as I did in my president, an administrator to back them up. My president was happy in his job. He liked holding committee meetings and he liked to maneuver people—all the things that I found very boring.

You couldn't have gone on and created more funds, acquired other interest to make Lexington grow?

No, it seemed impossible at the time. I thought my solution was to be acquired by an insurance company. At least my projections indicated that an insurance company and a mutual fund had to be married. Everybody else in the company was against it. So it was a continual struggle those last few years. Eventually, though, it happened in 1969, at the top of the market.

Did you tell associates at work about how you were feeling?

Some key men knew, but I never talked to them about my personal feelings, my shifting values. You can't in a company; you only end up frightening everybody. It's bad enough trying to talk about it at home. So you keep it quiet, and bottle it up inside you.

So for the last two years at Lexington you were carrying a number of burdens you couldn't share?

Yes, and that became one of the things that got me into psychiatry. It was about a year before the company was finally sold. I was feeling so torn apart I thought it was about time I talked to a psychiatrist; I had never done that. When I first went to see him, I said, "If I am so successful, how come I feel so bad?" It took two months before I felt any better.

What was the breakthrough?

About the third month of psychiatry, I woke up in the middle of the night and sat bolt upright in bed. My heart was going very fast; I didn't know if I was sick or what. I went downstairs and put all the lights on—didn't want to wake my wife—walked through all the rooms, and still the strange feeling of fear didn't go away. I was praying that dawn would come so I could see the sun. I felt full, as though I were being cramped in my chest. I finally went back upstairs, woke up my wife and said, "I'm scared. This feeling won't go away. I may be having a heart attack." I had never felt so frightened before. And so I said, "Call Ian"—he was my psychiatrist.

Ian came over at 2:00 in the morning. My wife couldn't stand to see me in this terrible state of fright and torment, so she went downstairs to get away. Ian held my hand, sat with me on the bed and said, "Let it out, let it out." And I began to cry. I cried for about two hours. I kept sobbing, "Get off my back, get off my back, get off my back." That's all I could say. But finally I had verbalized all of my fears. When I saw Ian the next day, he asked, "Who put them on your back?" I admitted, "I guess I did." Once you understand *that*, you can take them off.

So you had your own necessity to be the strong and reliable one.

Well, I felt responsible for everyone. For the employees, the stockholders, the investors, the clients, my children, my wife, my mother, and I forgot my own needs. I always felt much more comfortable, if there was something to be done, to say, "Oh, don't worry about it, I'll do it." But when you get into a business over a certain size, you can't do it all. And some day you realize you can't please everyone. I had to let go and that was hard.

When it finally came time to leave, were you afraid?

No, no, no, no. No fear. It was just turbulent turmoil in the last year of the company, when I knew I wanted to get out from under, sell it out, and everybody was fighting me on that. And my wife also knew I wanted to clear out and float free.

How did your wife feel about it?

Any time you make a change, everybody around you is affected by the change. And either they adjust or break away. In this case I was constantly getting freer and freer, and she became more and more worried. She'd cry, "What are we going to do? We won't have any money coming in."

But you had sufficient money by that time.

She knew that. It was the job, the *job*. Her daddy was a dentist; he always stood behind that chair and worked hard most of his life. People had jobs, with a capital J. She trembled whenever I said, "I'm not going to work for a salary any more", or, "I don't care what happens to our income."

Was she able to accept it finally?

She got her own psychiatrist eventually and got stronger. We had great ups and downs that last year. We were in fact more in love than ever. We also got angry, angrier than we ever had before. I would say things like, "Damn it, I won't behave only in ways that make you comfortable." I'd never said that before. We'd always been so nice.

What happened then? Did the marriage get stronger?

Well, no. Everything was happening at one time. I never realized there must have been more going on, more traumatic stuff happening, than I knew at the time. I see now that every change you make is a drain on you. I wonder now that I didn't bust apart. The crisis at home came before I actually quit my job. It occurred when I took off to Africa alone to do my first wildlife photography. That started my wife feeling that I was pulling away from her. And then one evening after I got back from Africa, while we were sitting on the couch, it was my wife who had the guts to say, "Maybe we ought to get a divorce." I said, "OK." The nearest I'd got to thinking about divorce was when I was angry one day and walked into my psychiatrist and said, "I wish I could pension her off."

How did your children feel about your separation? Were they as worried?

They took it remarkably well. The 15- and 17-year old wondered why we didn't separate a year earlier. The 13-year old was jolted but was OK in a day. Those boys are very independent souls. I remember my third year at Lexington; we had made several films of how the mutual funds operate, and I had brought the films home with me to show the kids what I was doing at the office. My middle son said, "I want your job when I grow up," and I said, "Too late, I'm not going to be there." I said, "I just want to show you what I'm doing, but don't ever think, any of you, that you're going to move into any part of this business. You're going to be on your own."

To get back to when you left, were you afraid of not finding something else that would sufficiently replace your work?

No, but there was an emptiness. At first I missed the camaraderie. So I tried to hold on. I went to luncheons, did things with my old contacts. Then you see that what they're talking about now you're not interested in. So you pull away from that. You wonder about your own identity. You wonder about what you are and who you are. And then you wonder if maybe you should take that job someplace and become president of another company.

So you didn't have anything else in particular that you wanted to do?

No. I didn't know what I wanted out of life. But for the first time I knew what I didn't want.

What about your friends? Were they surprised?

Business associates couldn't understand my action. My few friends did, and were supportive. Despite the miles, my friendship with those men goes on even today.

When you finally decided to walk away, how did you feel?

At times terrible. The trauma really is one of loss of identity. When someone says, "Hello, what do you do?" you can say you are president of an investment company, and they smile politely and won't ask any more questions. They've got you framed up there someplace. That's fine. I liked that feeling of being framed up there. But after you leave the business world and somebody says, "What do you do?" you say, "Well, I'm retired," and they say, "Oh, you're too young to retire." So you can gloat on that one for about two months, and then the novelty wears off. The next thing you say is, "Well, I *was* chairman of the board, but now I'm setting up a new company." "That's nice." And then that wears off. Finally, after a year of uncertainty, I started doing some serious wildlife photography and then I started saying, "Well, I'm doing a lot of wildlife photography, but I *used* to be chairman of the board."

Do you ever consider going back to business?

No. Sometimes I wonder where I can find the elements that I miss. I still enjoy people . . . but on my terms. I've been accused of wanting my cake and eating it, too. Exactly. I would consider an appointment to something at a college or in government, but again, on my terms. I could even see taking over a small foundation, provided I didn't have a big, clumsy board to report to. There are small foundations that are, say, between $5 million and $10 million. And, hell, with some creative ideas you could have a lot of fun with that and do quite a lot of good.

What can large corporations do to keep people like yourself, who have valuable years of experience, but who feel the need for new challenges as well as for excitement?

I think corporations have to accommodate the man with a new direction, or whatever it might take. At the production level, if you set up a system like Volvo's and build cars with different teams, you find that you improve production. It is no different when you go upstairs. The good executive in the corporation also forms his team. The organization wants team men—men who are comfortable being on the team. And they're necessary. The world is full of Indians and very few chiefs. But corporations couldn't continue with a lot of chiefs. They put fires under friends and shoot off in all directions. My God, you would never get a car tuned that way.

But if a guy who really is a potential chief, a steamroller, is in a job where he's simply trying to behave properly to get along, all the power, all the energy is being taken out of him. Before you lose him, somebody should be smart enough to stop this, to offer this man a new direction and gamble with him on a project.

And it takes somebody like yourself to give somebody else his head?

If you like to be your own man, you can see how somebody else would like it. So it takes a particular kind of top executive to take risks with this man, to give him a special project with a special budget. After all, the top executive is the one who is eventually going to have to face the board and say, "I gambled half a million on this man and backed this project."

How would you identify these people?

I think every good leader recognizes potential chiefs, the ones who might become discontented. You can tell a certain amount from what people talk about. They're not going to talk about comfortable things; they're talking about a meaningful life, adventure, about risk taking, new ideas, and new directions. You see signs in what they do with their private lives, what they do with their families. Even the way they walk tells there's a dynamic tension. You can tell by looking in their eyes. They usually turn out to be the ones who are almost little irritants. They're not the nice ones who are getting along, who look like they're going to be the next department head. They're mavericks, the guys who wouldn't be very happy even if you handed them a $30,000 raise. They'd say, "What? That's all?"

Would companies do themselves favors if they establish policies and encourage people to change careers at 45?

Discontent for the maverick can come at any age. If inside redirection isn't possible, then look outside, to a new division, a new acquisition. Also, a challenge for this man could be found in assignments that are not related to business, but that use all of his talents, like the foundation work I've gotten into. Big corporations wouldn't lose, lending executive talent to charitable foundations. A man who is from GM, for instance; contributing six months of an executive's time to the Nature Conservancy would help both organizations.

Were you ever conscious of wanting power?

Being able to dominate lives doesn't give me a kick. I prefer to discover and use my own creativity. Someone says, "Well, you could make another million dollars." Maybe so, but I can't eat it. Accumulating money is like accumulating photographs. Just taking a lot of pictures is no satisfaction. I've got to have the outlet for my creations. If I'm not making posters for some conservation organization or publishing a book or giving a wildlife exhibit to the local schools or doing something different, there's no fun. Photography has to have an end product.

So, the same with money. If I have a way to give it away and enjoy doing that,

that's fine. And then it's still working for myself. That's why I started my own foundation back in 1968.

What is the full name of the foundation?

Just me. Just The Damroth Foundation. It's small. I just took some of my winnings, $250,000, and put them aside. Most of it right now has got to do with preserving wildlife through the Sanibel-Captiva Conservation Foundation and The World Wildlife Fund. But I give grants to many worthy causes. The only stipulation is that all of the assets are used before I die. I enjoyed making the money. I want the pleasure of giving it away.

Are you finding the satisfactions that you thought you'd find?

I feel much better about my life. Let's say that I'm not frustrated, except that I'm seeking that new challenge that's waiting for me behind that seventh veil. But my time is my own. I can lie on my back for two hours if I want. Instead of saying, "This is what I want" and moving toward it, I've said, "This is what I don't like," and I've eliminated it. I've cut away all the things that make life unhappy for me. I don't have any tension headaches in the mornings.

What is your social life like now?

I have made a few new friends. But I have no close relationships with anybody down here in Sanibel where I live, although I've lived here three years. People are glad to see me, and we do get together. And when I go into the Conservation Foundation, they want to know, "Where the hell have you been? Let's have lunch and hear what you've been doing," and I give them a new idea and then I disappear. A modest social life. But no, no deep friendships here.

Have you remarried?

Yes, last year. A pretty Swiss miss. She's my vice president. My first wife is remarried, too. Funny, she's now in a decorating business on Martha's Vineyard and getting a real kick out of it.

Do you feel that if you suddenly decided that you wanted to go back into business yourself, that age would stand in the way?

No. I see that as no impediment at all. I can start for myself any time. My credentials are pretty good, and all I have to do is present them. I've done a hell of a lot. I can do a hell of a lot more. But it won't be a business for profit.

Do you miss the fast track?

I miss the pulse of being where things are happening and I'm in the wrong place for that on Sanibel. Two things bother me: one is that I feel I have the power to move mountains in terms of people, but just now that talent has no place to go. Not finding the way to fully use myself is very frustrating. Right now I'm living in these happy surroundings but have no way to use all of my strength. That's bothersome. Second: perhaps it would be better if we spent part of the year in a college town, or in Washington, D.C. — someplace with a pulse, and not limit my horizon to Sanibel. I want to feel the pulse, I want to be with people who talk about the pulse, to recommend creative ideas around that pulse. But I don't want you to hold my hand. And that opportunity is not easy to find.

You don't worry about the road not taken?

No, no. That's dead. Yesterday is dead.

Are you working on anything now?

Lots of things. All through my foundation and my photography. I've even written several children's books, one on sea gulls. Publishers liked the photographs, but not "another" gull story. But I like the idea and think the market is there. In New York I've had these same publishers take me to lunch, talk with me. One children's book editor said, "We've got to find something for you to do." I said, "Fine. But I usually find out what I want to do and I hope you like it." He said, "I've got it. How would you like to do a children's book about termites?" I said, "I couldn't care less." He said, "There's not a good book on termites. We could sell it." And he would. He would sign a contract and pay an advance, if I would do a book on termites. But I don't *have* to do a book on termites. I don't have to do anything I don't want to do.

5

The Financial and Emotional Sides of Selling Your Company

MICHAEL G. BEROLZHEIMER

Back in the spring of 1977, I seemed to have everything a man of 36 could possibly want. I was president and a principal shareholder of a company with about $25 million annual sales. Because the company was helping pioneer a new consumer product area, running the company was exciting and future prospects appeared bright.

I should have been looking forward to endlessly favorable growth curves, but I wasn't. Instead, I faced a number of disturbing business and personal problems that made me think seriously of selling the company. But that prospect suggested its own equally disturbing set of problems.

How would I go about finding serious bidders? Who could advise me? Should I have a business broker? What would I tell my employees? Should I talk to one potential buyer at a time or several?[1]

Since those anxiety-provoking days of 1977, much has changed in my life. I have successfully completed the task of selling my company, Duraflame Inc. I now have the unmistakable luxury of hindsight. My hope is that the advice I received, together with my actual experience, will aid others who face the deeply personal and emotional question of whether to sell their companies and, if so, how.

First, though, I should relate some history.

Duraflame's Birth and Growth

My brother and I founded Duraflame in 1969 in Stockton, California, with a $20,000 investment. The company's business was to market fireplace logs made of a mixture of mostly sawdust and wax together with a small amount of coloring agents. The firelogs were made by a subcontractor with specialized skills in wood processing and a need to dispose of wood waste. Three competitors were already in the $1 million processed firelog market at the time of our entry.

Duraflame's objective was to develop quickly a national brand based on superior product quality, premium price, and extensive distribution so as to obtain a dominant market share. This effort would be supported with a modest advertising program, strong sales management, and rapid production expansion.

Nine years later, in 1978, Duraflame's sales were $28 million, representing over 50% of the total firelog market. Yet the company had operated profitably in only five of these years. Losses occurred during the season of 1974–1975 when sales declined sharply because of recession, in 1975–1976 because of our excessive carry-over inventory, and in 1976–1977 because of heavy competitive pressure from a market entry by Colgate-Palmolive.

The nine years of operation were a mixture of triumph and disappointment. The triumph stemmed from our extremely successful marketing effort and fast sales growth. The disappointment was the result of the losses and also the occasional friction with my brother about Duraflame's policies and future directions.

For instance, I wanted to commit capital toward diversifying into new consumer products, but some family members argued—perhaps correctly—in favor of more conservative financial policies.

Business Considerations for Selling

In 1977, when I first thought seriously about selling Duraflame, the idea seemed to make good business sense. It would solve the problem of the internal disagreements over the company's future directions and also reward my brother and me quite handsomely on our original investment.

Selling the company would relieve me of several other business concerns, such as the risk of marketing a seasonal product, the product's sensitivity to economic conditions, increasing oil prices (wax is a byproduct of the manufacture of lubricating oil), and frequently shifting competitive pressures.

It all seemed reasonable provided an acquirer could be found who understood the fundamental value of the company in the future, who would pay for that value *today* (with no contingencies), and who would recognize the key factors in the business's success and not unwittingly destroy the Duraflame brand name. *Projected* net income justified close to $8 million in goodwill value alone, based on 20% pretax return objectives. But how would a potential buyer judge past performance?

Possibly more important, did I really want to sell the business—from a personal viewpoint? Answering that question meant doing some very intensive soul-searching.

Should I Sell My "Baby"?

In retrospect, the soul-searching started in 1976, when I attended a regional conference of the Young Presidents' Organization in Washington, D.C. Having always been interested in politics, I thought the conference would be an opportunity to find out more about the national political scene. But what I learned at that conference had less to do with national or international issues than with what I learned about myself.

Wayne Dyer, author of a number of books and articles about personal psychology, was there to speak about feelings and choices. He said that *we* make choices as to how we feel and should not blame our grandfathers, fathers, mothers, sisters, children, or wives for our feelings. For some time I had been unhappy with the way I was feeling. The concept that I could do something about it—if I so chose—was simple but very powerful. I proceeded to write down a projection of where I would be in ten years if I continued on the path of the previous ten years. Here is what I saw:

Continued difficulties in my marriage.

Continued responsibilities for a group of separate family companies in the wood-processing business—of which Duraflame was one—without the authority to build and lead the enterprises. That situation evolved because my father, brother, and I had differing viewpoints of company goals.

Increasing danger to the companies and their employees because of the family differences.

(As one small company, we could keep our differences in a single room. However, our group of companies had grown from less than $7 million sales in 1969 to more than $50 million in 1977—of which Duraflame was approximately one-half. No one appeared ready to sacrifice his or her own goals for someone else's, and our divergent viewpoints seemed likely to have an increasingly serious negative effect on profits and employee morale.)

A probable change in my role within the family businesses—from one of stimulating opportunities for creative business development to one of conservative financial custodianship for my relatives and my children.

Ten years of continued personal illiquidity.

These details may bore the reader, but I believe company owners must understand their personal objectives before they decide to sell (or buy) a company. By April 1977 I had decided to develop a strategy for selling the company *if* I chose to do so. However, I had not yet actually reached the emotional decision to sell.

Specific Pointers

The Young Presidents' Organization conducts an annual week-long international seminar, which includes an idea exchange session. I was given the honor of organizing the idea exchange for the 1977 meeting at Vienna University. Not surprisingly, I included a discussion of strategies for selling your business. The following basic principles emerged during that idea exchange and in subsequent conversations I had with executives:

You only sell your company once. Whoever is buying your company buys companies repeatedly. Therefore, you must prepare yourself very thoroughly and leave nothing to chance.

Selling your company is a personal affair. You cannot delegate the responsibility to someone else, including a business broker. A family company is *you*. Therefore, *you* have to sell it. I discarded the notion of keeping myself distant—as I might in labor negotiations—as unworkable.

Sell for cash if you want liquidity and if you do not want your assets tied up in someone else's company.

Negotiate with two or more willing buyers at the same time. Do *not* deal with only one company. This was especially important advice for me because I had come to believe that to deal with two or more people at the same time was somehow unethical. However, I approached potential buyers very discreetly and thus avoided tainting the company with a shopped-around image.

Do not tell your employees. This is another rule with ethical overtones that I found difficult to accept but I nevertheless followed. For nine months only one person at Duraflame knew I was trying to sell the company. Employees speculated about a possible sale, but I never answered them formally. Informally, I tried to give the impression of seeking to establish a positive value for Duraflame, in the eyes of the company's directors, by talking with potential buyers.

Carefully select those companies that your company will appeal to most. This was easy advice to follow because of the numerous inquiries I had received over the years from companies wanting to acquire Duraflame. I had always rejected these inquiries—but not before courteously greeting the acquisition people to gauge the depth of their interest.

After selecting the companies you would like to negotiate with, develop a substrategy for contacting them. That is, who will make the contacts, with whom, and what will be said? This is a delicate process that requires careful planning.

Plan on 18 months to complete the sale. This should include one year to select the buyer, followed by 6 months of final negotiations. In fact, I took approximately one year to select the finalist but needed only 3 months for the final negotiations because both parties had tax considerations and other incentives for quickly completing the transaction.

Once you negotiate the framework of the deal, select a lawyer who will negotiate the details in a style compatible with your own personality. A poor lawyer can disrupt the delicate negotiations and kill the deal.

Organize your company so that you can spend 100% of your time on the sale process. The time should include rest and relaxation to keep sane and cool. Early on, I appointed our national sales and marketing manager as general manager to take care of Duraflame's day-to-day operations. Without his dedicated leadership during a most critical period, I would not have had the time and energy necessary for the task.

Stay alert and healthy. In my experience, every day brought a potentially fatal new issue concerning the proposed transaction. You have to *will* the sale to happen. This takes a healthy mental attitude.

Finally, a company is not sold until the money is in your bank account. Horror stories abound about deals that have fallen through just before the closing papers were to be signed.

These principles eased my anxiety about *how* to sell the company. I knew the time had come to make the decision. And somehow—perhaps unconsciously—I came to the point one evening in April 1977 that, yes, the idea made sense. I consulted with other family members and directors and they agreed. I then settled on June 1978 as my target date for completing the sale.

Why June 1978? First, that would give me 14 months to go through the process and reach the final agreement.

Second, I thought the country would begin a recession by the fall of 1978, and I knew that most of our losses had occurred because of the 1974–1975 recession, when the firelog market dropped 40% after having doubled during each of the previous three years.

Third, I felt I would want liquidity by about mid-1978 if I decided to separate from my wife so as to maintain our previous individual standards of living.

Finally, why wait for another unforeseen event to create a new crisis in the business?

Now began the process of courtship—what a friend calls the Indian rain dance. This was a key part of the negotiations and perhaps the most delicate phase.

The Rain Dance

Over the years I had kept a file of all the prospective acquirers I had talked with as well as other possible candidates suggested by close friends familiar with leading consumer products companies. I then compiled a list of companies that would be logical acquirers of Duraflame.

Carefully selected intermediaries contacted a total of seven of these companies. All but two initial discussions were with the presidents or the executive vice presidents of potential acquirers. All were large, cash-rich companies that were in consumer products businesses and had policies of diversification.

My objective during this process was to keep three companies on an active list of potential acquirers. When one dropped out, I added another.

Of the seven companies, two declined nearly immediately because Duraflame did not interest them for one reason or another. Two more declined when they realized I would accept only cash and would not commit myself to an earn-out agreement coupled with a long-term management contract.

That left three companies to go through the serious process of financial review, plant visits, and so forth. One company dropped out because it concluded it would "kill Duraflame with overhead" since Duraflame was, in one official's words, the most complicated small business to manage in that company's history of acquisition analysis. That left two companies — one of which was Kingsford Co., a subsidiary of Clorox Co.

Bargaining with Kingsford

Kingsford acquired Duraflame because Kingsford was the logical company to do so. Its management knew it and I knew it. The idea had made sense since 1973 when Clorox acquired Kingsford, a charcoal briquet maker. In 1974, Kingsford entered the firelog business but abandoned it in 1976 because of poor product quality.

Nonetheless, it was obvious that Kingsford and Duraflame should be married. The space in the supermarket occupied by charcoal briquets during the summer months is occupied by firelogs during the winter, and distribution patterns for the two products are similar.

Since our suitability for each other was so obvious, I had gradually come to know various officials at Clorox and Kingsford. However, despite this fact, I decided that the best way to approach them would be through a close friend who would explain that he felt I could be convinced to sell the company if they were interested.

The negotiation process was long and arduous. It was, at the same time, an intellectual, business, and emotional challenge. It was an important learning experience, and a few lessons stand out today as being particularly valuable:

Keep a notebook on your desk. Make notes of every conversation regarding the negotiations. These notes can become important when you or the potential buyer have memory lapses concerning previous understandings. I learned this lesson after such a lapse over a small detail cost us $40,000.

Negotiate to keep the escrow amount as low as possible. The escrow amount is a percentage of the sale price held back to protect the buyer from inventory and other variations discovered later. In our case, it was less than 3% of the nearly $14 million total purchase price. The escrow amount should be the *exclusive* remedy for inaccuracies in the transaction. The seller must be careful to protect his value of the transaction from unknown, unforeseen, or forgotten events which could impair that value.

Write your own draft of the letter of intent or memo of understanding. Do this at the conclusion of the initial negotiations, preferably during a quiet weekend so you can concentrate. It will guide your lawyer and serve as the document from which you and your team will negotiate the final contract. Include as much information as possible because details agreed on during the months of preliminary discussions tend to be forgotten during the final negotiations.

Including such items in the original memo of understanding will give the buyer less room to make subsequent changes. Remember that during the period following the handshake, many people will become involved who will want to show their business acumen by improving the deal for whichever party they represent.

Be totally honest and candid about your business. That does not mean you have to confess speculative concerns about the future, but avoid being devious. Include bad news as well as good news. Your forthrightness will improve your credibility with the buyer and also help put him or her more at ease.

Determine how the buyer intends to allocate his acquisition price. For example, high allocation to fixed assets gives the buyer a greater base of depreciation but raises the issue of income recapture for the seller. In my case, it was important to limit the buyer's valuation of the noncompete clause to avoid the possibility of that part of the transaction being taxed as ordinary income rather than capital gains.

Do not be afraid to reject an offer. Kingsford's first offer totaled $2 million in goodwill and required complicated restructuring of the company prior to the sale. It was rejected as an insult to the investment made to build Duraflame as the firelog industry leader. We parted company, and I continued the rain dance with another possible corporate suitor.

Then one day, about a month later, I received a call from a Clorox executive who thought we should meet because there had been "misunderstandings." We met for dinner and that night agreed to the central principle of the transaction. My insight into Clorox's objectives and its past analytical assumptions allowed me to tailor our discussions to its perspective.

As an example Clorox officials had assumed no price increase for the 1978–1979 season, but I explained we had just announced a 10% price increase to the trade, which meant their pretax profit estimates were significantly understated. I was therefore able to lend support to my price objective and also suggest that Clorox could reasonably expect to meet its return-on-investment objectives.

Be assertive regarding your own worth. This is important if you want to arrange a consulting agreement or continue employment with the company. I, for one, had no idea how much to seek from my employment contract, which covered half of my time for one year. On the advice of several business friends, I selected the highest sum I had considered and told Clorox officials. They agreed.

Avoid becoming complacent about the transaction. After you have reached an agreement in principle, the hard work has really just begun—as the reader will see.

The Negotiating Team

I reached a preliminary agreement without assembling a negotiating team. The reason was simple: I did not know whether I could create the deal.

My goals had been high from the outset, and I did not intend to deviate from them. But once a sale was in sight, the negotiations over the final contract needed to be properly managed.

My initial step was to hire the best lawyer I could find. I made my choice based on interviews and reference checks of two specialists in mergers and acquisitions. One of the lawyer's first actions was to obtain Kingsford's agreement to pay all our legal and accounting expenses—about $50,000—*if* it acquired Duraflame.

Apart from professional competence, I wanted the lawyer to be personally committed. My lawyer promised to play that role. He was always available—days, nights, weekends. He never visited my office nor I his. I discovered that nearly all meetings are unnecessary if one is willing to spend countless hours on the telephone and make use of speedy mail delivery service.

The rest of the team was assembled after April 3, 1978, which was opening day of Duraflame's three-day sales meeting at Lake Tahoe. The meeting represented our kickoff for the 1978–1979 season. At 11:00 the previous evening, I telephoned the company's three key executives and asked them to meet me for breakfast at 7:30 A.M. Over breakfast I told them of the agreement.

Afterward, I had the dubious pleasure of being the leadoff speaker at our sales meeting and spent two hours explaining the sale and answering questions about it. Most of the answers had been worked out prior to the meeting through joint consultation with Kingsford. That afternoon we informed food brokers who sold our logs to retailers, and the following morning we issued a press release, which was relayed over various wire services. To the credit of our staff, the sales meeting continued in a somber but professional manner.

I met with our key executives in the afternoon and asked the chief controller to participate with me during the final negotiating process. He indicated that he was unhappy at not having been included earlier in the negotiating process. While he was tremendously valuable during the final negotiating phases, I do not see what might have been gained by having him or other staff members involved in the early stages. He, our accountants, a second controller, and our lawyer made up the negotiating team.

We met about eight times over a three-month period at Clorox's headquarters in Oakland to negotiate the final agreement. Each company's staff attended all these meetings. Every word of the one-foot-high legal document was negotiated. Hundreds of thousands of dollars rode on the language. Tens of thousands were at stake in the placement of commas and periods. Each day my staff would alert me to some new item that had developed into a potential crisis.

This was the most emotionally difficult period for me. It seemed a time of constant crisis. I was extremely sensitive to anything and anyone who might kill the deal. A few examples will show the importance of maintaining your mental and physical health during this period of tremendous stress.

Emotional Trials

Six weeks into the final negotiations, a family member dropped by my office to complain that I was being too soft in the negotiations. He cited several examples to illustrate his point. Apart from his abrupt, critical manner, I was upset at being second-guessed when Duraflame was about to be sold for more than two-and-a-half times the value that the same family member would have sold Duraflame for ten months earlier.

Eight weeks into the final negotiations, Kingsford representatives and I were at odds over the language of a clause regarding the firelog production plant. During a break from the formal negotiating sessions, I met privately with one of Kingsford's chief negotiators and suddenly found each of us accusing the other of being stubborn and cheap. About an hour later, we broke the bottleneck over the language issue. I raise this point because I feel both parties must get their feelings on the table and risk emotional crises in order to make progress.

I also felt extreme tension during the Duraflame shareholders' meeting called to review and approve the final transaction documents. This meeting was timed to occur approximately three or four days before the final signing—only when all the wording in the various documents had been carefully negotiated and typed in final form and approved by Clorox and my staff.

Present at that meeting in addition to the shareholders were four lawyers. During the six hours of discussion about the contract I feared that any revision would jeopardize the overall transaction.

Happily, the stockholders' questions and concerns were answered without any material changes being required in the various documents. With the meeting behind me, I went to Clorox's offices for the final signing. However, even that meeting consumed more than four hours of negotiations over such things as out-of-state income taxes and the wording of one press release. Finally, we had the signing ceremony!

The Aftermath

Selling your company is a deeply emotional experience. It is also a tough experience.

I have since been able to concentrate on my real love—nurturing new consumer products—by forming a venture capital partnership devoted to backing consumer companies. The Early Stages Company's objective is to be the leading venture capital firm specializing in consumer products; other venture capital firms tend to invest in high-technology companies or leveraged buyouts.

Selling Duraflame has thus given me a new career opportunity, personal liquidity, and a sense of freedom. And this last benefit is the most precious one of all.

About the Contributors

Joseph C. Bailey

Joseph C. Bailey was Professor of Human Relations, Emeritus, Harvard Business School, and Professor of Human Relations, Graduate School of Business, Northeastern University. He died in 1980.

Fernando Bartolomé

Fernando Bartolomé is Professor of Management, Bentley College, Waltham, Massachusetts, and a human resources management consultant. He is coauthor of *Must Success Cost So Much?* (Basic Books, 1981) and a recent *Harvard Business Review* article, "The Manager: Master and Servant of Power."

Michael G. Berolzheimer

Michael G. Berolzheimer is president, P & M Products Incorporated; general partner, Rockwood Holdings International; and president, China Swan Associates Incorporated. All of these firms are located in San Francisco.

James F. Bolt

James F. Bolt is president of Executive Development Associates, an executive education consulting firm in Westport, Connecticut. His most recent publication, "Global Competitors: Some Criteria for Success," appeared in *Business Horizons*.

Floyd A. Bond

Floyd A. Bond is Dean Emeritus and Donald C. Cook Distinguished Professor of Business Economics, Graduate School of Business Administration, University of Michigan.

David P. Boyd

David P. Boyd is dean of the College of Business Administration, Northeastern University, and a consultant.

Leland P. Bradford

Leland P. Bradford was a founder of the National Training Laboratories, a pioneer in sensitivity training. He served as its director until his retirement in 1970.

Paul J. Brouwer

Paul J. Brouwer, now retired, was a general partner, Rohrer, Hibler, and Replogle Incorporated, Cleveland, Ohio, and president, RH&R International. He is a coauthor of *Performance Appraisal and Human Development* (Addison-Wesley, 1977).

David H. Burnham

David H. Burnham is president, David H. Burnham and Associates, an organizational development consulting firm with offices in Boston and London. He is the author of *The Rise of the Computer State* (Random House, 1983).

Albert Z. Carr

The late Albert Z. Carr was a consultant and author of *Business as a Game* (New American Library, 1968). During World War II he was assistant to the chairman, War Production Board, and later a special assistant to President Harry Truman.

Basil Robert Cuddihy

Basil Robert Cuddihy is personnel director, Alcan International Kingston Research and Development Center, Kingston, Ontario, Canada.

William G. Damroth

William G. Damroth was president and chairman of the board, Lexington Research and Management Corporation, a mutual fund and investment counseling firm. He died in 1987.

Peter F. Drucker

Peter F. Drucker is Clarke Professor of Social Science and Management, Claremont Graduate School, Claremont, California. He is also a management consultant, a columnist, and the author of twenty-five books, including *The Effective Executive* (Harper & Row, 1966), *The Age of Discontinuity* (Harper & Row, 1969), and, most recently, *Frontiers of Management* (Truman Talley Books, 1986).

Paul A. Lee Evans

Paul A. Lee Evans is Professor of Organizational Behavior, European Institute of Business Administration. He has published journal articles on managerial careers and is coauthor of *Must Success Cost So Much?* (Basic Books, 1981).

Thomas H. Fitzgerald

Thomas H. Fitzgerald was director, Organizational Planning and Development, General Motors Corporation. Since his retirement from GM, he has been affiliated with the Corporate Education Center, Eastern Michigan University.

John J. Gabarro

John J. Gabarro is Professor of Organizational Behavior and Human Resource Management, Harvard Business School. He has written or edited numerous publications. His most recent book is *The Dynamics of Taking Charge* (Harvard Business School Press, 1987), winner of the 1988 Johnson, Smith & Kinsley Award for New Perspectives on Executive Leaders.

Saul W. Gellerman

Saul W. Gellerman is Dean of the Graduate School of Management, University of Dallas. An industrial psychologist, he formerly headed his own consulting firm. His most recent *Harvard Business Review* article is "Cyanamid's New Take on Performance Appraisal."

David E. Gumpert

David E. Gumpert, a former associate editor of the *Harvard Business Review*, is the owner of Enterprise Communication Company, a publisher of newsletters on entrepreneurship and small business.

Rosabeth Moss Kanter

Rosabeth Moss Kanter is Class of 1960 Professor of Business Administration, Harvard Business School. She has written several books, including *Men and Women of the Corporation* (Basic Books, 1979), *The Change Masters: Innovation and Entrepreneurship in the American Corporation* (Simon and Schuster, 1983), and, most recently, with Governor Michael S. Dukakis, *Creating the Future* (Summit Books, 1988).

Robert L. Katz

Robert L. Katz is president of Robert L. Katz and Associates, a consulting firm specializing in corporate strategy. He has taught at the graduate schools of business at Dartmouth, Harvard, and Stanford and has written three textbooks.

Harry Levinson

Harry Levinson is president of the Levinson Institute, a consulting firm in Cambridge, Massachusetts, specializing in the psychological aspects of leadership and the management of stress and change. He is Clinical Professor of Psychology, Department of Psychiatry, Harvard Medical School, and has been a visiting professor at the Harvard Business School. His books include *Emotional Health in the World of Work* (Harper & Row, 1964), *Casebook for Psychological Man* (Levinson Institute, 1982), and *Ready, Fire, Aim* (Levinson Institute, 1986).

Jay Lorsch

Jay Lorsch is Louis E. Kirstein Professor of Human Relations, Harvard Business School. He is the author of numerous books, including *Organization and Environment* (Harvard Business School, 1967), with Paul R. Lawrence; *Managing Diversity and Interdependence* (Harvard Business School, 1973), with Stephen A. Allen III; and *Decision Making at the Top* (Basic Books, 1983), with Gordon Donaldson.

David C. McClelland

David C. McClelland is Professor Emeritus, Harvard University, and Distinguished Research Professor of Psychology, Boston University. His most recent book is *Human Motivation* (Cambridge University Press, 1985).

Henry Mintzberg

Henry Mintzberg is Bronfman Professor of Management, McGill University. He recently won a second McKinsey Award for his *Harvard Business Review* article, "Crafting Strategy." His first McKinsey Award was for the article included in this book.

Derek A. Newton

Derek A. Newton is John Tyler Professor of Business Administration, Darden School, University of Virginia. His most recent book is *Sales Force Management* (Business Publications Incorporated, 1988).

Arch Patton

Now retired, Arch Patton was a director of McKinsey & Co. An authority on executive personnel and compensation, he has written twenty-six articles on these subjects for the *Harvard Business Review* over thirty-seven years. His most recent article, "Why Won't Directors Rock the Boat?," appeared in the November–December 1987 issue.

Jeffrey Sonnenfeld

Jeffrey Sonnenfeld is Associate Professor of Business Administration, Harvard Business School. His latest book is *The Hero's Farewell: Retirement and Renewal for Chief Executives* (Oxford University Press, 1988).

Howard H. Stevenson

Howard H. Stevenson is the Sarofim-Rock Professor of Business Administration, Harvard Business School. He has published numerous articles on entrepreneurship and is a coauthor of *Policy Formulation and Administration* (Irwin, 1984), and *New Business Ventures and the Entrepreneur* (Irwin, 1985).

Alfred W. Swinyard

Alfred W. Swinyard is Emeritus Professor of Business Administration and former director of the Division of Research, Graduate School of Business Administration, University of Michigan.

Haruo Takagi

Haruo Takagi is Associate Professor, Keio University, Tokyo, and the author of *The Flaw in Japanese Management* (UMI Research Press, 1985).

John F. Veiga

John F. Veiga is professor and chairman of the Management Department, University of Connecticut.

Wheelock Whitney

Wheelock Whitney is chairman of Whitney Management Company, a private investment company in Minneapolis, Minnesota.

Abraham Zaleznik

A practicing psychoanalyst and organizational consultant, Abraham Zaleznik is the Cahners-Rabb Professor of Social Psychology at Harvard Business School. He is the author of *Human Dilemmas of Leadership* (Harper & Row, 1966) and coauthor of *Power and the Corporate Mind* (Houghton Mifflin, 1975).

Index